This is the final volume.

Thank you so very much for your support these past 15 years.

I'd be honored if, in the future, you occasionally recall that there once was a character named Naruto.

Well then, please enjoy the conclusion of Naruto.

—Masashi Kishimoto, 2015

岸本斉史

Author/artist Masashi Kishimoto was born in 1974 in rural Okayama Prefecture, Japan. After spending time in art college, he won the Hop Step Award for new manga artists with his manga **Karakuri** (Mechanism). Kishimoto decided to base his next story on traditional Japanese culture. His first version of **Naruto**, drawn in 1997, was a one-shot story about fox spirits; his final version, which debuted in **Weekly Shonen Jump** in 1999, quickly became the most popular ninja manga in Japan.

NARUTO VOL. 72
SHONEN JUMP Manga Edition

STORY AND ART BY MASASHI KISHIMOTO

Translation/Mari Morimoto
Touch-up Art & Lettering/John Hunt
Design/Sam Elzway
Editor/Alexis Kirsch

NARUTO © 1999 by Masashi Kishimoto. All rights reserved. First
published in Japan in 1999 by SHUEISHA Inc., Tokyo. English translation
rights arranged by SHUEISHA Inc.

The stories, characters and incidents
mentioned in this publication are entirely fictional.

Printed in the U.S.A.

Published by VIZ Media, LLC
P.O. Box 77010
San Francisco, CA 94107

10 9 8 7 6 5 4 3 2 1
First printing, October 2015

PARENTAL ADVISORY
NARUTO is rated T for Teen and is recommended
for ages 13 and up. This volume contains realistic
and fantasy violence.
ratings.viz.com

www.viz.com

THE WORLD'S
MOST POPULAR MANGA
www.shonenjump.com

[redacted]DITION

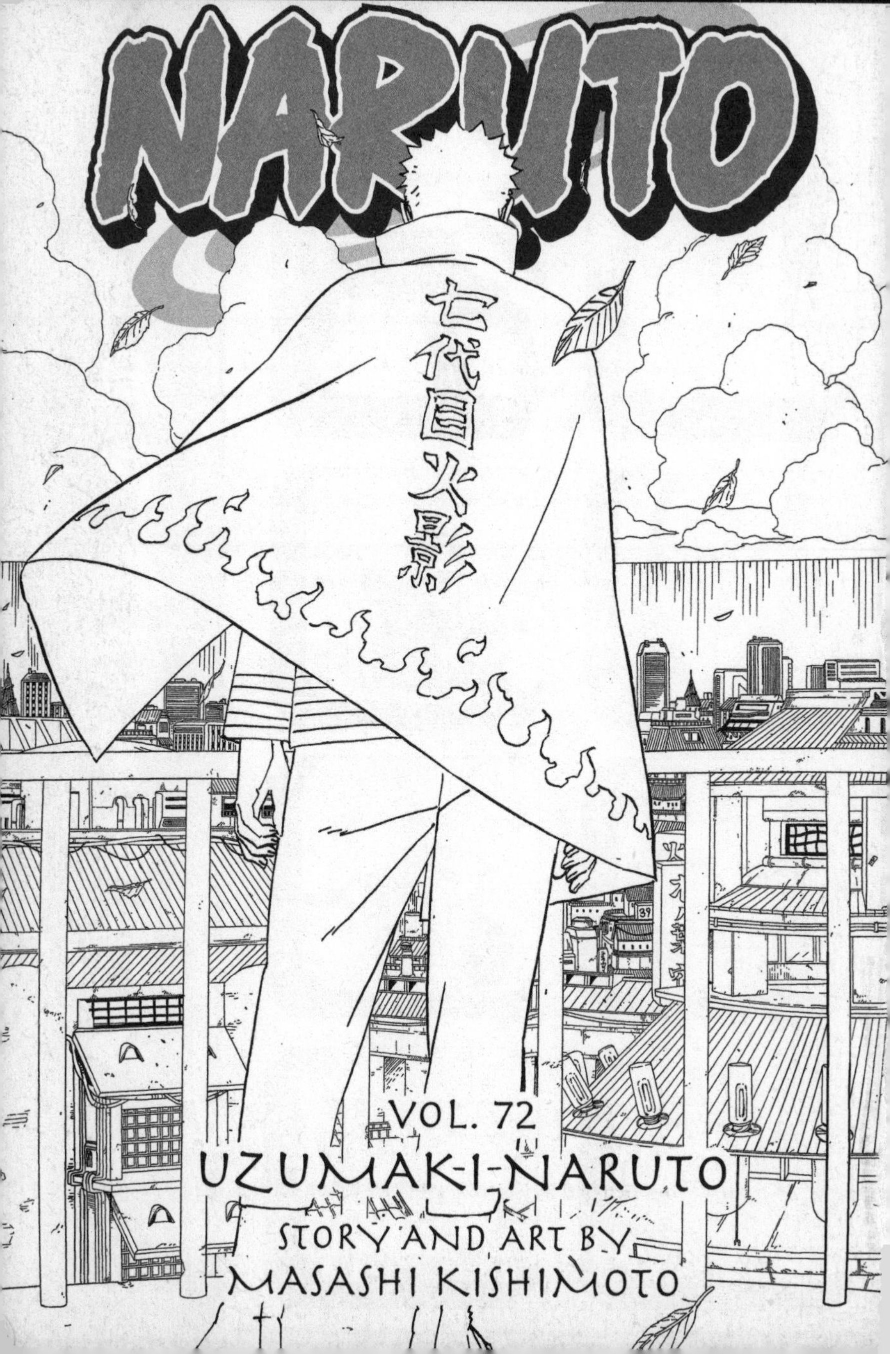
七代目火影

NARUTO

VOL. 72
UZUMAKI NARUTO

STORY AND ART BY
MASASHI KISHIMOTO

CHARACTERS

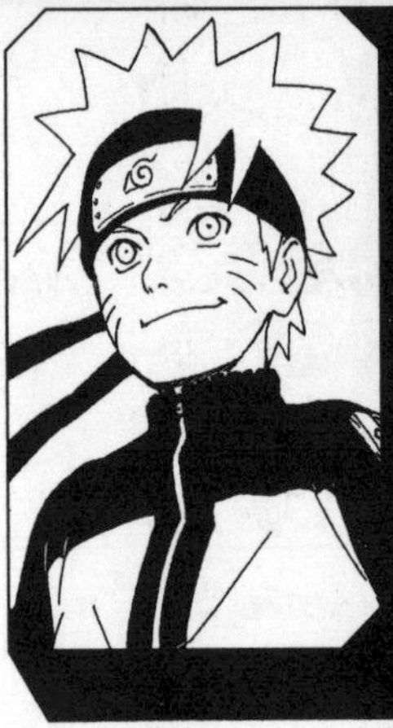

Naruto うずまきナルト

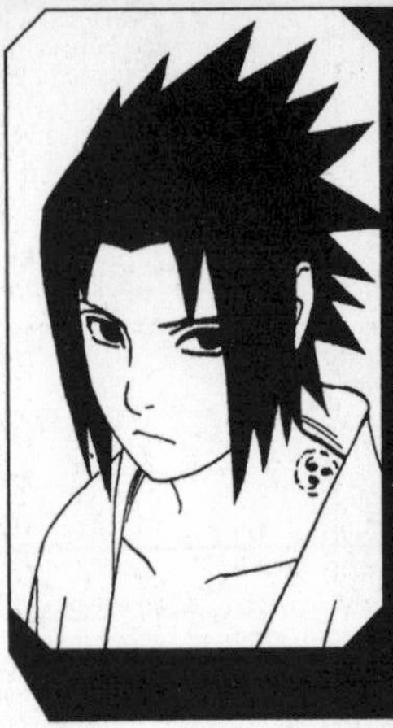

Sasuke うちはサスケ

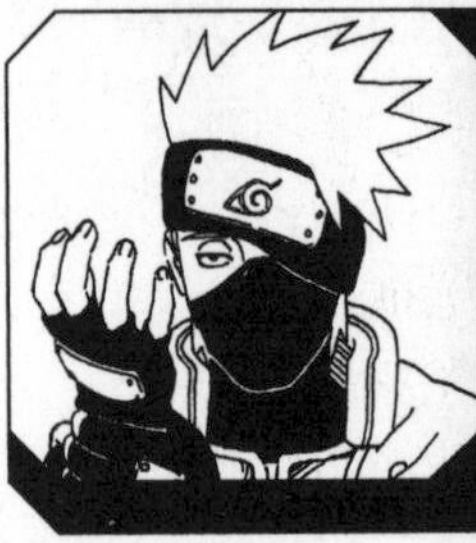

Kakashi はたけカカシ

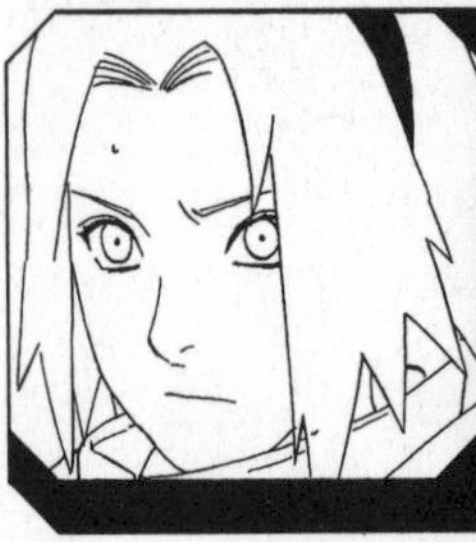

Sakura 春野サクラ

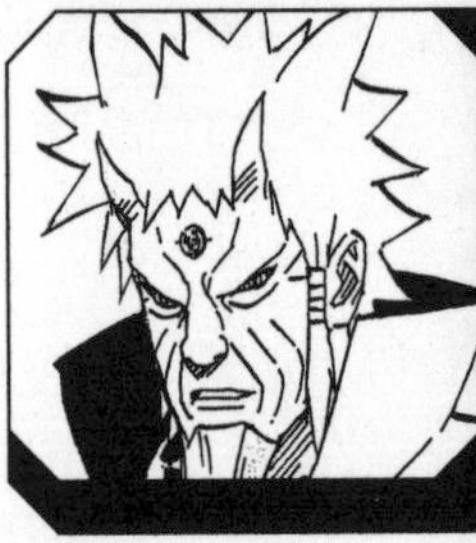

Sage of Six Paths 六道仙人

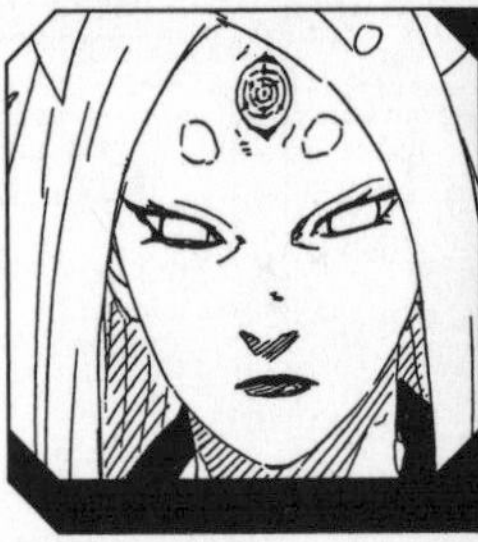

Kaguya 大筒木カグヤ

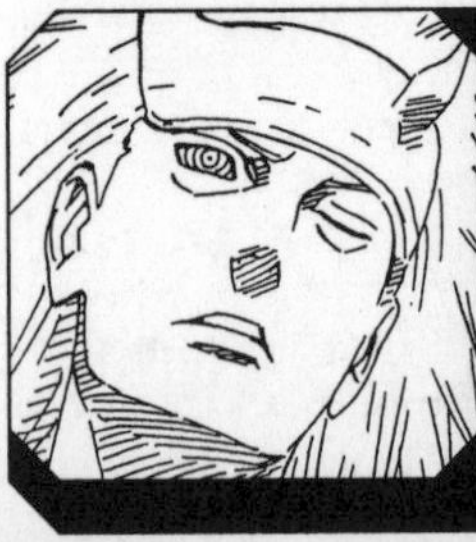

Madara うちはマダラ

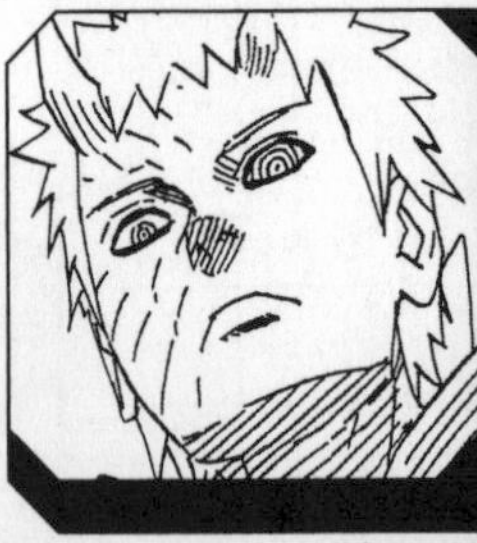

Obito うちはオビト

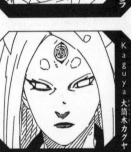

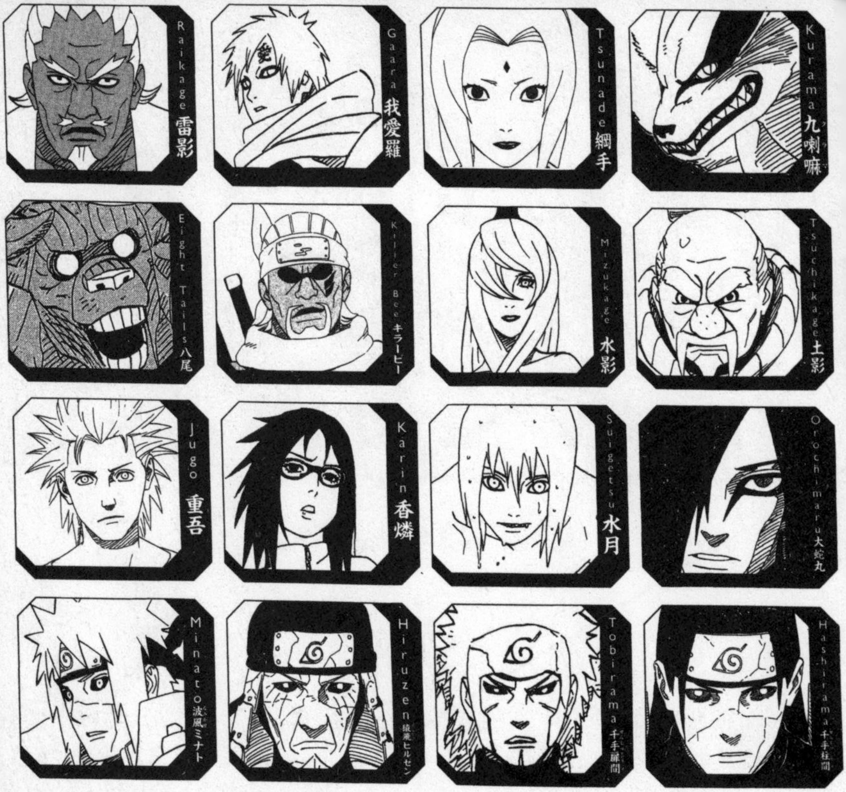
Kurama 九喇嘛
Tsunade 綱手
Gaara 我愛羅
Raikage 雷影
Tsuchikage 土影
Mizukage 水影
Killer Bee キラービー
Eight Tails 八尾
Orochimaru 大蛇丸
Suigetsu 水月
Karin 香燐
Jugo 重吾
Hashirama 千手柱間
Tobirama 千手扉間
Hiruzen 猿飛ヒルゼン
Minato 波風ミナト

THE STORY SO FAR...

Naruto, the biggest troublemaker at the Ninja Academy in the Village of Konohagakure, finally becomes a ninja along with his classmates Sasuke and Sakura. They grow and mature through countless trials and battles. However, Sasuke, unable to give up his quest for vengeance, leaves Konohagakure to seek Orochimaru and his power…

Two years pass. Naruto grows up and engages in fierce battles against the Tailed Beast-targeting Akatsuki. And the Fourth Great Ninja War against the Akatsuki finally begins. Having regained a living body thanks to the Rinne Rebirth jutsu, Madara activates the Infinite Tsukuyomi and the people are sucked into a dream world. Immediately afterwards, Black Zetsu betrays Madara and revives the Rabbit Goddess Kaguya, who attacks Naruto and the others! Naruto joins forces with Sasuke and succeeds in sealing away Kaguya, but...?!

NARUTO

VOL. 72
UZUMAKI NARUTO

CONTENTS

Number 691: Congratulations

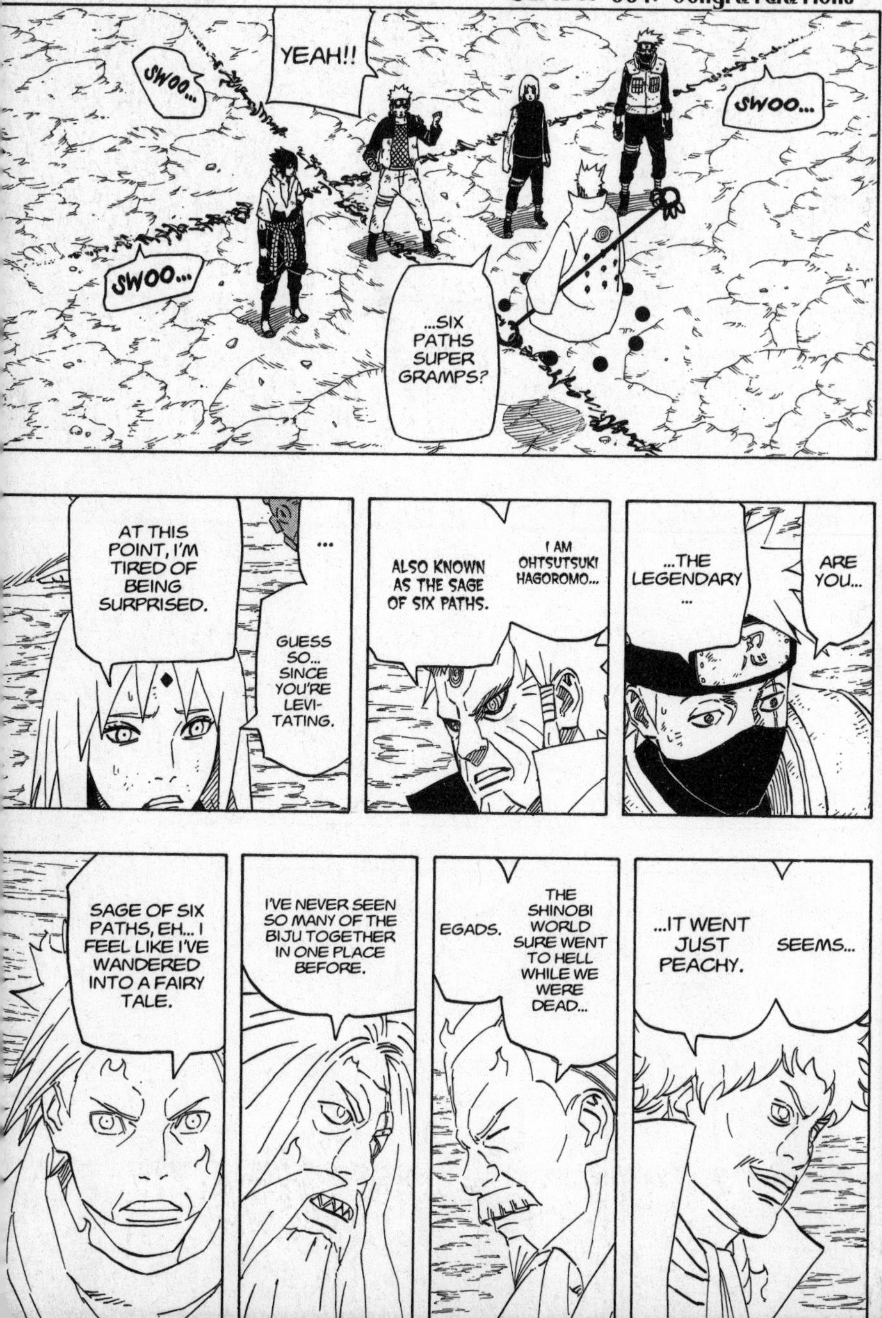
SWOO...
YEAH!!
SWOO...
...SIX PATHS SUPER GRAMPS?
SWOO...
ARE YOU...
...THE LEGENDARY ...
I AM OHTSUTSUKI HAGOROMO...
ALSO KNOWN AS THE SAGE OF SIX PATHS.
...
GUESS SO... SINCE YOU'RE LEVI-TATING.
AT THIS POINT, I'M TIRED OF BEING SURPRISED.
SEEMS...
...IT WENT JUST PEACHY.
THE SHINOBI WORLD SURE WENT TO HELL WHILE WE WERE DEAD...
EGADS.
I'VE NEVER SEEN SO MANY OF THE BIJU TOGETHER IN ONE PLACE BEFORE.
SAGE OF SIX PATHS, EH... I FEEL LIKE I'VE WANDERED INTO A FAIRY TALE.

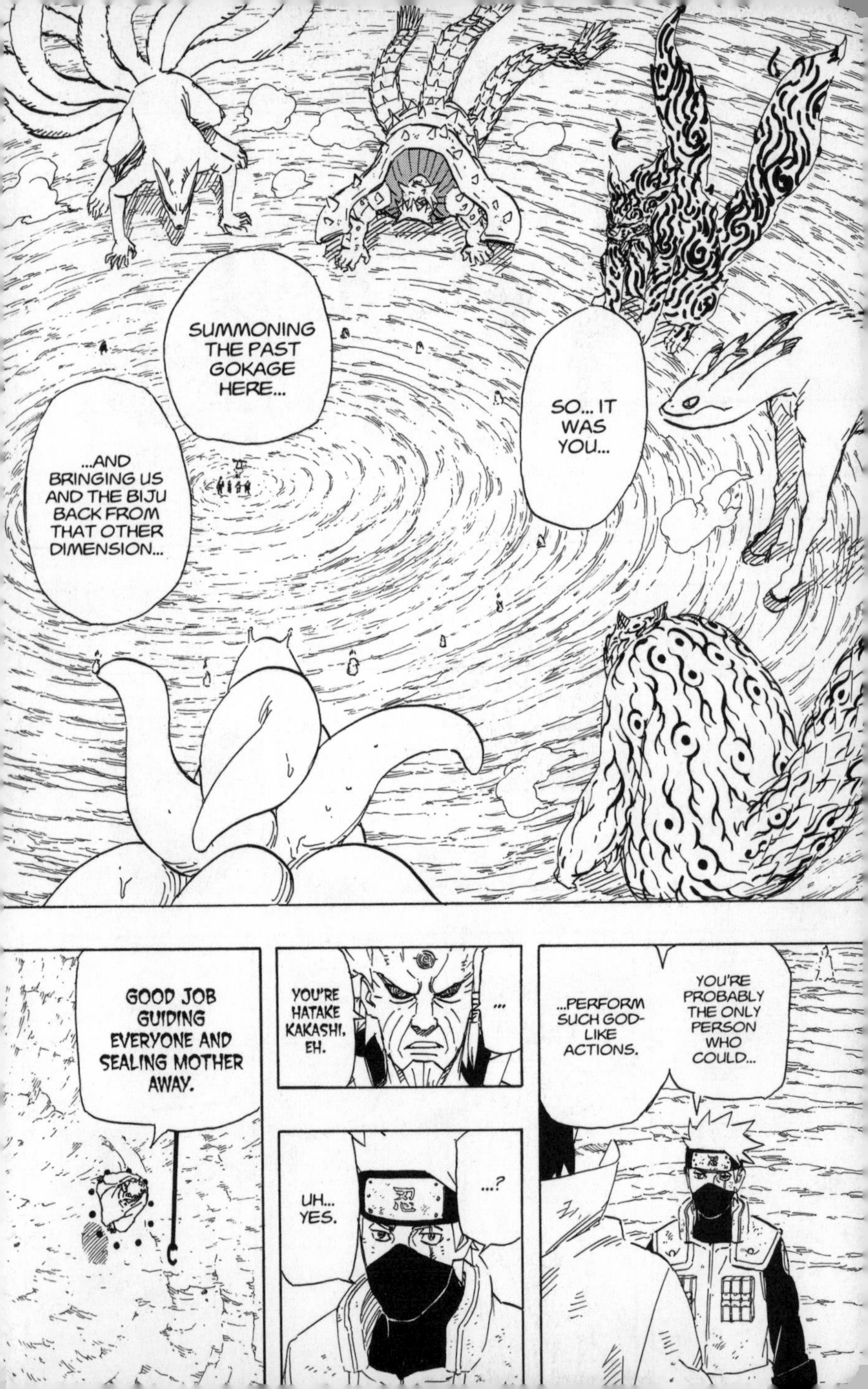
SO... IT WAS YOU...
SUMMONING THE PAST GOKAGE HERE...
...AND BRINGING US AND THE BIJU BACK FROM THAT OTHER DIMENSION...
YOU'RE PROBABLY THE ONLY PERSON WHO COULD...
...PERFORM SUCH GOD-LIKE ACTIONS.
...
YOU'RE HATAKE KAKASHI, EH.
...?
UH... YES.
GOOD JOB GUIDING EVERYONE AND SEALING MOTHER AWAY.

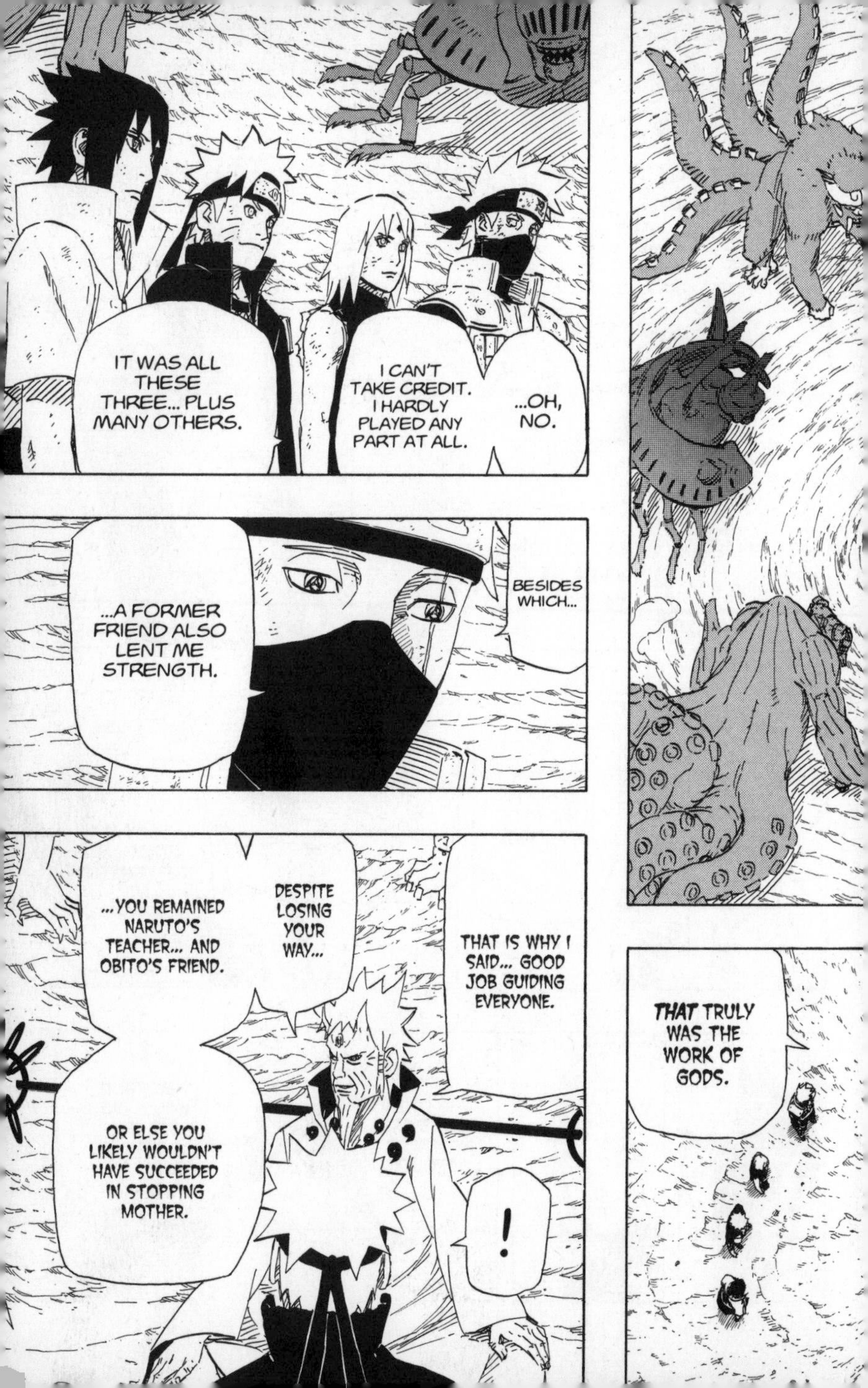

THAT TRULY WAS THE WORK OF GODS.
...OH, NO.
I CAN'T TAKE CREDIT. I HARDLY PLAYED ANY PART AT ALL.
IT WAS ALL THESE THREE... PLUS MANY OTHERS.
BESIDES WHICH...
...A FORMER FRIEND ALSO LENT ME STRENGTH.
DESPITE LOSING YOUR WAY...
...YOU REMAINED NARUTO'S TEACHER... AND OBITO'S FRIEND.
OR ELSE YOU LIKELY WOULDN'T HAVE SUCCEEDED IN STOPPING MOTHER.
THAT IS WHY I SAID... GOOD JOB GUIDING EVERYONE.
!

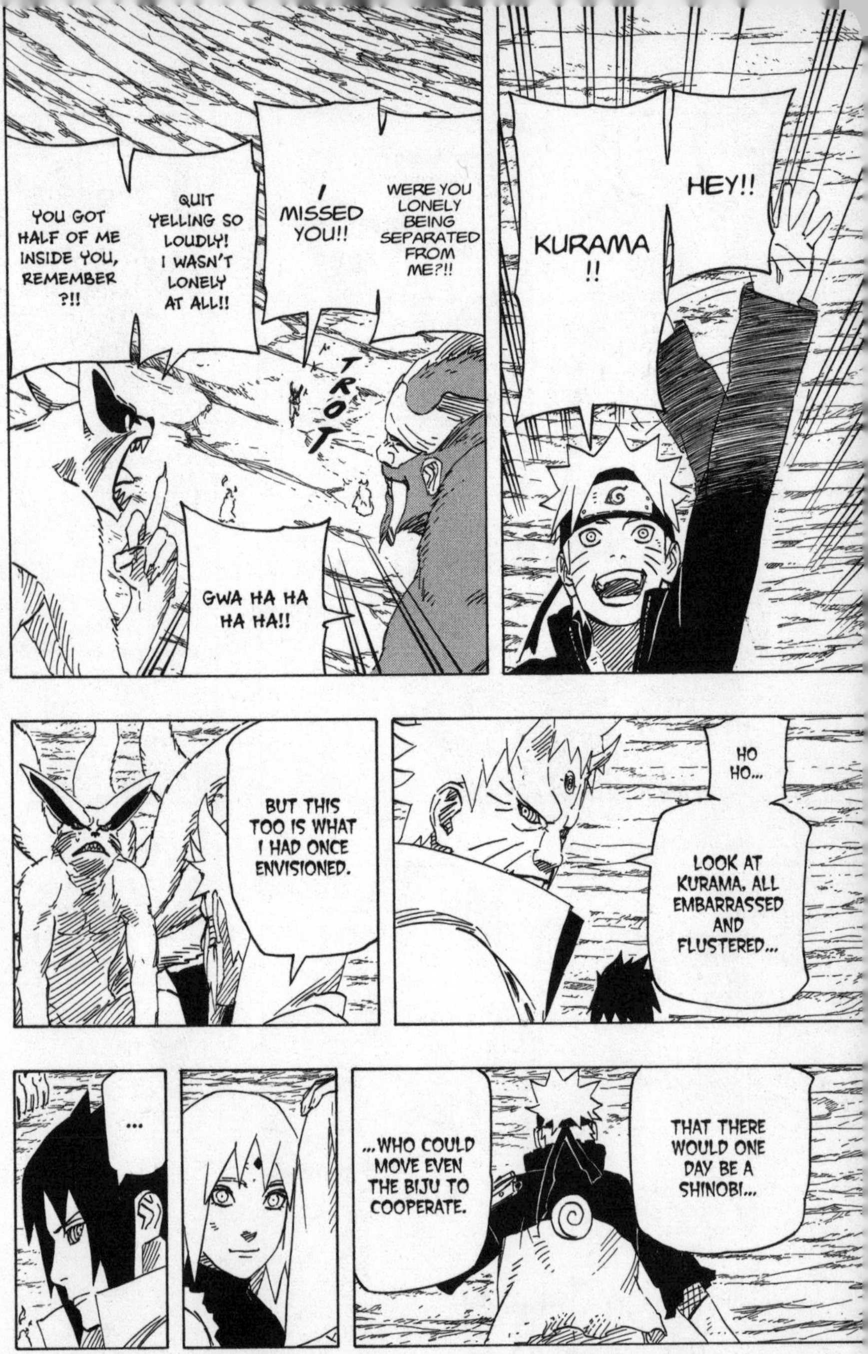
HEY!!
KURAMA !!
WERE YOU LONELY BEING SEPARATED FROM ME?!!
I MISSED YOU!!
QUIT YELLING SO LOUDLY! I WASN'T LONELY AT ALL!!
YOU GOT HALF OF ME INSIDE YOU, REMEMBER ?!!
TROT
GWA HA HA HA HA!!
HO HO...
LOOK AT KURAMA, ALL EMBARRASSED AND FLUSTERED...
BUT THIS TOO IS WHAT I HAD ONCE ENVISIONED.
THAT THERE WOULD ONE DAY BE A SHINOBI...
...WHO COULD MOVE EVEN THE BIJU TO COOPERATE.
...

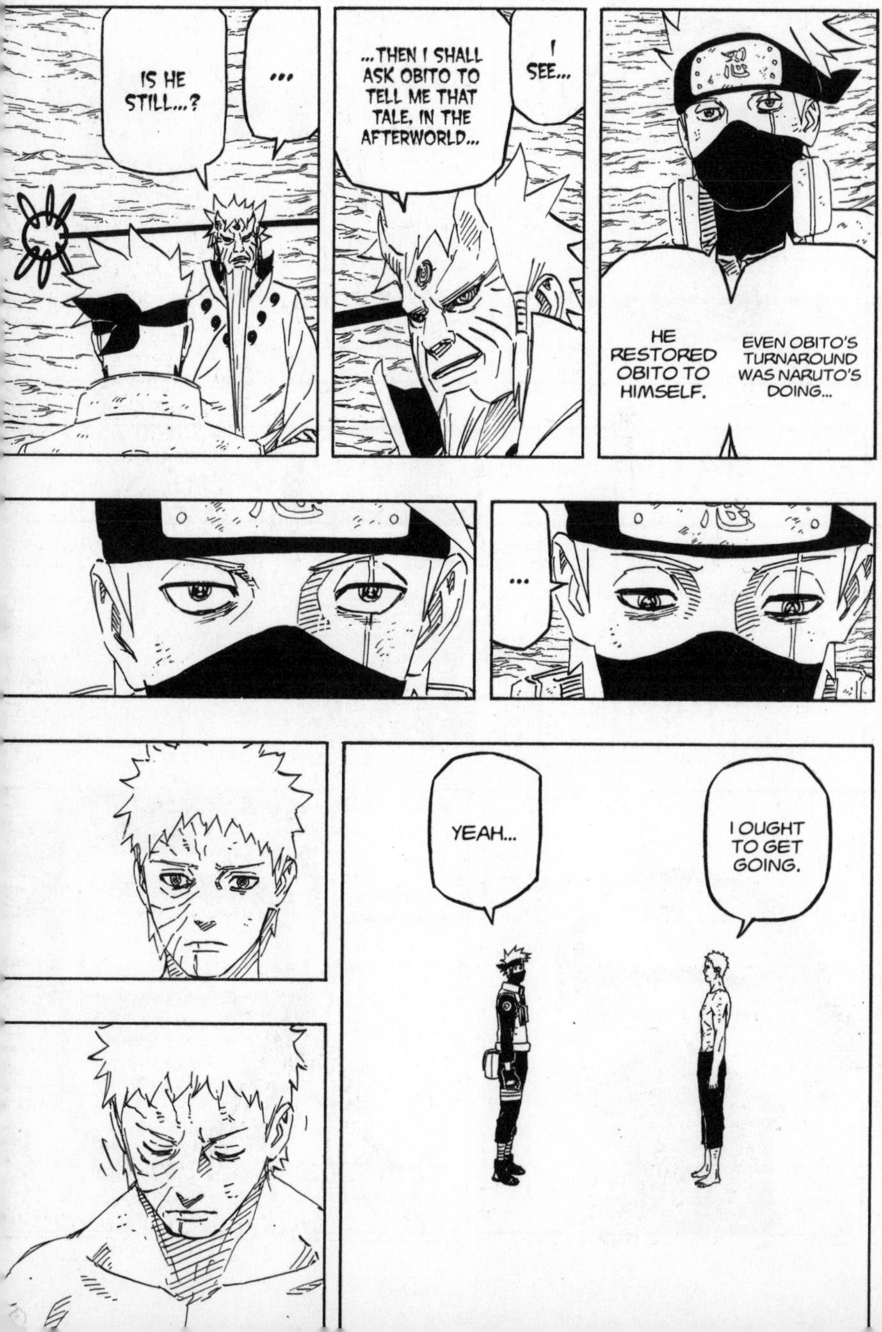
EVEN OBITO'S TURNAROUND WAS NARUTO'S DOING...
HE RESTORED OBITO TO HIMSELF.
I SEE...
...THEN I SHALL ASK OBITO TO TELL ME THAT TALE, IN THE AFTERWORLD...
...
IS HE STILL...?
...
I OUGHT TO GET GOING.
YEAH...

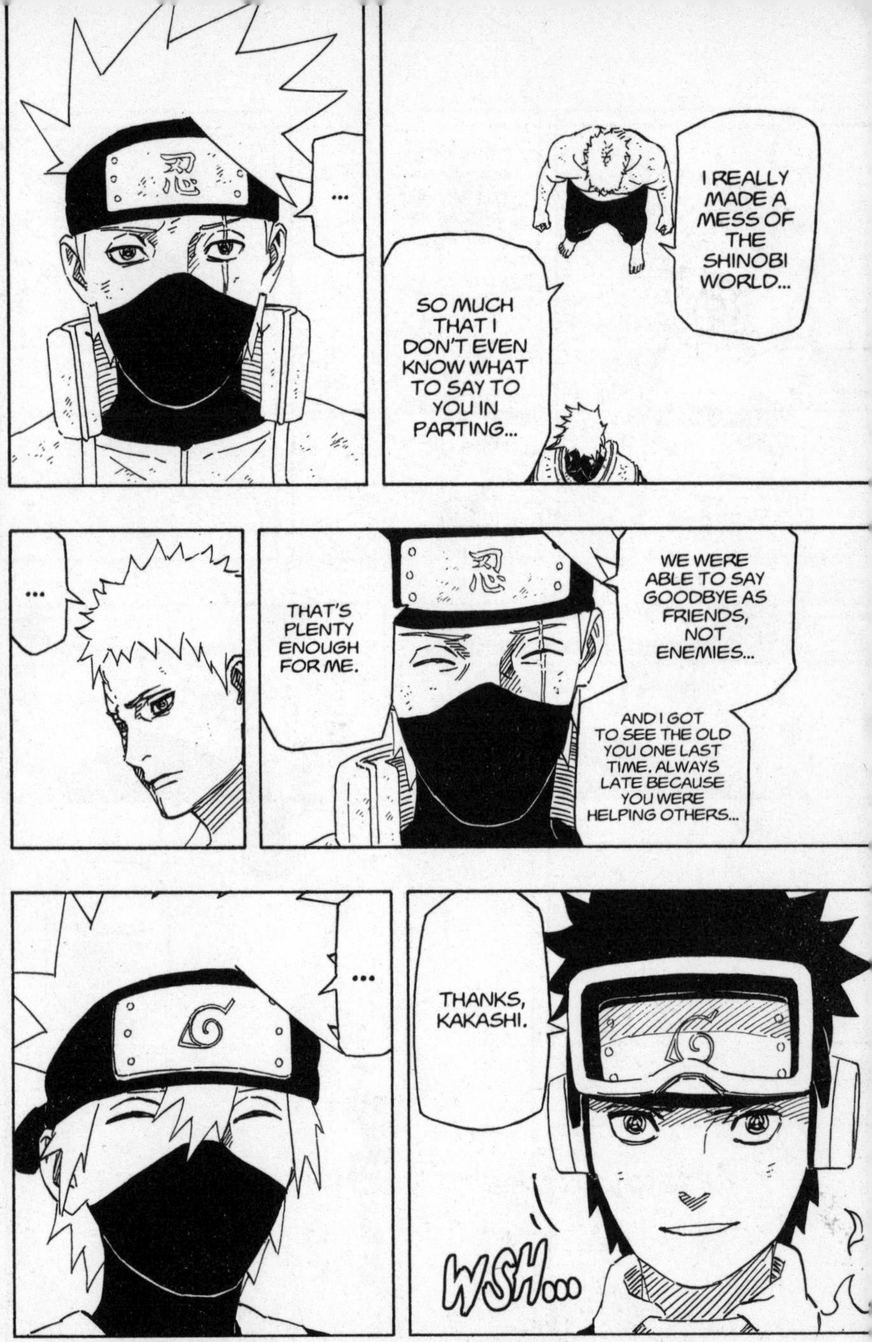
I REALLY MADE A MESS OF THE SHINOBI WORLD...
SO MUCH THAT I DON'T EVEN KNOW WHAT TO SAY TO YOU IN PARTING...
...
WE WERE ABLE TO SAY GOODBYE AS FRIENDS, NOT ENEMIES...
AND I GOT TO SEE THE OLD YOU ONE LAST TIME. ALWAYS LATE BECAUSE YOU WERE HELPING OTHERS...
THAT'S PLENTY ENOUGH FOR ME.
...
THANKS, KAKASHI.
WSH...
...

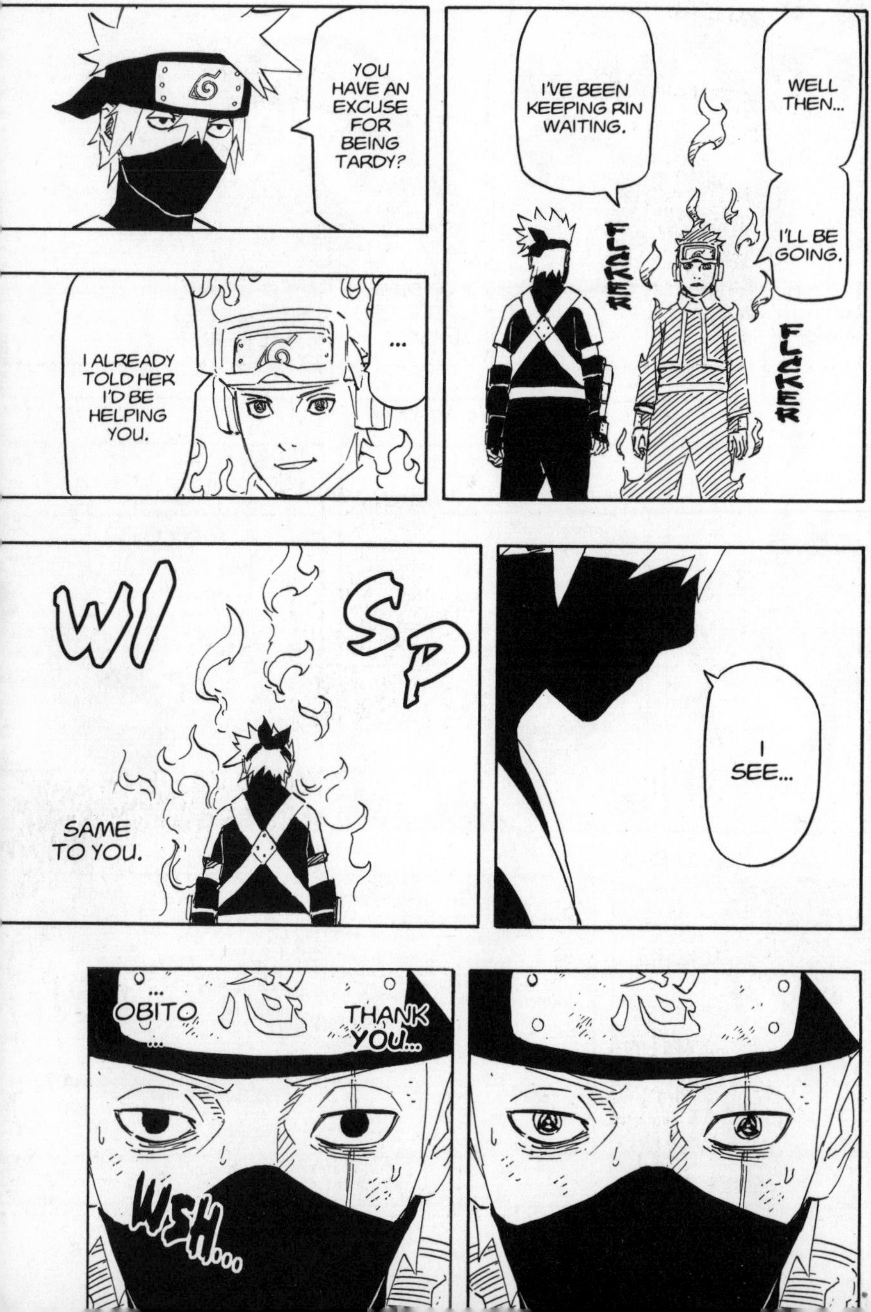

WELL THEN...
I'VE BEEN KEEPING RIN WAITING.
I'LL BE GOING.
FLICKER
FLICKER
YOU HAVE AN EXCUSE FOR BEING TARDY?
...
I ALREADY TOLD HER I'D BE HELPING YOU.
I SEE...
WI SP
SAME TO YOU.
THANK YOU...
...OBITO...
WSH...

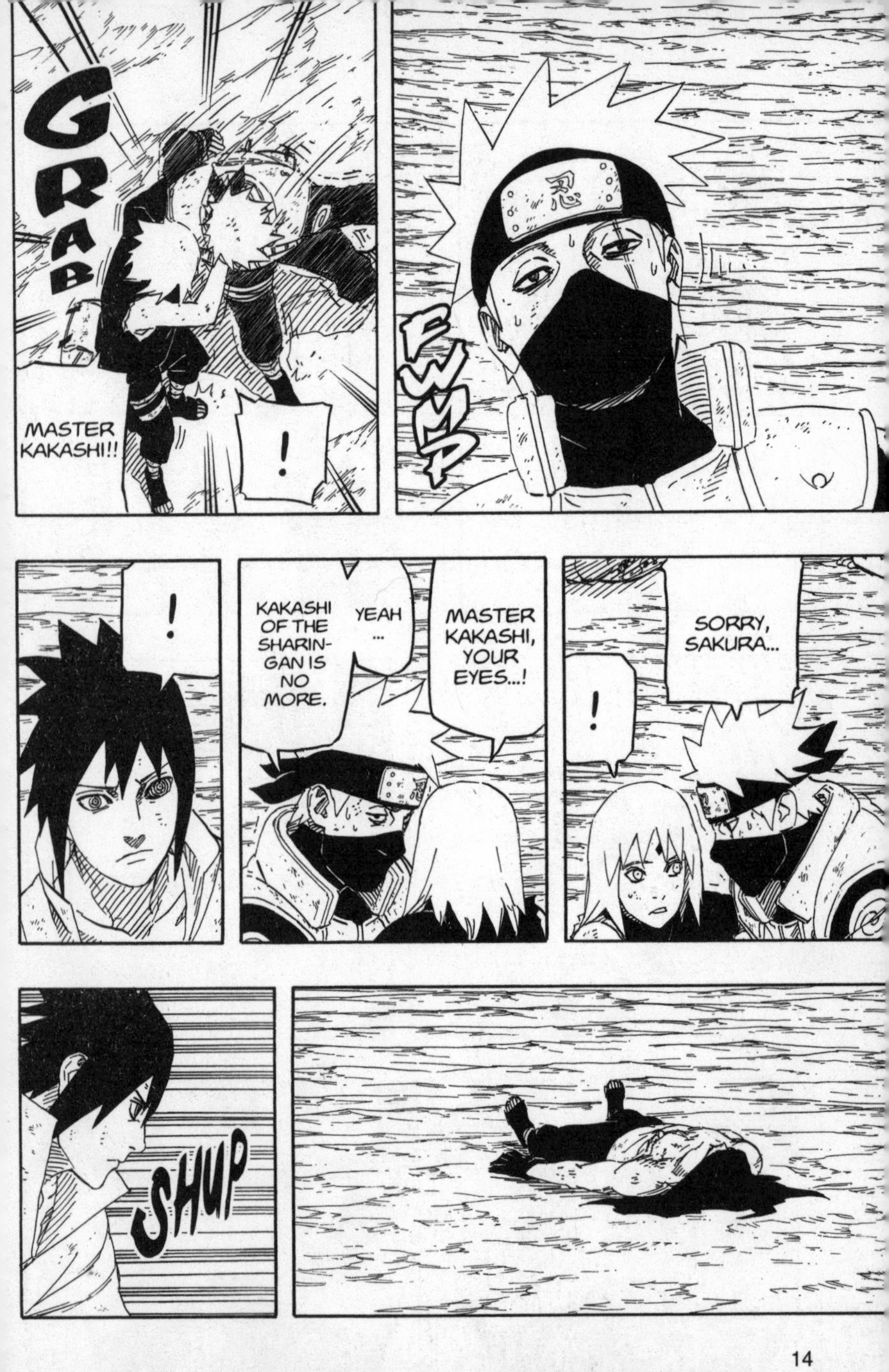
FWMP
GRAB
!
MASTER KAKASHI!!
SORRY, SAKURA...
!
MASTER KAKASHI, YOUR EYES...!
YEAH...
KAKASHI OF THE SHARINGAN IS NO MORE.
!
SHUP

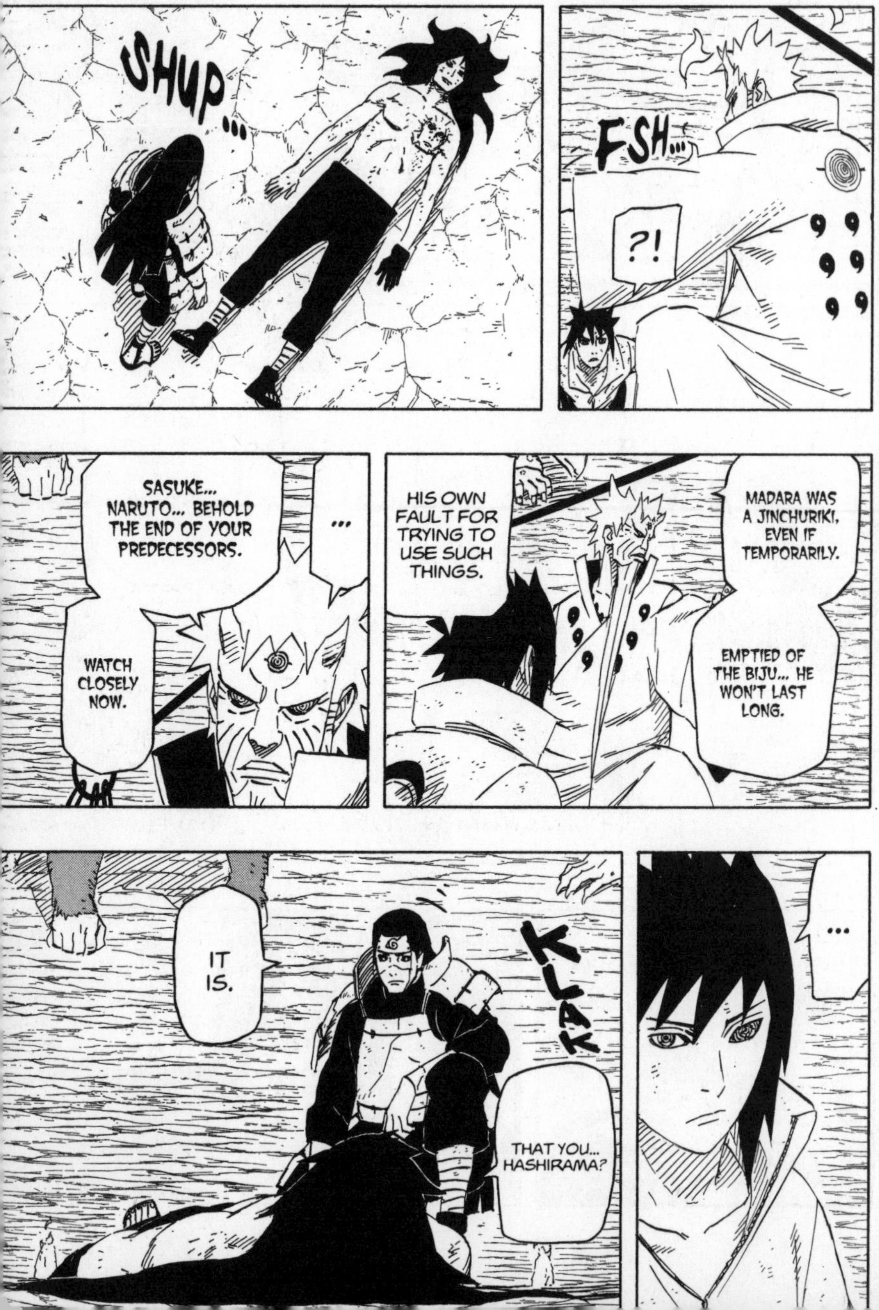
FSH...
?!
SHUP...
MADARA WAS A JINCHURIKI, EVEN IF TEMPORARILY.
EMPTIED OF THE BIJU... HE WON'T LAST LONG.
HIS OWN FAULT FOR TRYING TO USE SUCH THINGS.
...
SASUKE... NARUTO... BEHOLD THE END OF YOUR PREDECESSORS.
WATCH CLOSELY NOW.
...
KLAK
THAT YOU... HASHIRAMA?
IT IS.

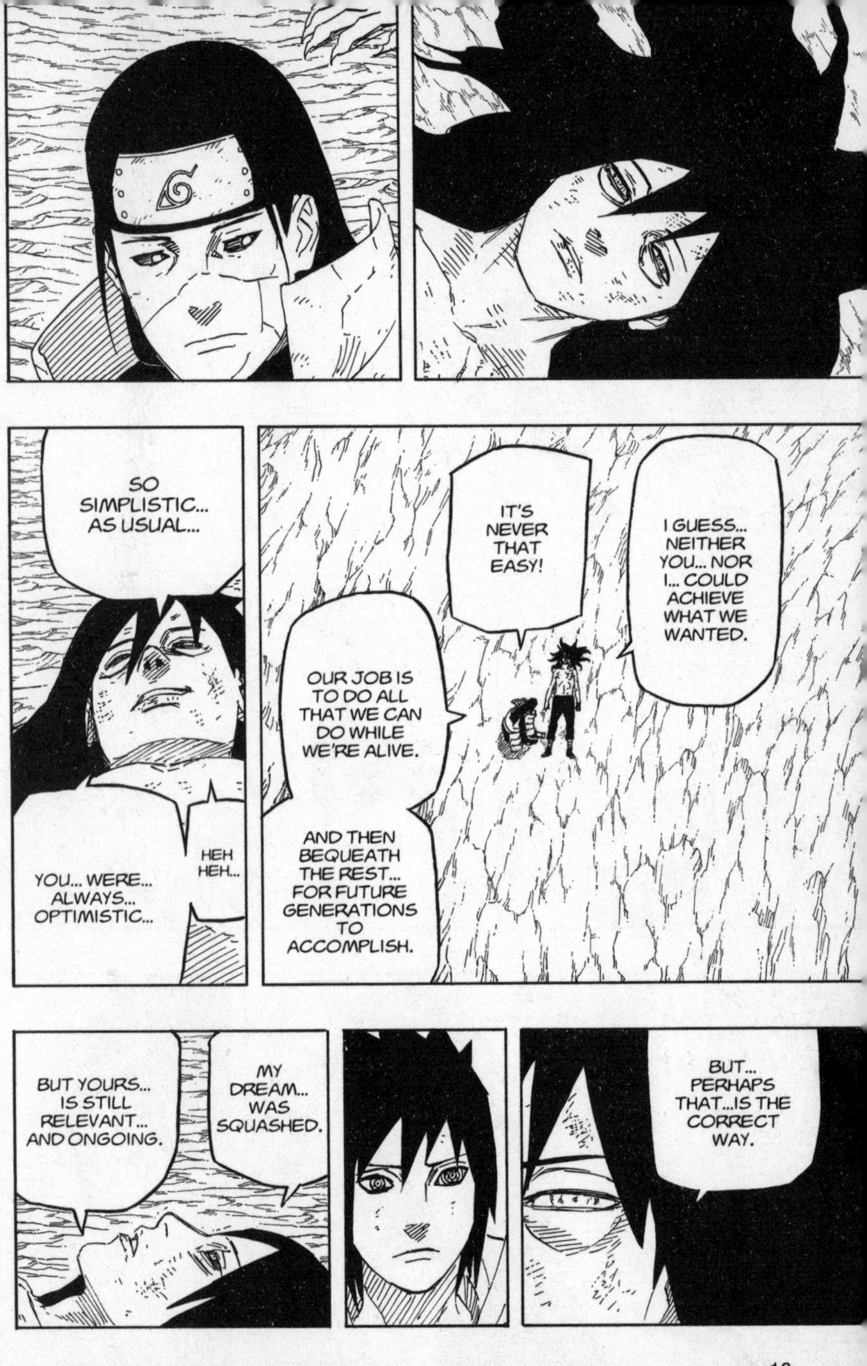
I GUESS... NEITHER YOU... NOR I... COULD ACHIEVE WHAT WE WANTED.
IT'S NEVER THAT EASY!
OUR JOB IS TO DO ALL THAT WE CAN DO WHILE WE'RE ALIVE.
AND THEN BEQUEATH THE REST... FOR FUTURE GENERATIONS TO ACCOMPLISH.
SO SIMPLISTIC... AS USUAL...
HEH HEH...
YOU... WERE... ALWAYS... OPTIMISTIC...
BUT... PERHAPS THAT...IS THE CORRECT WAY.
MY DREAM... WAS SQUASHED.
BUT YOURS... IS STILL RELEVANT... AND ONGOING.

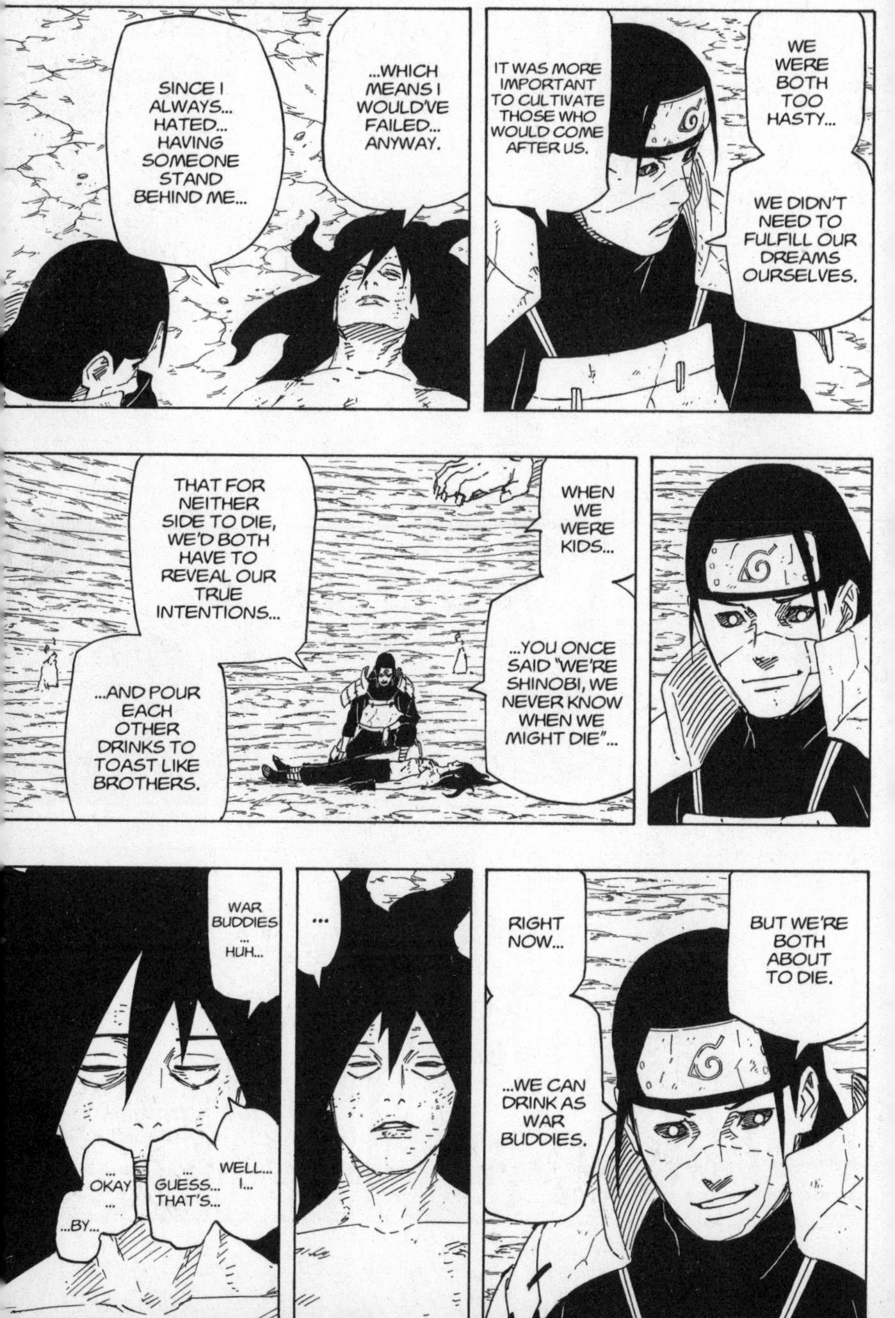
WE WERE BOTH TOO HASTY...
WE DIDN'T NEED TO FULFILL OUR DREAMS OURSELVES.
IT WAS MORE IMPORTANT TO CULTIVATE THOSE WHO WOULD COME AFTER US.
...WHICH MEANS I WOULD'VE FAILED... ANYWAY.
SINCE I ALWAYS... HATED... HAVING SOMEONE STAND BEHIND ME...
WHEN WE WERE KIDS...
...YOU ONCE SAID "WE'RE SHINOBI, WE NEVER KNOW WHEN WE MIGHT DIE"...
THAT FOR NEITHER SIDE TO DIE, WE'D BOTH HAVE TO REVEAL OUR TRUE INTENTIONS...
...AND POUR EACH OTHER DRINKS TO TOAST LIKE BROTHERS.
BUT WE'RE BOTH ABOUT TO DIE.
RIGHT NOW...
...WE CAN DRINK AS WAR BUDDIES.
...
WAR BUDDIES ... HUH...
WELL... I...
... GUESS... THAT'S...
... OKAY ...
...BY...

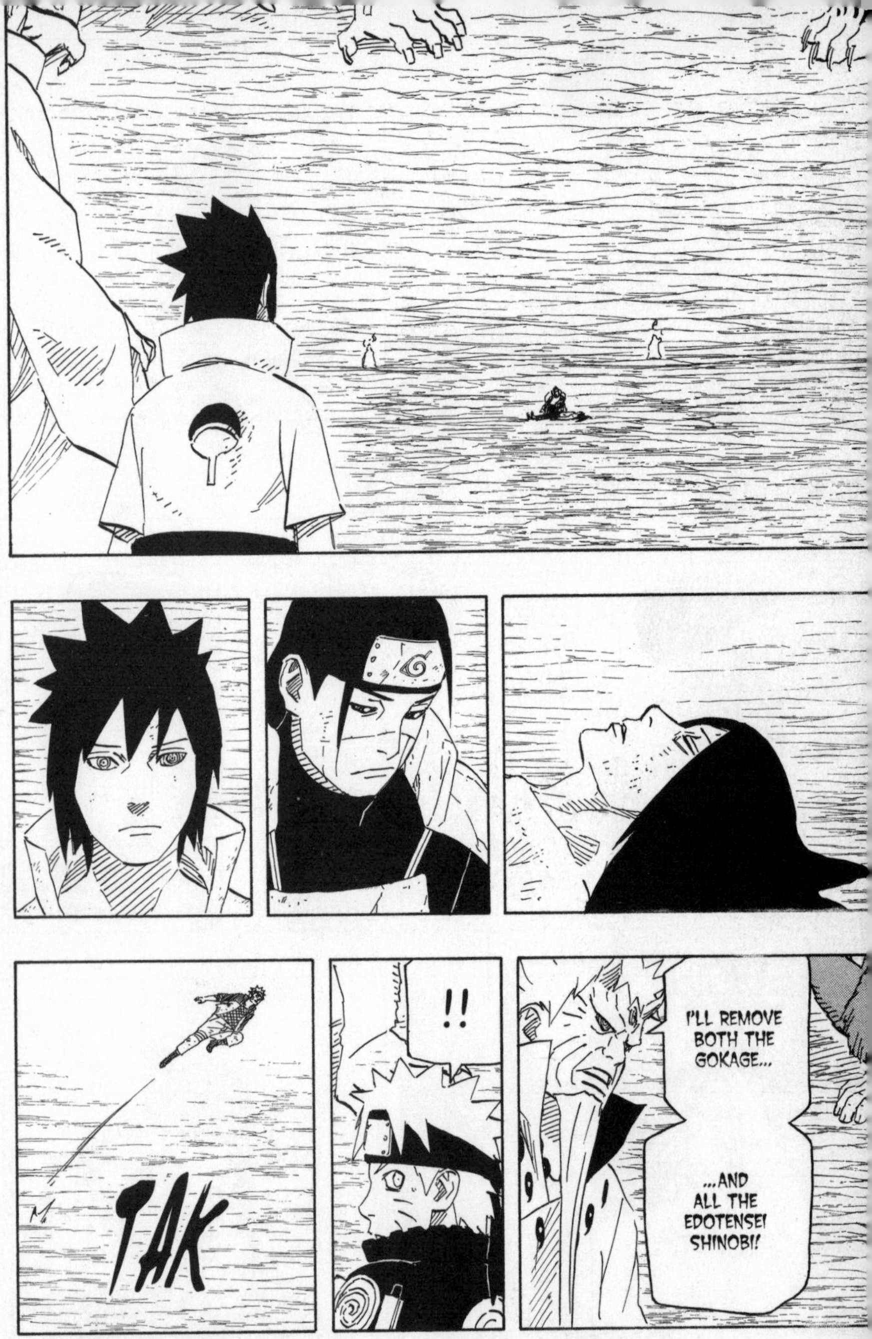
I'LL REMOVE BOTH THE GOKAGE...
...AND ALL THE EDOTENSEI SHINOBI!
!!
TAK

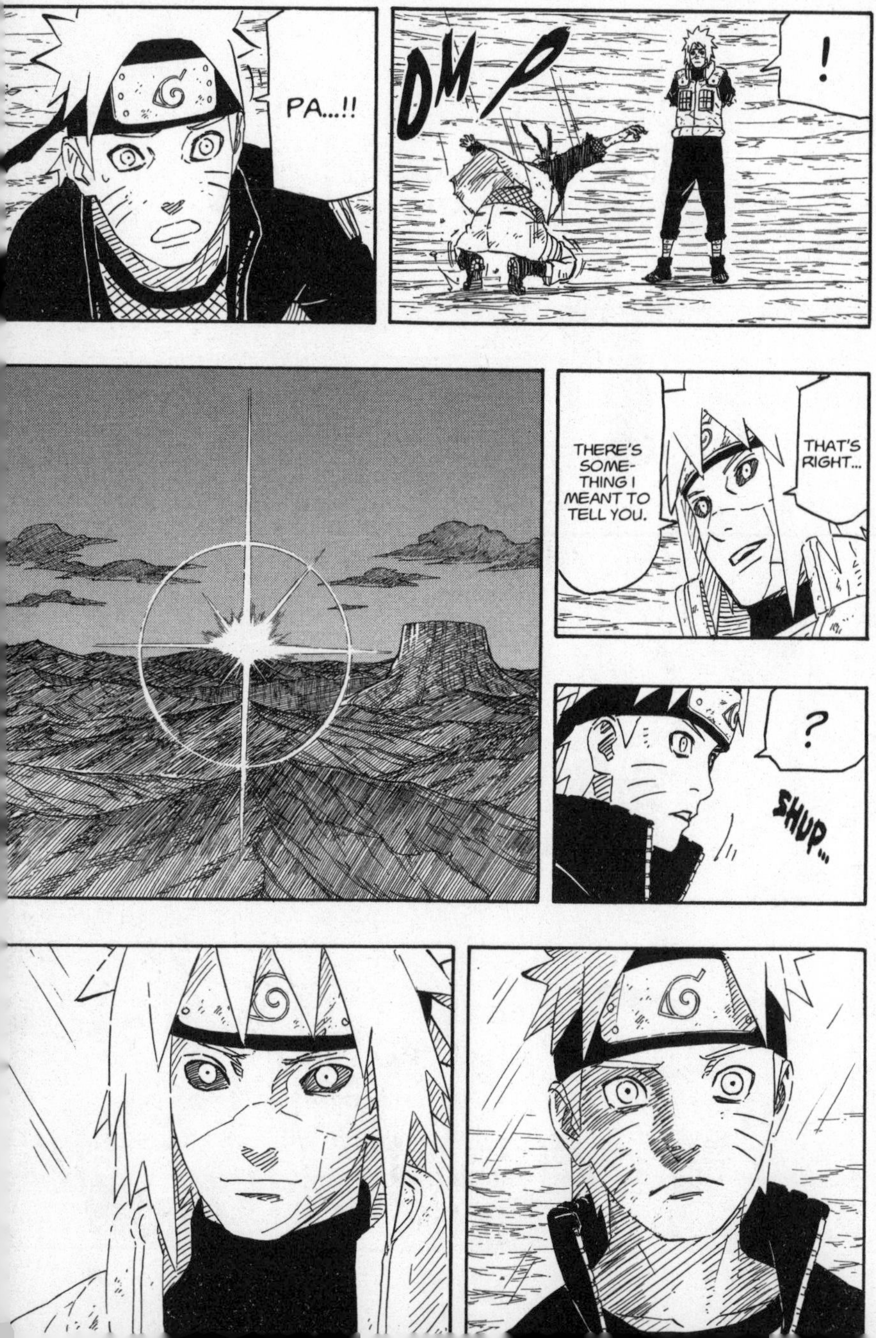
DMP
!
PA...!!
THAT'S RIGHT...
THERE'S SOME-THING I MEANT TO TELL YOU.
?
SHUP...

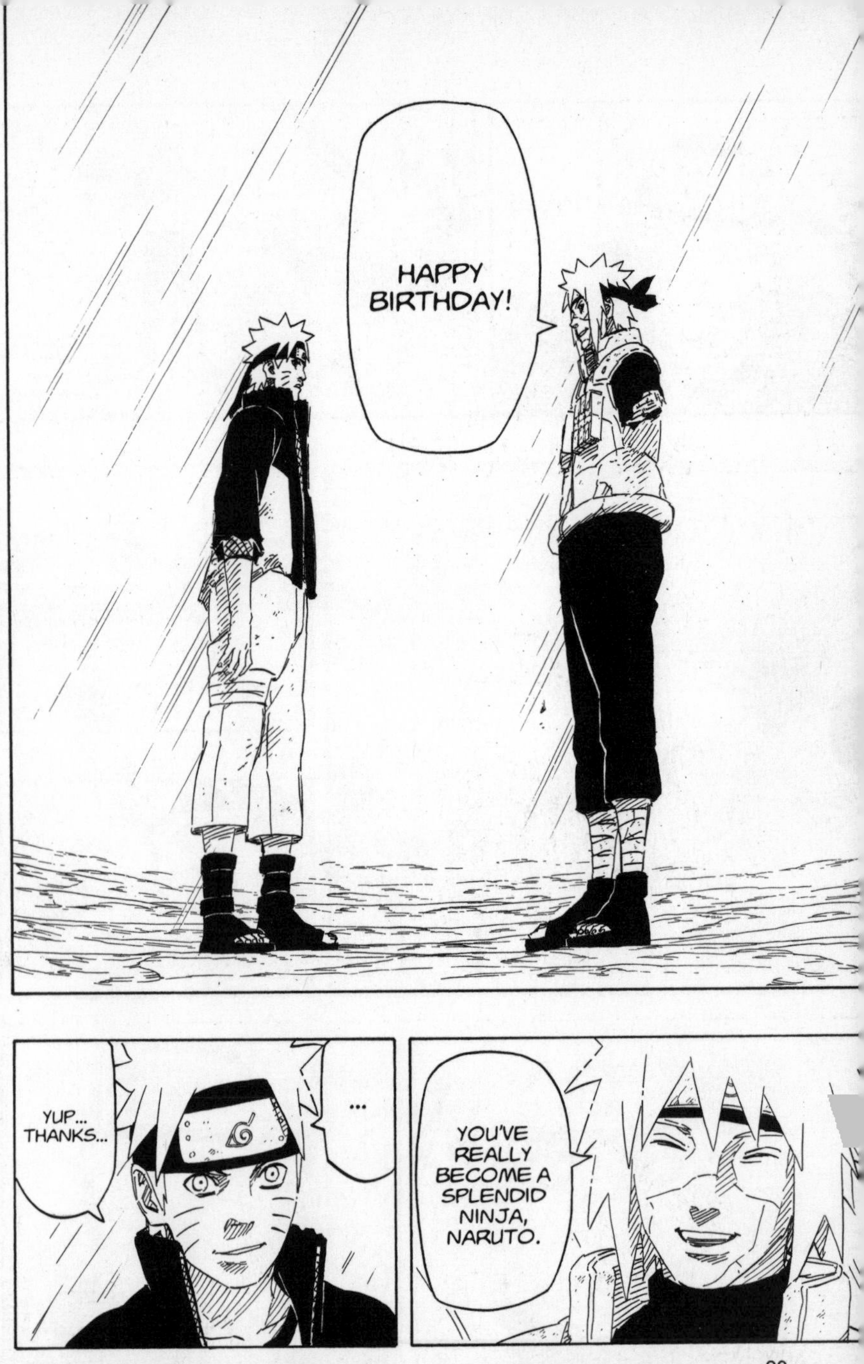
HAPPY BIRTHDAY!
YOU'VE REALLY BECOME A SPLENDID NINJA, NARUTO.
...
YUP... THANKS...

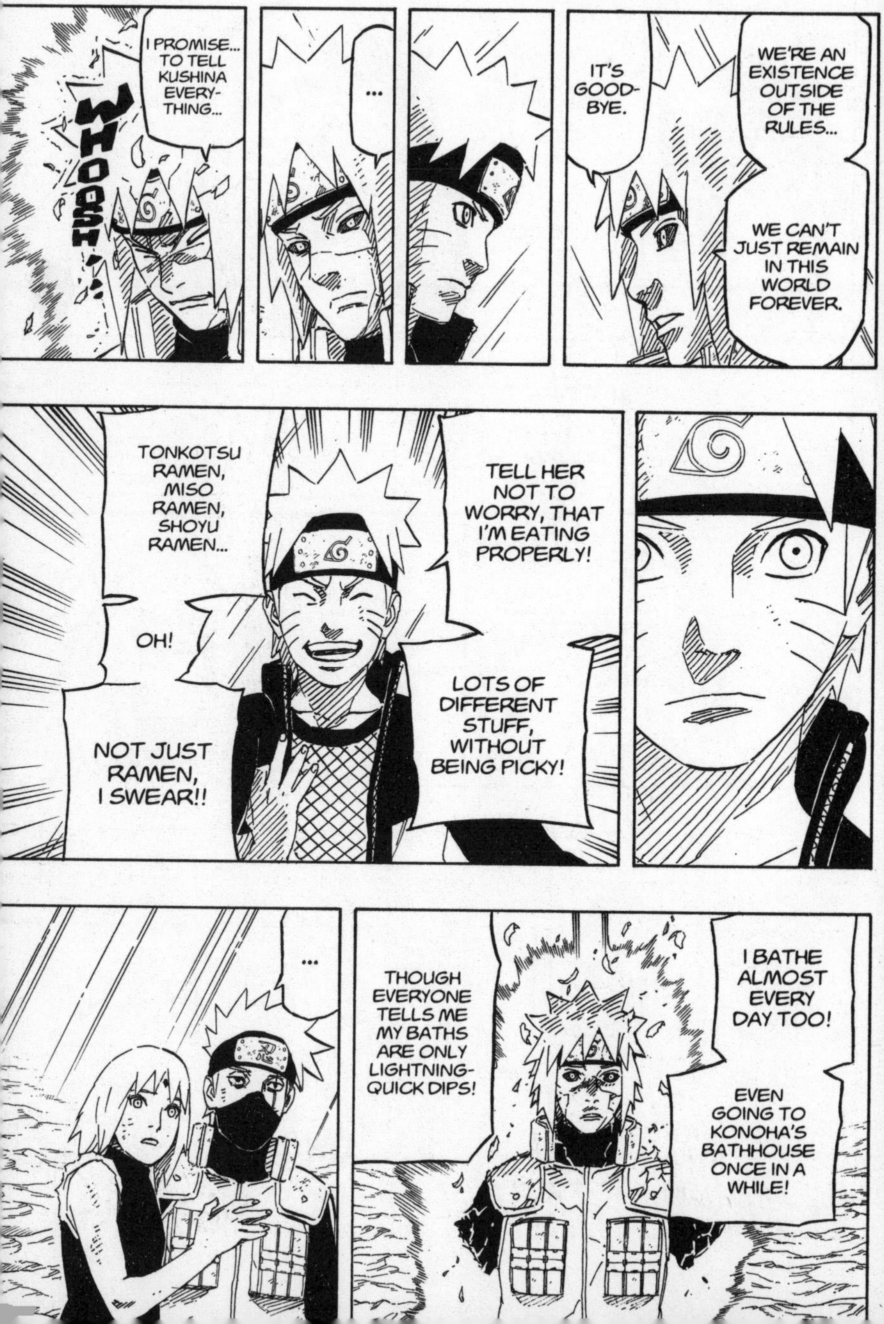
WE'RE AN EXISTENCE OUTSIDE OF THE RULES...
WE CAN'T JUST REMAIN IN THIS WORLD FOREVER.
IT'S GOOD-BYE.
...
I PROMISE... TO TELL KUSHINA EVERY-THING...
WHOOSH
TELL HER NOT TO WORRY, THAT I'M EATING PROPERLY!
LOTS OF DIFFERENT STUFF, WITHOUT BEING PICKY!
TONKOTSU RAMEN, MISO RAMEN, SHOYU RAMEN...
OH!
NOT JUST RAMEN, I SWEAR!!
I BATHE ALMOST EVERY DAY TOO!
EVEN GOING TO KONOHA'S BATHHOUSE ONCE IN A WHILE!
THOUGH EVERYONE TELLS ME MY BATHS ARE ONLY LIGHTNING-QUICK DIPS!
...

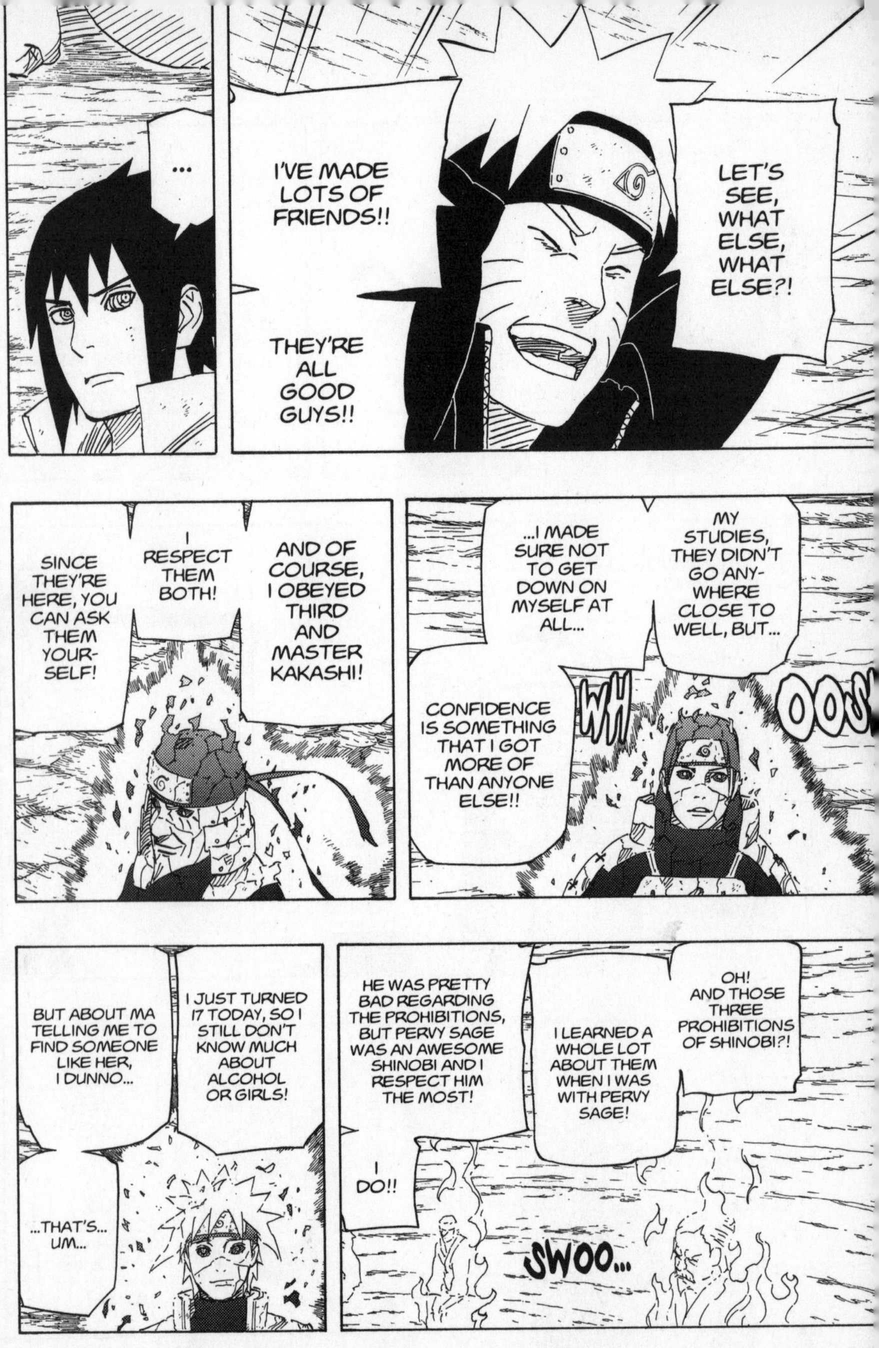

LET'S SEE, WHAT ELSE, WHAT ELSE?!
I'VE MADE LOTS OF FRIENDS!!
THEY'RE ALL GOOD GUYS!!
...
MY STUDIES, THEY DIDN'T GO ANYWHERE CLOSE TO WELL, BUT...
...I MADE SURE NOT TO GET DOWN ON MYSELF AT ALL...
CONFIDENCE IS SOMETHING THAT I GOT MORE OF THAN ANYONE ELSE!!
WH
OOS
AND OF COURSE, I OBEYED THIRD AND MASTER KAKASHI!
I RESPECT THEM BOTH!
SINCE THEY'RE HERE, YOU CAN ASK THEM YOURSELF!
OH! AND THOSE THREE PROHIBITIONS OF SHINOBI?!
I LEARNED A WHOLE LOT ABOUT THEM WHEN I WAS WITH PERVY SAGE!
HE WAS PRETTY BAD REGARDING THE PROHIBITIONS, BUT PERVY SAGE WAS AN AWESOME SHINOBI AND I RESPECT HIM THE MOST!
I DO!!
SWOO...
I JUST TURNED 17 TODAY, SO I STILL DON'T KNOW MUCH ABOUT ALCOHOL OR GIRLS!
BUT ABOUT MA TELLING ME TO FIND SOMEONE LIKE HER, I DUNNO...
...THAT'S... UM...

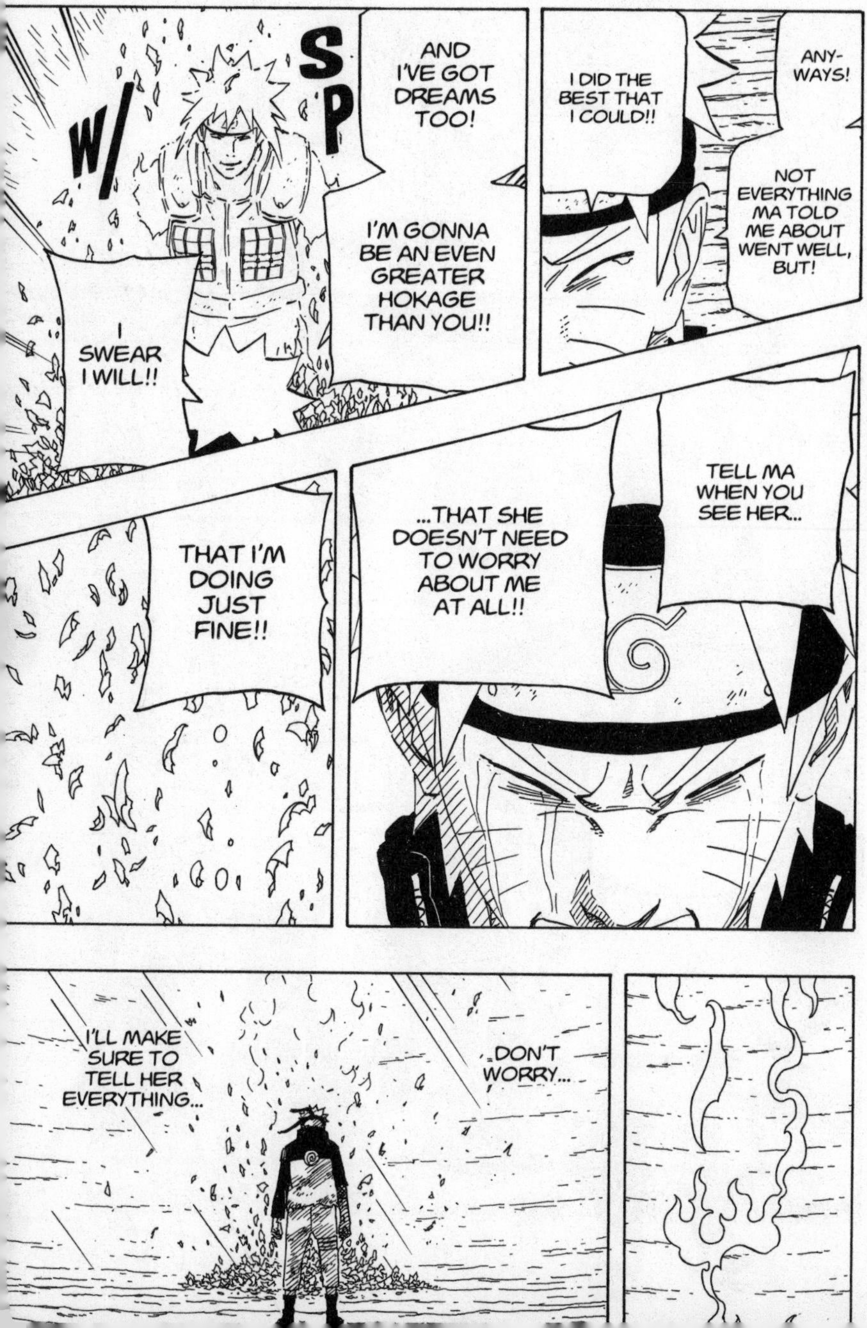
ANYWAYS!
NOT EVERYTHING MA TOLD ME ABOUT WENT WELL, BUT!
I DID THE BEST THAT I COULD!!
AND I'VE GOT DREAMS TOO!
I'M GONNA BE AN EVEN GREATER HOKAGE THAN YOU!!
I SWEAR I WILL!!
TELL MA WHEN YOU SEE HER...
...THAT SHE DOESN'T NEED TO WORRY ABOUT ME AT ALL!!
THAT I'M DOING JUST FINE!!
DON'T WORRY...
I'LL MAKE SURE TO TELL HER EVERYTHING...

END OF SERIES COMMEMORATION ILLUSTRATION (1) KENJI TAIRA

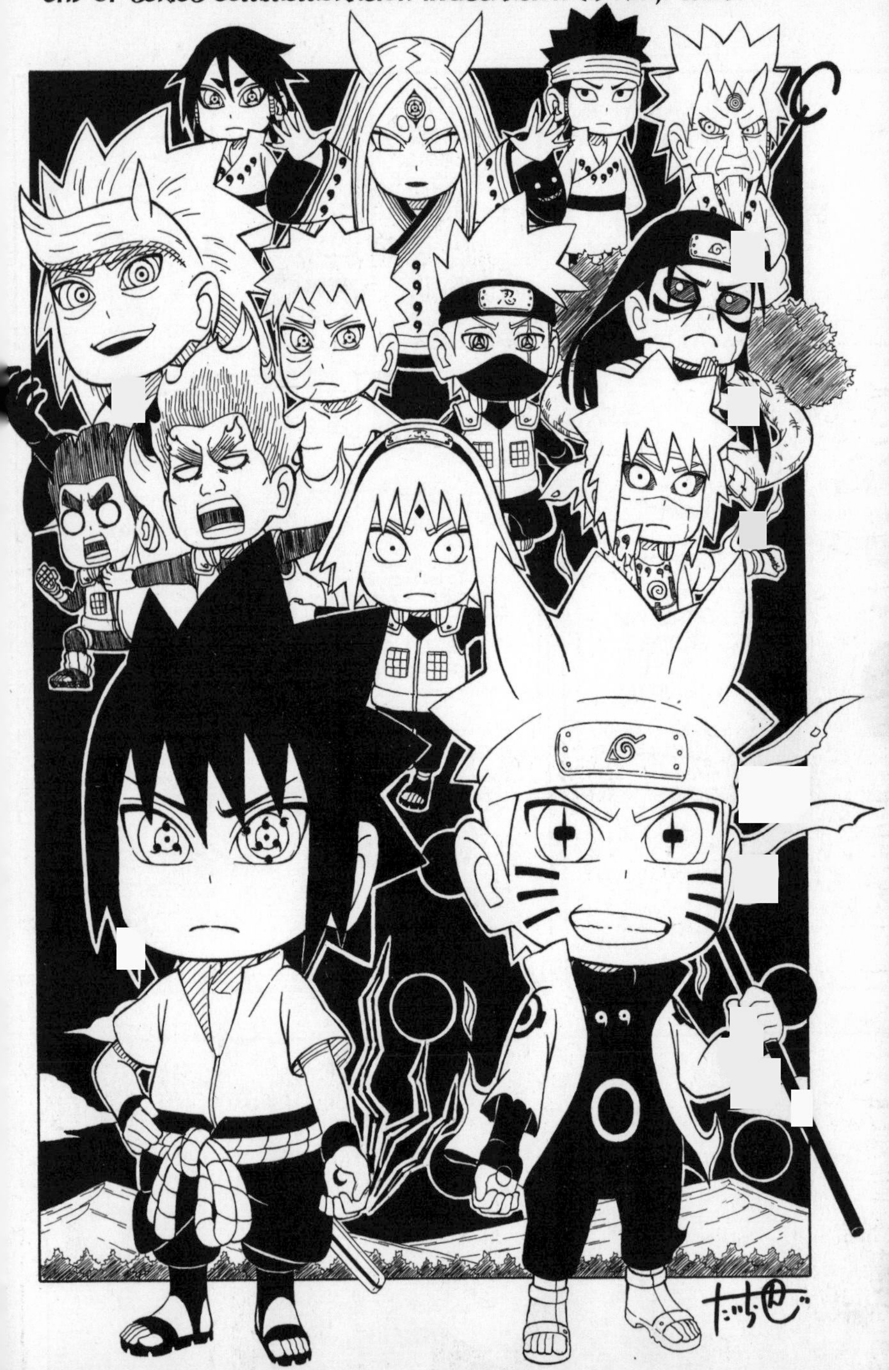

Number 692: Revolution

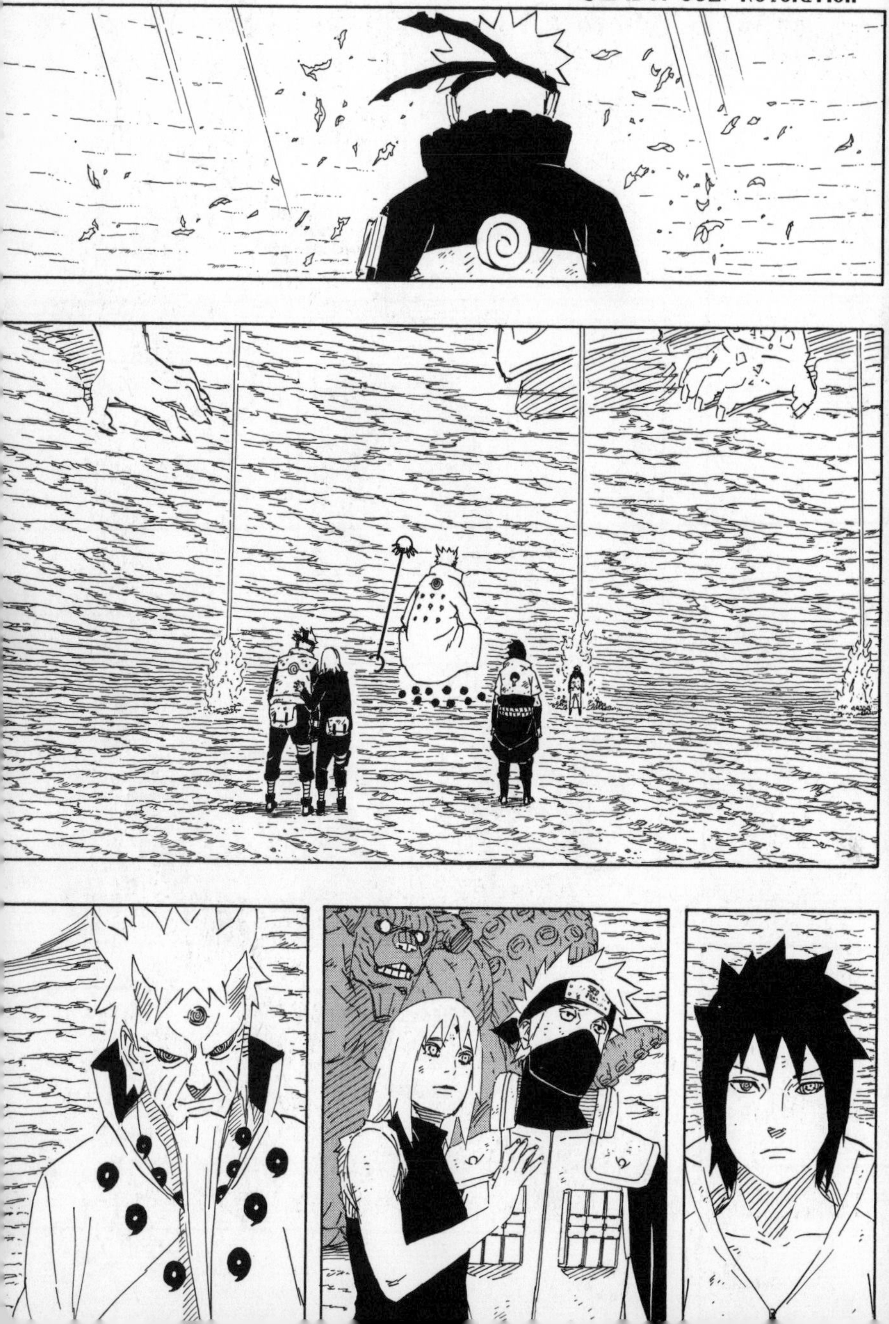

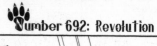

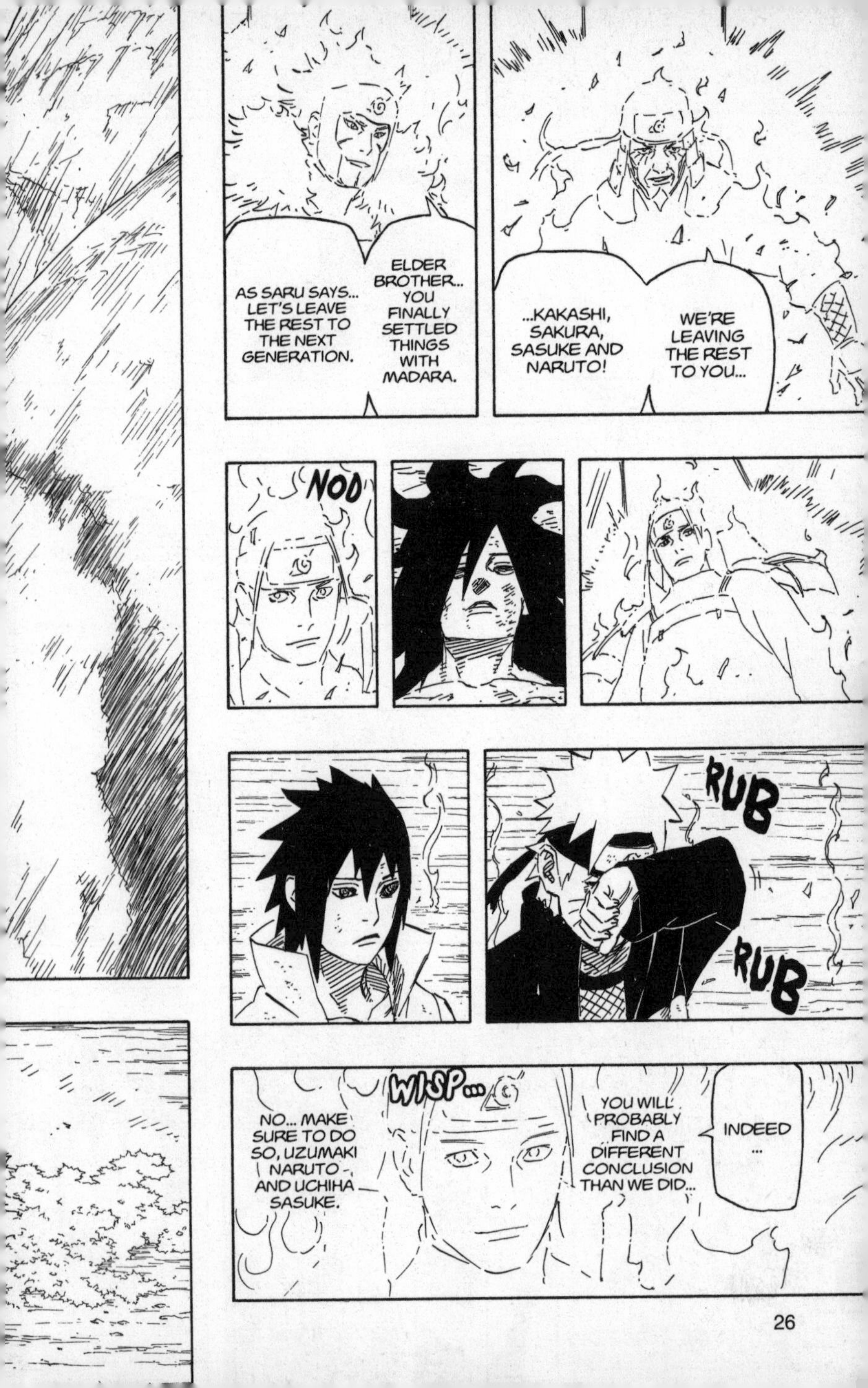
WE'RE LEAVING THE REST TO YOU...
...KAKASHI, SAKURA, SASUKE AND NARUTO!
ELDER BROTHER... YOU FINALLY SETTLED THINGS WITH MADARA.
AS SARU SAYS... LET'S LEAVE THE REST TO THE NEXT GENERATION.
NOD
RUB
RUB
INDEED...
YOU WILL PROBABLY FIND A DIFFERENT CONCLUSION THAN WE DID...
WISP...
NO... MAKE SURE TO DO SO, UZUMAKI NARUTO AND UCHIHA SASUKE.

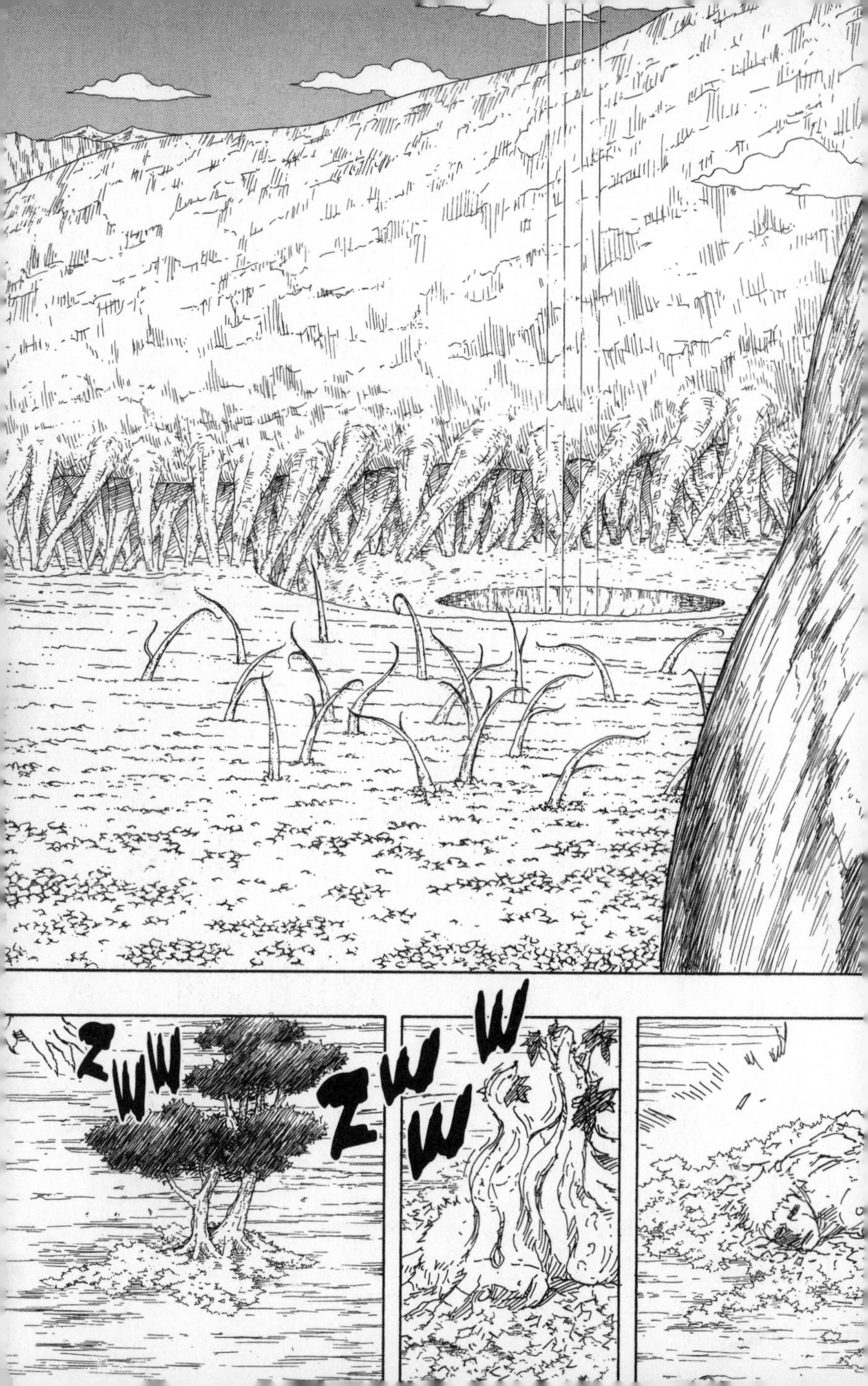
ZWWW
ZWW

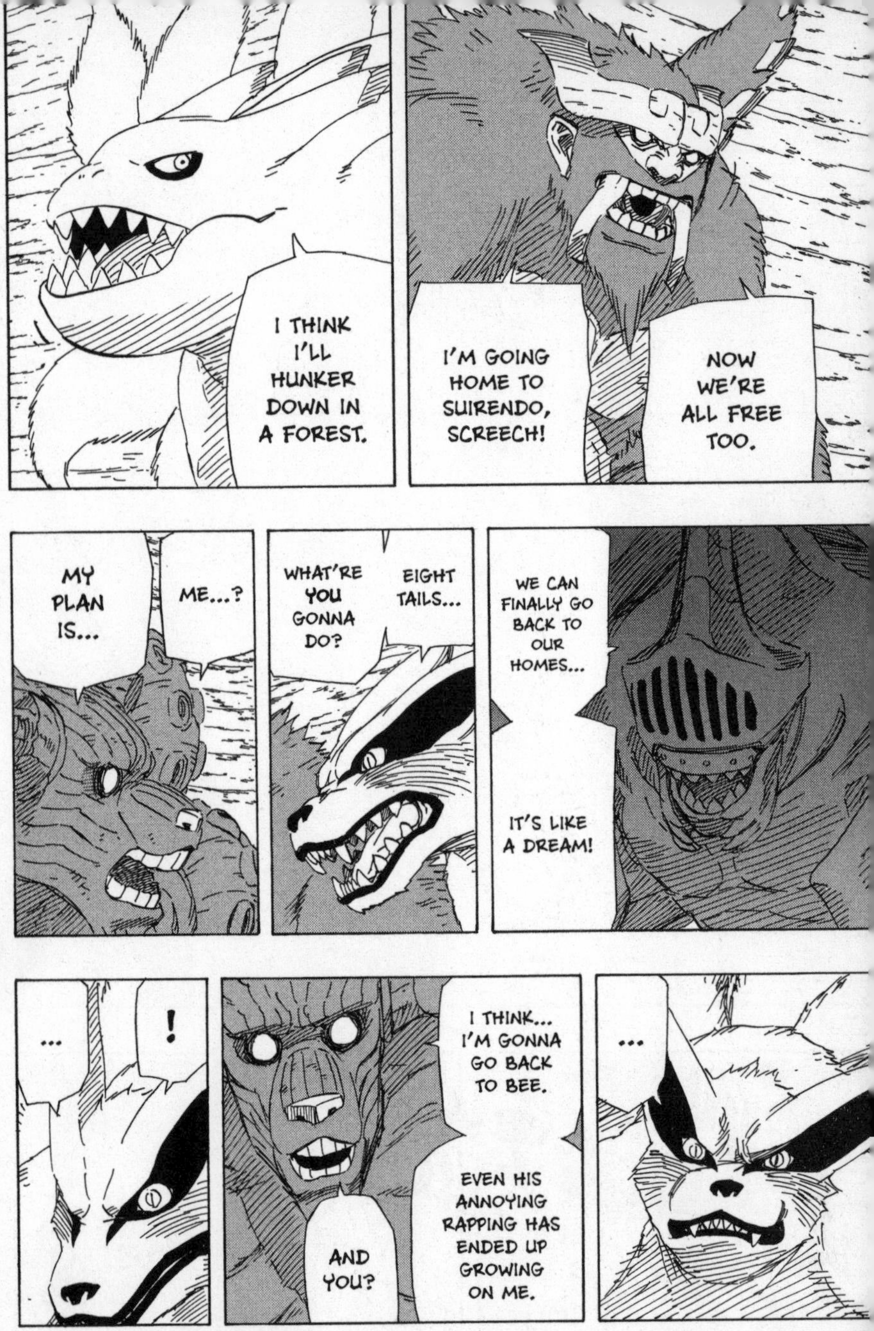
NOW WE'RE ALL FREE TOO.
I'M GOING HOME TO SUIRENDO, SCREECH!
I THINK I'LL HUNKER DOWN IN A FOREST.
WE CAN FINALLY GO BACK TO OUR HOMES...
IT'S LIKE A DREAM!
EIGHT TAILS...
WHAT'RE YOU GONNA DO?
ME...?
MY PLAN IS...
...
I THINK... I'M GONNA GO BACK TO BEE.
EVEN HIS ANNOYING RAPPING HAS ENDED UP GROWING ON ME.
AND YOU?
!
...

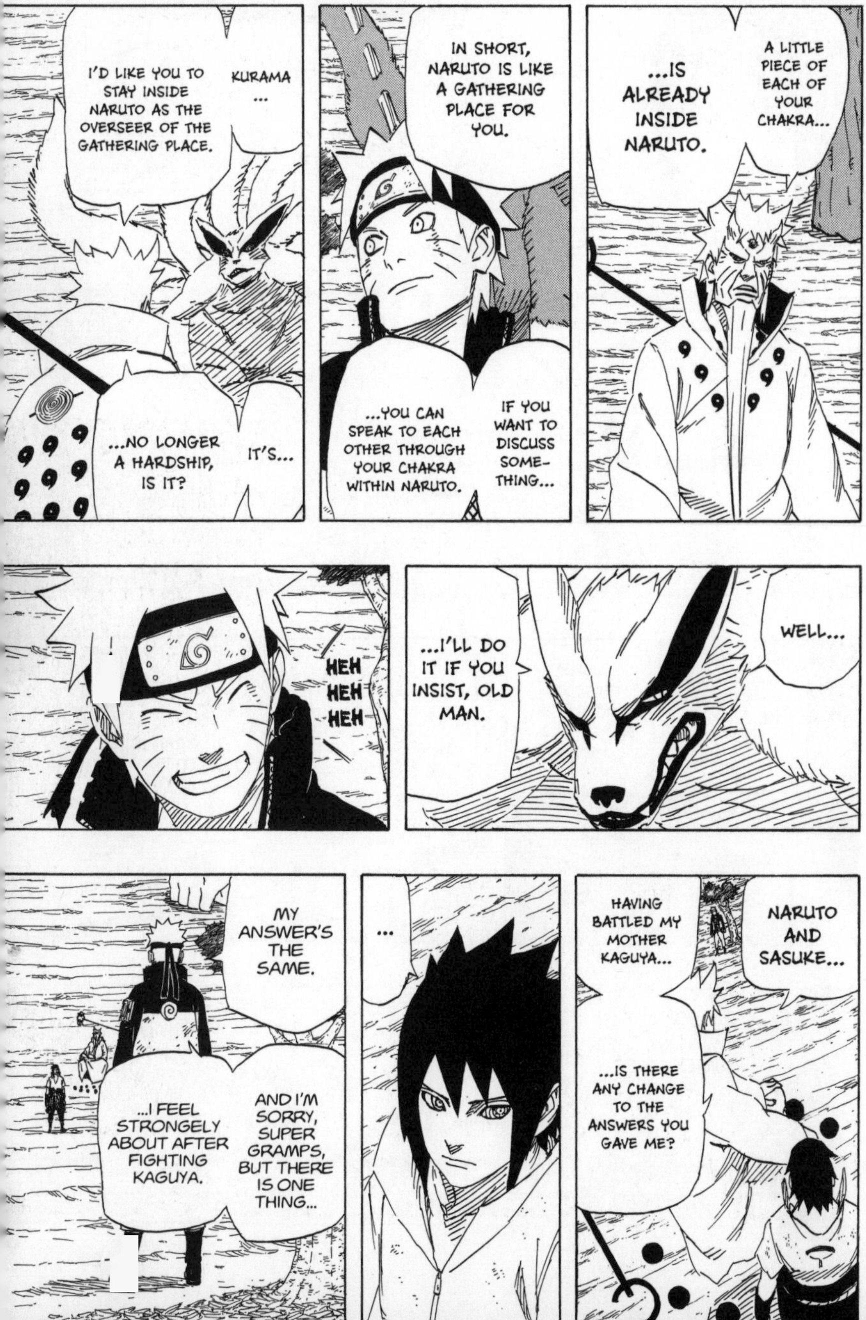
A LITTLE PIECE OF EACH OF YOUR CHAKRA...
...IS ALREADY INSIDE NARUTO.
IN SHORT, NARUTO IS LIKE A GATHERING PLACE FOR YOU.
IF YOU WANT TO DISCUSS SOME-THING...
...YOU CAN SPEAK TO EACH OTHER THROUGH YOUR CHAKRA WITHIN NARUTO.
KURAMA...
I'D LIKE YOU TO STAY INSIDE NARUTO AS THE OVERSEER OF THE GATHERING PLACE.
IT'S...
...NO LONGER A HARDSHIP, IS IT?
WELL...
...I'LL DO IT IF YOU INSIST, OLD MAN.
!
HEH HEH HEH
NARUTO AND SASUKE...
HAVING BATTLED MY MOTHER KAGUYA...
...IS THERE ANY CHANGE TO THE ANSWERS YOU GAVE ME?
...
MY ANSWER'S THE SAME.
AND I'M SORRY, SUPER GRAMPS, BUT THERE IS ONE THING...
...I FEEL STRONGELY ABOUT AFTER FIGHTING KAGUYA.

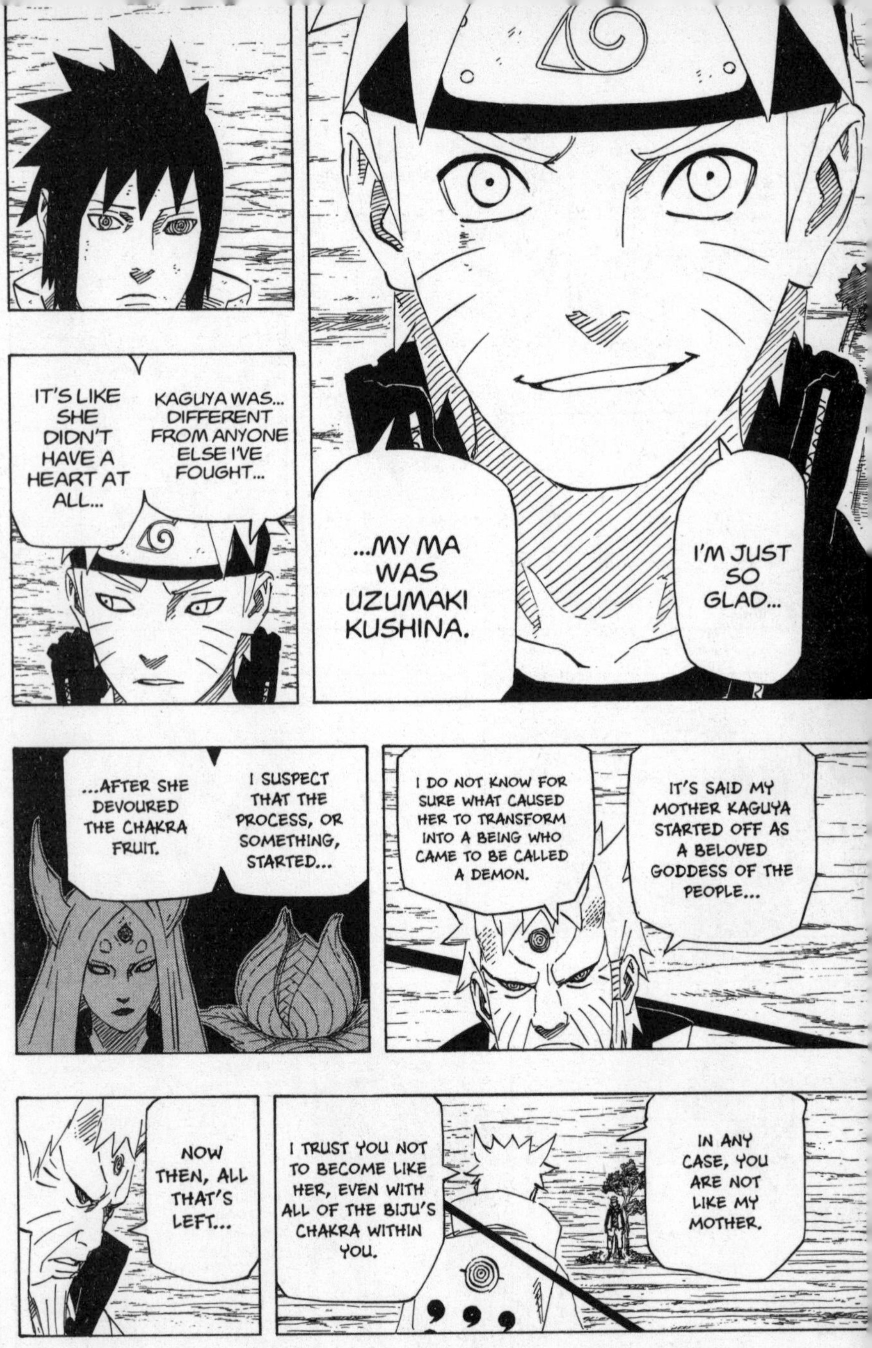
I'M JUST SO GLAD...
...MY MA WAS UZUMAKI KUSHINA.
KAGUYA WAS... DIFFERENT FROM ANYONE ELSE I'VE FOUGHT...
IT'S LIKE SHE DIDN'T HAVE A HEART AT ALL...
IT'S SAID MY MOTHER KAGUYA STARTED OFF AS A BELOVED GODDESS OF THE PEOPLE...
I DO NOT KNOW FOR SURE WHAT CAUSED HER TO TRANSFORM INTO A BEING WHO CAME TO BE CALLED A DEMON.
I SUSPECT THAT THE PROCESS, OR SOMETHING, STARTED...
...AFTER SHE DEVOURED THE CHAKRA FRUIT.
IN ANY CASE, YOU ARE NOT LIKE MY MOTHER.
I TRUST YOU NOT TO BECOME LIKE HER, EVEN WITH ALL OF THE BIJU'S CHAKRA WITHIN YOU.
NOW THEN, ALL THAT'S LEFT...

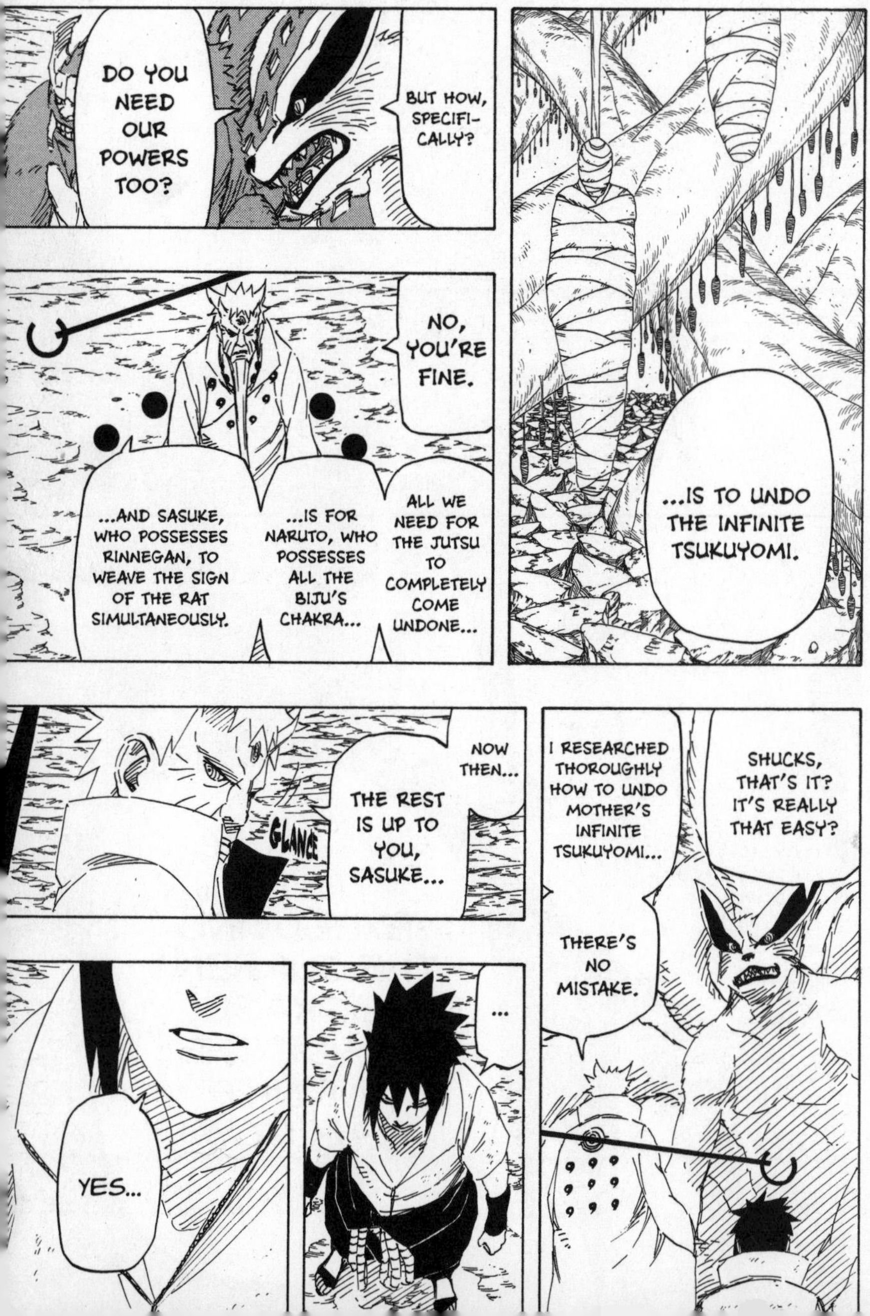
...IS TO UNDO THE INFINITE TSUKUYOMI.
BUT HOW, SPECIFI-CALLY?
DO YOU NEED OUR POWERS TOO?
NO, YOU'RE FINE.
ALL WE NEED FOR THE JUTSU TO COMPLETELY COME UNDONE...
...IS FOR NARUTO, WHO POSSESSES ALL THE BIJU'S CHAKRA...
...AND SASUKE, WHO POSSESSES RINNEGAN, TO WEAVE THE SIGN OF THE RAT SIMULTANEOUSLY.
SHUCKS, THAT'S IT? IT'S REALLY THAT EASY?
I RESEARCHED THOROUGHLY HOW TO UNDO MOTHER'S INFINITE TSUKUYOMI...
THERE'S NO MISTAKE.
NOW THEN...
THE REST IS UP TO YOU, SASUKE...
GLANCE
...
YES...

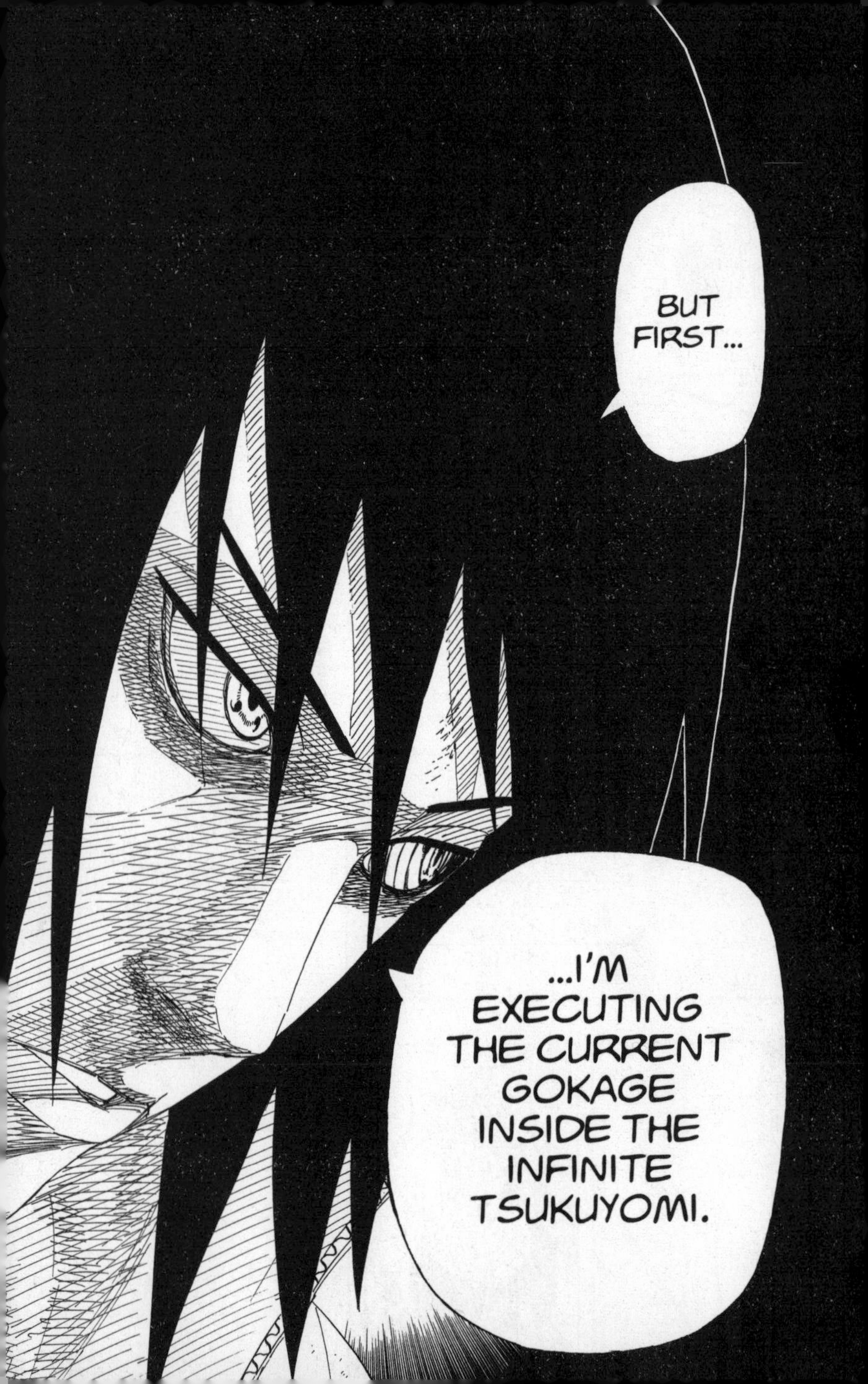
BUT FIRST...
...I'M EXECUTING THE CURRENT GOKAGE INSIDE THE INFINITE TSUKUYOMI.

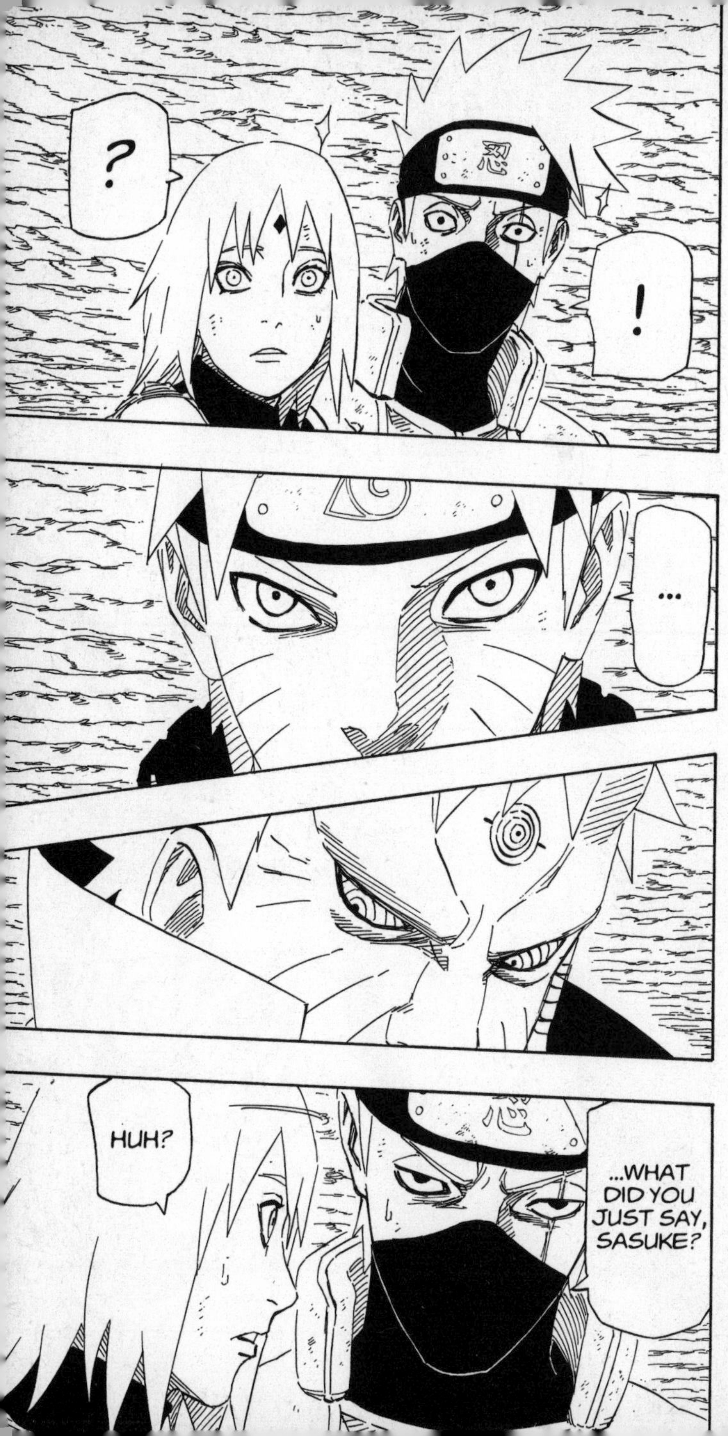
!
?
...
...WHAT DID YOU JUST SAY, SASUKE?
HUH?

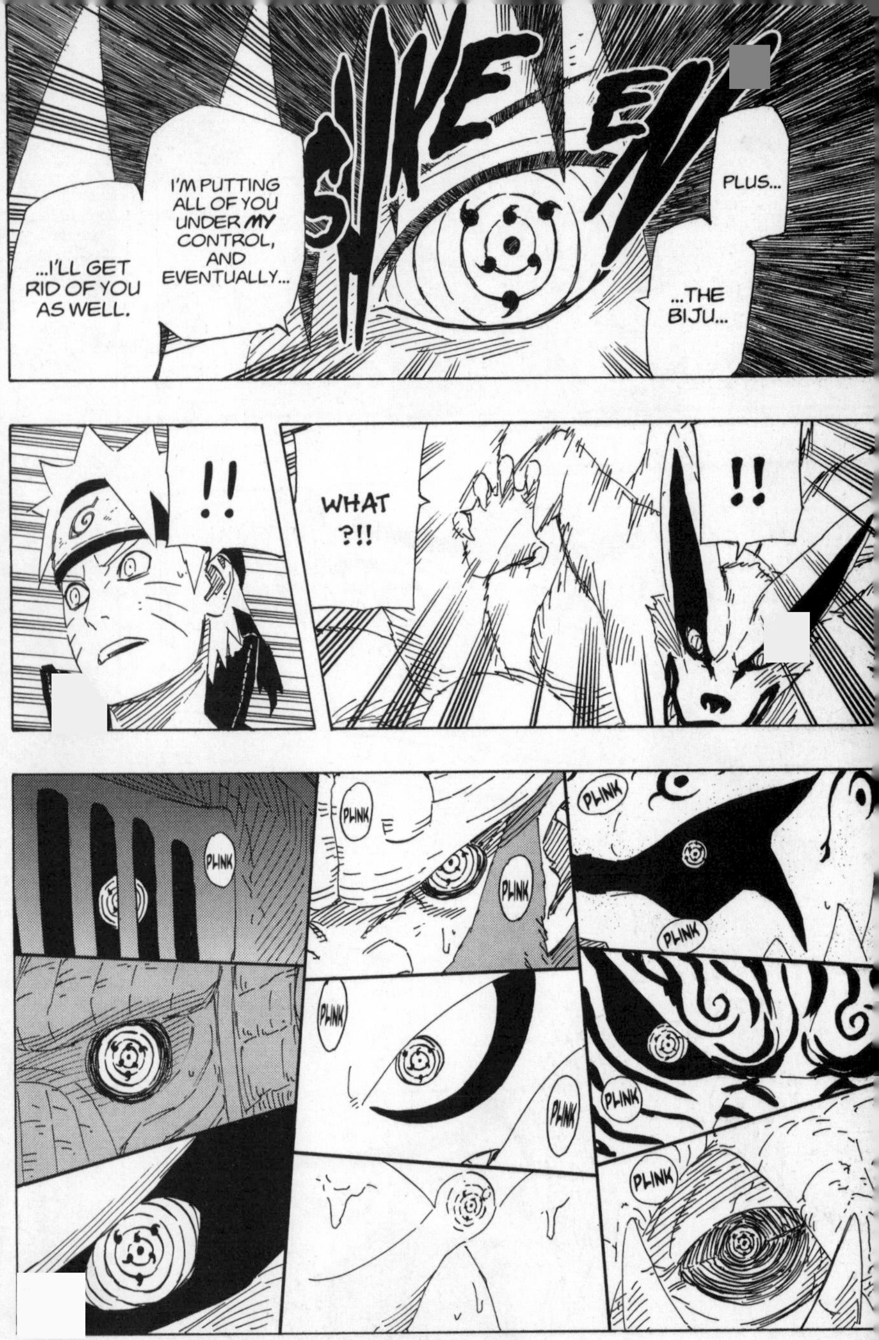
PLUS...
...THE BIJU...
I'M PUTTING ALL OF YOU UNDER MY CONTROL, AND EVENTUALLY...
...I'LL GET RID OF YOU AS WELL.
!!
WHAT ?!!
!!
PLINK
PLINK
PLINK
PLINK
PLINK
PLINK
PLINK
PLINK
PLINK

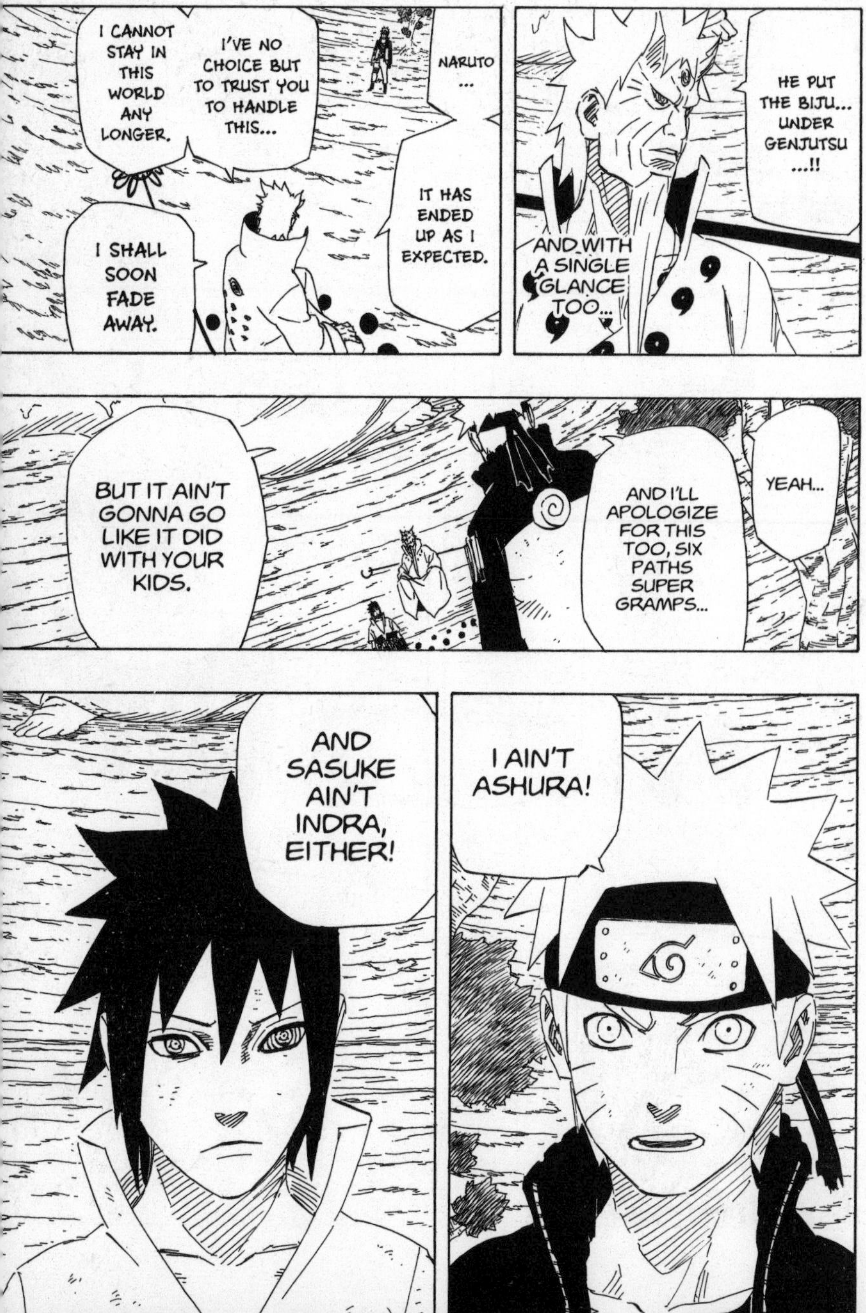
HE PUT THE BIJU... UNDER GENJUTSU ...!!
AND WITH A SINGLE GLANCE TOO...
NARUTO ...
IT HAS ENDED UP AS I EXPECTED.
I'VE NO CHOICE BUT TO TRUST YOU TO HANDLE THIS...
I CANNOT STAY IN THIS WORLD ANY LONGER.
I SHALL SOON FADE AWAY.
YEAH...
AND I'LL APOLOGIZE FOR THIS TOO, SIX PATHS SUPER GRAMPS...
BUT IT AIN'T GONNA GO LIKE IT DID WITH YOUR KIDS.
I AIN'T ASHURA!
AND SASUKE AIN'T INDRA, EITHER!

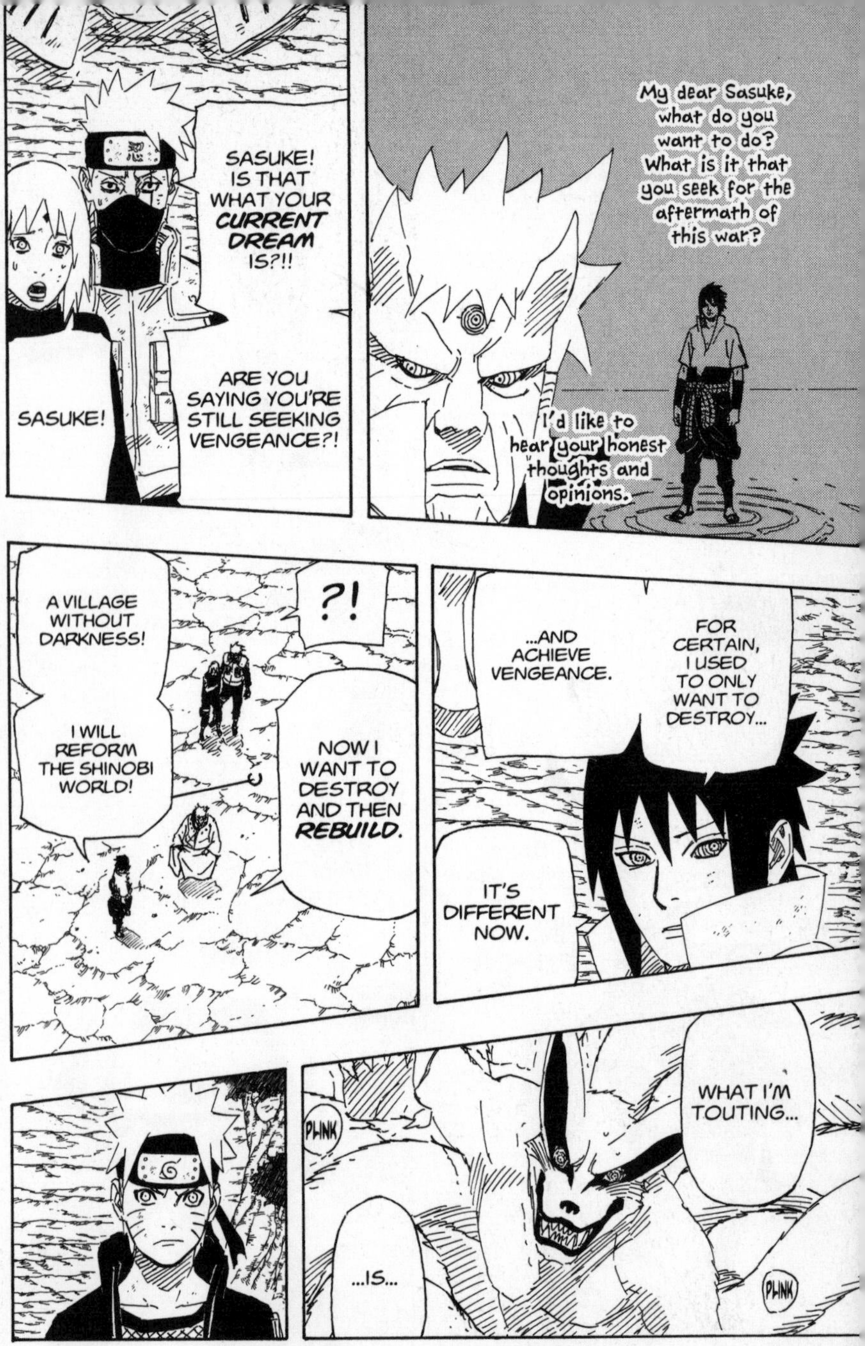
My dear Sasuke, what do you want to do? What is it that you seek for the aftermath of this war?
I'd like to hear your honest thoughts and opinions.
SASUKE! IS THAT WHAT YOUR *CURRENT DREAM* IS?!!
ARE YOU SAYING YOU'RE STILL SEEKING VENGEANCE?!
SASUKE!
FOR CERTAIN, I USED TO ONLY WANT TO DESTROY...
...AND ACHIEVE VENGEANCE.
IT'S DIFFERENT NOW.
?!
NOW I WANT TO DESTROY AND THEN *REBUILD*.
A VILLAGE WITHOUT DARKNESS!
I WILL REFORM THE SHINOBI WORLD!
WHAT I'M TOUTING...
PLINK
...IS...
PLINK

REVOLUTION... YOU SAY?!

....!

!

ALL OF THE PREVIOUS KAGE CREATED THESE CURRENT CIRCUMSTANCES.

SO, I WILL BECOME HOKAGE AND CHANGE THE VILLAGE.

THIS HOKAGE THAT YOU HAVE MENTIONED...

WHAT MEAN YOU BY IT...?

...I'LL TELL YOU.

IF YOU WANT TO KNOW SO BADLY...

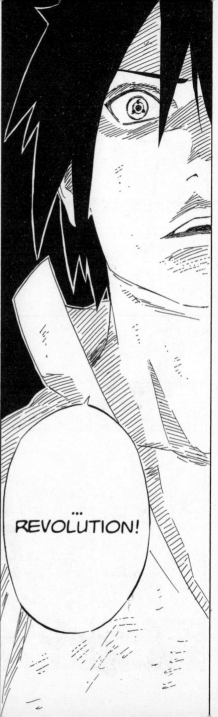

...REVOLUTION!

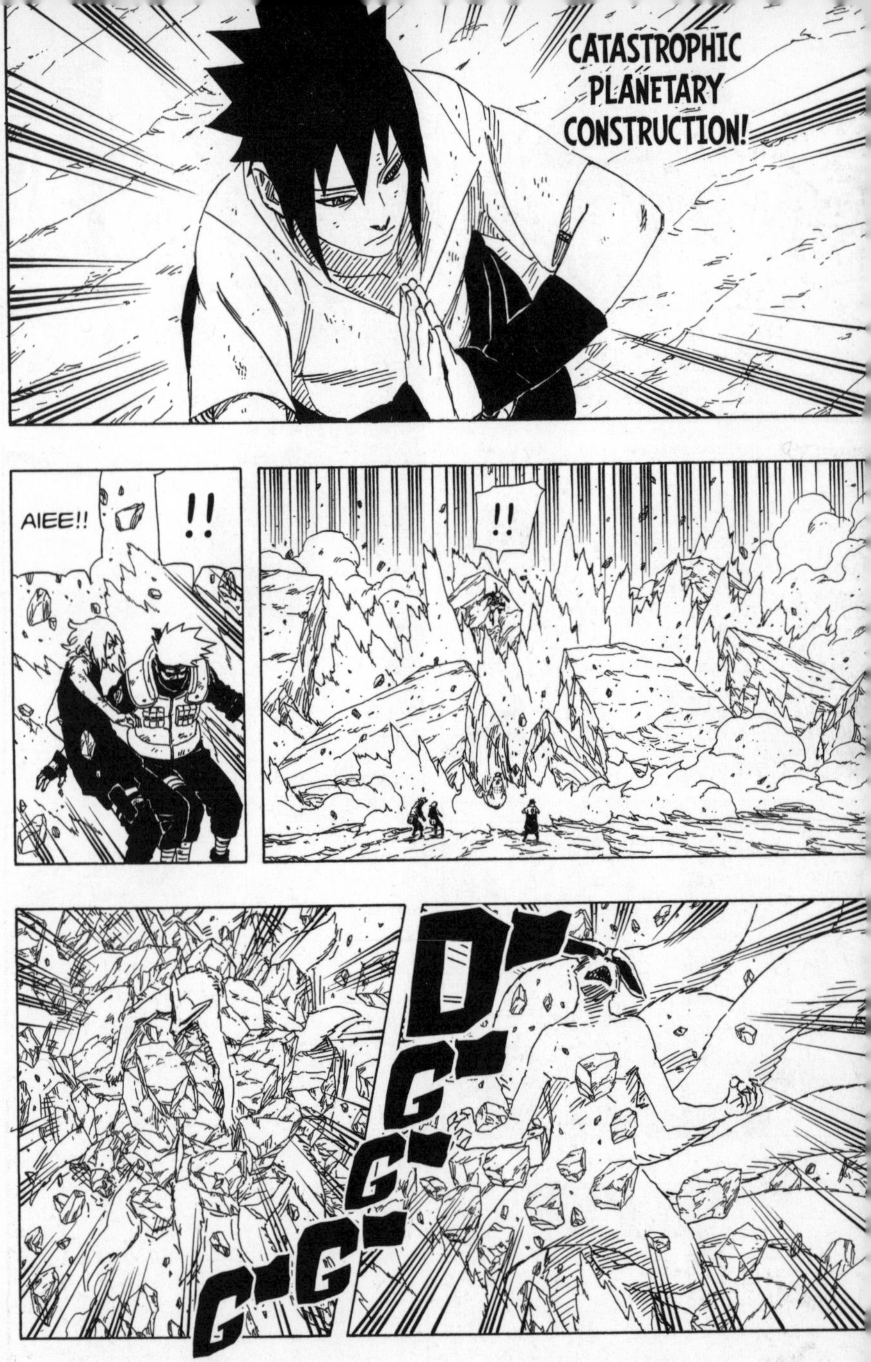
CATASTROPHIC PLANETARY CONSTRUCTION!
!!
!!
AIEE!!
D-G-G-G-G-G

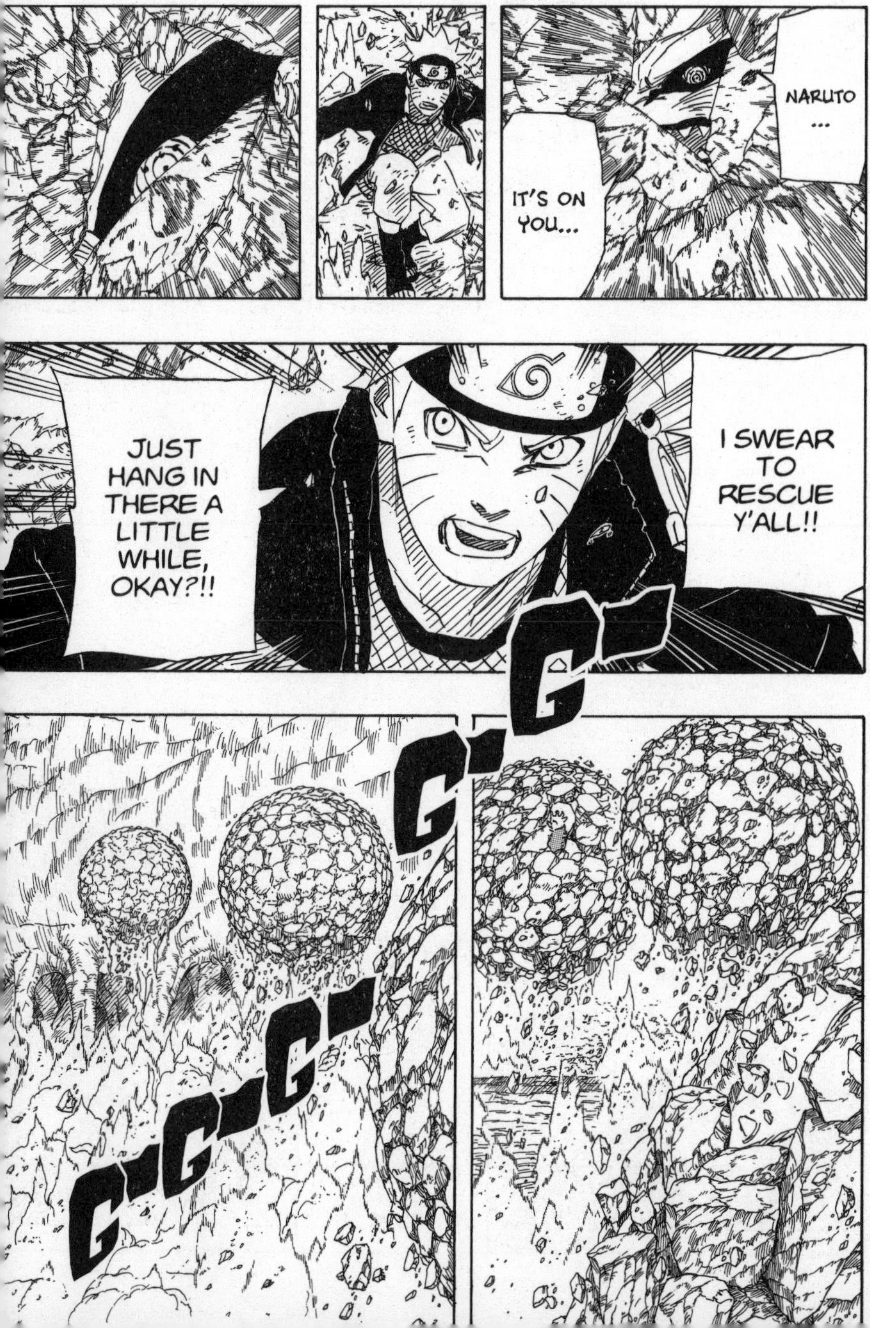
NARUTO ...
IT'S ON YOU...
I SWEAR TO RESCUE Y'ALL!!
JUST HANG IN THERE A LITTLE WHILE, OKAY?!!
G-G-G-G-G-G

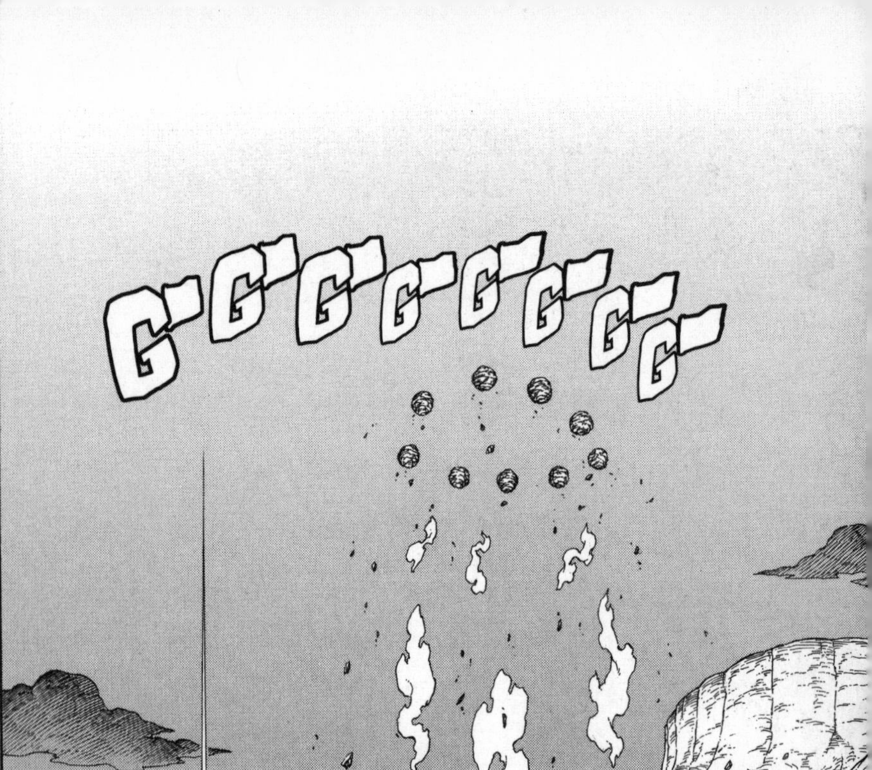
G-G-G-G-G-G-G-G-

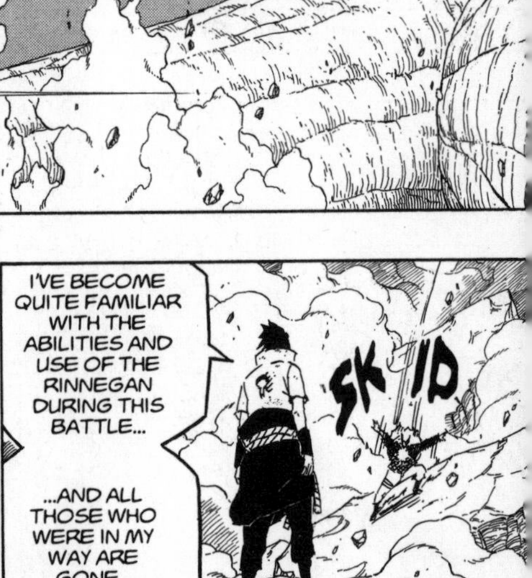
I'VE BECOME QUITE FAMILIAR WITH THE ABILITIES AND USE OF THE RINNEGAN DURING THIS BATTLE...
...AND ALL THOSE WHO WERE IN MY WAY ARE GONE...
SKID

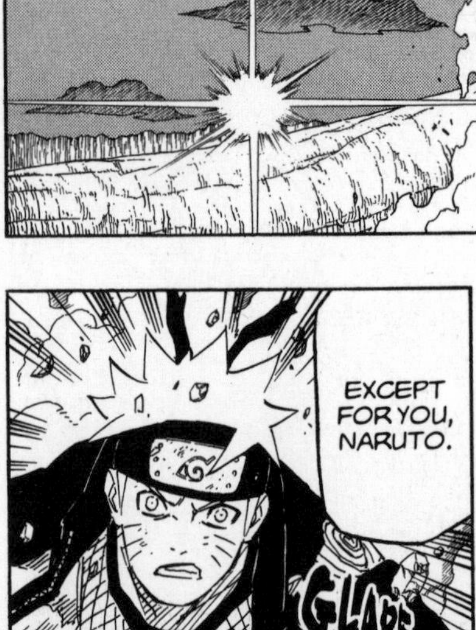
EXCEPT FOR YOU, NARUTO.
GLARE

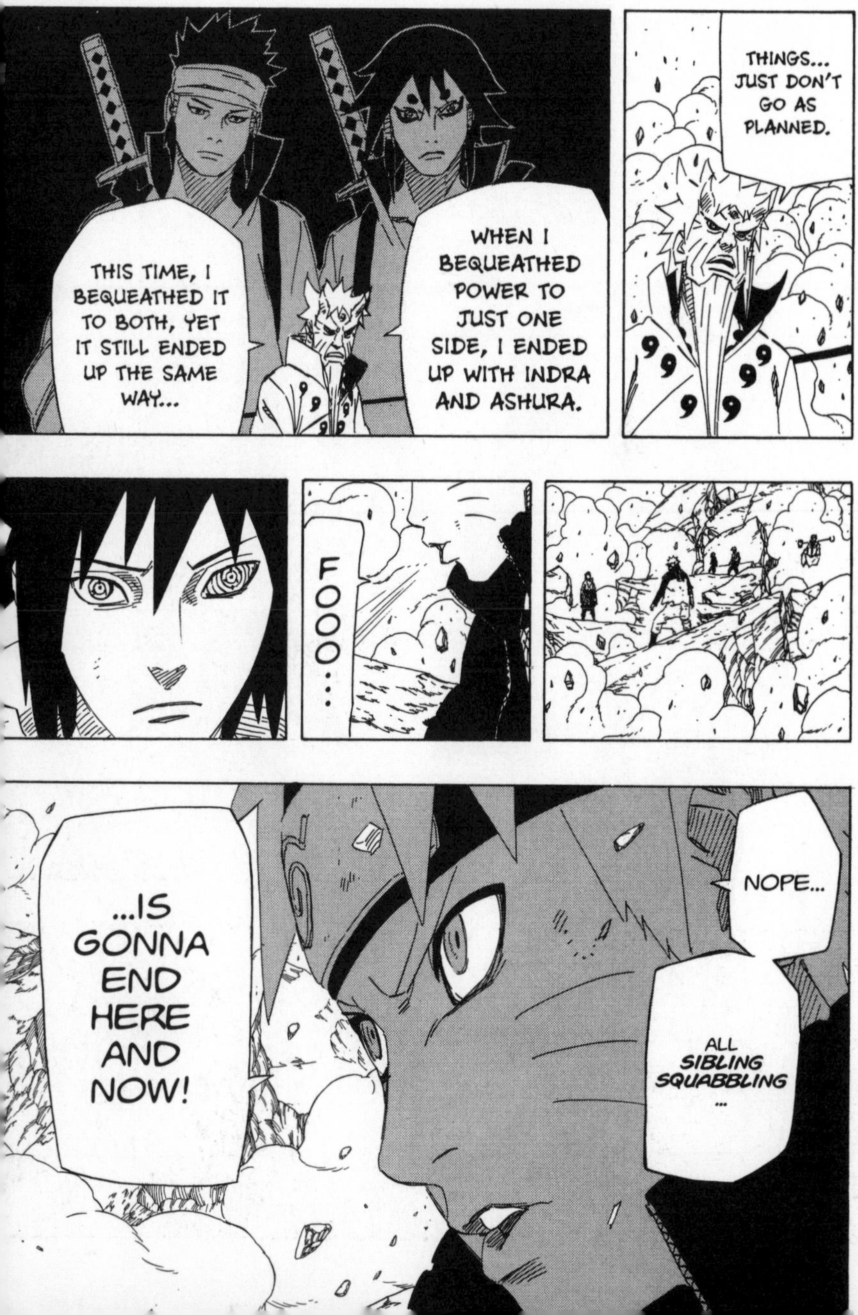
THINGS... JUST DON'T GO AS PLANNED.
WHEN I BEQUEATHED POWER TO JUST ONE SIDE, I ENDED UP WITH INDRA AND ASHURA.
THIS TIME, I BEQUEATHED IT TO BOTH, YET IT STILL ENDED UP THE SAME WAY...
FOOOO...
NOPE...
ALL SIBLING SQUABBLING ...
...IS GONNA END HERE AND NOW!

END OF SERIES COMMEMORATION ILLUSTRATION (2) MIKIO IKEMOTO

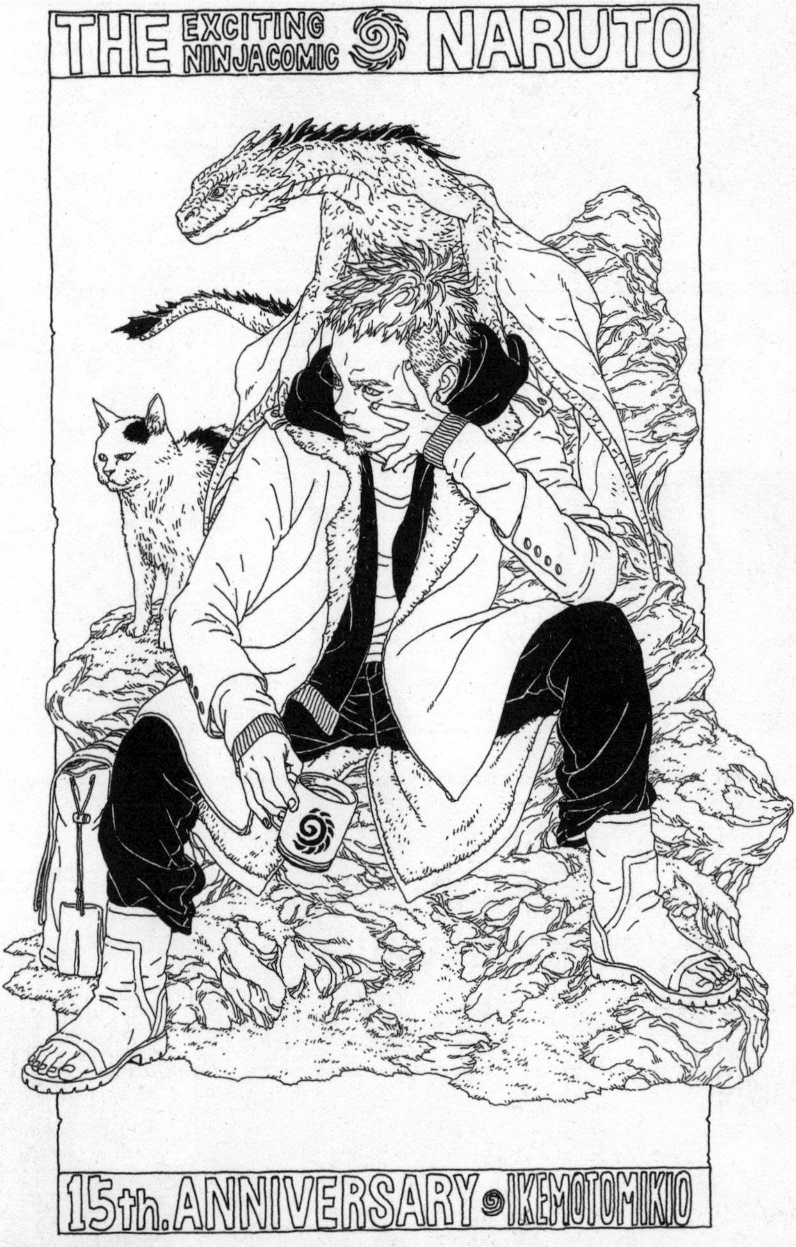
THE EXCITING NINJACOMIC NARUTO
15th. ANNIVERSARY IKEMOTOMIKIO

Number 693: Here Once Again

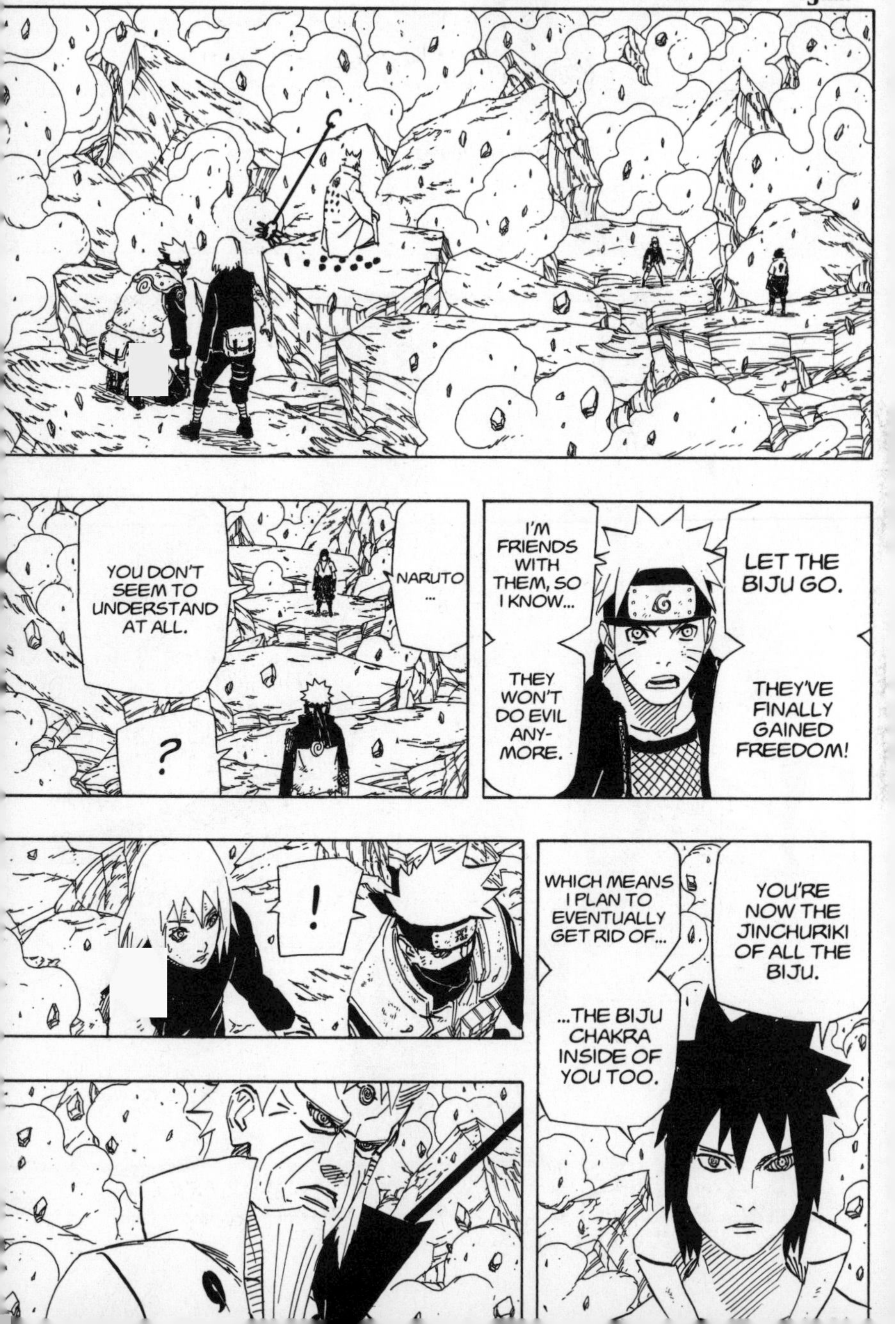
LET THE BIJU GO.
THEY'VE FINALLY GAINED FREEDOM!
I'M FRIENDS WITH THEM, SO I KNOW...
THEY WON'T DO EVIL ANYMORE.
NARUTO...
YOU DON'T SEEM TO UNDERSTAND AT ALL.
?
YOU'RE NOW THE JINCHURIKI OF ALL THE BIJU.
WHICH MEANS I PLAN TO EVENTUALLY GET RID OF...
...THE BIJU CHAKRA INSIDE OF YOU TOO.
!

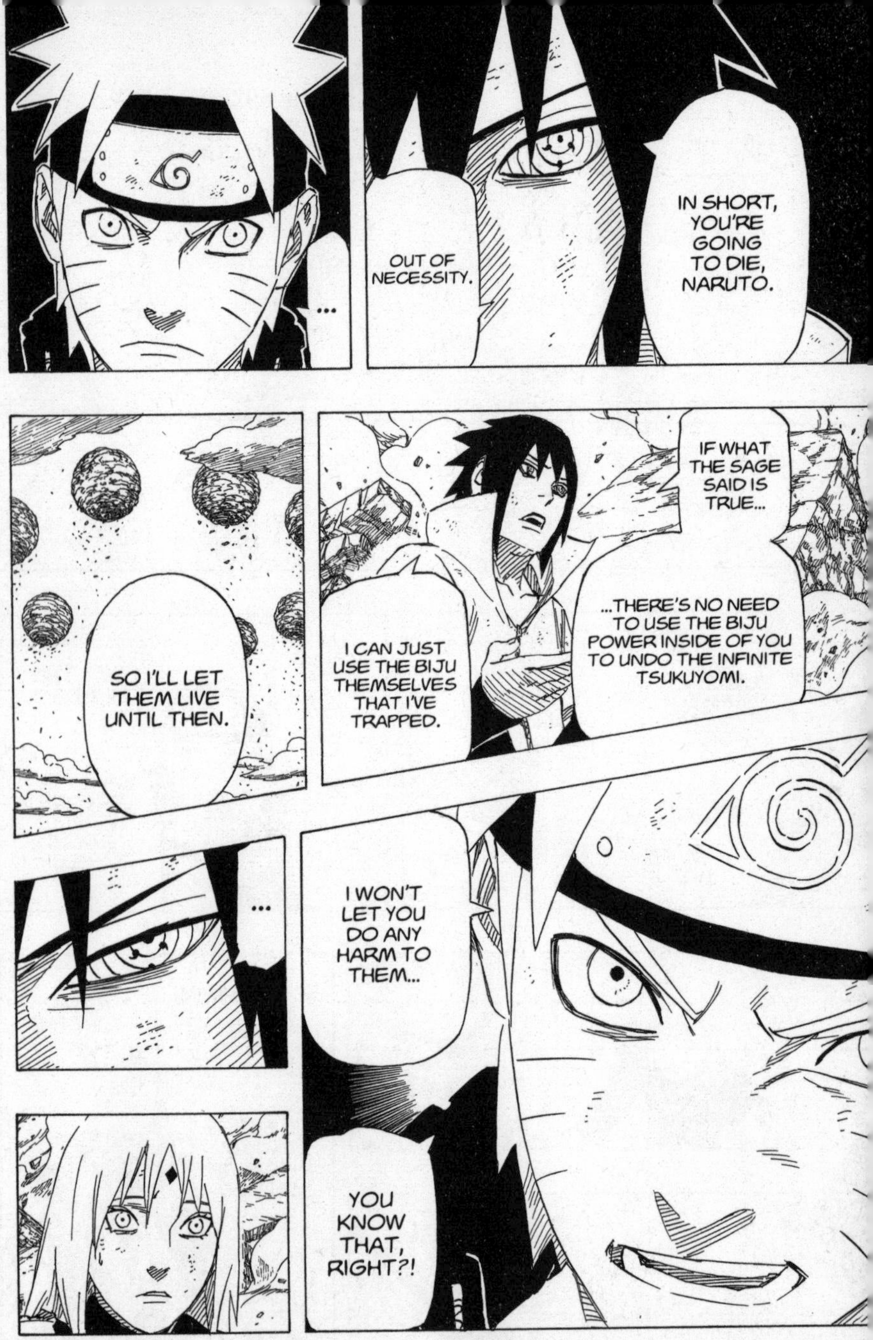
IN SHORT, YOU'RE GOING TO DIE, NARUTO.
OUT OF NECESSITY.
...
IF WHAT THE SAGE SAID IS TRUE...
...THERE'S NO NEED TO USE THE BIJU POWER INSIDE OF YOU TO UNDO THE INFINITE TSUKUYOMI.
I CAN JUST USE THE BIJU THEMSELVES THAT I'VE TRAPPED.
SO I'LL LET THEM LIVE UNTIL THEN.
I WON'T LET YOU DO ANY HARM TO THEM...
YOU KNOW THAT, RIGHT?!
...

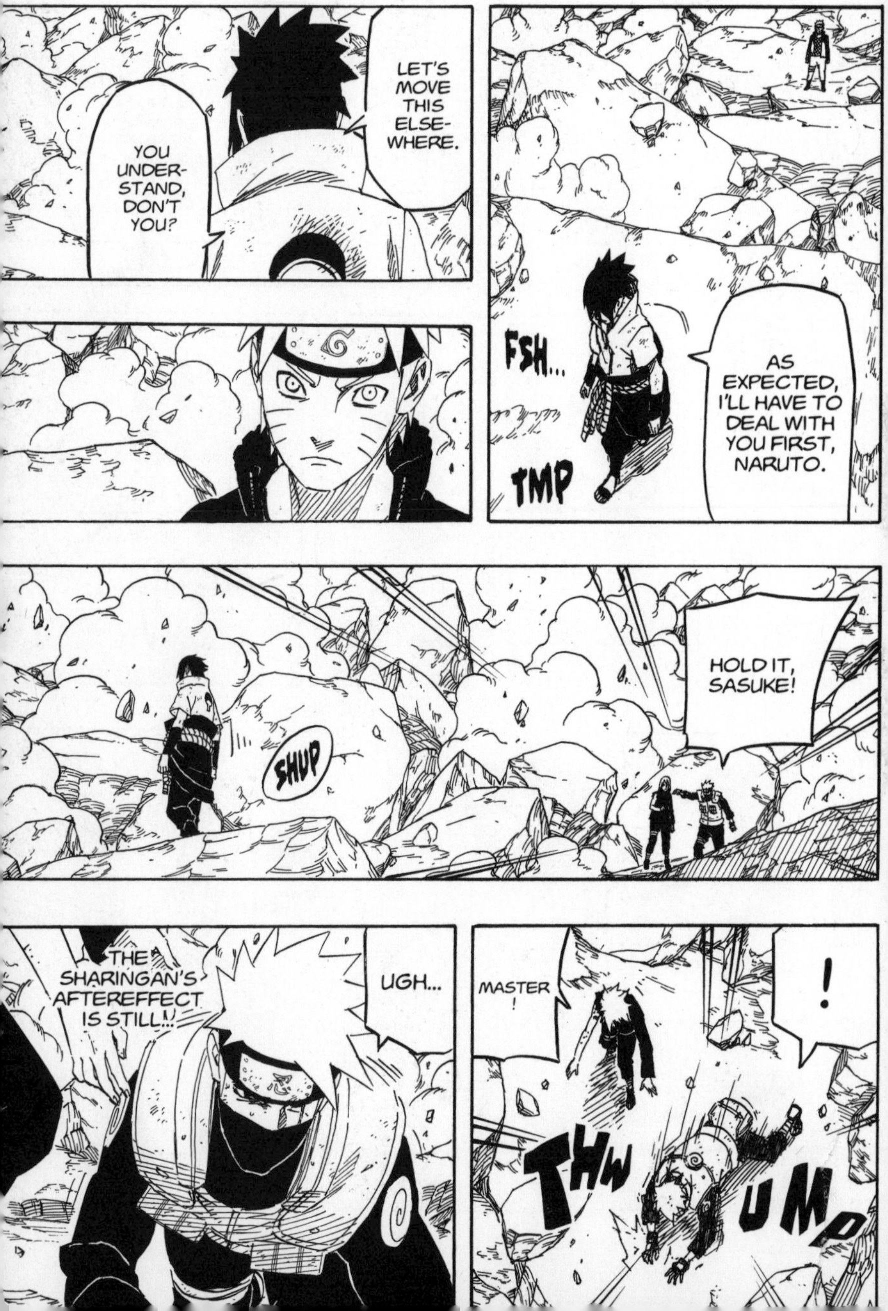
FSH...
TMP
AS EXPECTED, I'LL HAVE TO DEAL WITH YOU FIRST, NARUTO.
LET'S MOVE THIS ELSEWHERE.
YOU UNDERSTAND, DON'T YOU?
HOLD IT, SASUKE!
SHUP
!
MASTER!
THWUMP
UGH...
THE SHARINGAN'S AFTEREFFECT IS STILL...!!

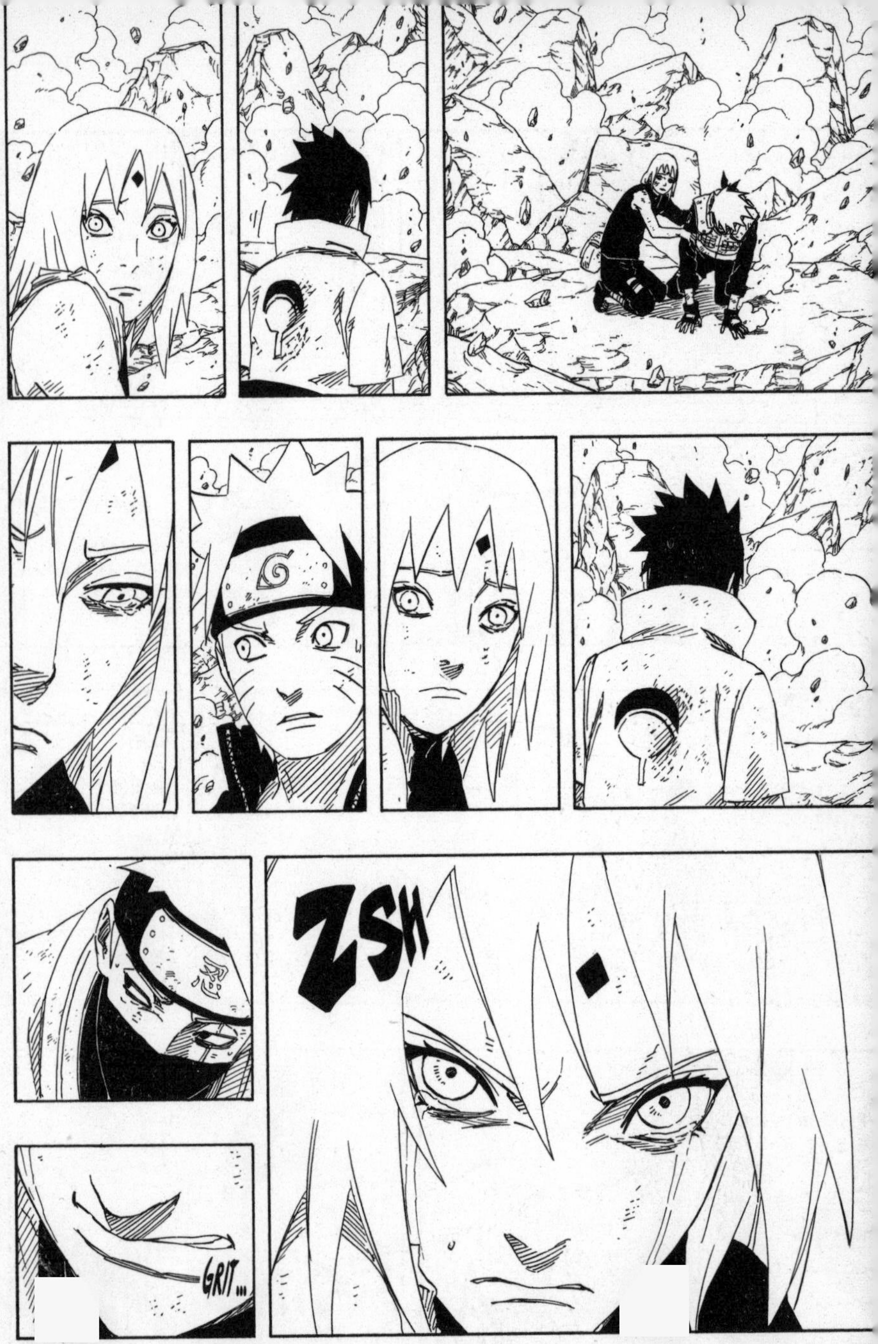
ZSH
GRIT...

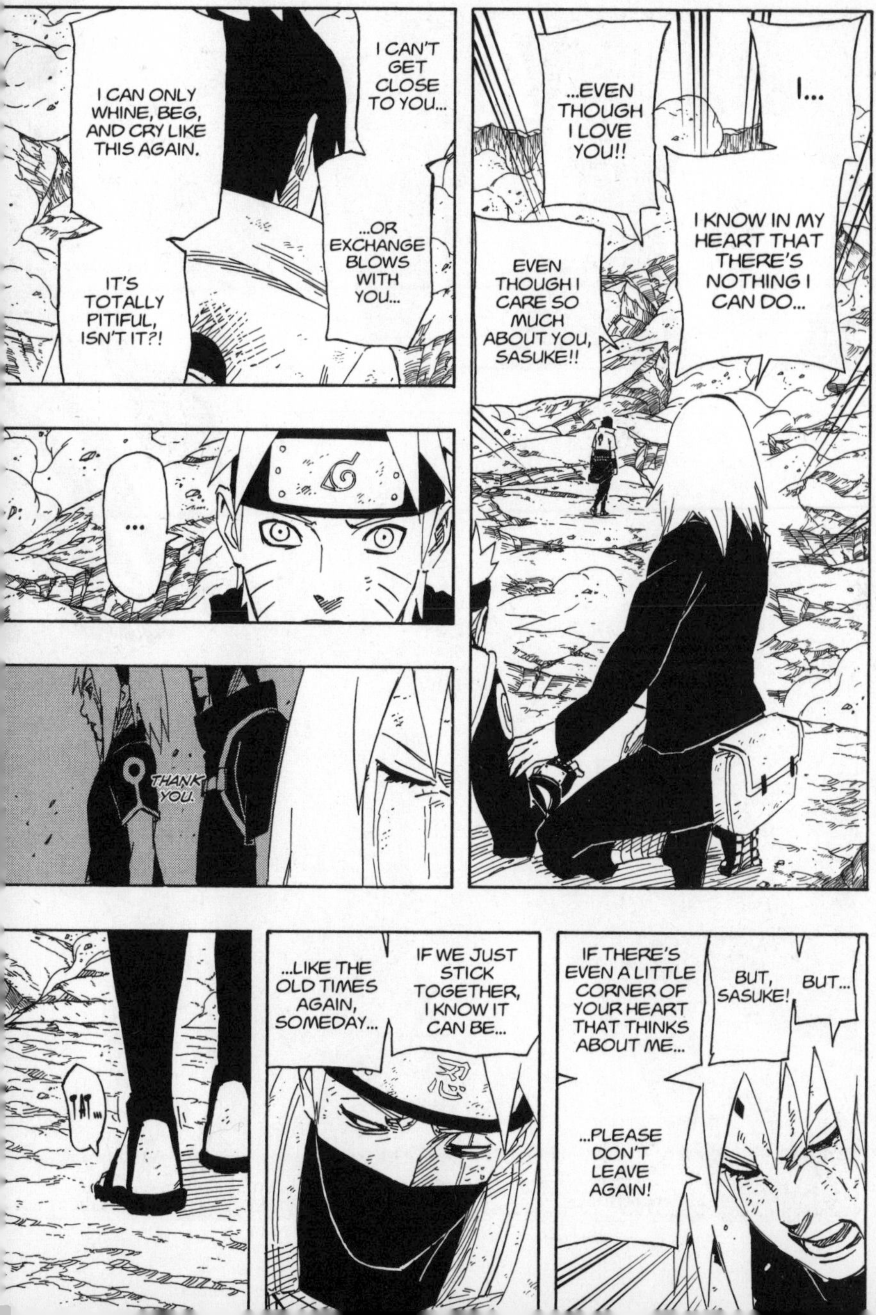
I...
...EVEN THOUGH I LOVE YOU!!
I KNOW IN MY HEART THAT THERE'S NOTHING I CAN DO...
EVEN THOUGH I CARE SO MUCH ABOUT YOU, SASUKE!!
I CAN'T GET CLOSE TO YOU...
...OR EXCHANGE BLOWS WITH YOU...
I CAN ONLY WHINE, BEG, AND CRY LIKE THIS AGAIN.
IT'S TOTALLY PITIFUL, ISN'T IT?!
...
THANK YOU.
BUT...
BUT, SASUKE!
IF THERE'S EVEN A LITTLE CORNER OF YOUR HEART THAT THINKS ABOUT ME...
...PLEASE DON'T LEAVE AGAIN!
IF WE JUST STICK TOGETHER, I KNOW IT CAN BE...
...LIKE THE OLD TIMES AGAIN, SOMEDAY...
TAT...

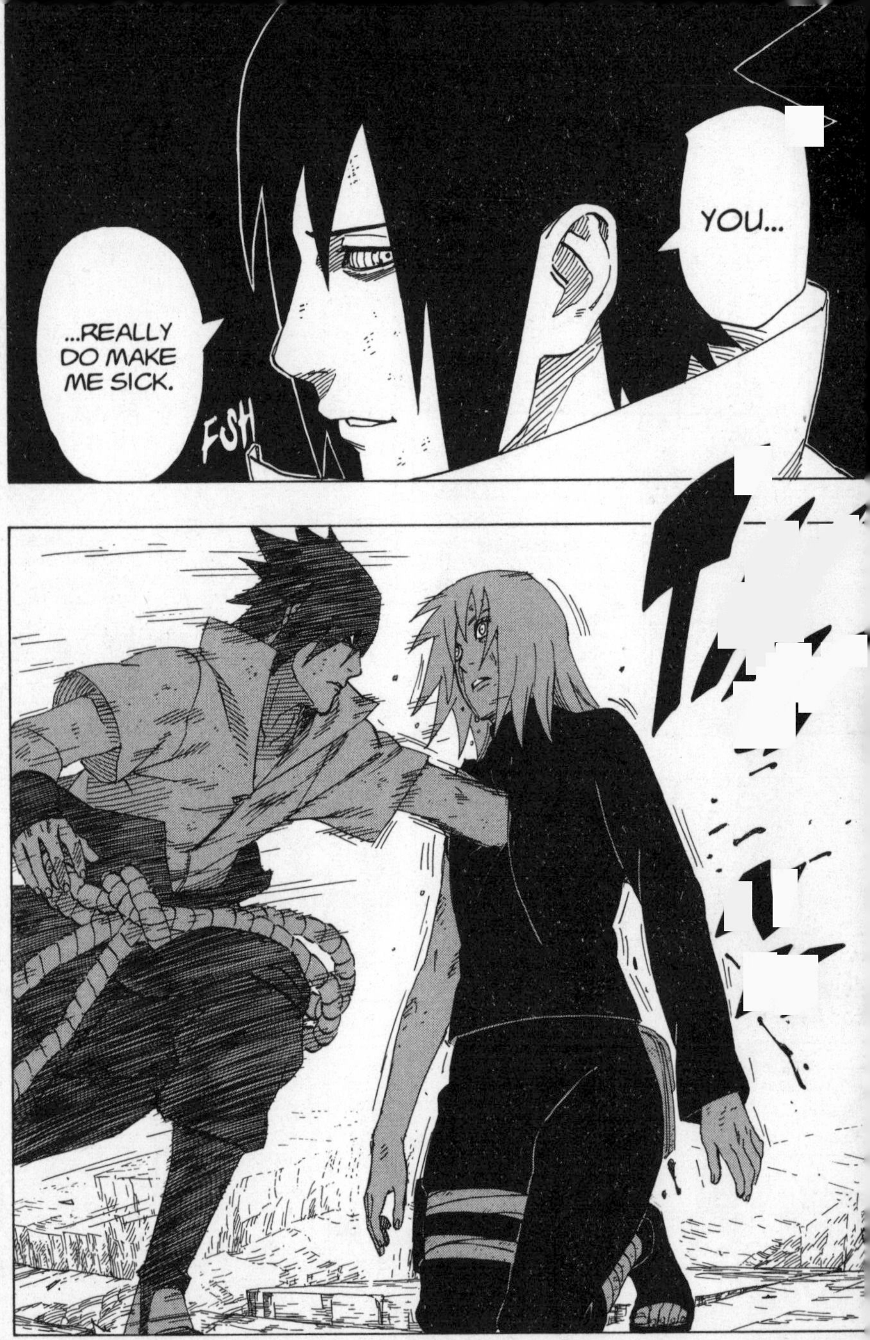
YOU...
...REALLY DO MAKE ME SICK.
FSH

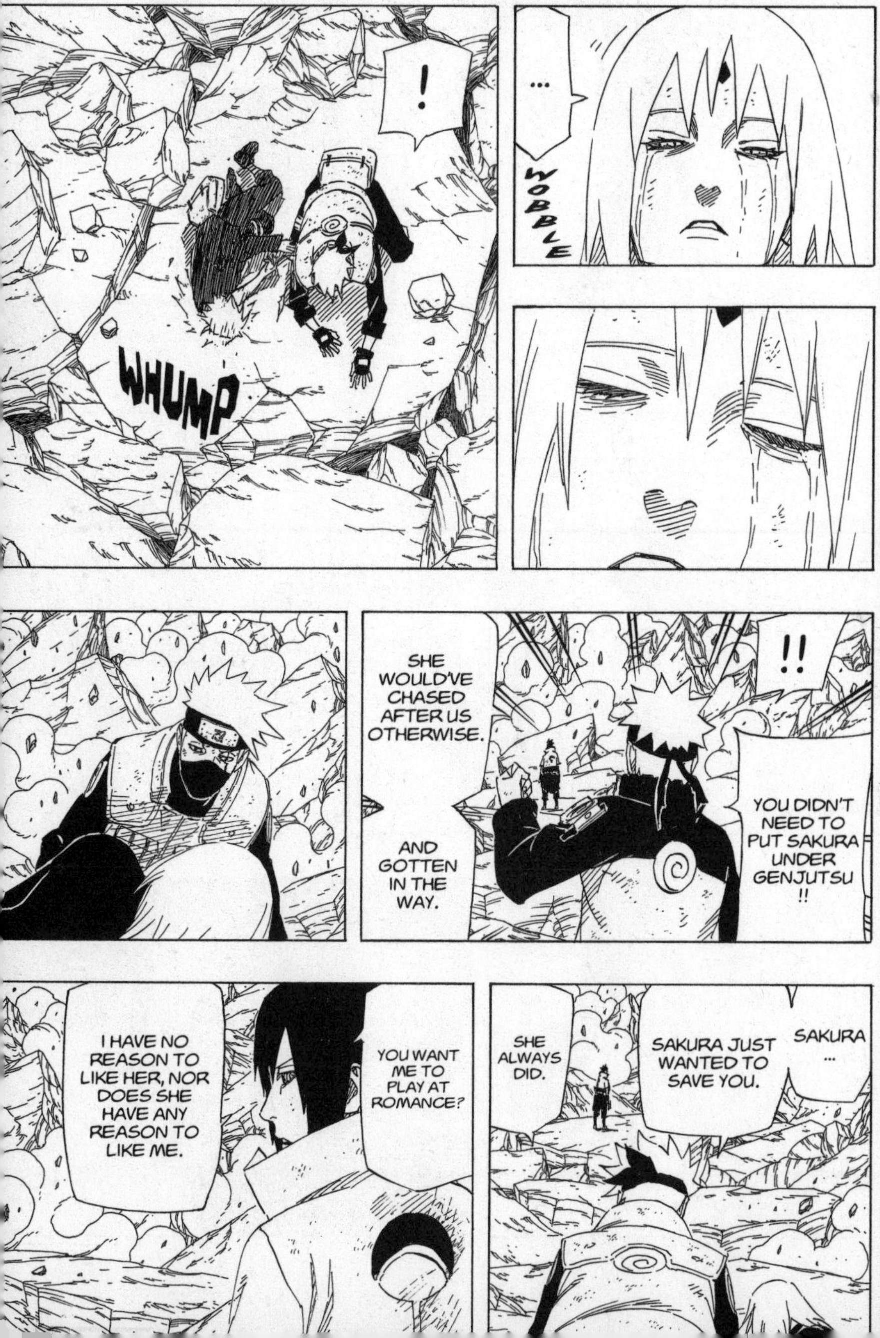
...
WOBBLE
!
WHUMP
!!
YOU DIDN'T NEED TO PUT SAKURA UNDER GENJUTSU !!
SHE WOULD'VE CHASED AFTER US OTHERWISE.
AND GOTTEN IN THE WAY.
SAKURA ...
SAKURA JUST WANTED TO SAVE YOU.
SHE ALWAYS DID.
YOU WANT ME TO PLAY AT ROMANCE?
I HAVE NO REASON TO LIKE HER, NOR DOES SHE HAVE ANY REASON TO LIKE ME.

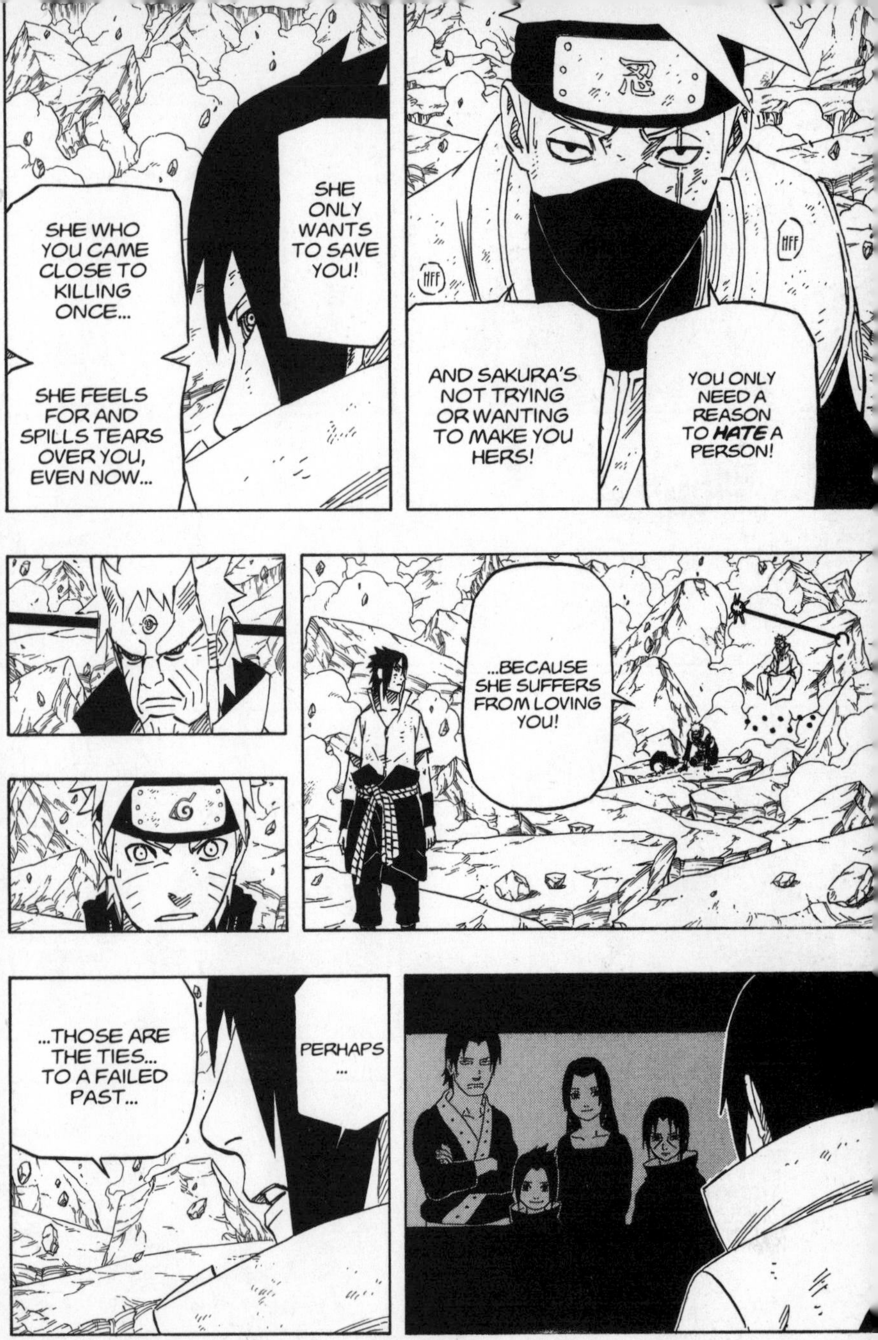
HFF
HFF
YOU ONLY NEED A REASON TO *HATE* A PERSON!
AND SAKURA'S NOT TRYING OR WANTING TO MAKE YOU HERS!
SHE ONLY WANTS TO SAVE YOU!
SHE WHO YOU CAME CLOSE TO KILLING ONCE...
SHE FEELS FOR AND SPILLS TEARS OVER YOU, EVEN NOW...
...BECAUSE SHE SUFFERS FROM LOVING YOU!
PERHAPS ...
...THOSE ARE THE TIES... TO A FAILED PAST...

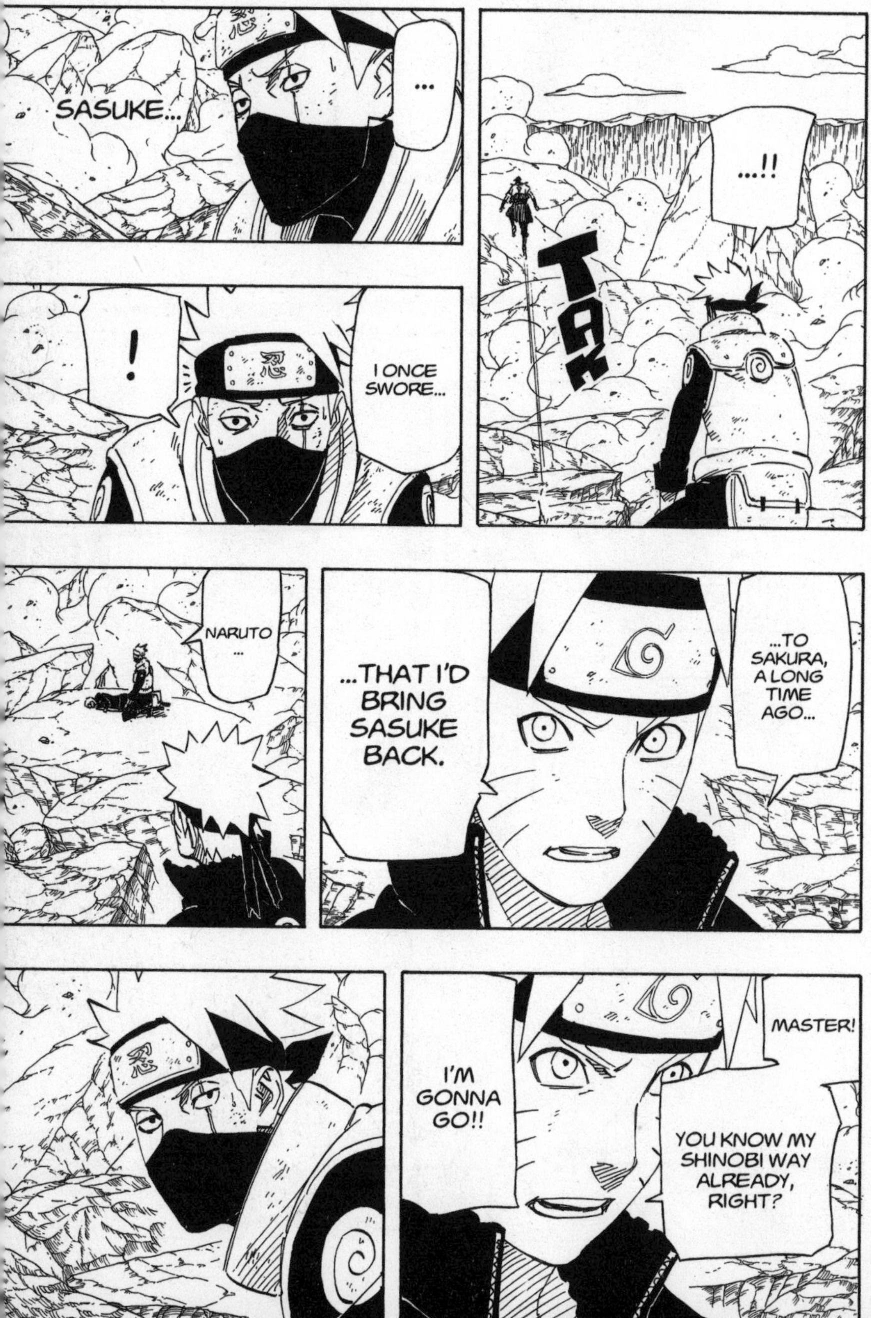
...!!
TAK
...
SASUKE...
I ONCE SWORE...
!
...TO SAKURA, A LONG TIME AGO...
...THAT I'D BRING SASUKE BACK.
NARUTO ...
MASTER!
I'M GONNA GO!!
YOU KNOW MY SHINOBI WAY ALREADY, RIGHT?

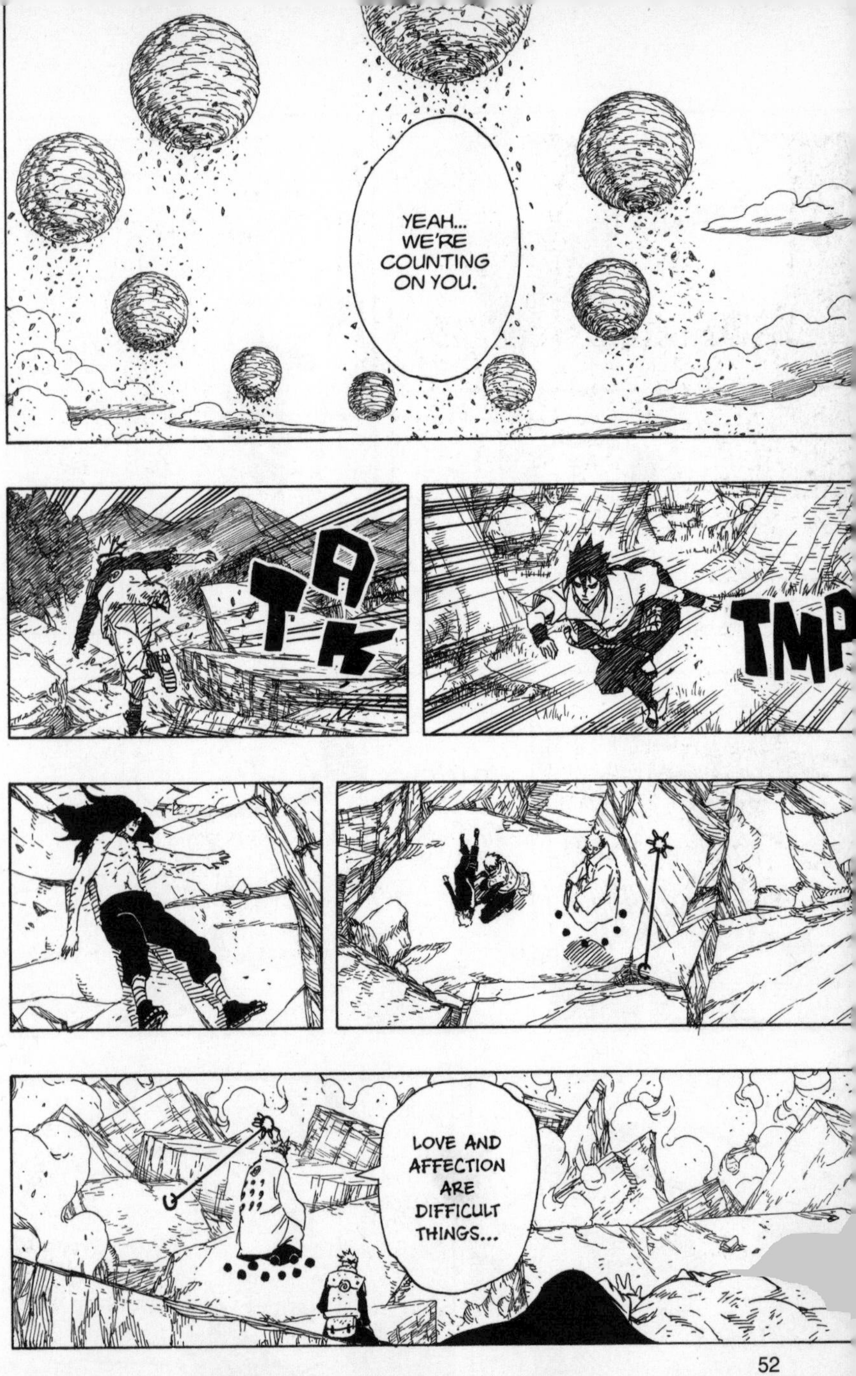
YEAH... WE'RE COUNTING ON YOU.
TMP
TA TK
LOVE AND AFFECTION ARE DIFFICULT THINGS...

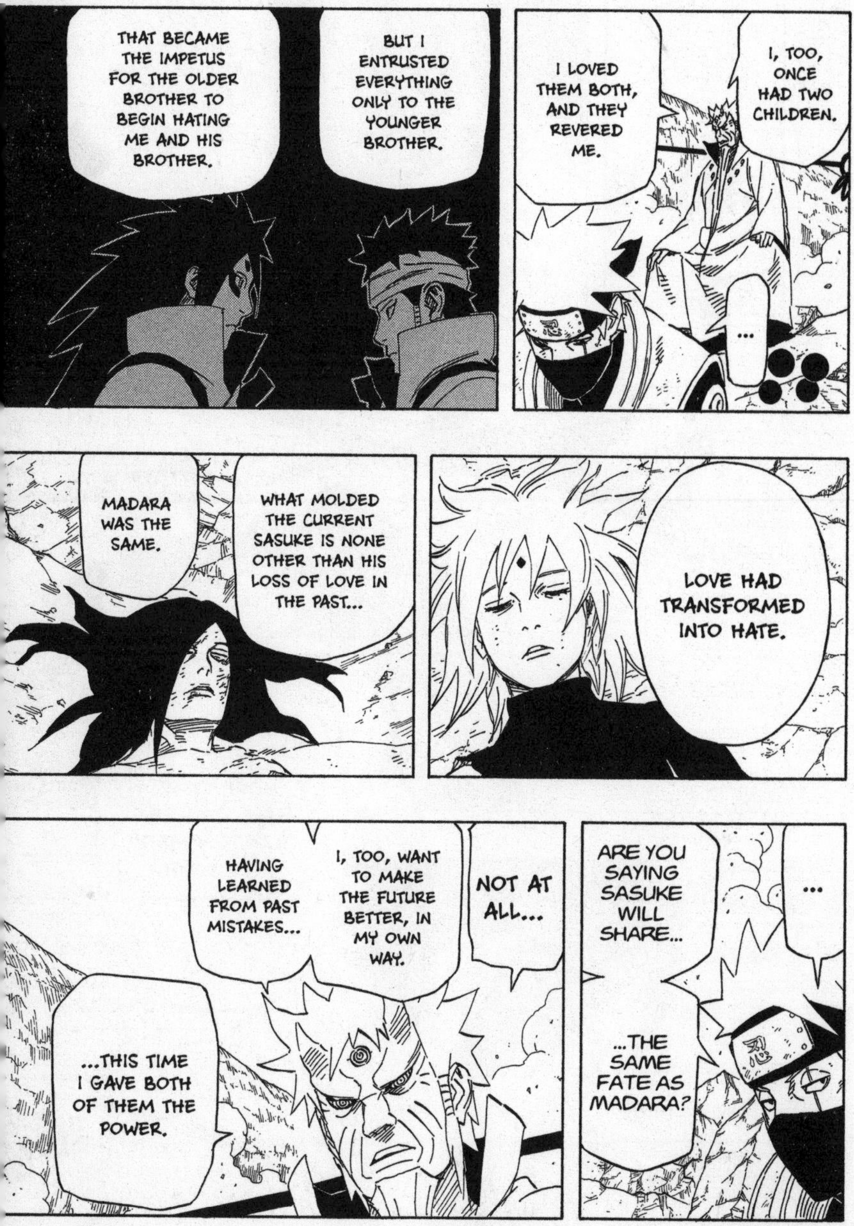
I, TOO, ONCE HAD TWO CHILDREN.
I LOVED THEM BOTH, AND THEY REVERED ME.
...
BUT I ENTRUSTED EVERYTHING ONLY TO THE YOUNGER BROTHER.
THAT BECAME THE IMPETUS FOR THE OLDER BROTHER TO BEGIN HATING ME AND HIS BROTHER.
LOVE HAD TRANSFORMED INTO HATE.
WHAT MOLDED THE CURRENT SASUKE IS NONE OTHER THAN HIS LOSS OF LOVE IN THE PAST...
MADARA WAS THE SAME.
...
ARE YOU SAYING SASUKE WILL SHARE...
...THE SAME FATE AS MADARA?
NOT AT ALL...
I, TOO, WANT TO MAKE THE FUTURE BETTER, IN MY OWN WAY.
HAVING LEARNED FROM PAST MISTAKES...
...THIS TIME I GAVE BOTH OF THEM THE POWER.

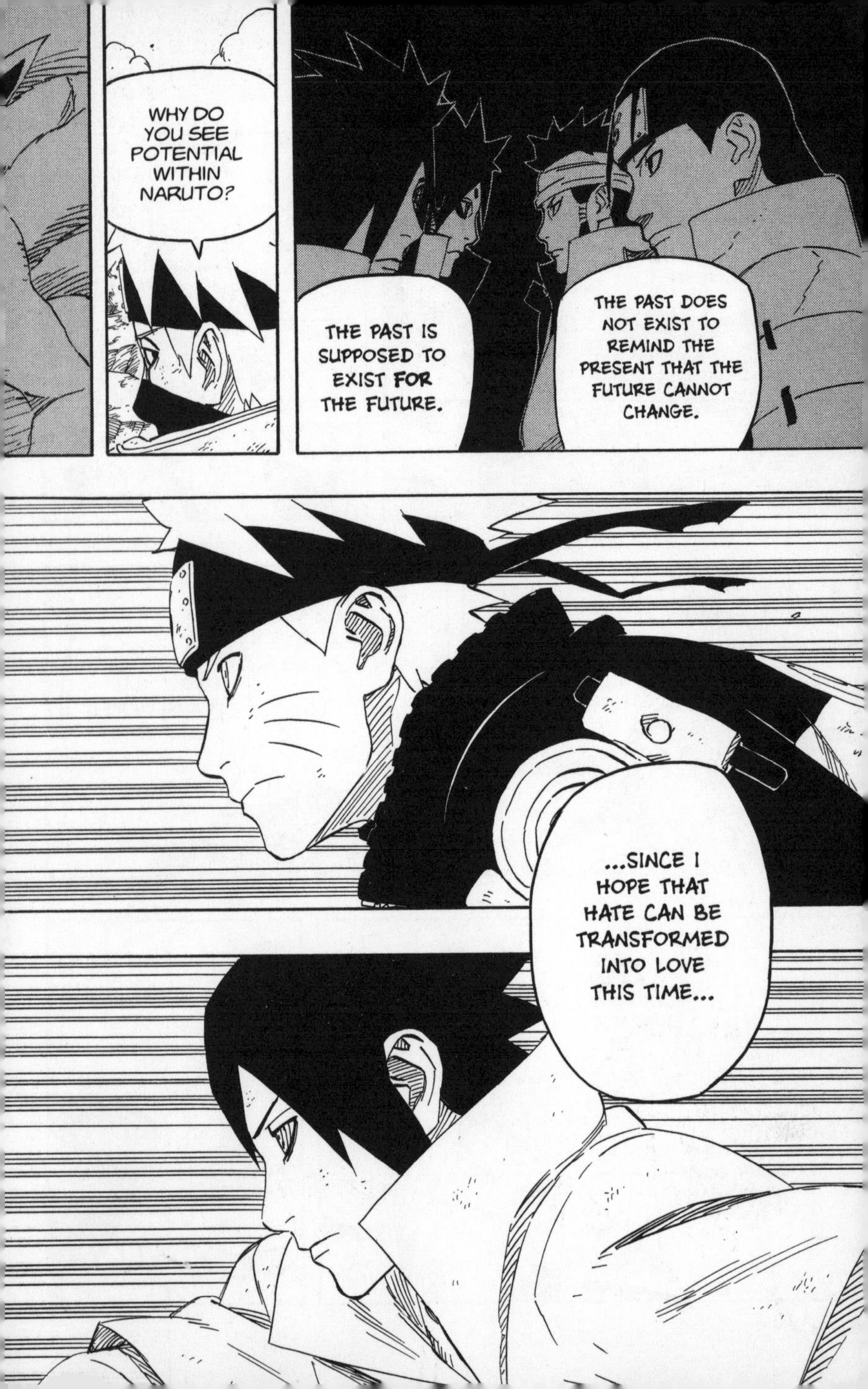
THE PAST DOES NOT EXIST TO REMIND THE PRESENT THAT THE FUTURE CANNOT CHANGE.
THE PAST IS SUPPOSED TO EXIST FOR THE FUTURE.
WHY DO YOU SEE POTENTIAL WITHIN NARUTO?
...SINCE I HOPE THAT HATE CAN BE TRANSFORMED INTO LOVE THIS TIME...

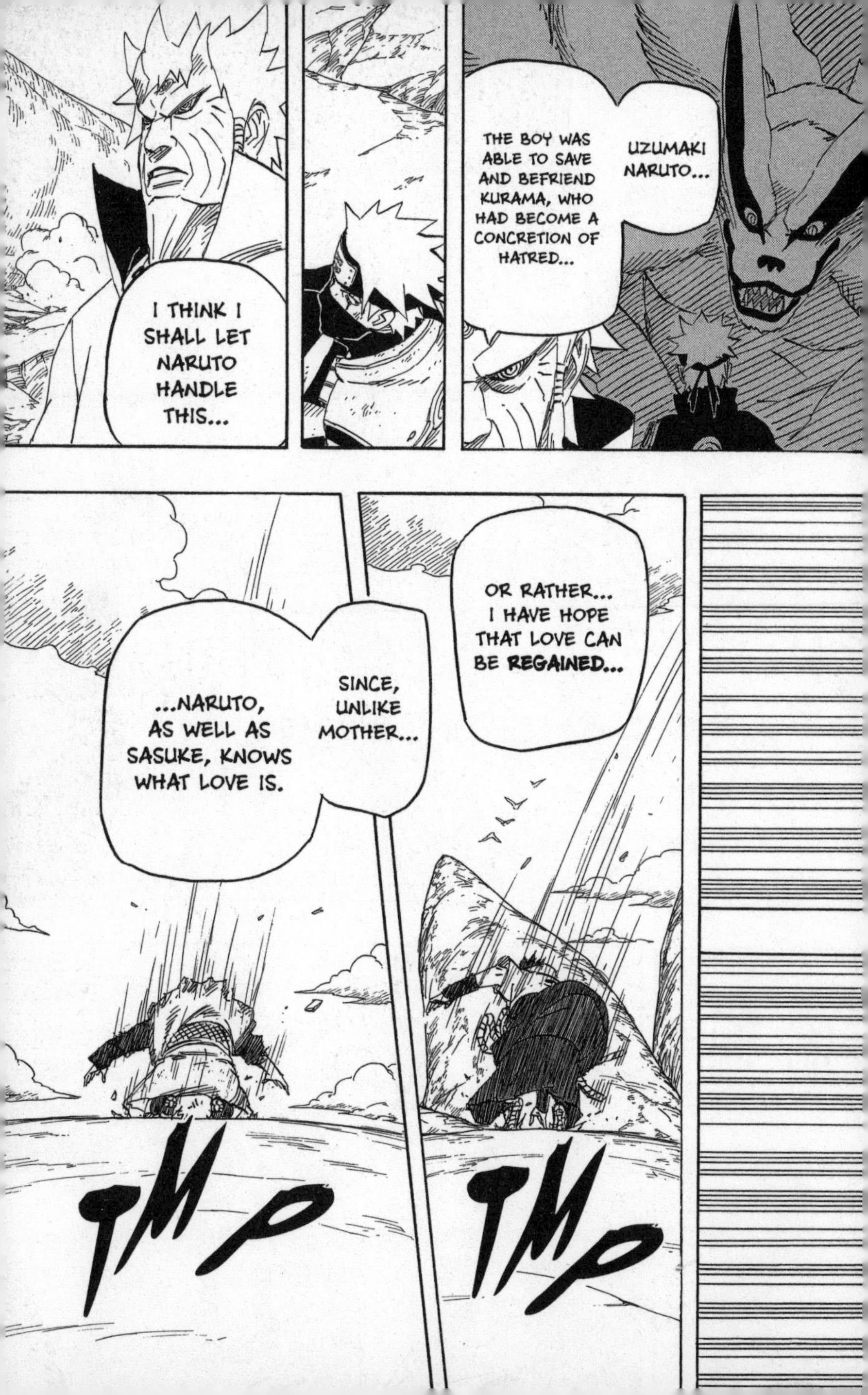
UZUMAKI NARUTO...
THE BOY WAS ABLE TO SAVE AND BEFRIEND KURAMA, WHO HAD BECOME A CONCRETION OF HATRED...
I THINK I SHALL LET NARUTO HANDLE THIS...
OR RATHER... I HAVE HOPE THAT LOVE CAN BE REGAINED...
TMP
SINCE, UNLIKE MOTHER...
...NARUTO, AS WELL AS SASUKE, KNOWS WHAT LOVE IS.
TMP

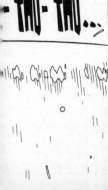

THO - THO...

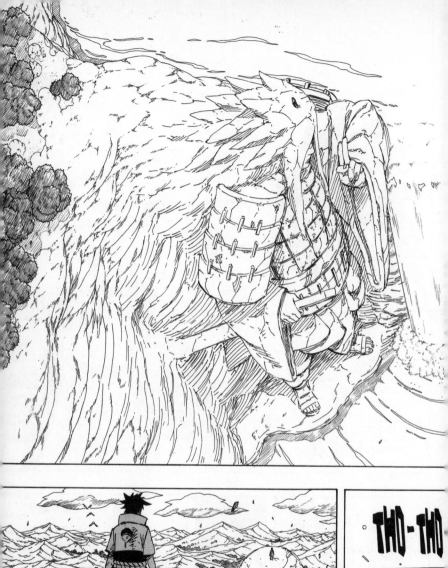

THO-THO

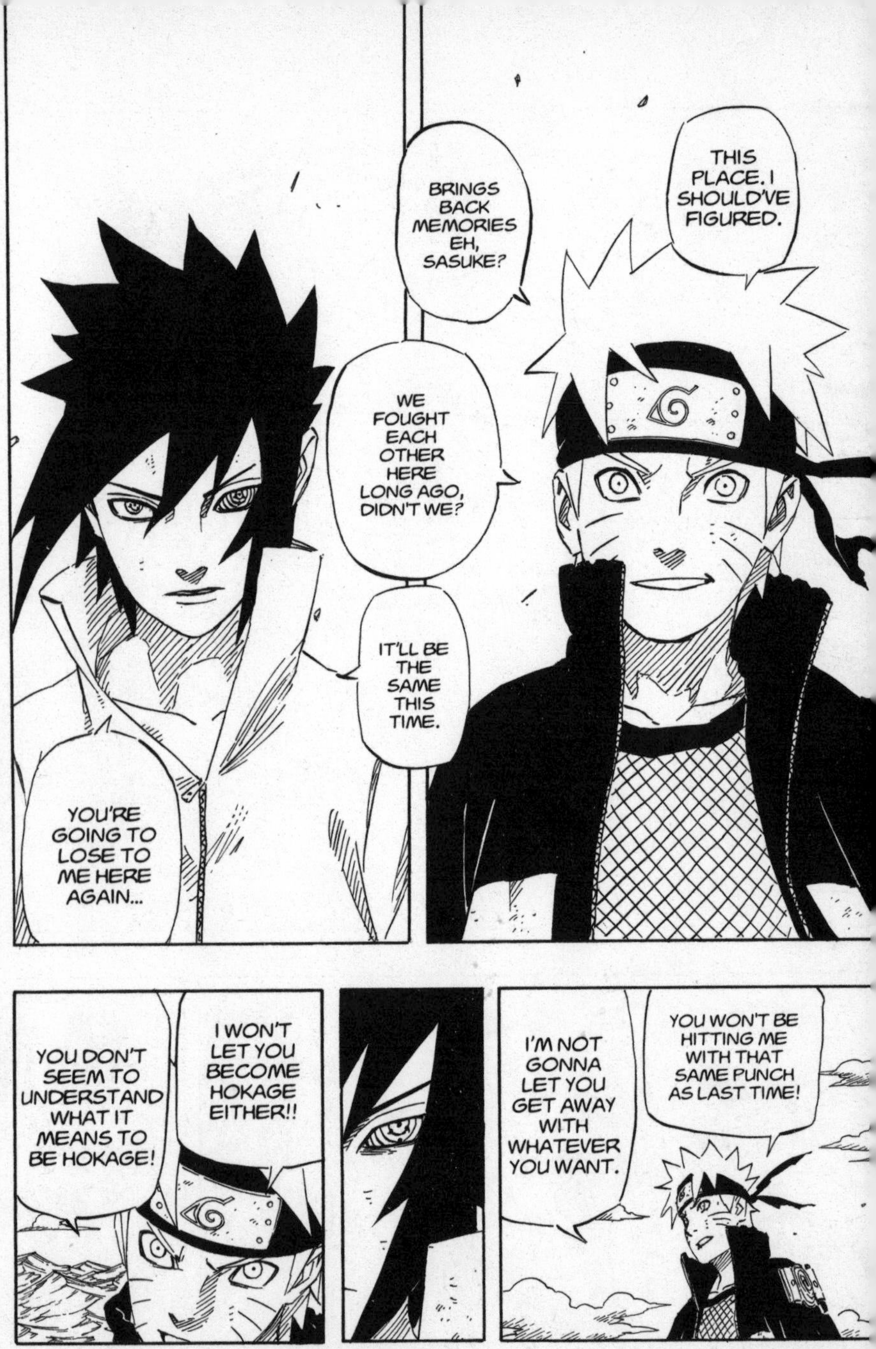
THIS PLACE. I SHOULD'VE FIGURED.
BRINGS BACK MEMORIES EH, SASUKE?
WE FOUGHT EACH OTHER HERE LONG AGO, DIDN'T WE?
IT'LL BE THE SAME THIS TIME.
YOU'RE GOING TO LOSE TO ME HERE AGAIN...
YOU WON'T BE HITTING ME WITH THAT SAME PUNCH AS LAST TIME!
I'M NOT GONNA LET YOU GET AWAY WITH WHATEVER YOU WANT.
I WON'T LET YOU BECOME HOKAGE EITHER!!
YOU DON'T SEEM TO UNDERSTAND WHAT IT MEANS TO BE HOKAGE!

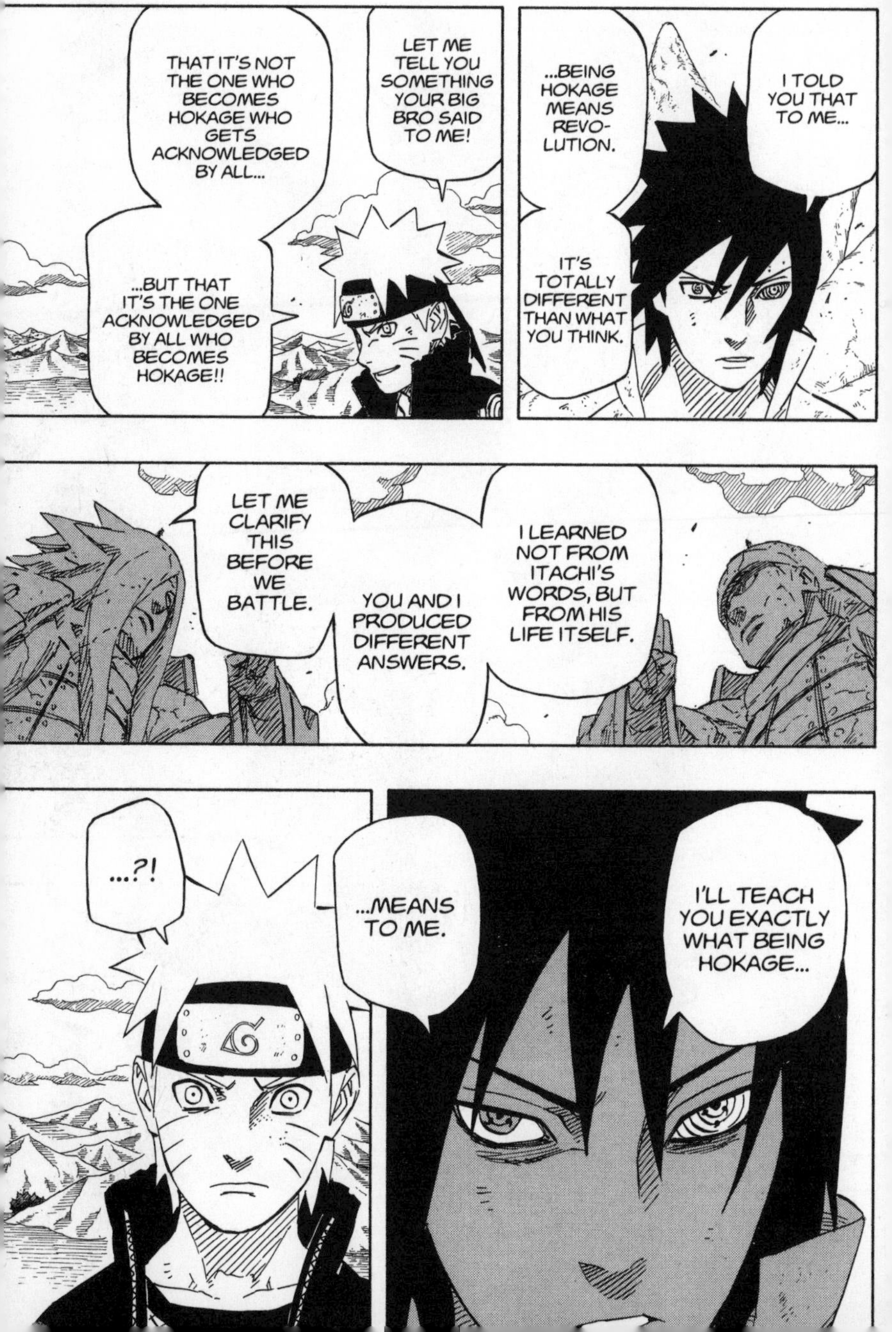
I TOLD YOU THAT TO ME...
...BEING HOKAGE MEANS REVOLUTION.
IT'S TOTALLY DIFFERENT THAN WHAT YOU THINK.
LET ME TELL YOU SOMETHING YOUR BIG BRO SAID TO ME!
THAT IT'S NOT THE ONE WHO BECOMES HOKAGE WHO GETS ACKNOWLEDGED BY ALL...
...BUT THAT IT'S THE ONE ACKNOWLEDGED BY ALL WHO BECOMES HOKAGE!!
I LEARNED NOT FROM ITACHI'S WORDS, BUT FROM HIS LIFE ITSELF.
YOU AND I PRODUCED DIFFERENT ANSWERS.
LET ME CLARIFY THIS BEFORE WE BATTLE.
I'LL TEACH YOU EXACTLY WHAT BEING HOKAGE...
...MEANS TO ME.
...?!

END OF SERIES COMMEMORATION ILLUSTRATION (3) KOUICHI NISHIYA

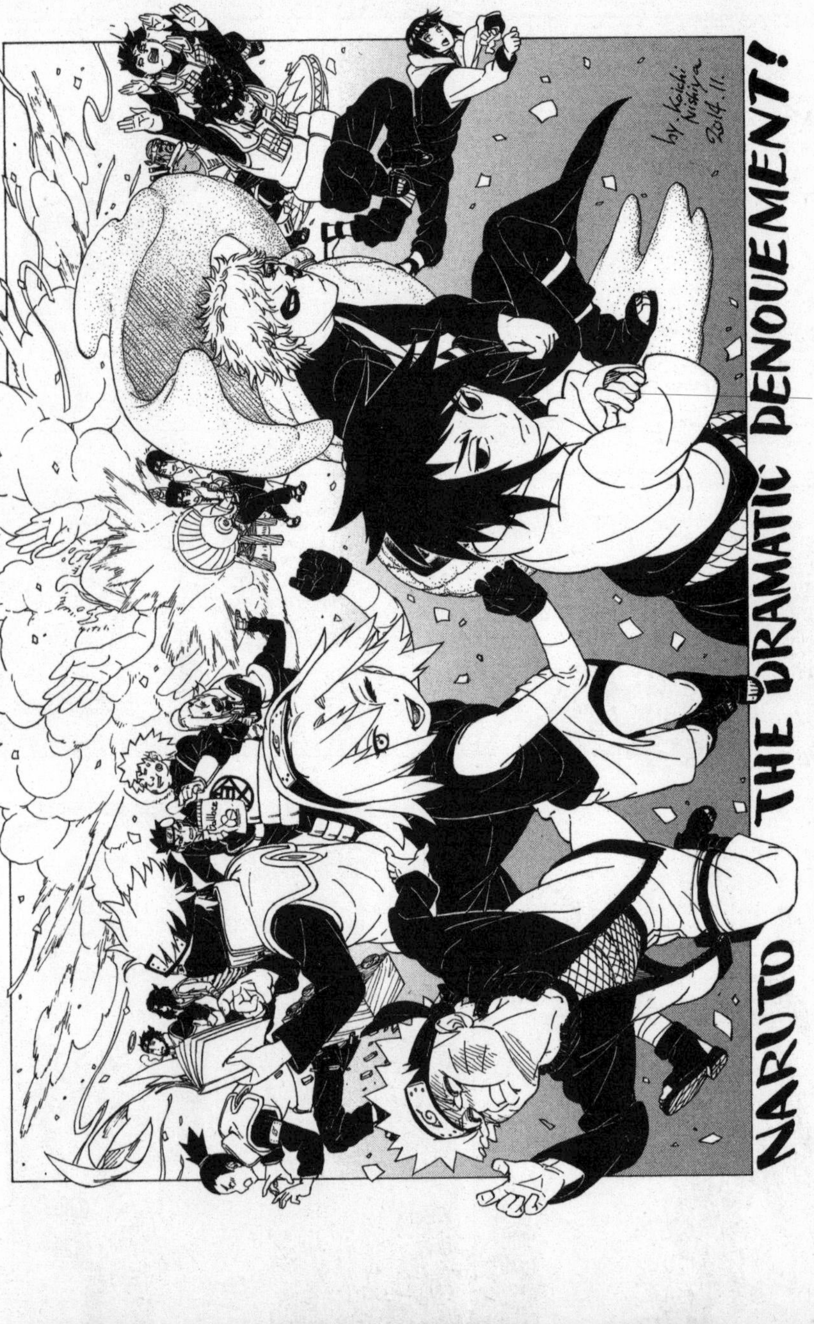
NARUTO THE DRAMATIC DENOUEMENT!
by Koichi Nishiya 2014.11.

Number 694: Naruto and Sasuke, Part 1

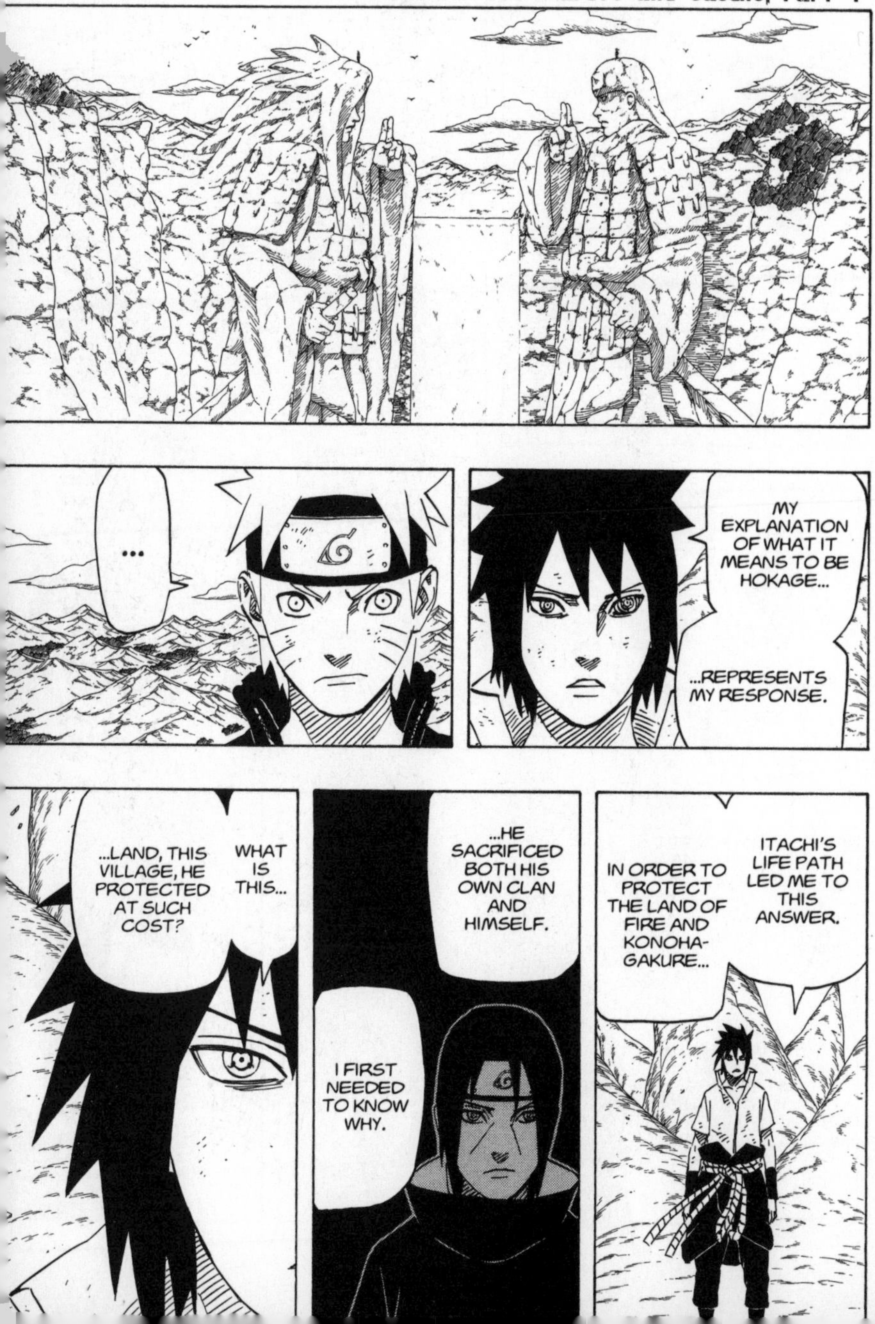
MY EXPLANATION OF WHAT IT MEANS TO BE HOKAGE...
...REPRESENTS MY RESPONSE.
...
ITACHI'S LIFE PATH LED ME TO THIS ANSWER.
IN ORDER TO PROTECT THE LAND OF FIRE AND KONOHA-GAKURE...
...HE SACRIFICED BOTH HIS OWN CLAN AND HIMSELF.
I FIRST NEEDED TO KNOW WHY.
WHAT IS THIS...
...LAND, THIS VILLAGE, HE PROTECTED AT SUCH COST?

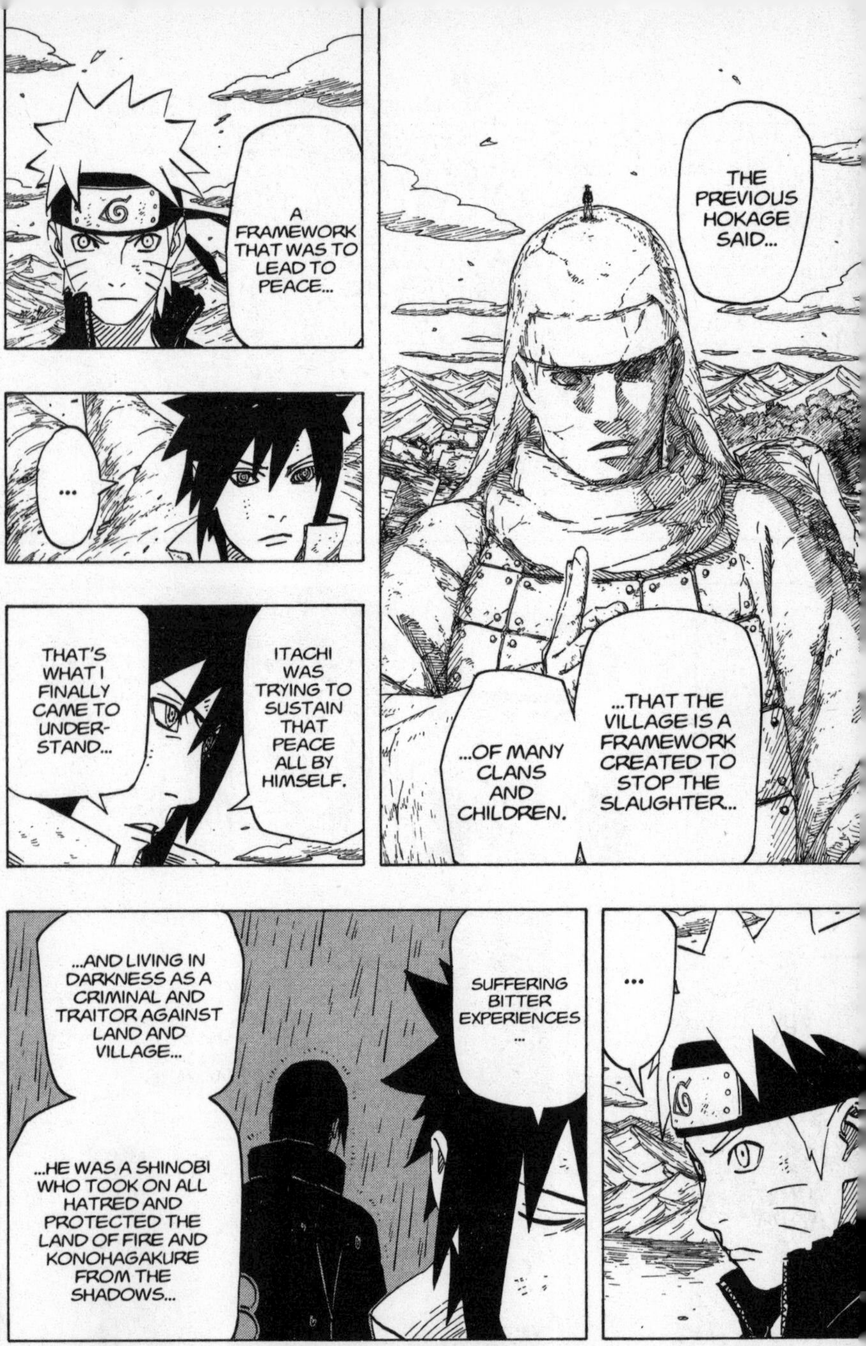
THE PREVIOUS HOKAGE SAID...
...THAT THE VILLAGE IS A FRAMEWORK CREATED TO STOP THE SLAUGHTER...
...OF MANY CLANS AND CHILDREN.
A FRAMEWORK THAT WAS TO LEAD TO PEACE...
...
ITACHI WAS TRYING TO SUSTAIN THAT PEACE ALL BY HIMSELF.
THAT'S WHAT I FINALLY CAME TO UNDER-STAND...
...
SUFFERING BITTER EXPERIENCES ...
...AND LIVING IN DARKNESS AS A CRIMINAL AND TRAITOR AGAINST LAND AND VILLAGE...
...HE WAS A SHINOBI WHO TOOK ON ALL HATRED AND PROTECTED THE LAND OF FIRE AND KONOHAGAKURE FROM THE SHADOWS...

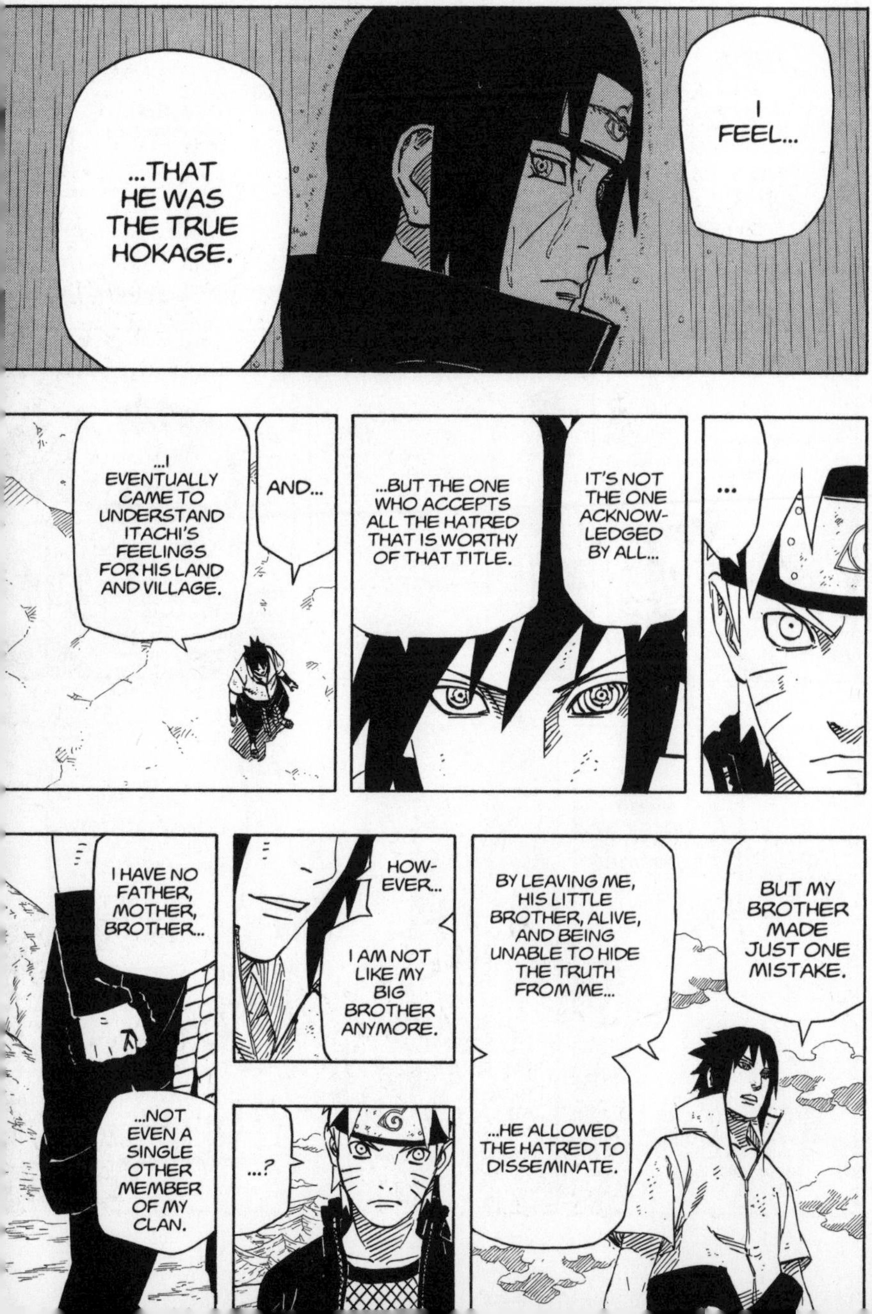
I FEEL...
...THAT HE WAS THE TRUE HOKAGE.
...
IT'S NOT THE ONE ACKNOWLEDGED BY ALL...
...BUT THE ONE WHO ACCEPTS ALL THE HATRED THAT IS WORTHY OF THAT TITLE.
AND...
...I EVENTUALLY CAME TO UNDERSTAND ITACHI'S FEELINGS FOR HIS LAND AND VILLAGE.
BUT MY BROTHER MADE JUST ONE MISTAKE.
BY LEAVING ME, HIS LITTLE BROTHER, ALIVE, AND BEING UNABLE TO HIDE THE TRUTH FROM ME...
...HE ALLOWED THE HATRED TO DISSEMINATE.
HOW-EVER...
I AM NOT LIKE MY BIG BROTHER ANYMORE.
...?
I HAVE NO FATHER, MOTHER, BROTHER...
...NOT EVEN A SINGLE OTHER MEMBER OF MY CLAN.

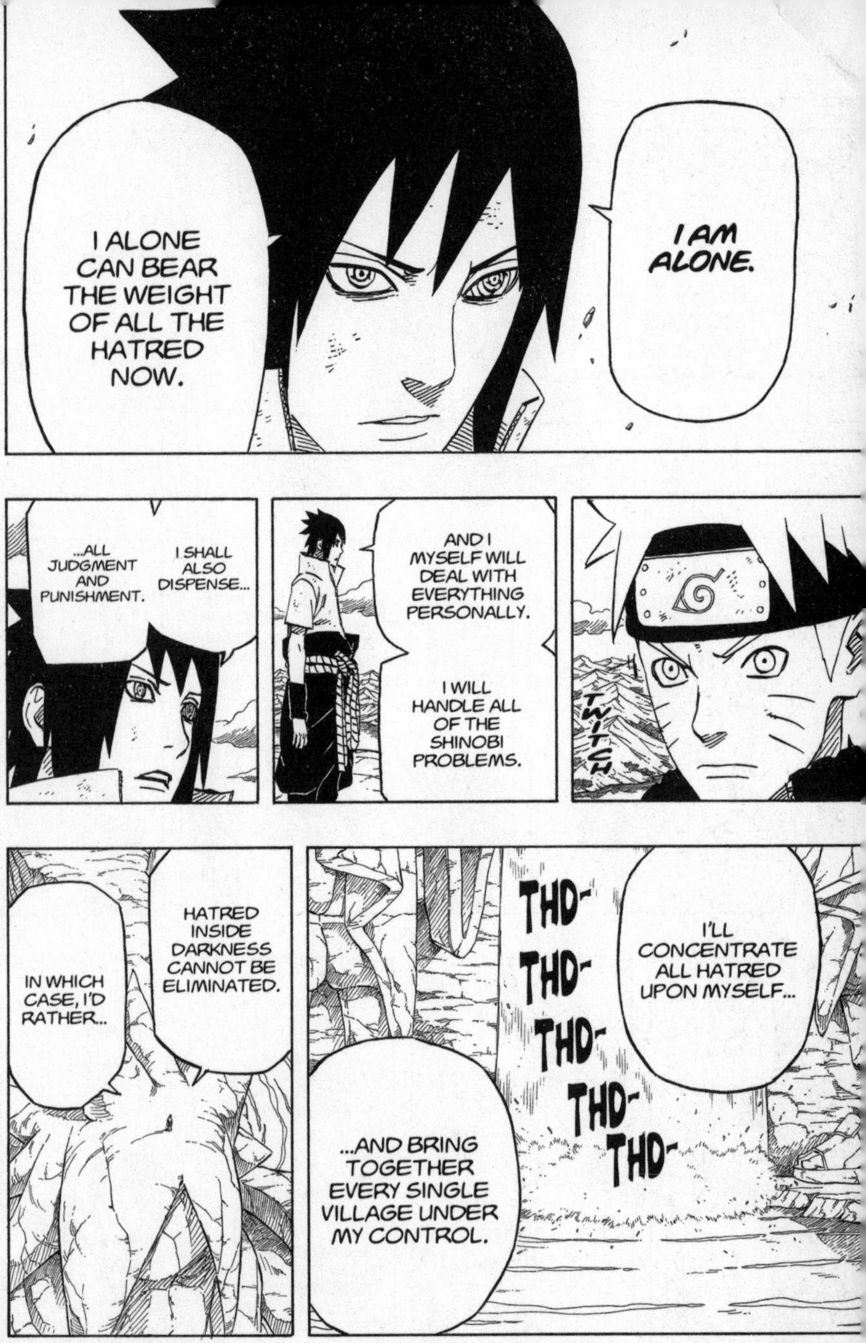
I AM ALONE.
I ALONE CAN BEAR THE WEIGHT OF ALL THE HATRED NOW.
TWITCH
AND I MYSELF WILL DEAL WITH EVERYTHING PERSONALLY.
I WILL HANDLE ALL OF THE SHINOBI PROBLEMS.
I SHALL ALSO DISPENSE...
...ALL JUDGMENT AND PUNISHMENT.
I'LL CONCENTRATE ALL HATRED UPON MYSELF...
THD- THD- THD- THD- THD-
...AND BRING TOGETHER EVERY SINGLE VILLAGE UNDER MY CONTROL.
HATRED INSIDE DARKNESS CANNOT BE ELIMINATED.
IN WHICH CASE, I'D RATHER...

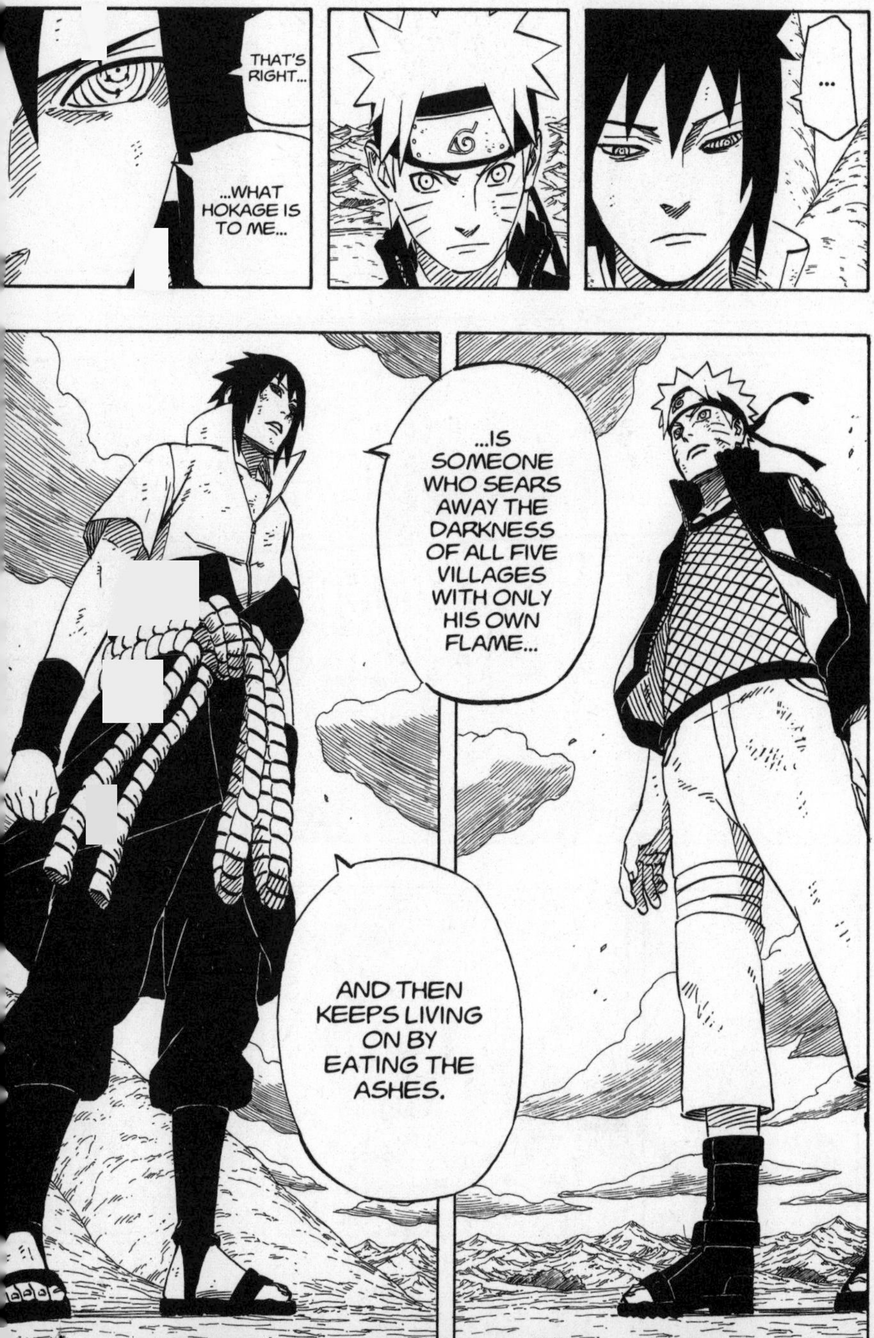
...
THAT'S RIGHT...
...WHAT HOKAGE IS TO ME...
...IS SOMEONE WHO SEARS AWAY THE DARKNESS OF ALL FIVE VILLAGES WITH ONLY HIS OWN FLAME...
AND THEN KEEPS LIVING ON BY EATING THE ASHES.

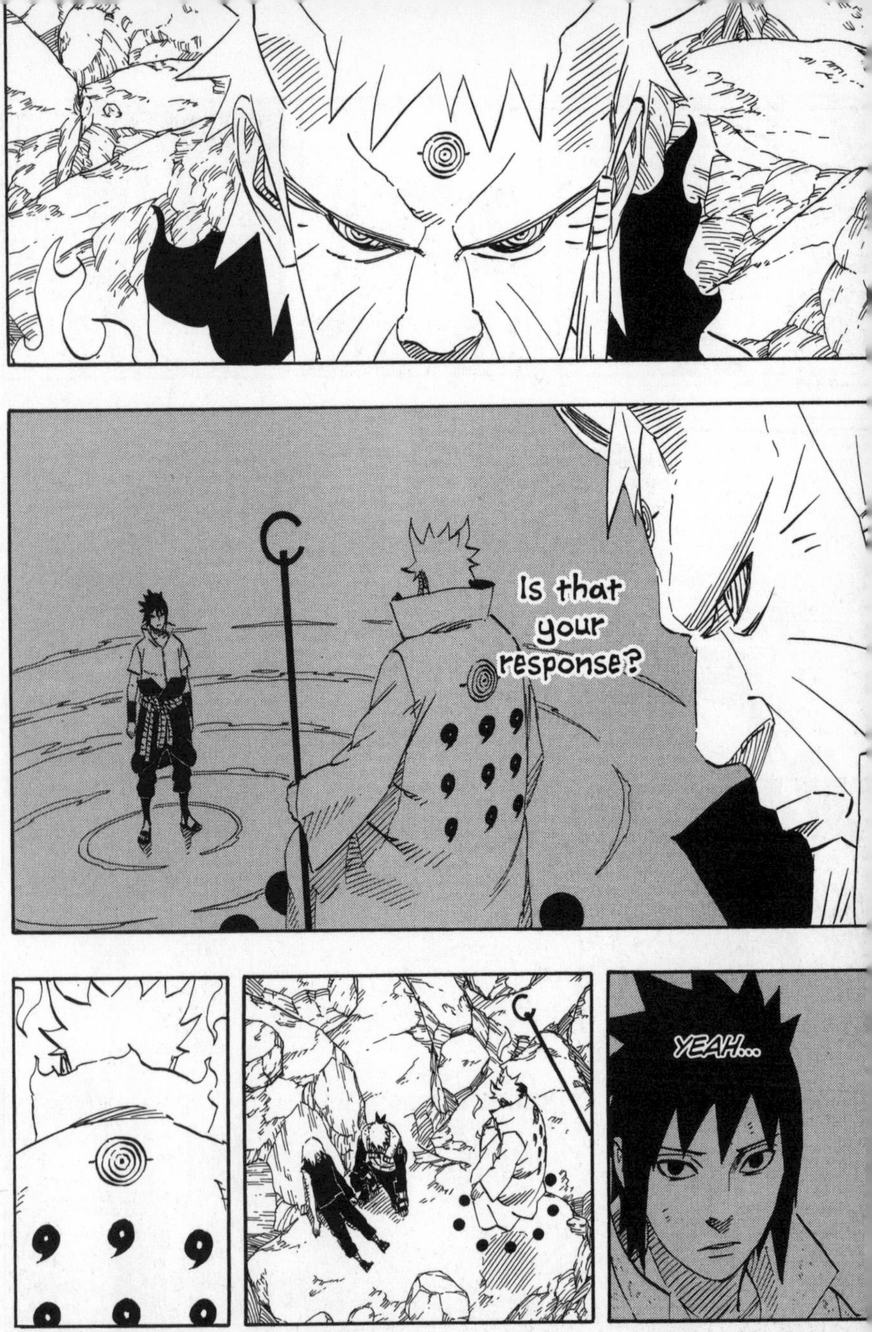

Is that your response?
YEAH...

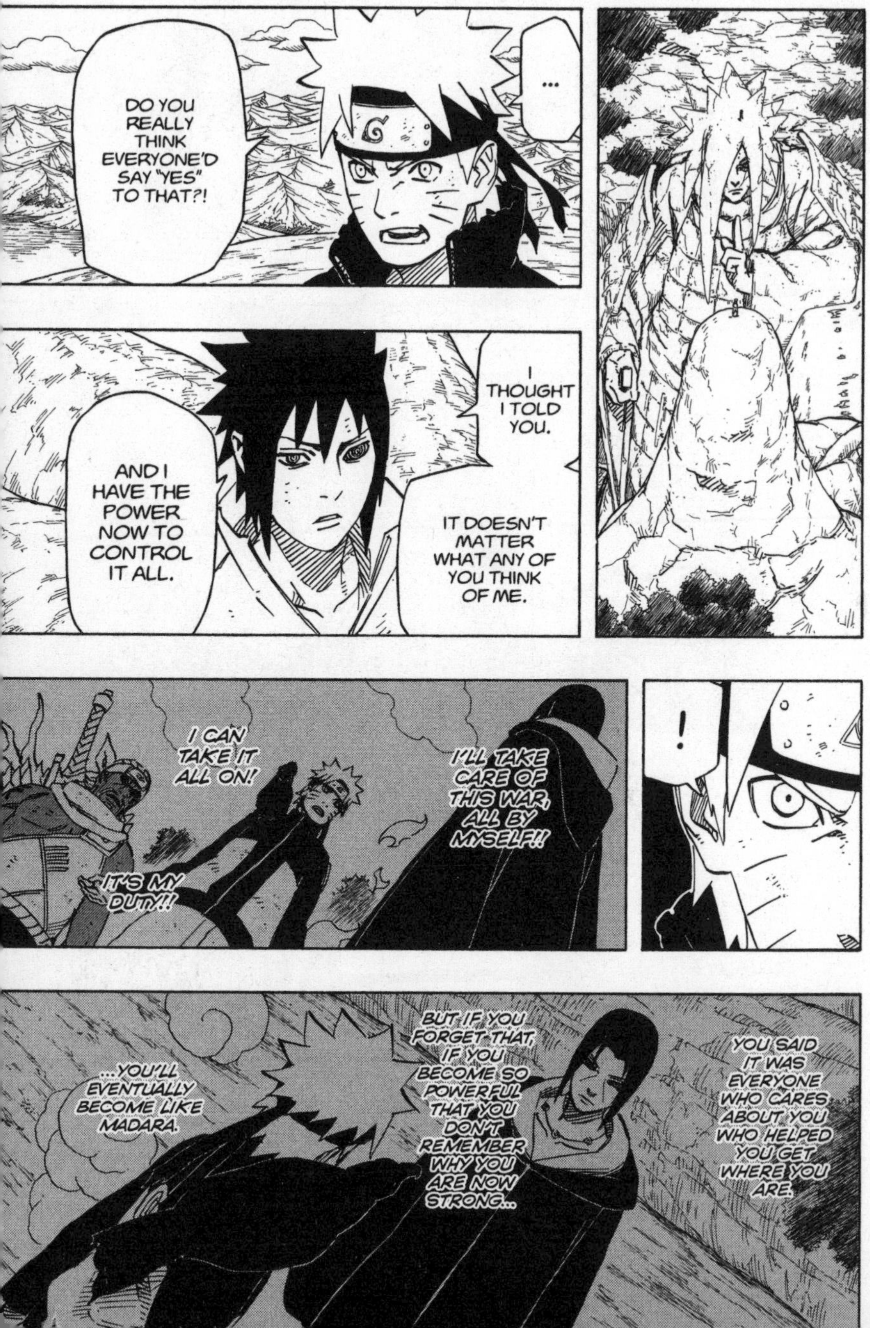
...
DO YOU REALLY THINK EVERYONE'D SAY "YES" TO THAT?!
I THOUGHT I TOLD YOU.
IT DOESN'T MATTER WHAT ANY OF YOU THINK OF ME.
AND I HAVE THE POWER NOW TO CONTROL IT ALL.
!
I'LL TAKE CARE OF THIS WAR, ALL BY MYSELF!!
I CAN TAKE IT ALL ON!
IT'S MY DUTY!!
YOU SAID IT WAS EVERYONE WHO CARES ABOUT YOU WHO HELPED YOU GET WHERE YOU ARE.
BUT IF YOU FORGET THAT, IF YOU BECOME SO POWERFUL THAT YOU DON'T REMEMBER WHY YOU ARE NOW STRONG...
...YOU'LL EVENTUALLY BECOME LIKE MADARA.

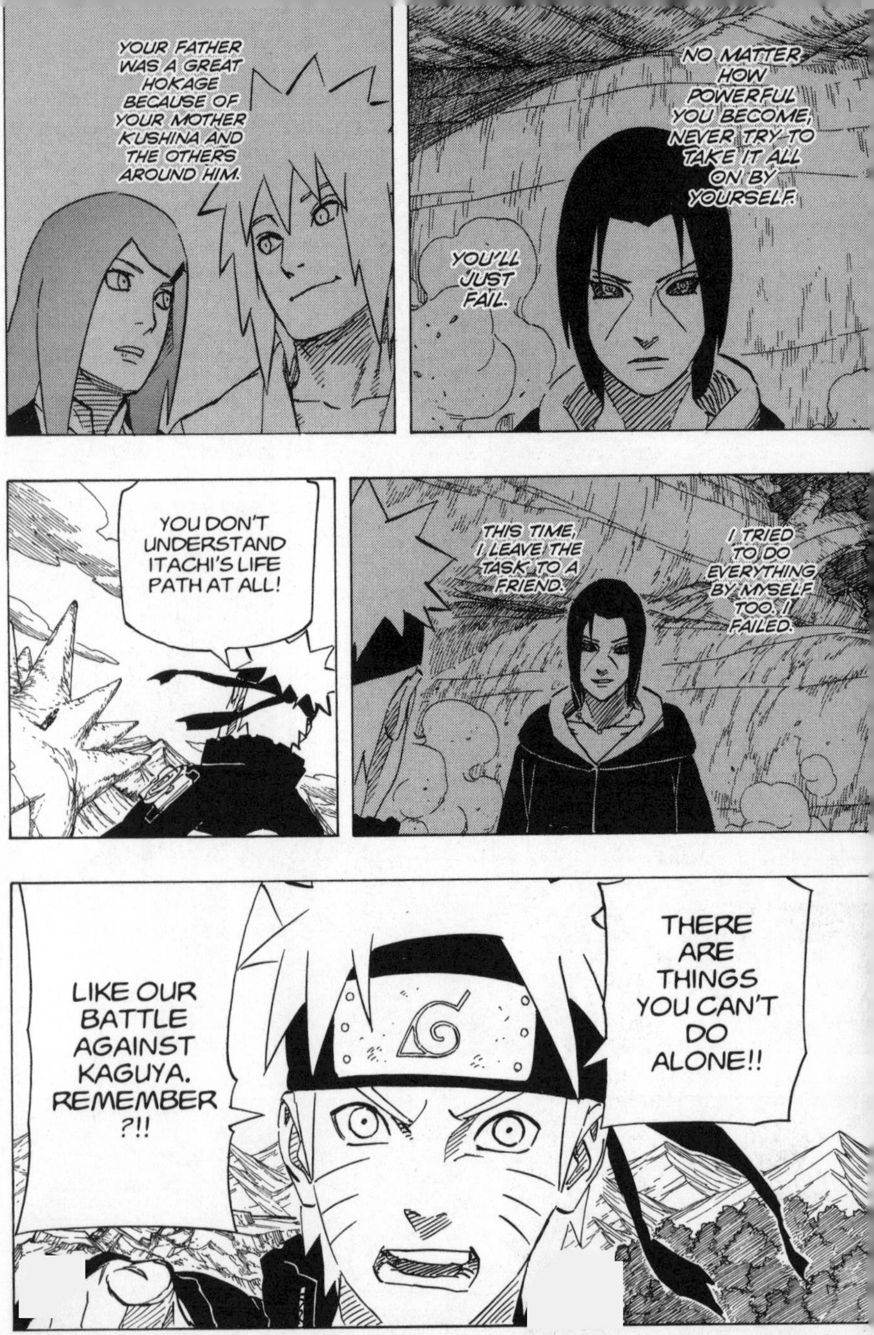
NO MATTER HOW POWERFUL YOU BECOME, NEVER TRY TO TAKE IT ALL ON BY YOURSELF.
YOU'LL JUST FAIL.
YOUR FATHER WAS A GREAT HOKAGE BECAUSE OF YOUR MOTHER KUSHINA AND THE OTHERS AROUND HIM.
I TRIED TO DO EVERYTHING BY MYSELF TOO. I FAILED.
THIS TIME, I LEAVE THE TASK TO A FRIEND.
YOU DON'T UNDERSTAND ITACHI'S LIFE PATH AT ALL!
THERE ARE THINGS YOU CAN'T DO ALONE!!
LIKE OUR BATTLE AGAINST KAGUYA. REMEMBER?!!

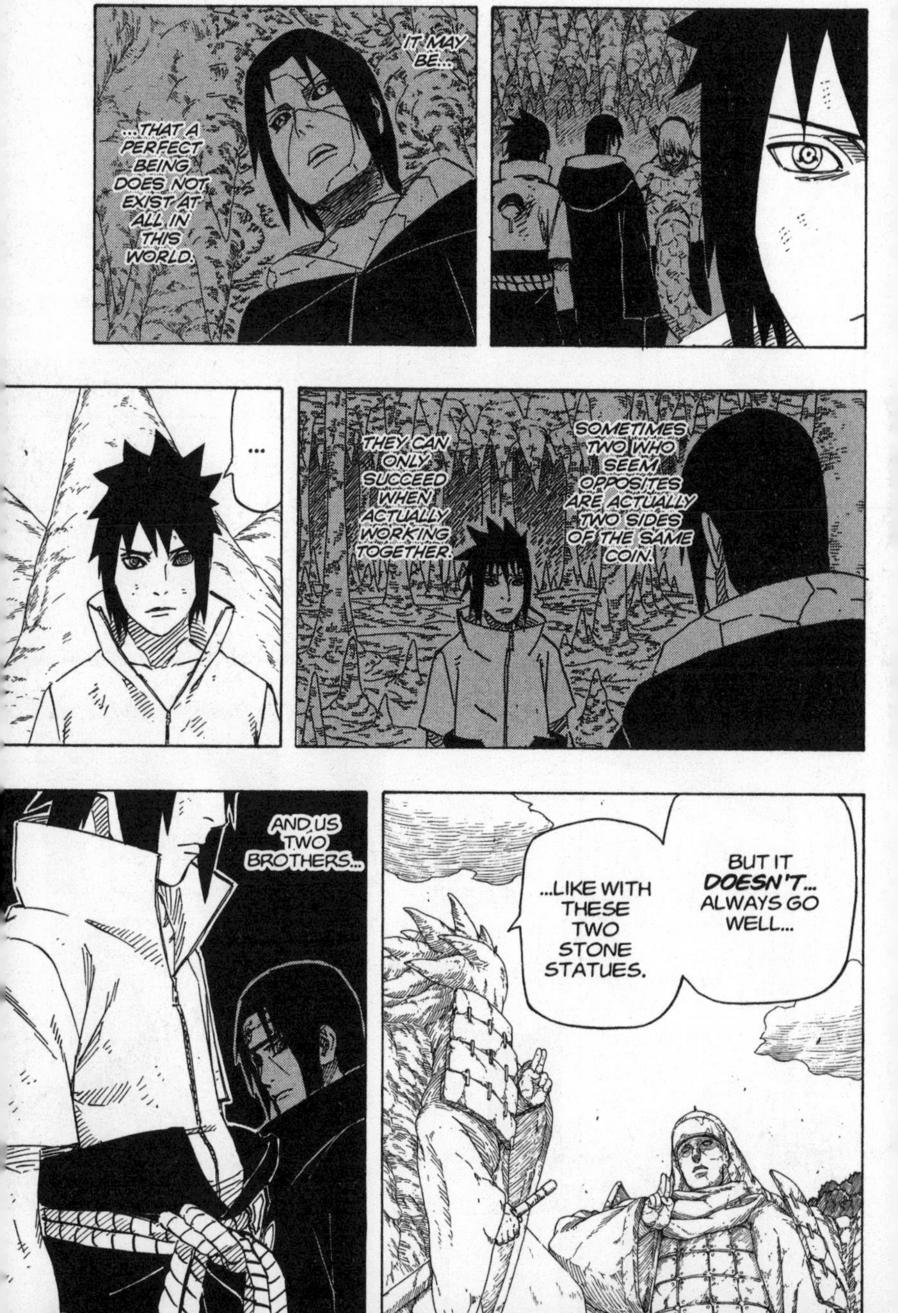
IT MAY BE...
...THAT A PERFECT BEING DOES NOT EXIST AT ALL IN THIS WORLD.
SOMETIMES TWO WHO SEEM OPPOSITES ARE ACTUALLY TWO SIDES OF THE SAME COIN.
THEY CAN ONLY SUCCEED WHEN ACTUALLY WORKING TOGETHER.
...
BUT IT **DOESN'T**... ALWAYS GO WELL...
...LIKE WITH THESE TWO STONE STATUES.
AND US TWO BROTHERS...

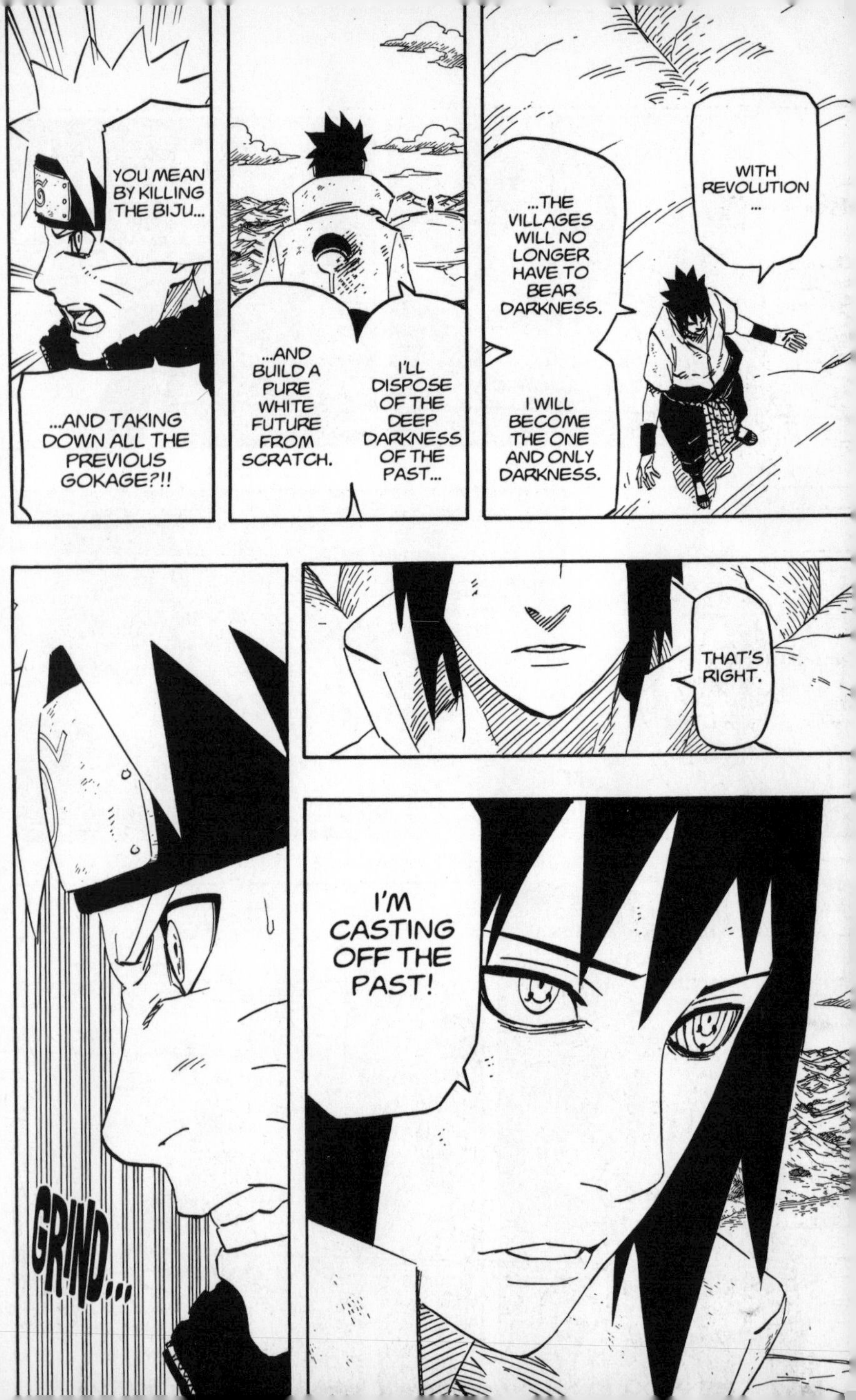
WITH REVOLUTION ...
...THE VILLAGES WILL NO LONGER HAVE TO BEAR DARKNESS.
I WILL BECOME THE ONE AND ONLY DARKNESS.
I'LL DISPOSE OF THE DEEP DARKNESS OF THE PAST...
...AND BUILD A PURE WHITE FUTURE FROM SCRATCH.
YOU MEAN BY KILLING THE BIJU...
...AND TAKING DOWN ALL THE PREVIOUS GOKAGE?!!
THAT'S RIGHT.
I'M CASTING OFF THE PAST!
GRIND...

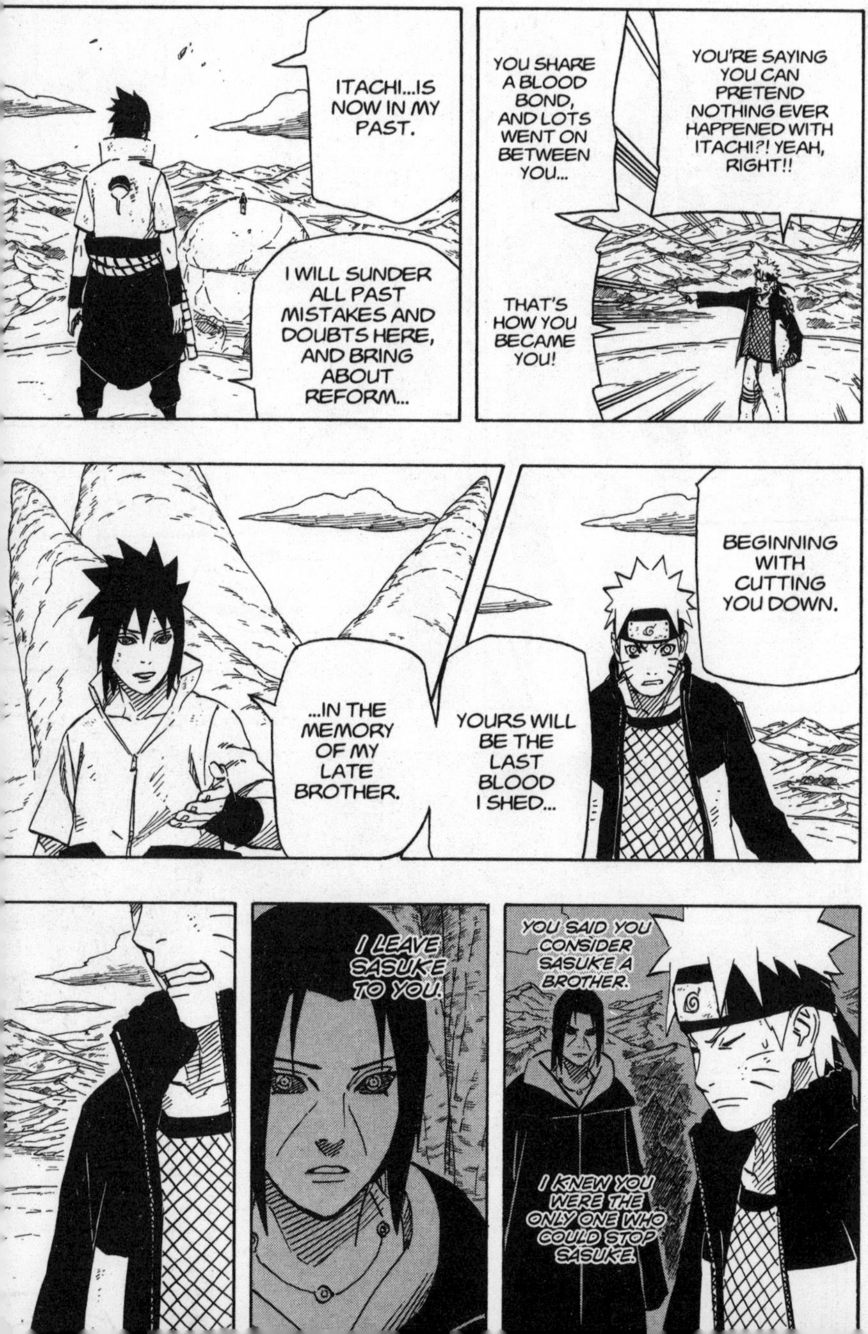
YOU'RE SAYING YOU CAN PRETEND NOTHING EVER HAPPENED WITH ITACHI?! YEAH, RIGHT!!
YOU SHARE A BLOOD BOND, AND LOTS WENT ON BETWEEN YOU...
THAT'S HOW YOU BECAME YOU!
ITACHI...IS NOW IN MY PAST.
I WILL SUNDER ALL PAST MISTAKES AND DOUBTS HERE, AND BRING ABOUT REFORM...
BEGINNING WITH CUTTING YOU DOWN.
YOURS WILL BE THE LAST BLOOD I SHED...
...IN THE MEMORY OF MY LATE BROTHER.
YOU SAID YOU CONSIDER SASUKE A BROTHER.
I KNEW YOU WERE THE ONLY ONE WHO COULD STOP SASUKE.
I LEAVE SASUKE TO YOU.

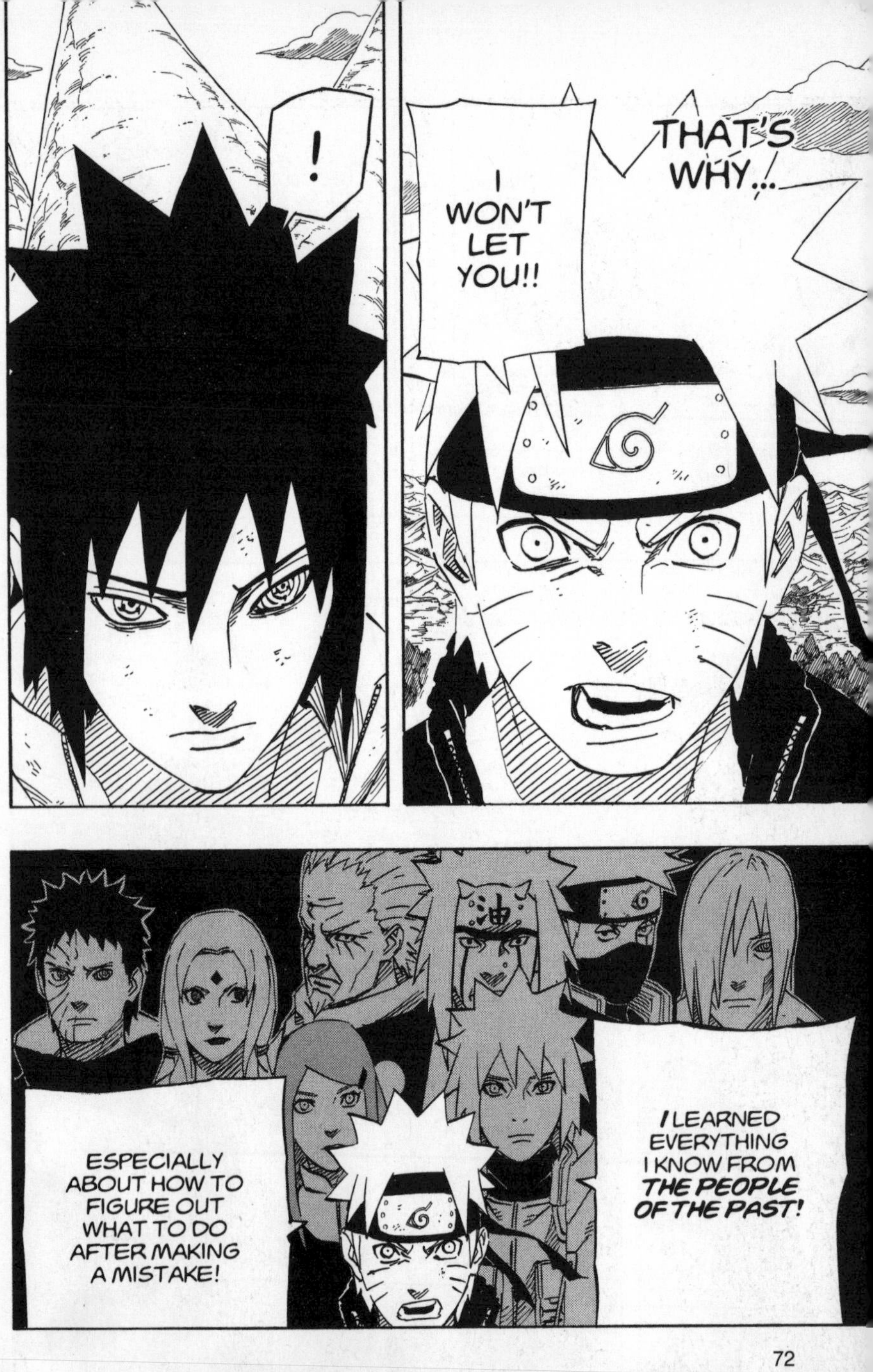
THAT'S WHY...
I WON'T LET YOU!!
!
I LEARNED EVERYTHING I KNOW FROM *THE PEOPLE OF THE PAST!*
ESPECIALLY ABOUT HOW TO FIGURE OUT WHAT TO DO AFTER MAKING A MISTAKE!

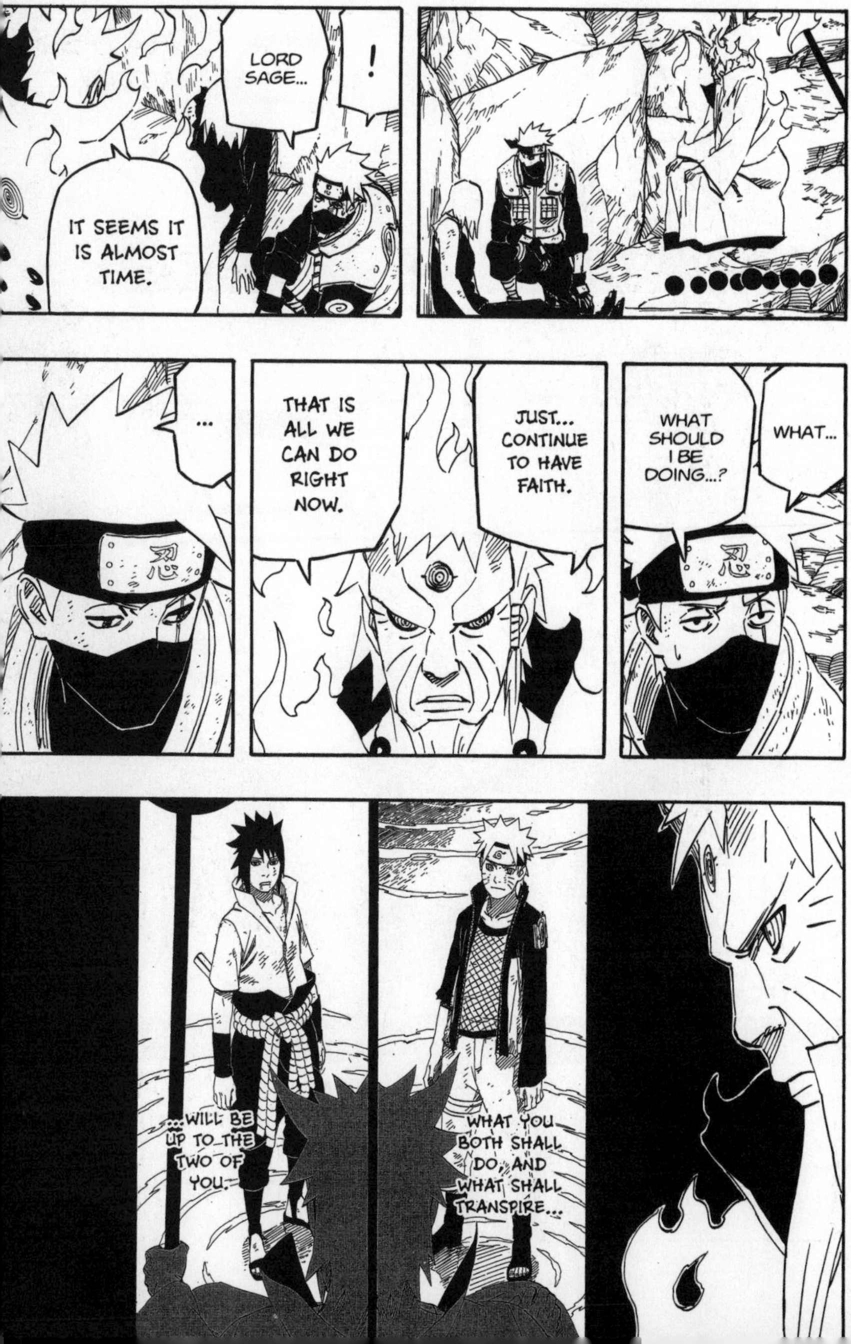
!
LORD SAGE...
IT SEEMS IT IS ALMOST TIME.
WHAT...
WHAT SHOULD I BE DOING...?
JUST... CONTINUE TO HAVE FAITH.
THAT IS ALL WE CAN DO RIGHT NOW.
...
WHAT YOU BOTH SHALL DO, AND WHAT SHALL TRANSPIRE...
...WILL BE UP TO THE TWO OF YOU.

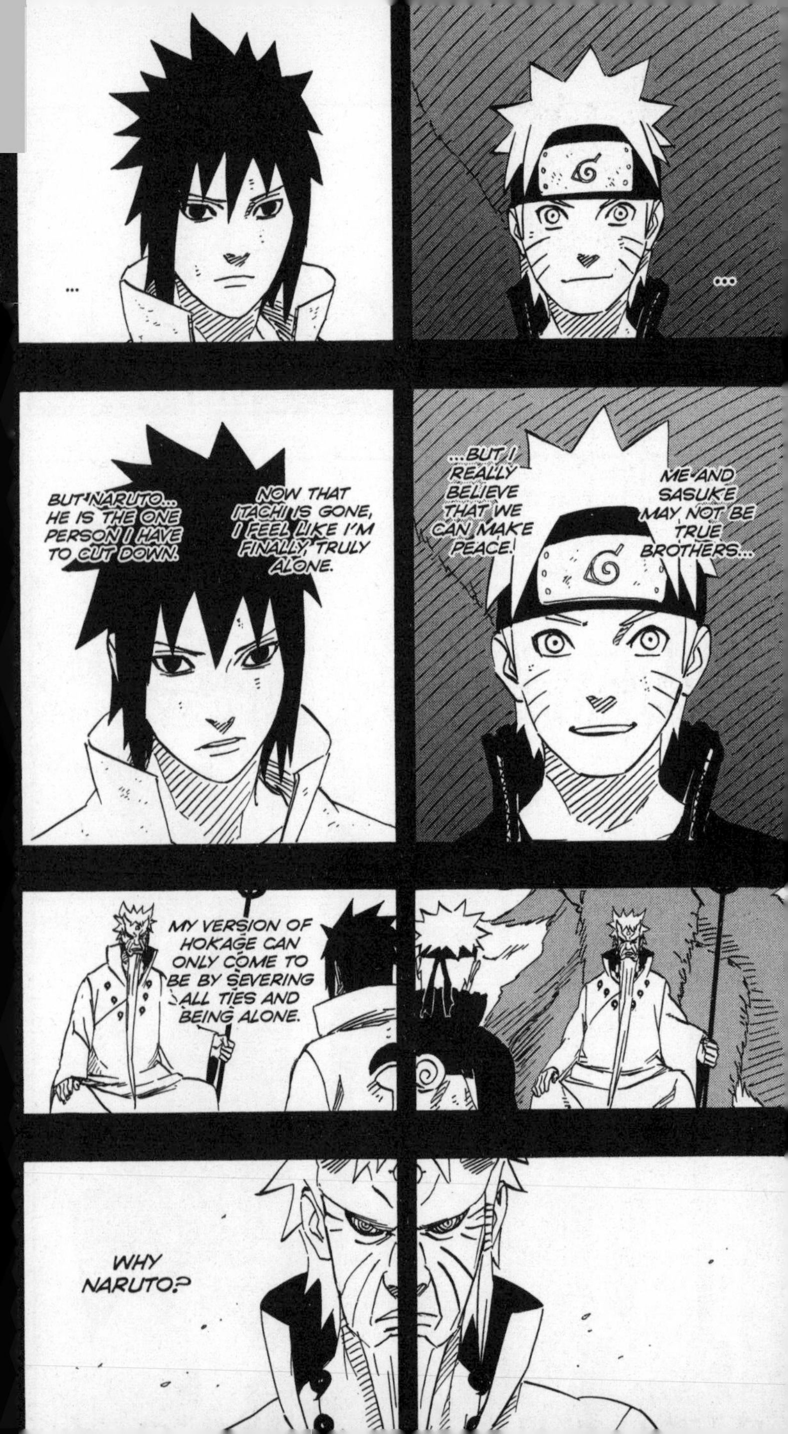
...
...
ME AND SASUKE MAY NOT BE TRUE BROTHERS...
...BUT I REALLY BELIEVE THAT WE CAN MAKE PEACE.
NOW THAT ITACHI IS GONE, I FEEL LIKE I'M FINALLY, TRULY ALONE.
BUT NARUTO... HE IS THE ONE PERSON I HAVE TO CUT DOWN.
MY VERSION OF HOKAGE CAN ONLY COME TO BE BY SEVERING ALL TIES AND BEING ALONE.
WHY NARUTO?

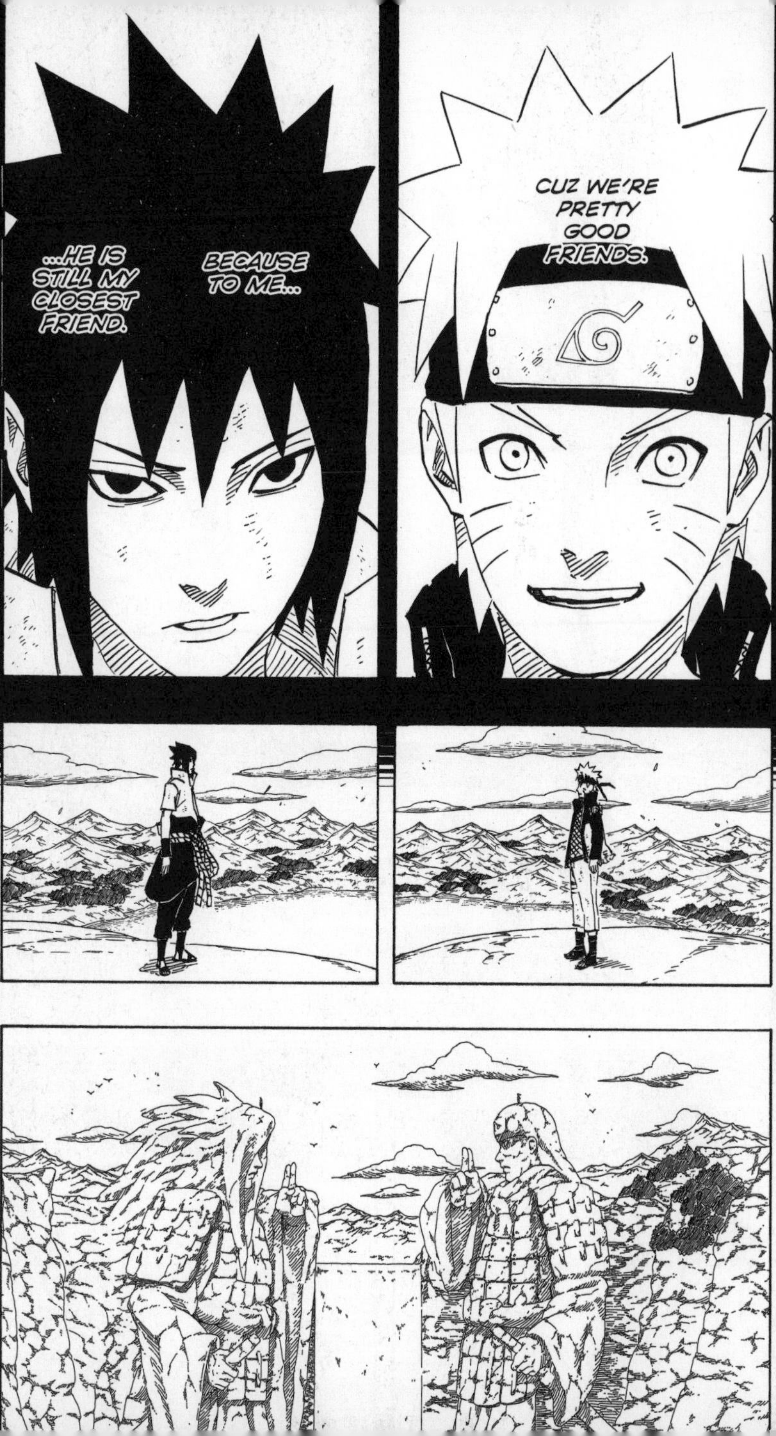
CUZ WE'RE PRETTY GOOD FRIENDS.
BECAUSE TO ME...
...HE IS STILL MY CLOSEST FRIEND.

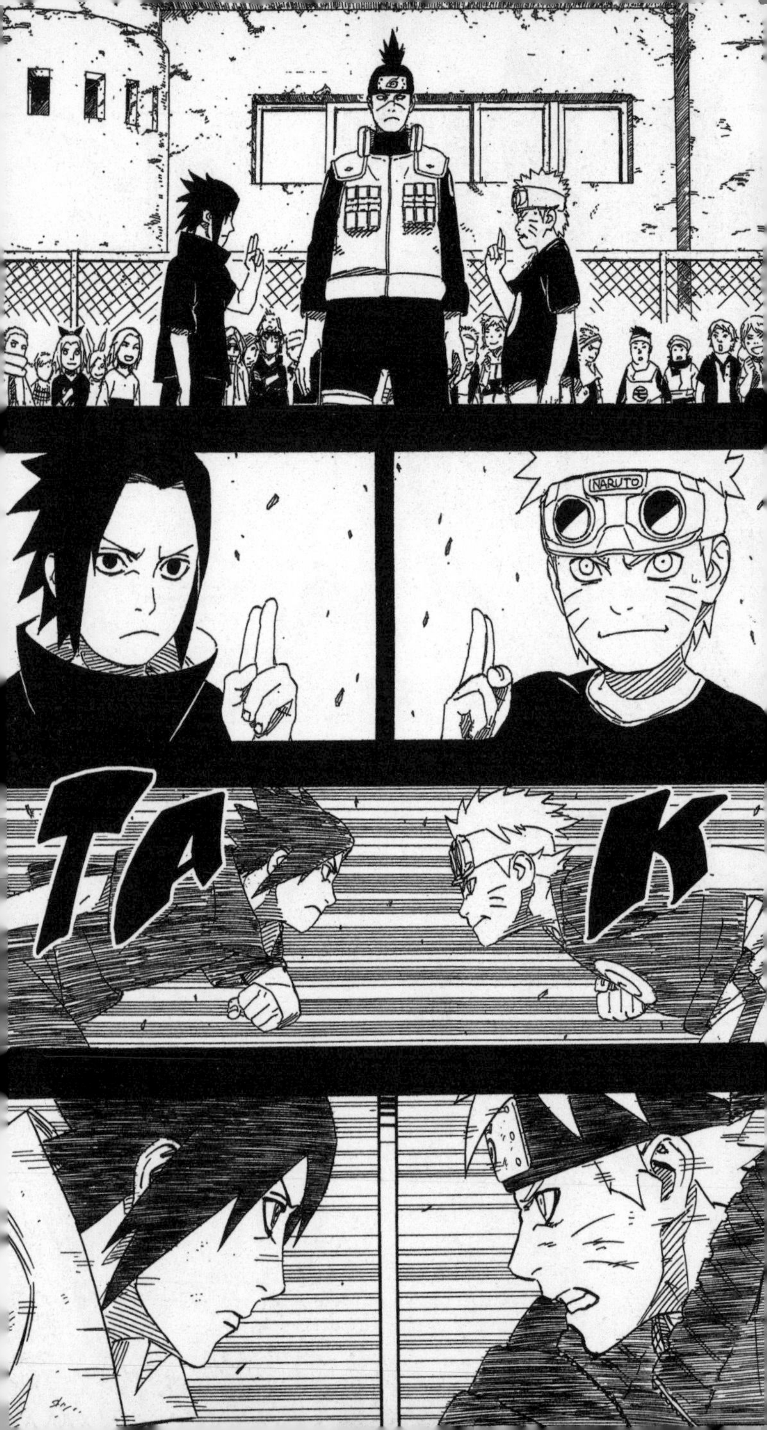
NARUTO
TAK

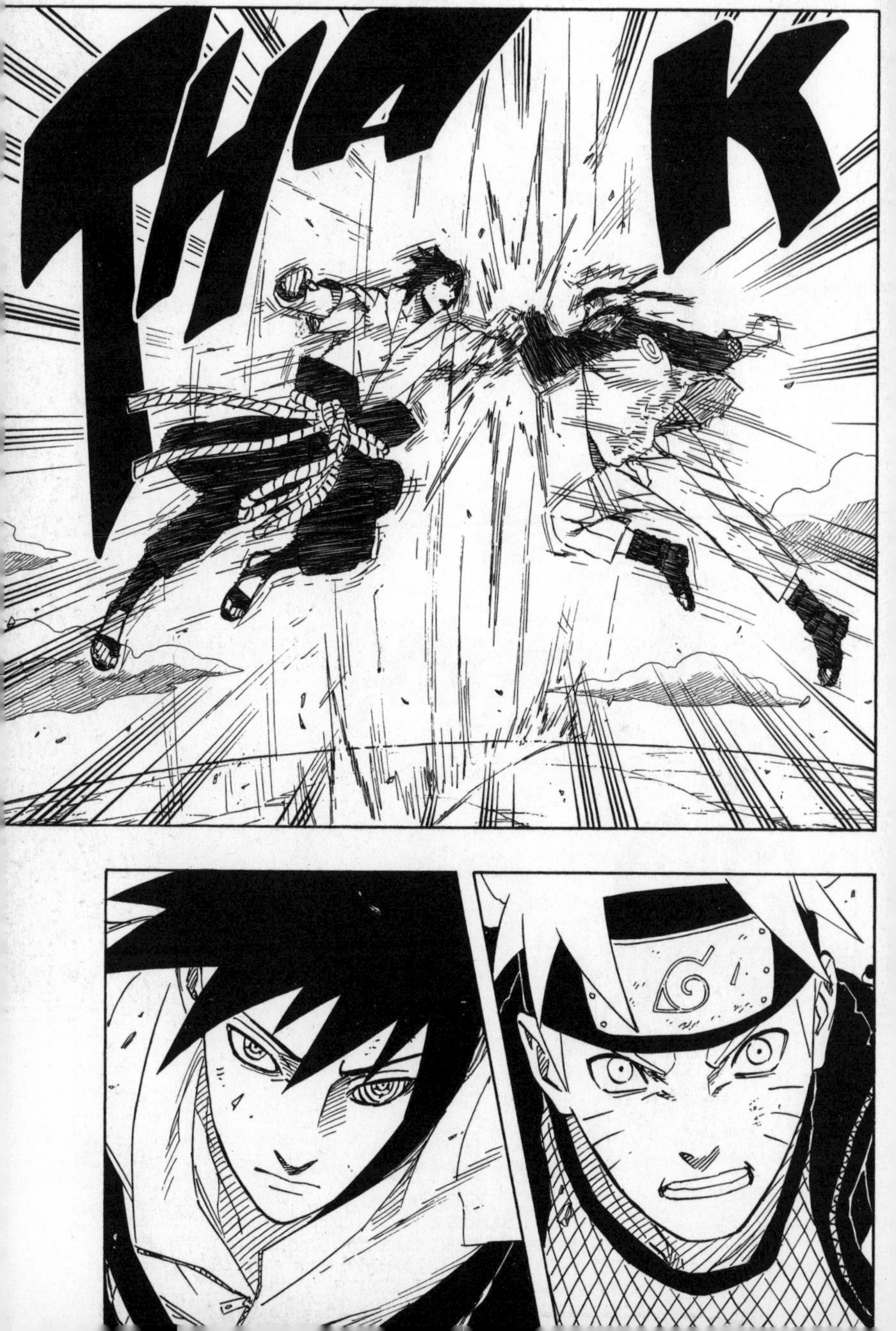
THAK

END OF SERIES COMMEMORATION ILLUSTRATION (4)

BANNER: CONGRATS ON 15 YEARS!

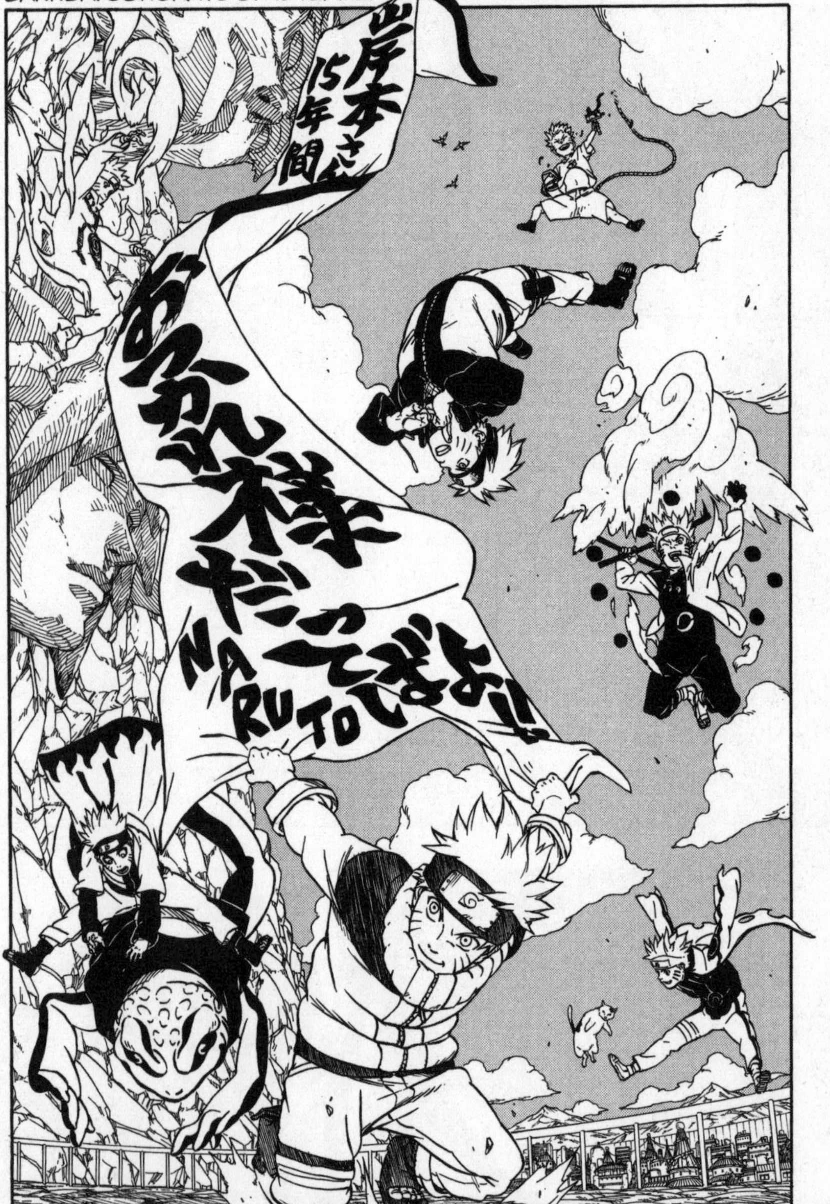
岸本さ
15年間
おつかれ様だってばよ!!
NARUTO

IT IS A LIFETIME HONOR THAT I, WHO WAS ORIGINALLY JUST A FAN, GOT TO BE INVOLVED WITH NARUTO FOR 8 YEARS. -AKIO SHIRASAKA

Number 695: Naruto and Sasuke, Part 2

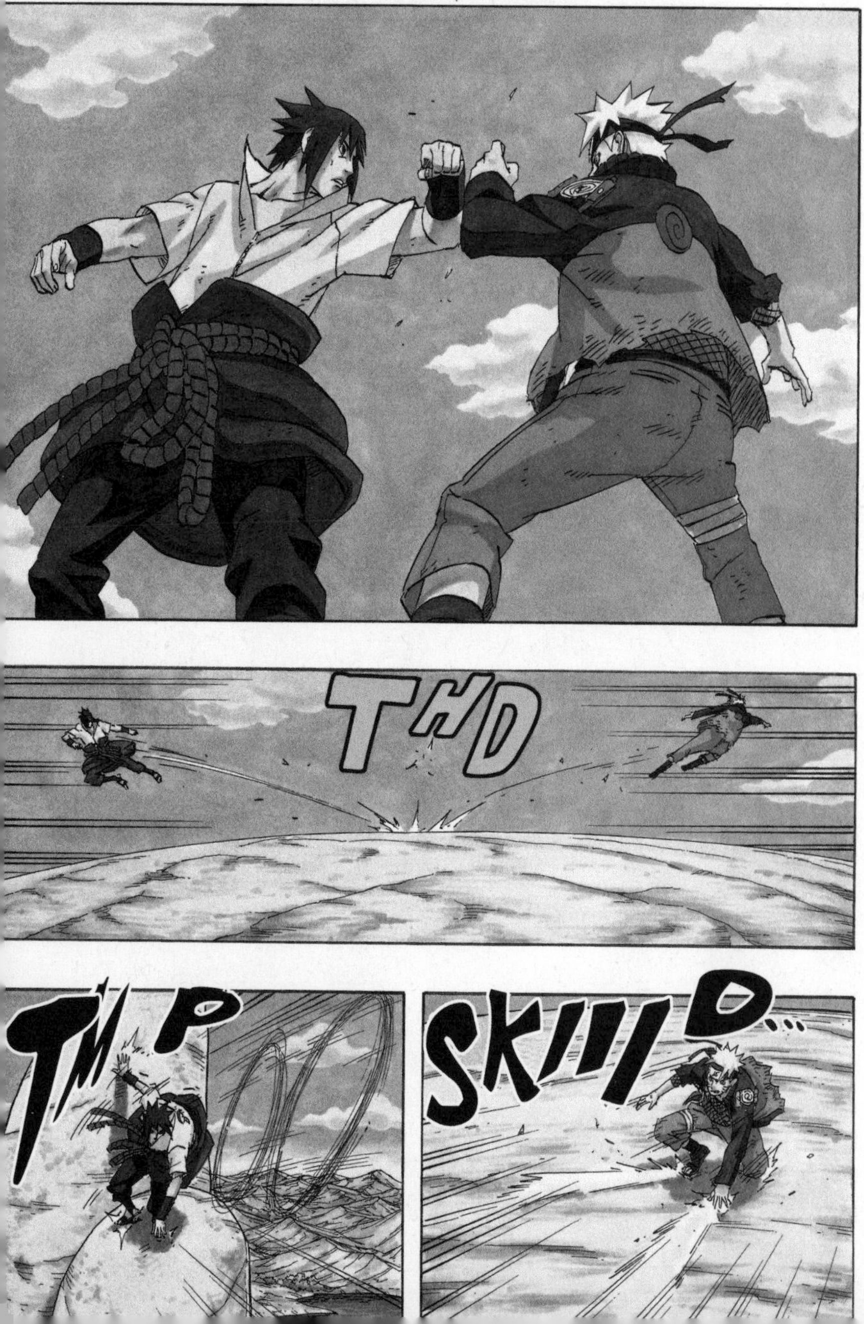

THD
SKIIID...
THP

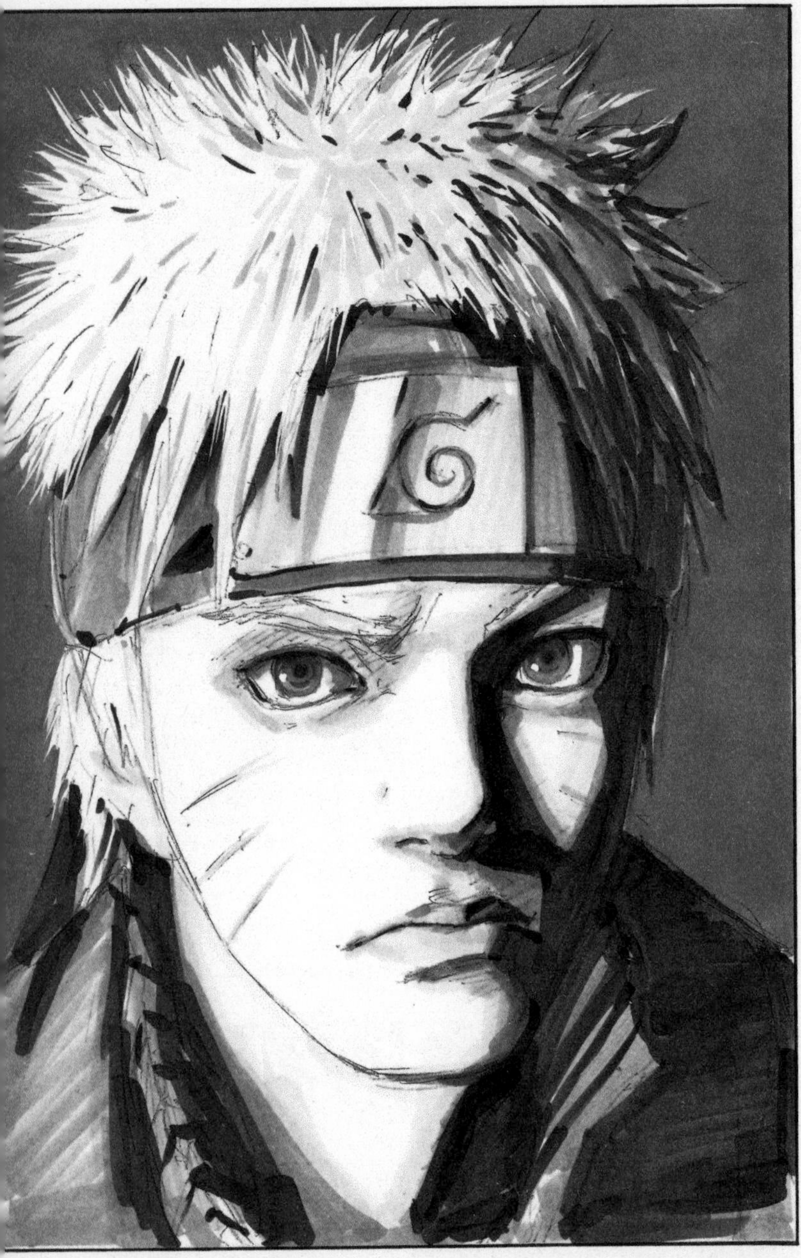

Number 695: Naruto and Sasuke, Part 2

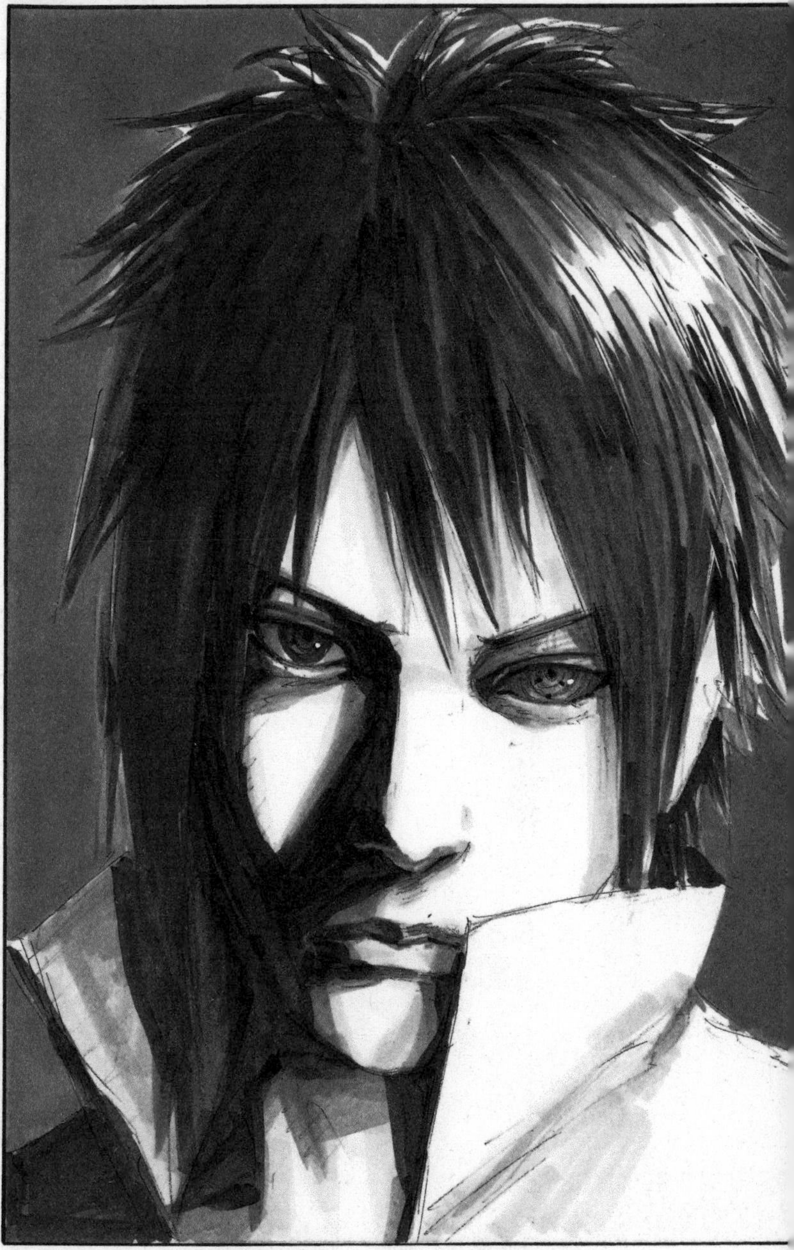

NARUTO

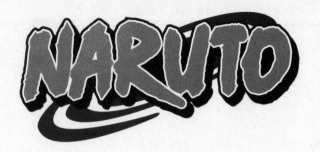

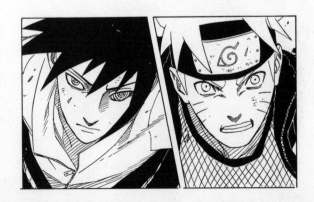

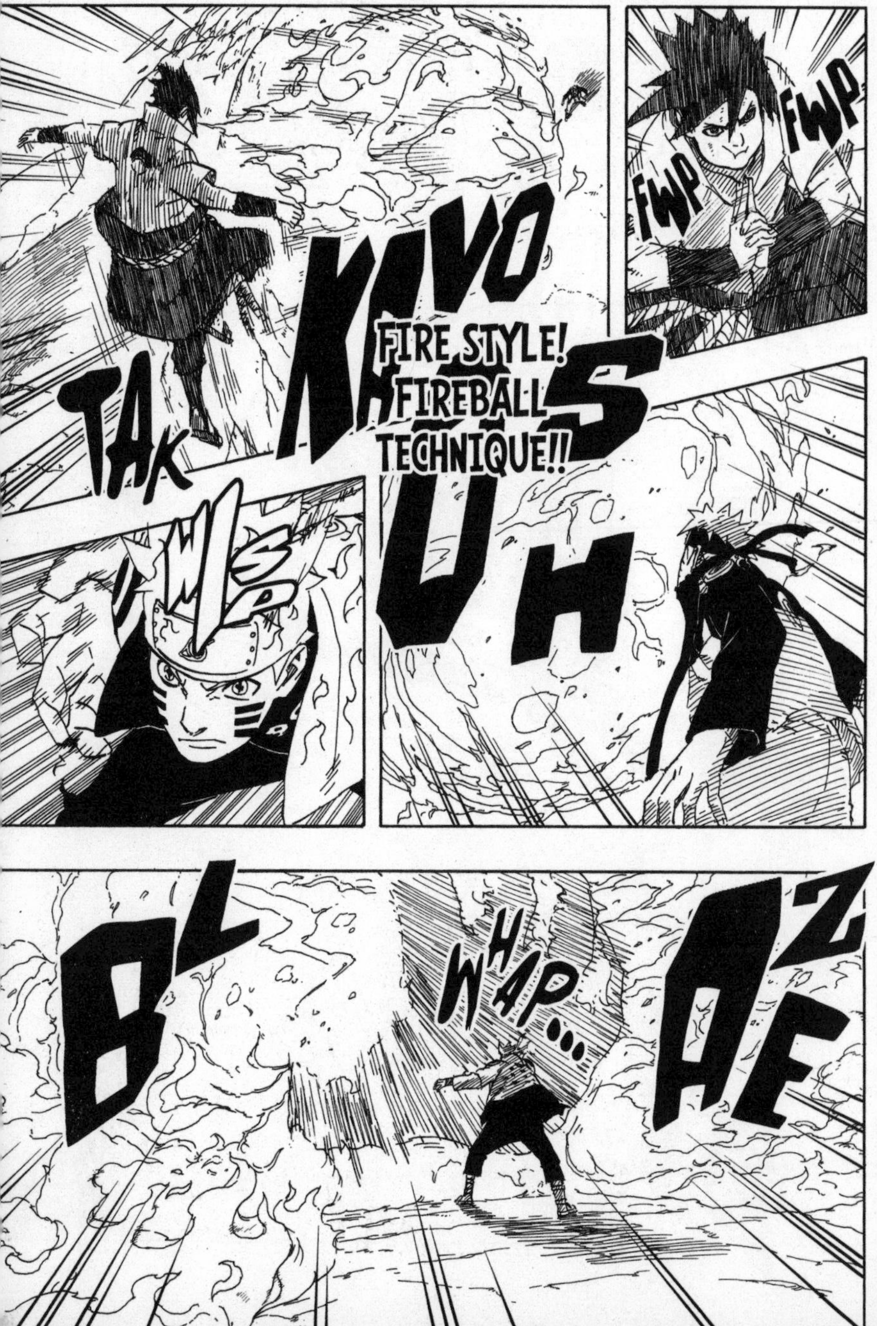
FWP
FWP
FWP
FIRE STYLE! FIREBALL TECHNIQUE!!
TAK
WHAP...

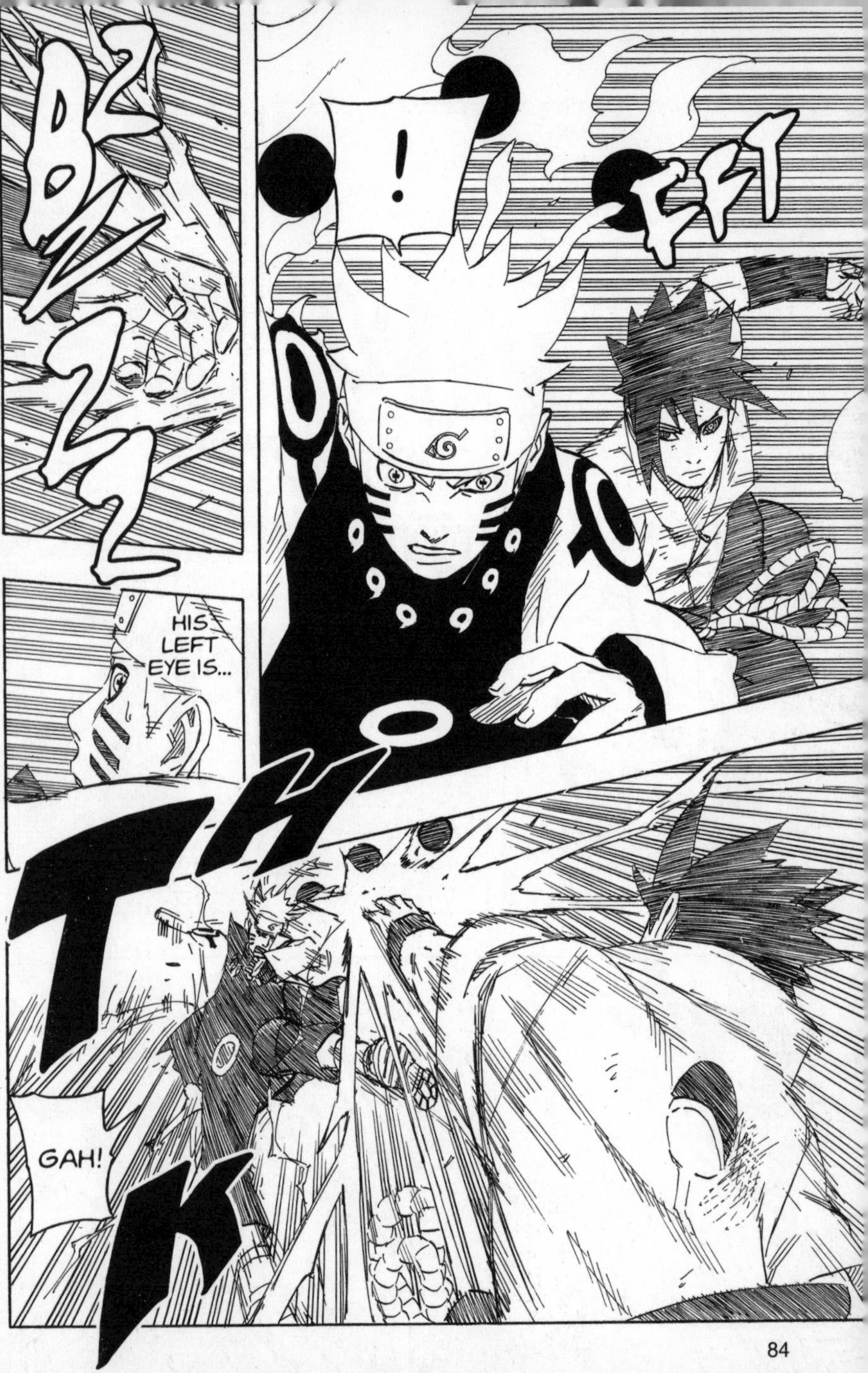
!
EFT
HIS LEFT EYE IS...
GAH!

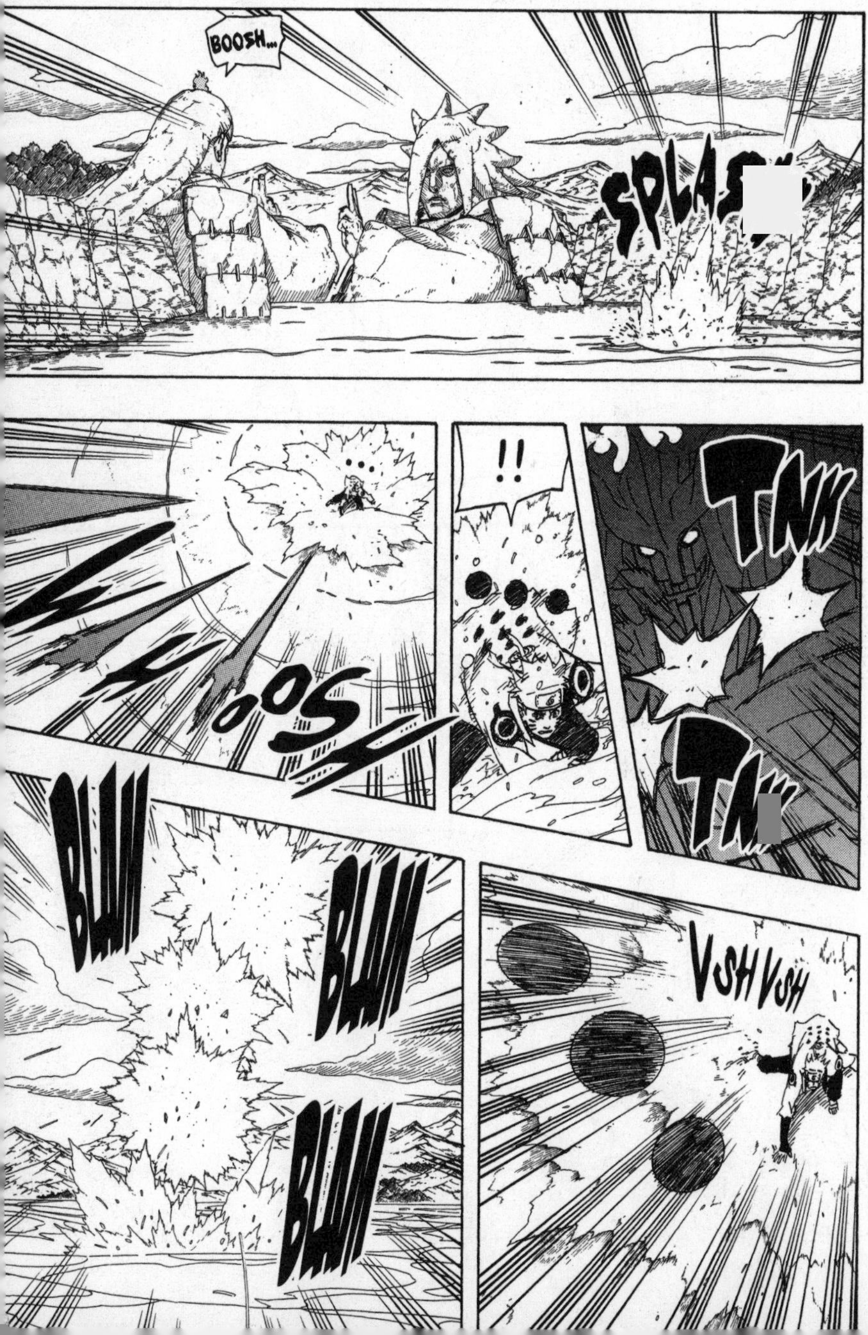
BOOSH...
SPLAS
TNK
TN
!!
...
WHOOSH
VSH VSH
BLAM
BLAM
BLAM

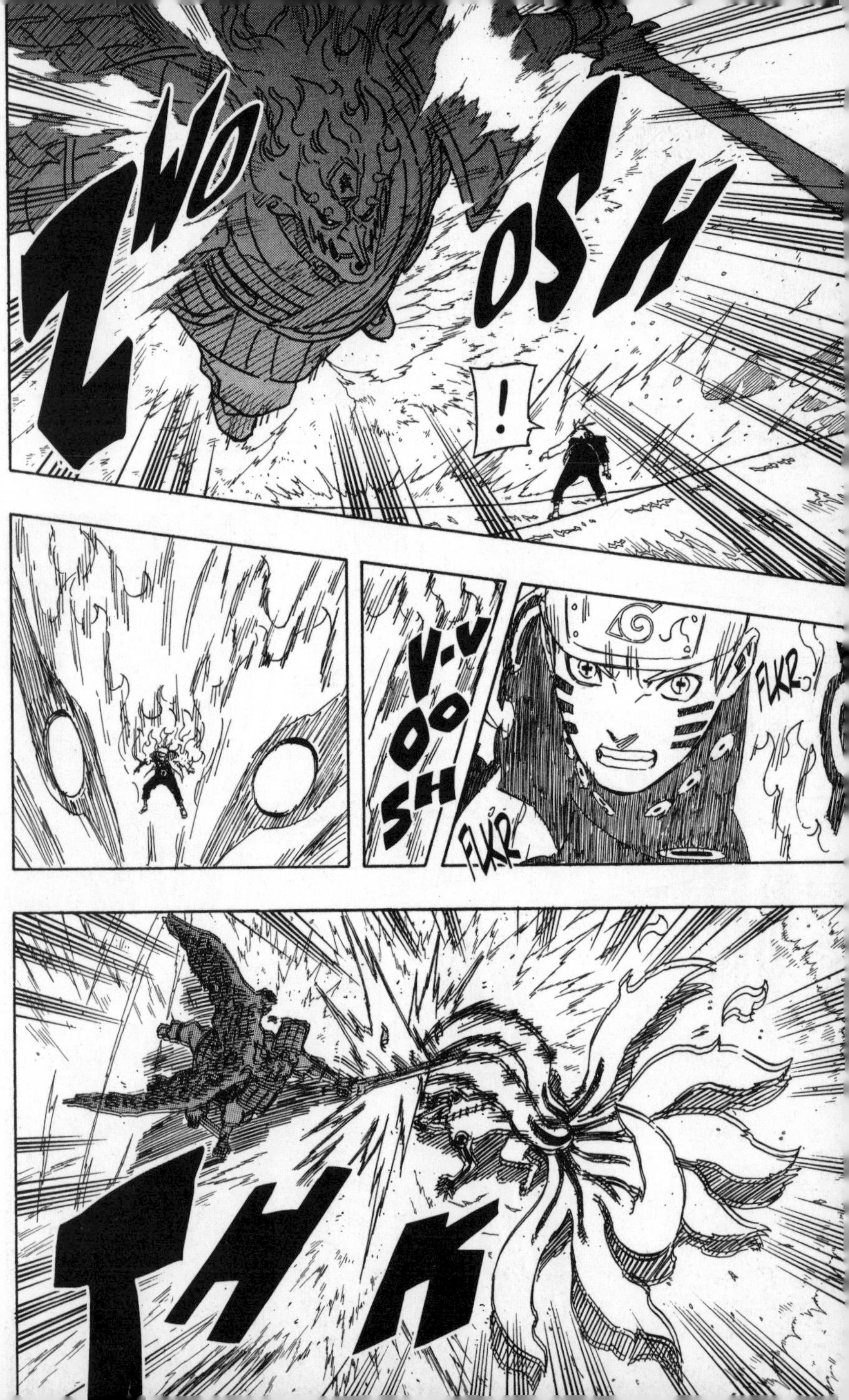
ZWOOSH
!
FLKR
FLKR
V-VOOOSH

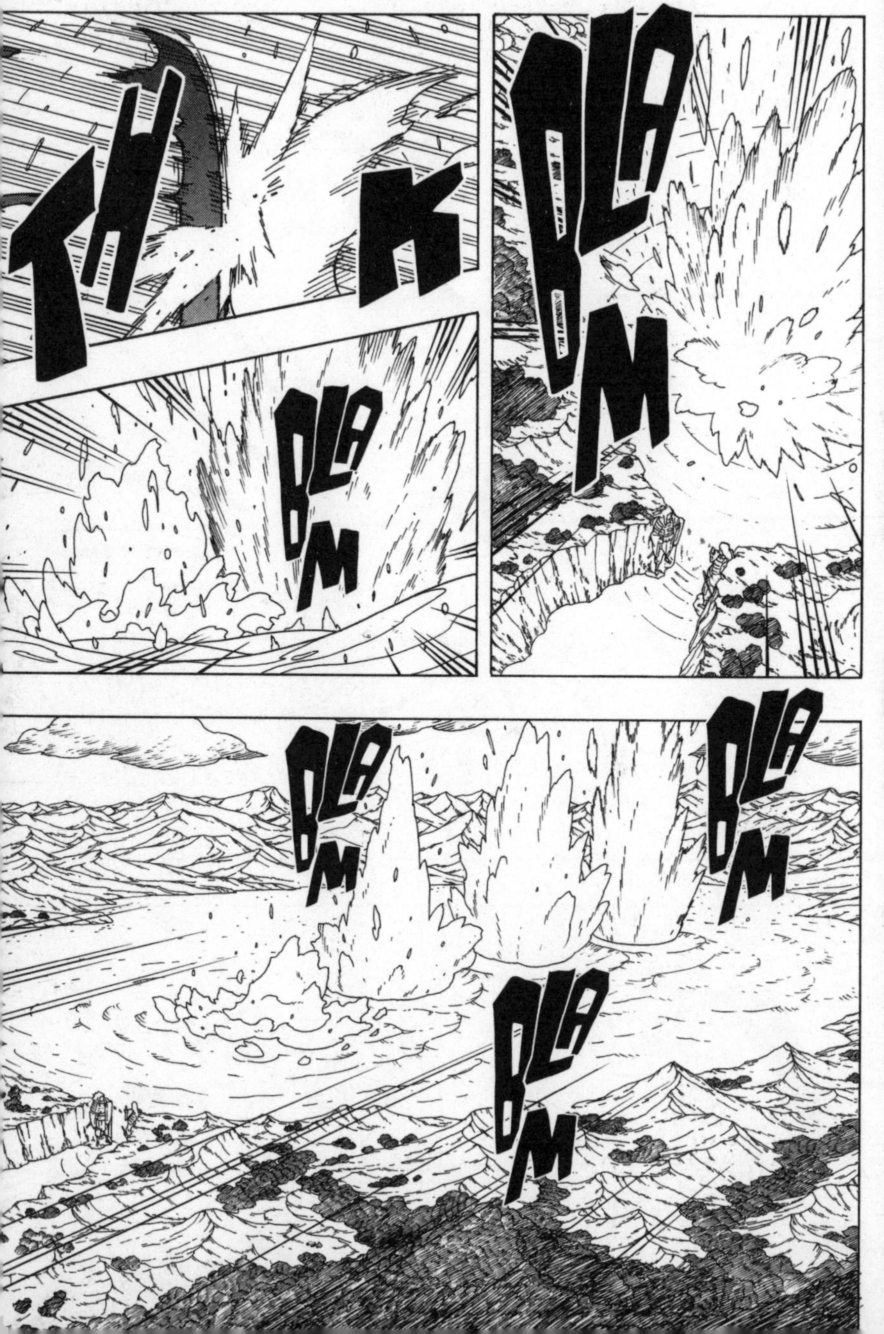
BLAM
THK
BLAM
BLAM
BLAM
BLAM

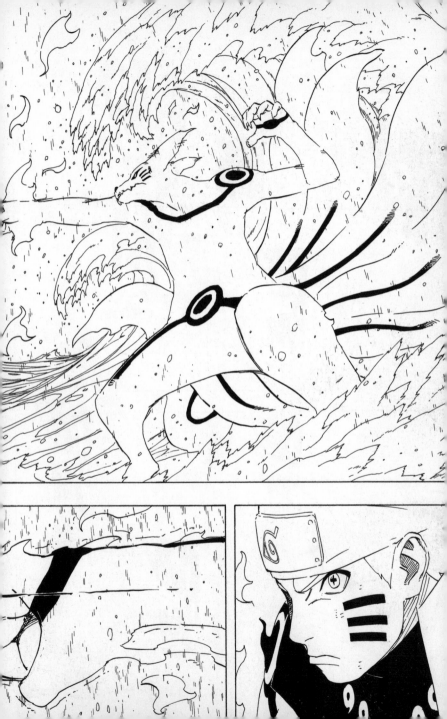

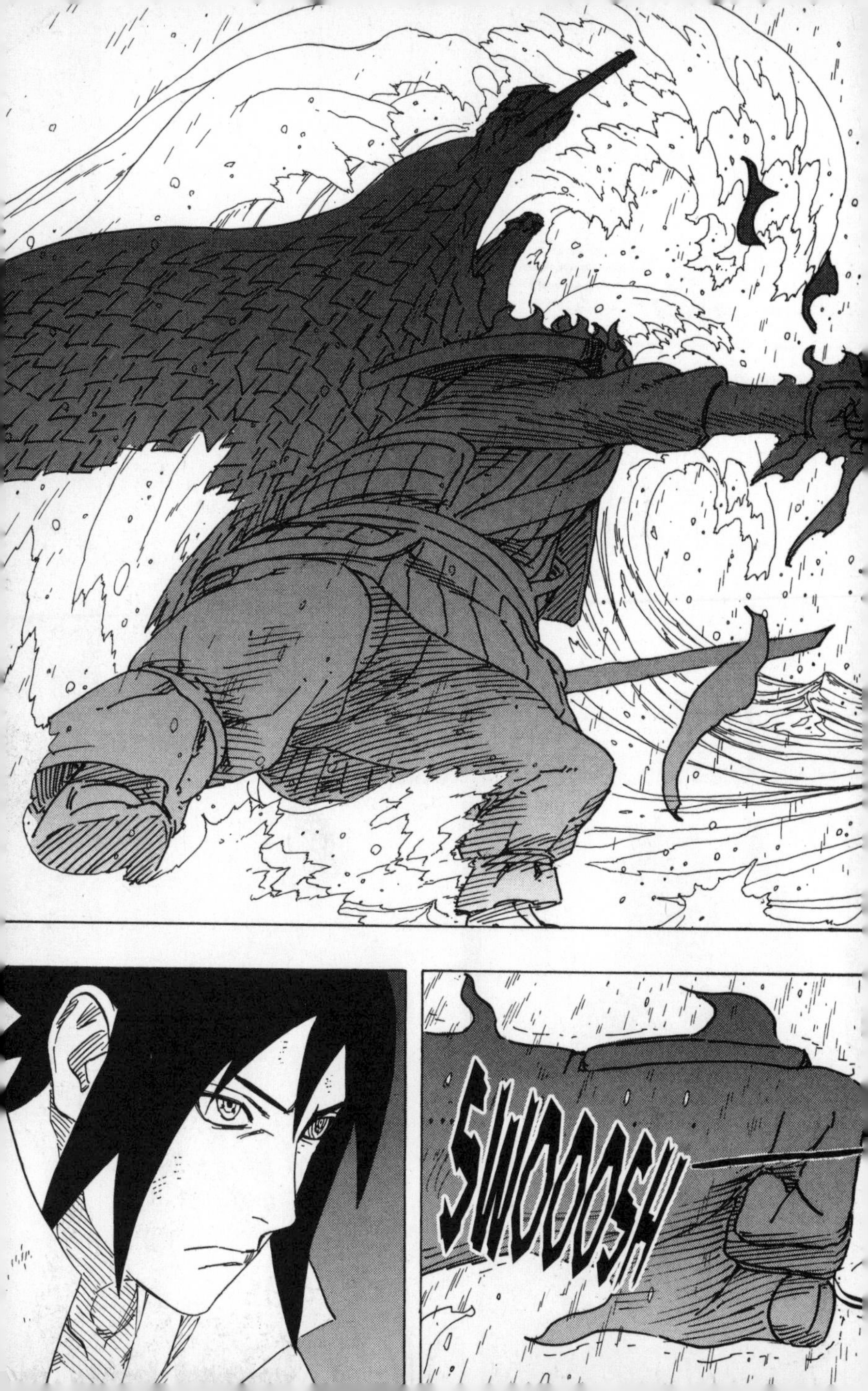
SWOOOSH

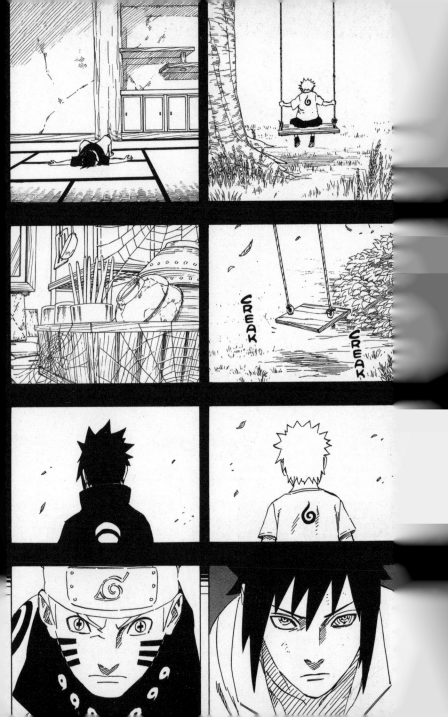

CREAK

CREAK

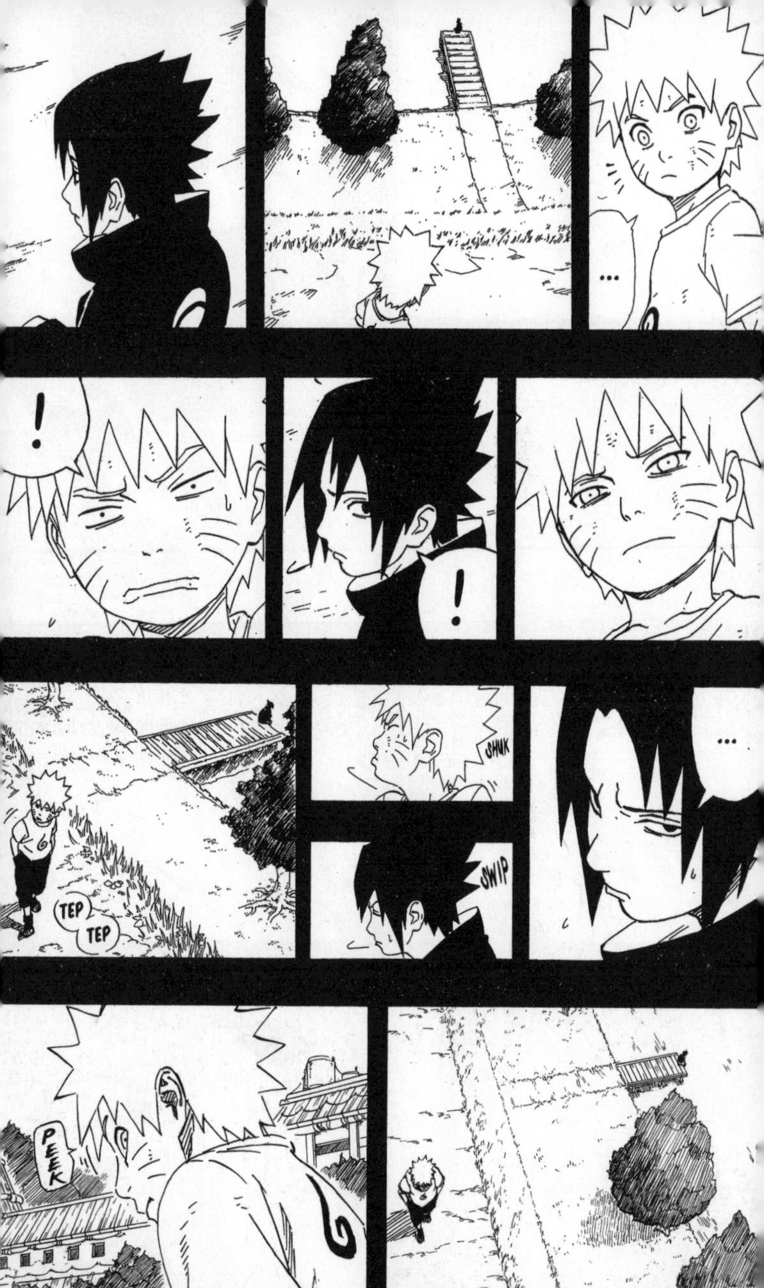
...
!
!
...
SHUK
SWIP
TEP
TEP
PEEK

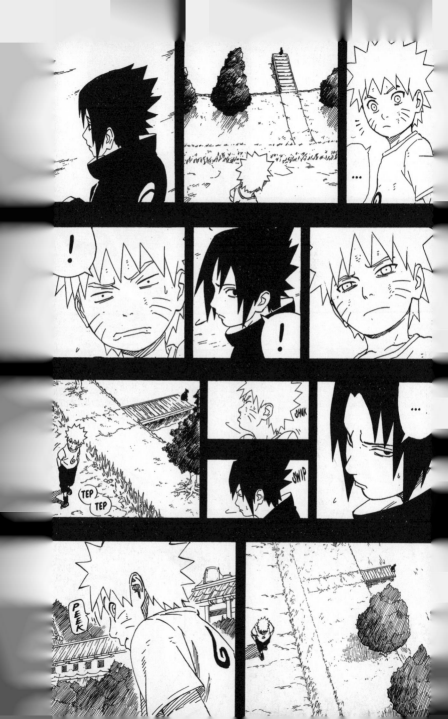

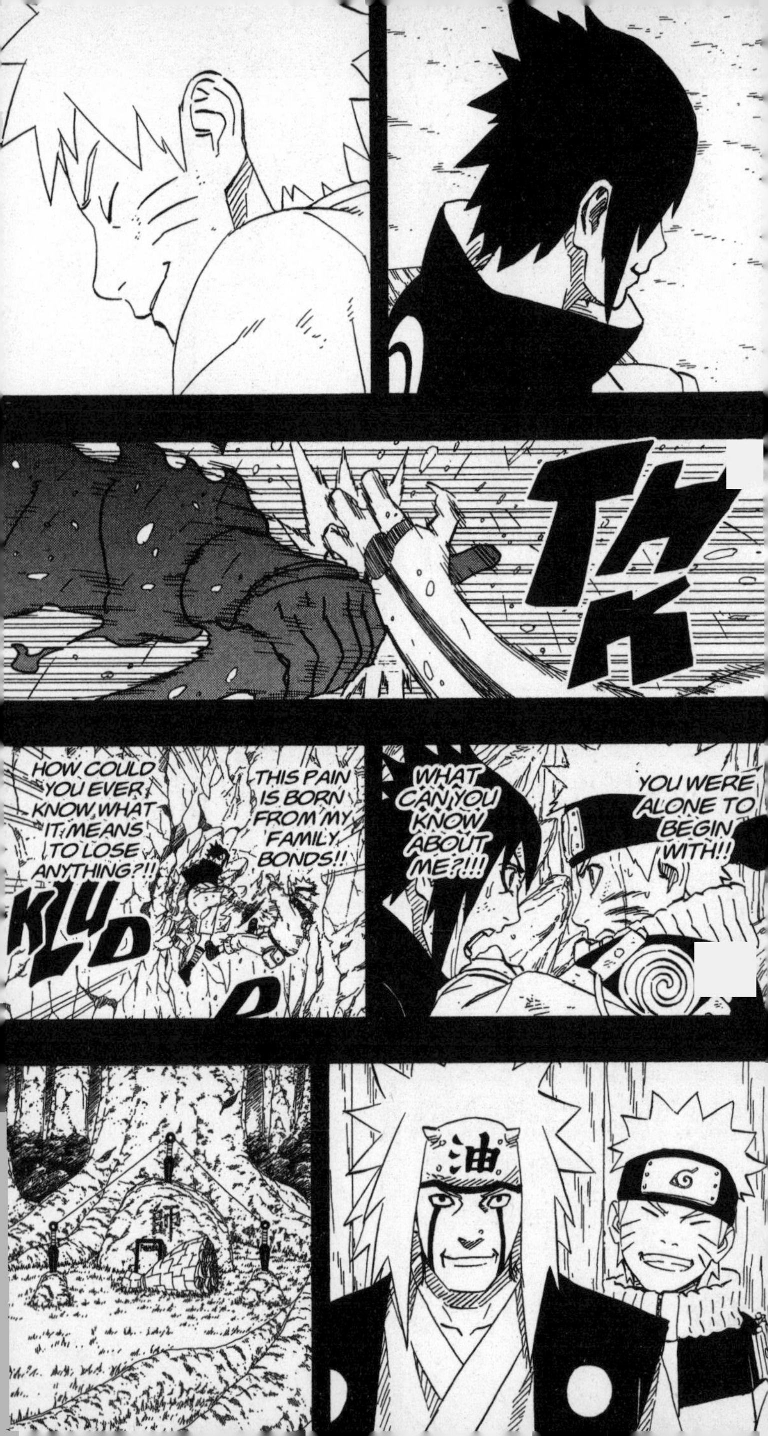

THA
YOU WERE ALONE TO BEGIN WITH!!
WHAT CAN YOU KNOW ABOUT ME?!!!
THIS PAIN IS BORN FROM MY FAMILY BONDS!!
HOW COULD YOU EVER KNOW WHAT IT MEANS TO LOSE ANYTHING?!!
KLUD
油
師

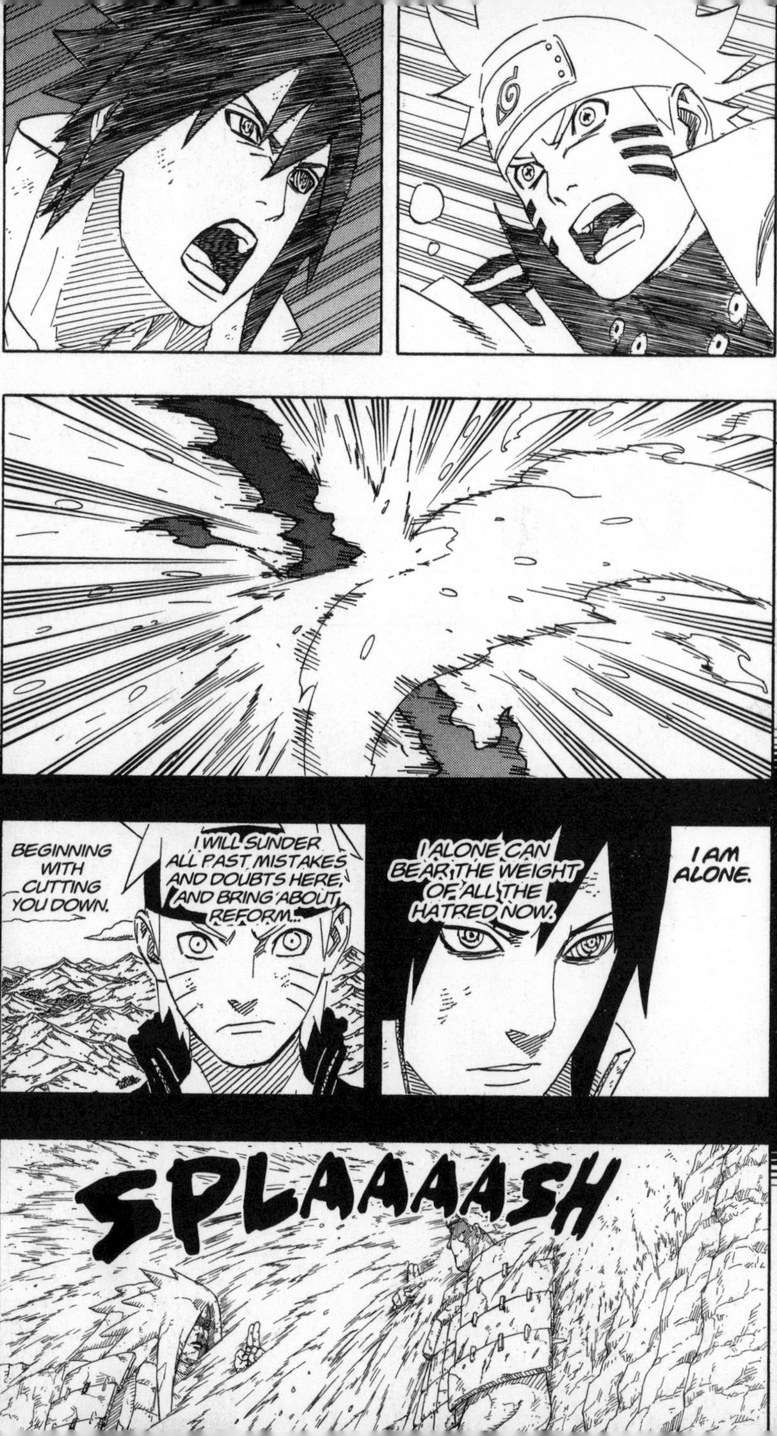
I AM ALONE.
I ALONE CAN BEAR THE WEIGHT OF ALL THE HATRED NOW.
I WILL SUNDER ALL PAST MISTAKES AND DOUBTS HERE, AND BRING ABOUT REFORM...
BEGINNING WITH CUTTING YOU DOWN.
SPLAAAASH

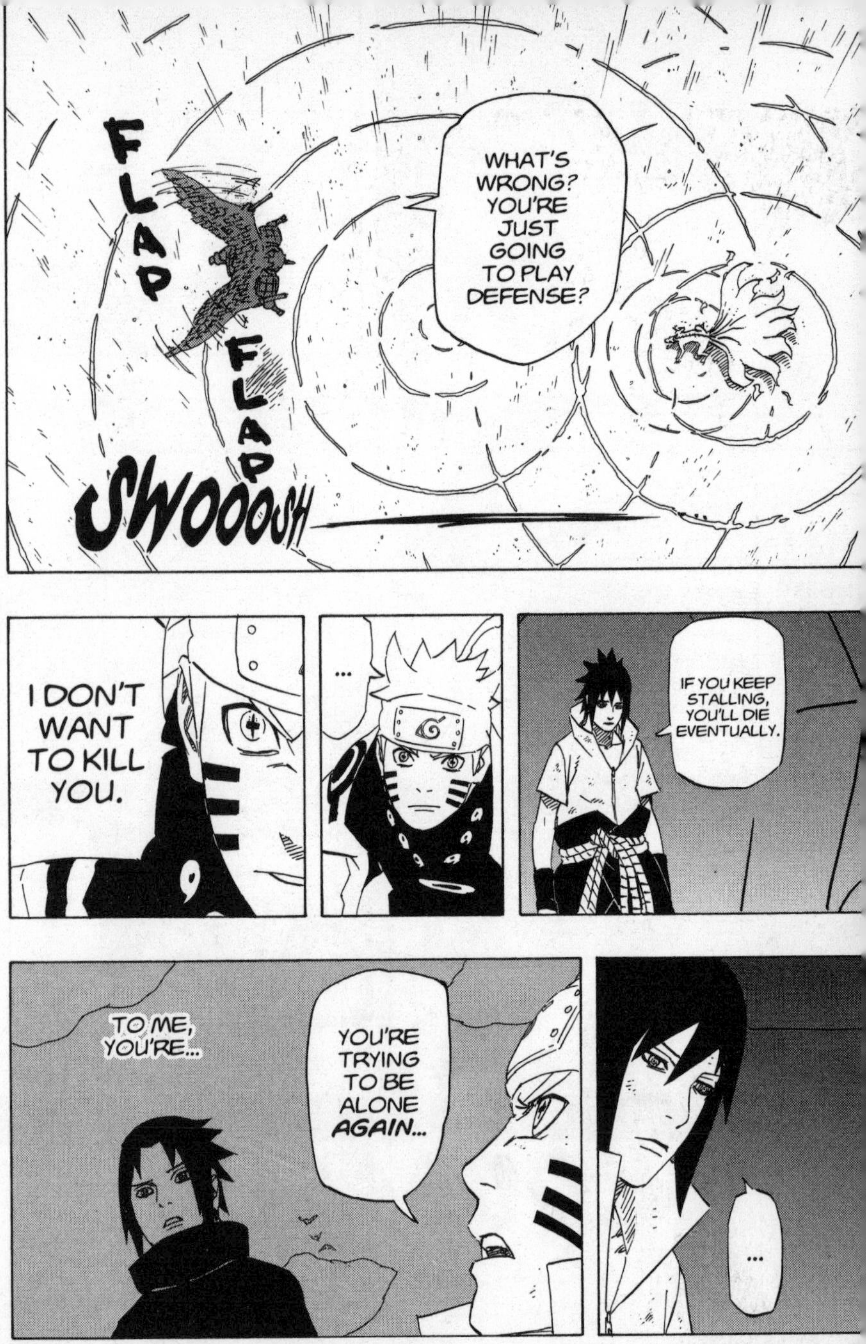
WHAT'S WRONG? YOU'RE JUST GOING TO PLAY DEFENSE?
FLAP
FLAP
SWOOOSH
IF YOU KEEP STALLING, YOU'LL DIE EVENTUALLY.
...
I DON'T WANT TO KILL YOU.
...
YOU'RE TRYING TO BE ALONE *AGAIN*...
TO ME, YOU'RE...

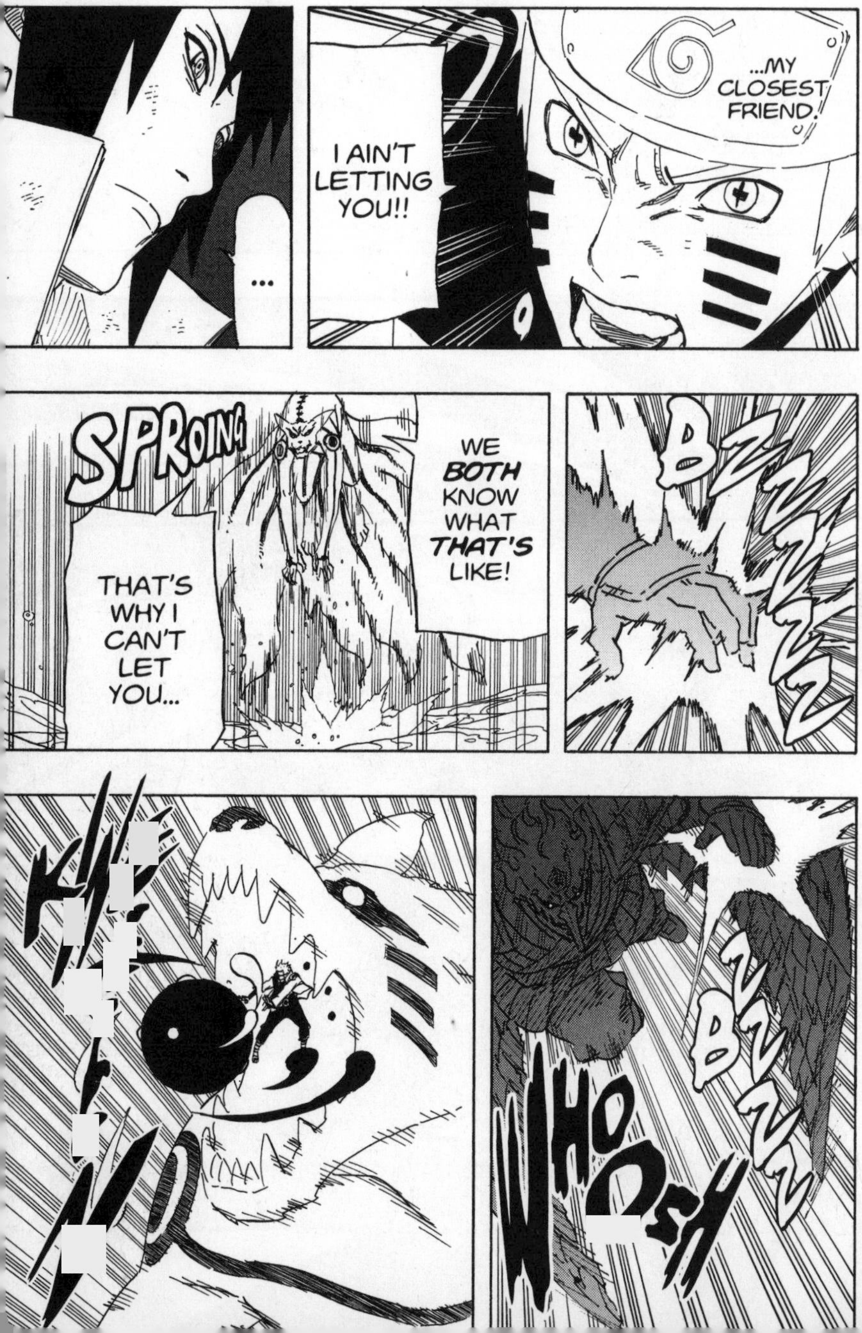
...MY CLOSEST FRIEND.
I AIN'T LETTING YOU!!
...
WE *BOTH* KNOW WHAT *THAT'S* LIKE!
THAT'S WHY I CAN'T LET YOU...
SPROING
WHOOSH

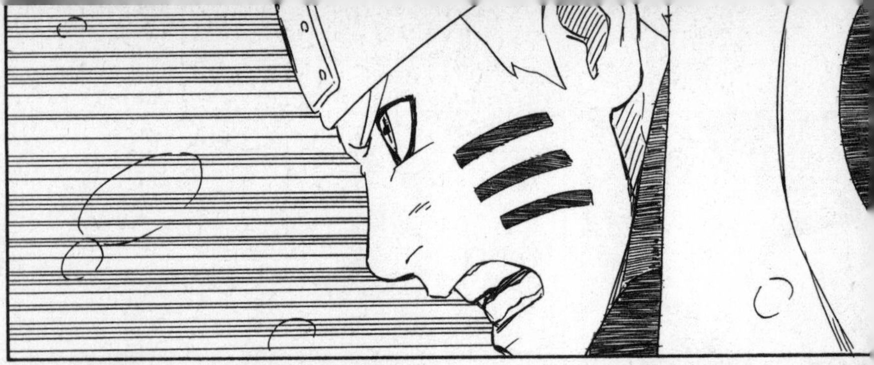

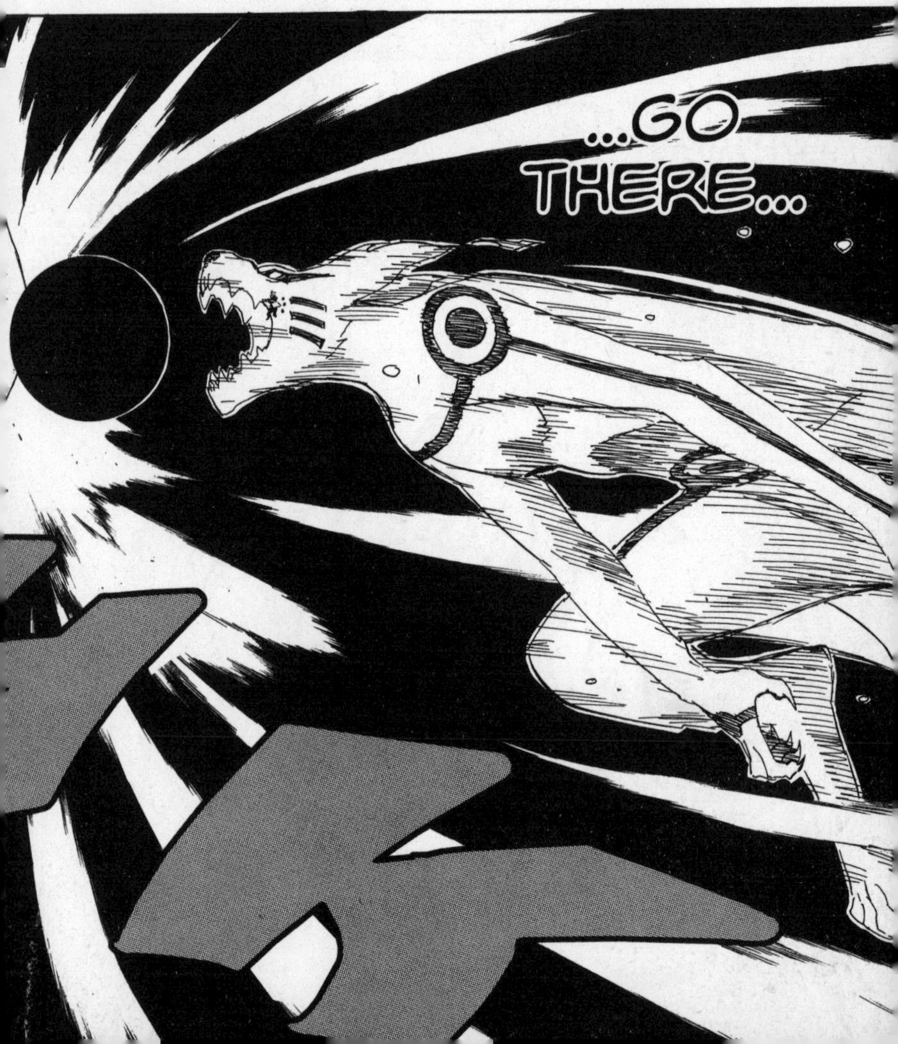
...GO THERE...

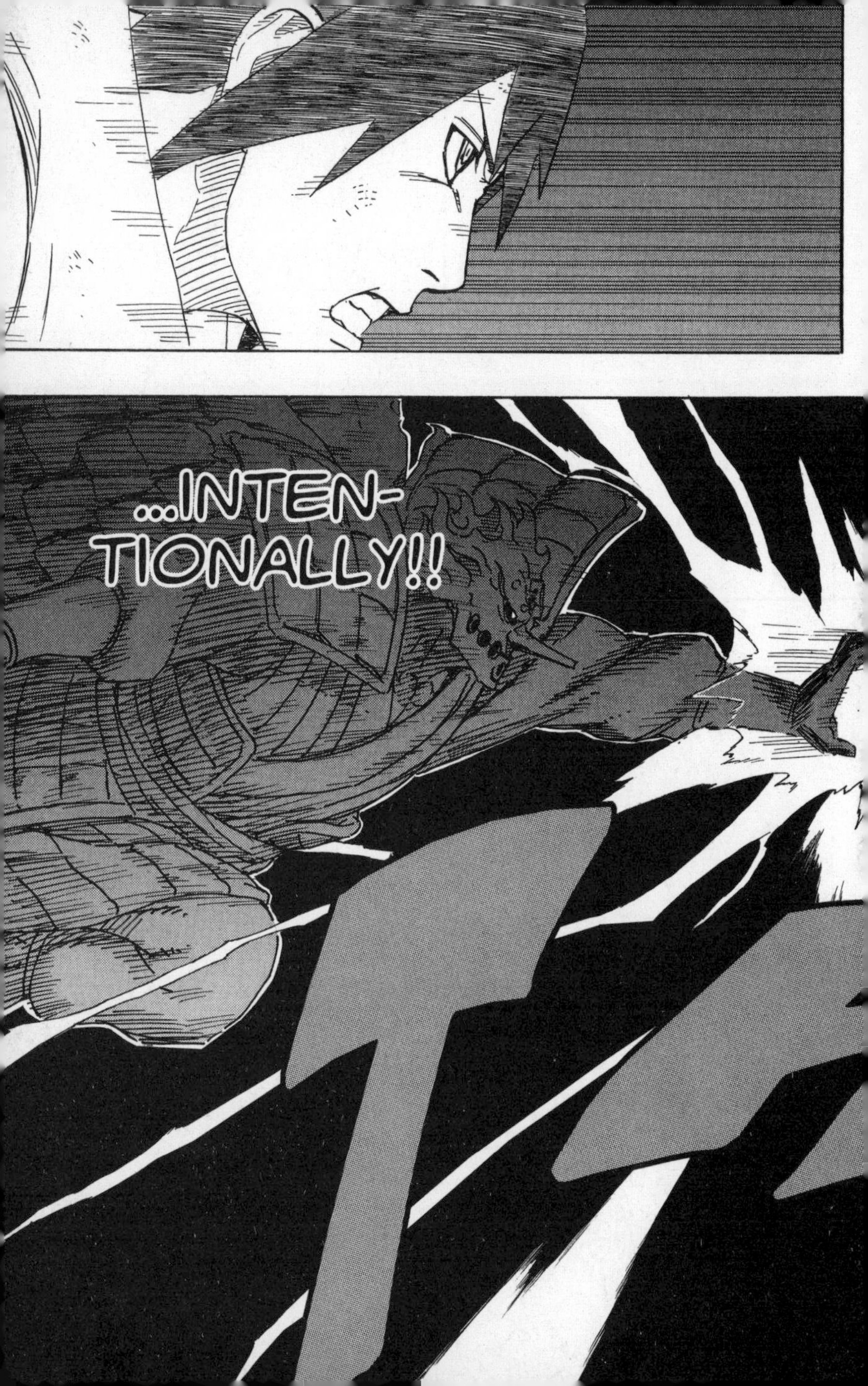
...INTEN-
TIONALLY!!

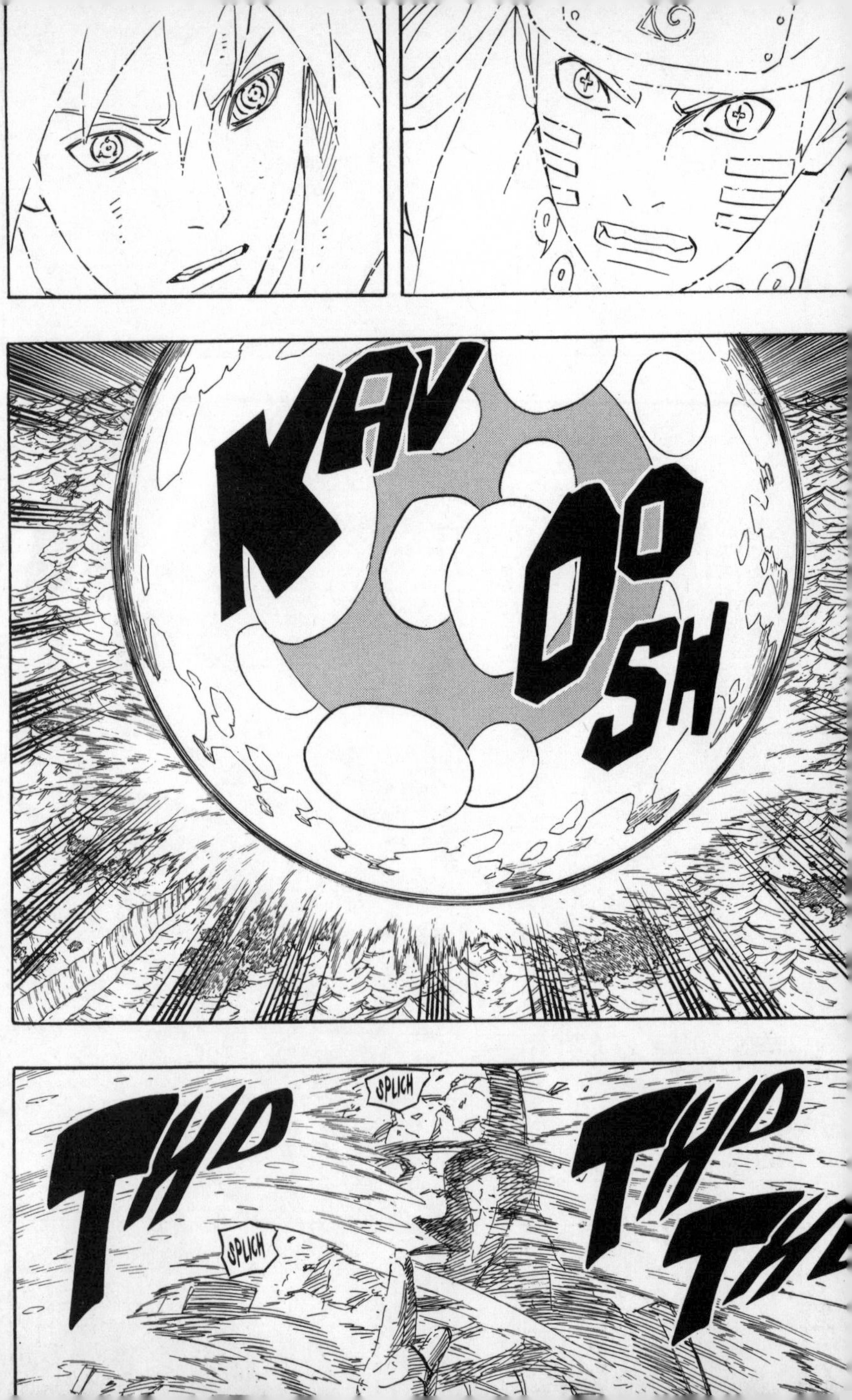
THD
SPLICH
THD
SPLICH

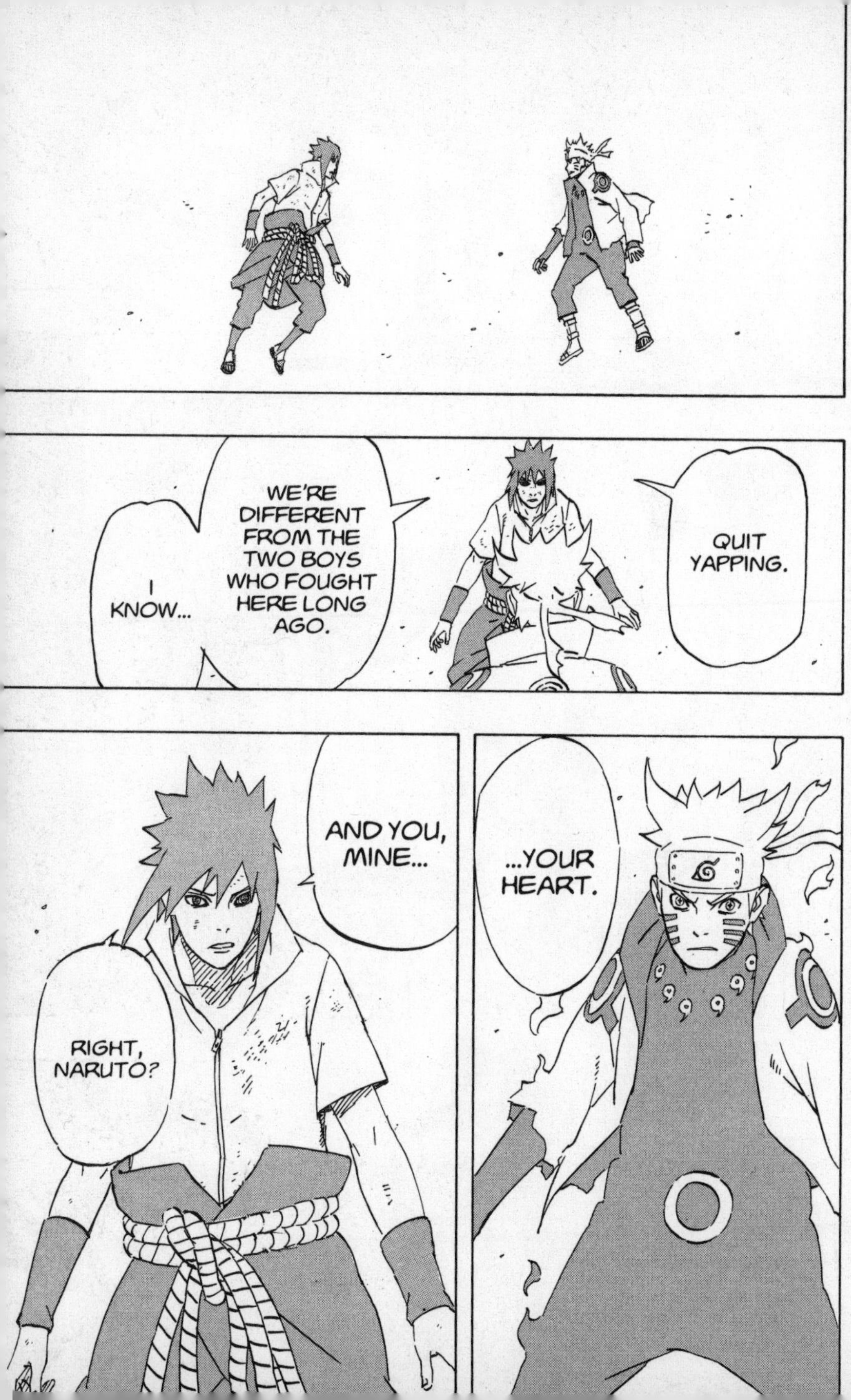
QUIT YAPPING.
WE'RE DIFFERENT FROM THE TWO BOYS WHO FOUGHT HERE LONG AGO.
I KNOW...
...YOUR HEART.
AND YOU, MINE...
RIGHT, NARUTO?

END OF SERIES COMMEMORATION ILLUSTRATION (5)

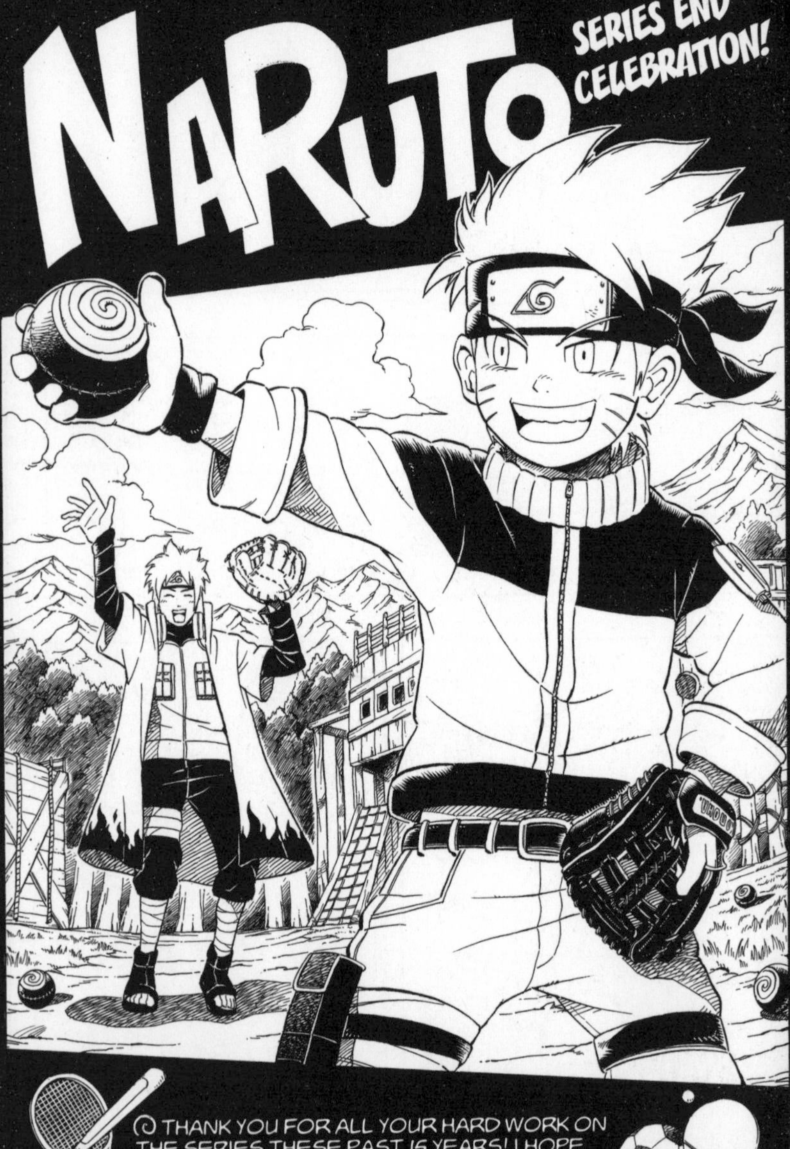
NARUTO
SERIES END CELEBRATION!

© THANK YOU FOR ALL YOUR HARD WORK ON THE SERIES THESE PAST 15 YEARS! I HOPE YOU'LL BE ABLE TO PLAY WITH YOUR FAMILY AS HARD AS YOU'VE WORKED!

TAKAHIRO HIRAISHI

Number 696: Naruto and Sasuke, Part 3

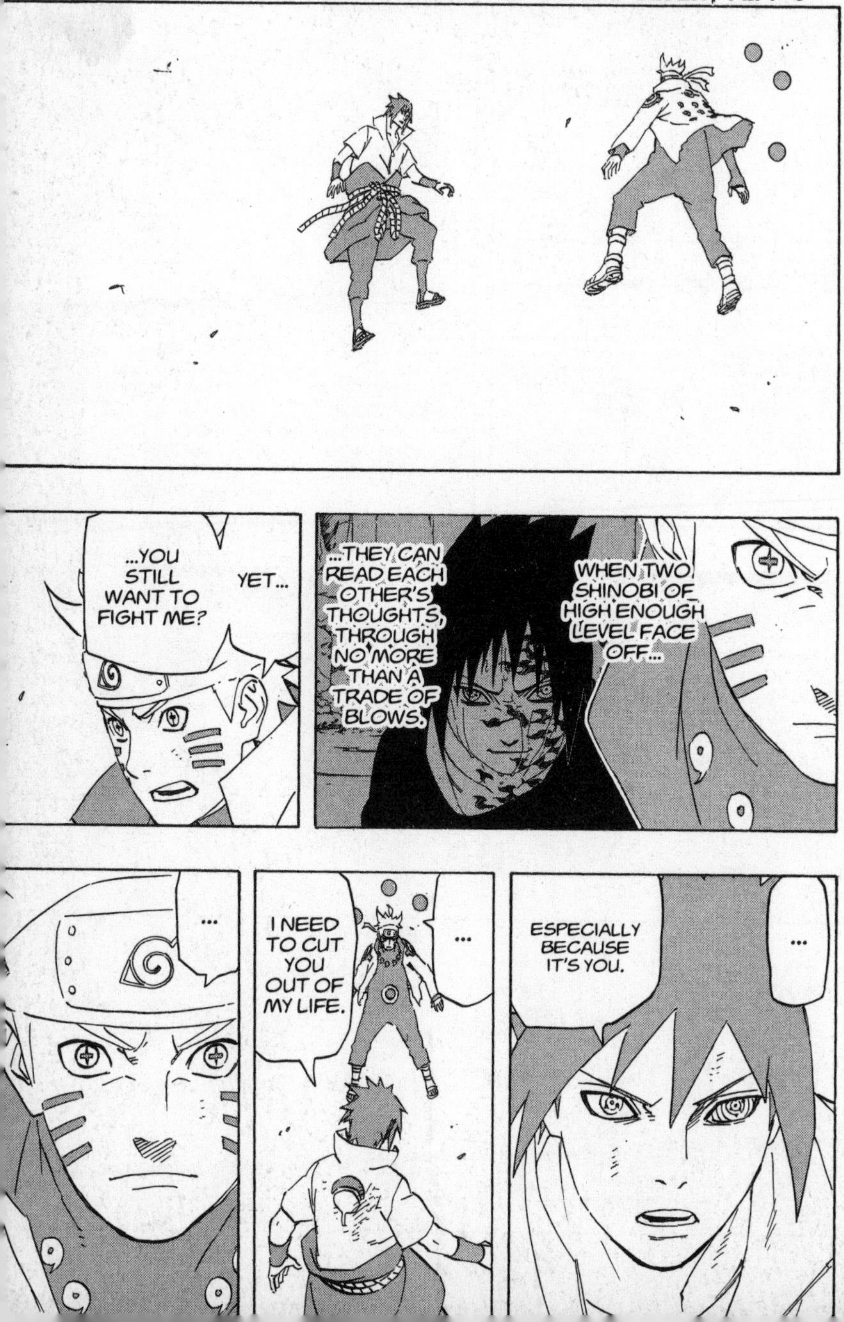
WHEN TWO SHINOBI OF HIGH ENOUGH LEVEL FACE OFF...
...THEY CAN READ EACH OTHER'S THOUGHTS, THROUGH NO MORE THAN A TRADE OF BLOWS.
YET...
...YOU STILL WANT TO FIGHT ME?
...
ESPECIALLY BECAUSE IT'S YOU.
...
I NEED TO CUT YOU OUT OF MY LIFE.
...

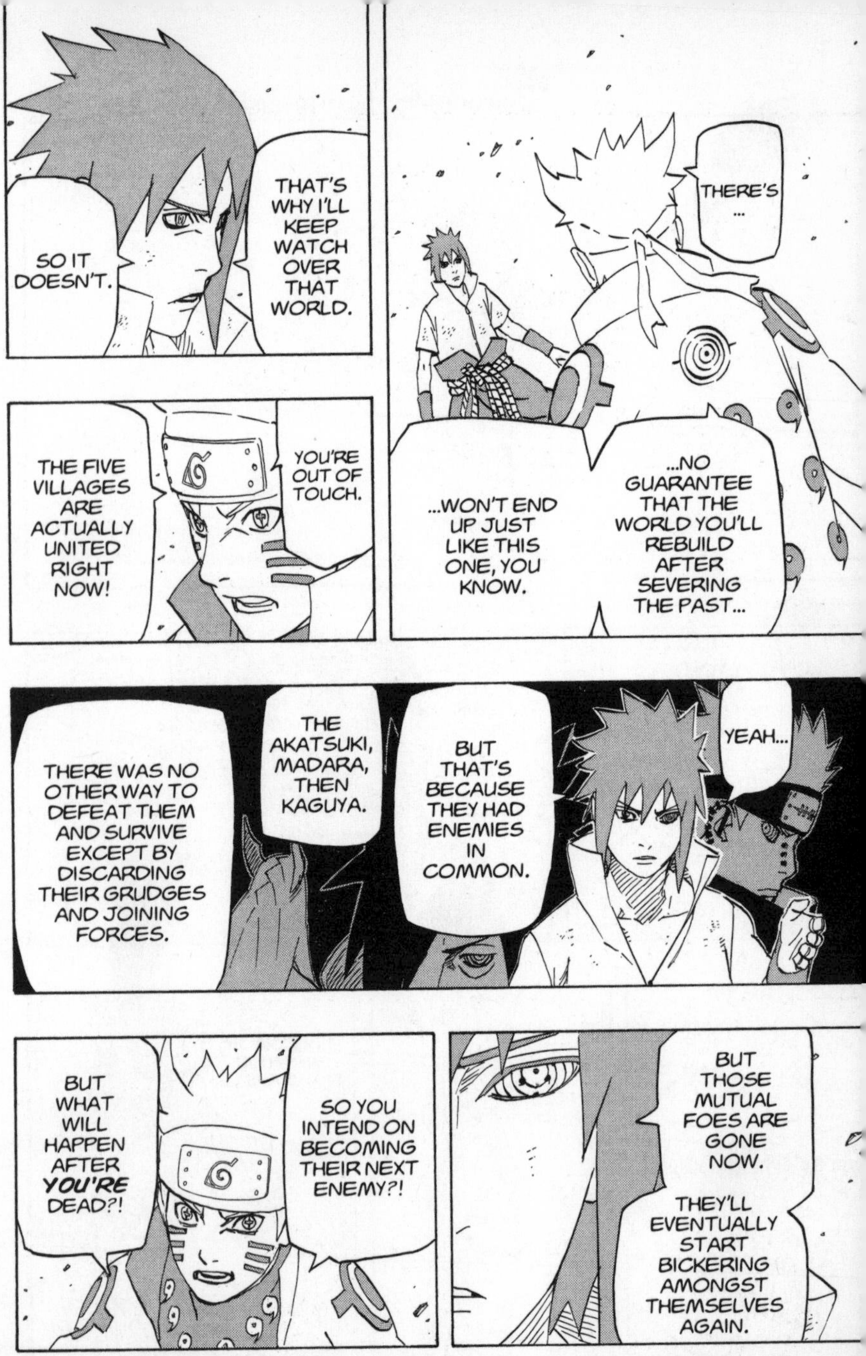
THERE'S ...
...NO GUARANTEE THAT THE WORLD YOU'LL REBUILD AFTER SEVERING THE PAST...
...WON'T END UP JUST LIKE THIS ONE, YOU KNOW.
SO IT DOESN'T.
THAT'S WHY I'LL KEEP WATCH OVER THAT WORLD.
YOU'RE OUT OF TOUCH.
THE FIVE VILLAGES ARE ACTUALLY UNITED RIGHT NOW!
YEAH...
BUT THAT'S BECAUSE THEY HAD ENEMIES IN COMMON.
THE AKATSUKI, MADARA, THEN KAGUYA.
THERE WAS NO OTHER WAY TO DEFEAT THEM AND SURVIVE EXCEPT BY DISCARDING THEIR GRUDGES AND JOINING FORCES.
BUT THOSE MUTUAL FOES ARE GONE NOW.
THEY'LL EVENTUALLY START BICKERING AMONGST THEMSELVES AGAIN.
SO YOU INTEND ON BECOMING THEIR NEXT ENEMY?!
BUT WHAT WILL HAPPEN AFTER ***YOU'RE*** DEAD?!

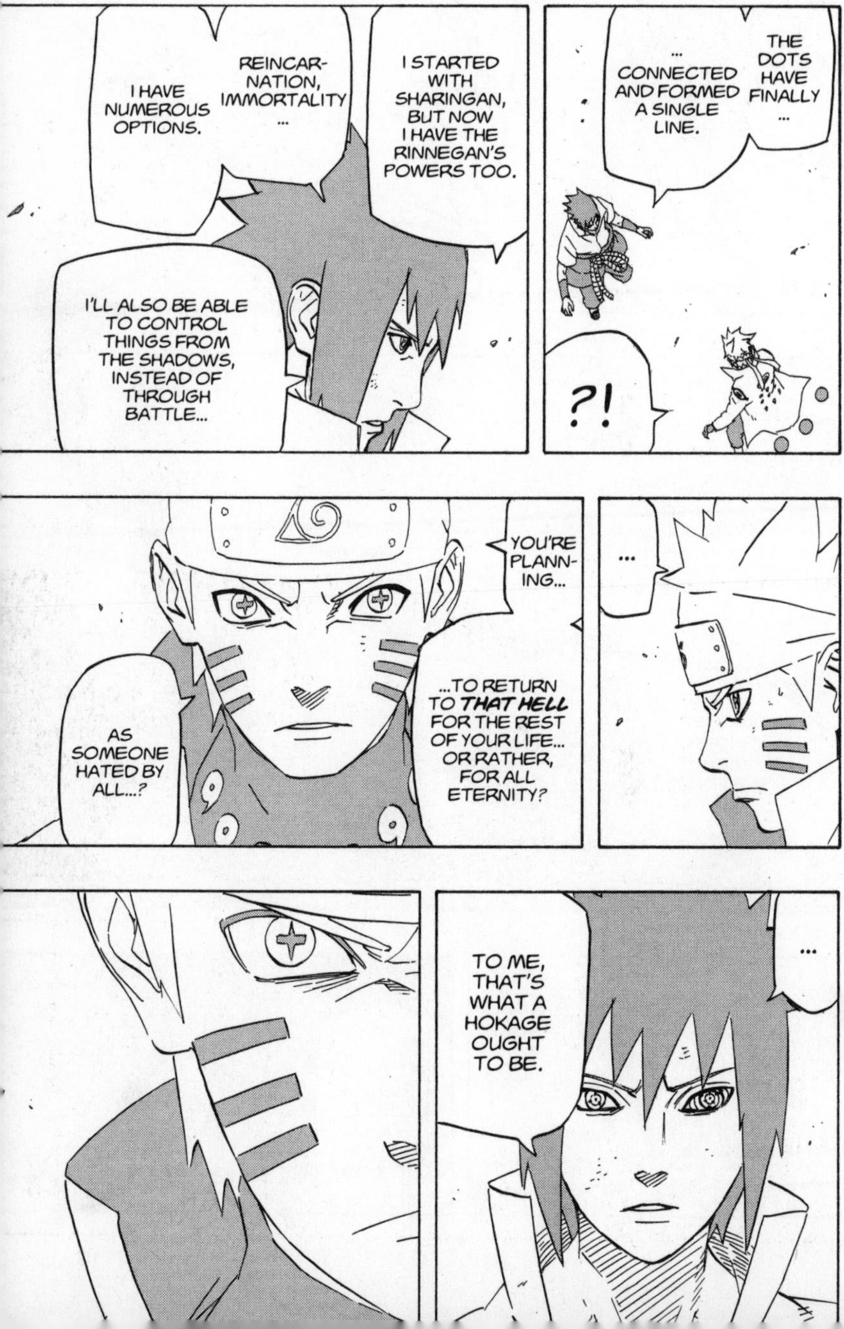
THE DOTS HAVE FINALLY...
...CONNECTED AND FORMED A SINGLE LINE.
?!
I STARTED WITH SHARINGAN, BUT NOW I HAVE THE RINNEGAN'S POWERS TOO.
REINCAR-NATION, IMMORTALITY...
I HAVE NUMEROUS OPTIONS.
I'LL ALSO BE ABLE TO CONTROL THINGS FROM THE SHADOWS, INSTEAD OF THROUGH BATTLE...
...
YOU'RE PLANN-ING...
...TO RETURN TO THAT HELL FOR THE REST OF YOUR LIFE... OR RATHER, FOR ALL ETERNITY?
AS SOMEONE HATED BY ALL...?
...
TO ME, THAT'S WHAT A HOKAGE OUGHT TO BE.

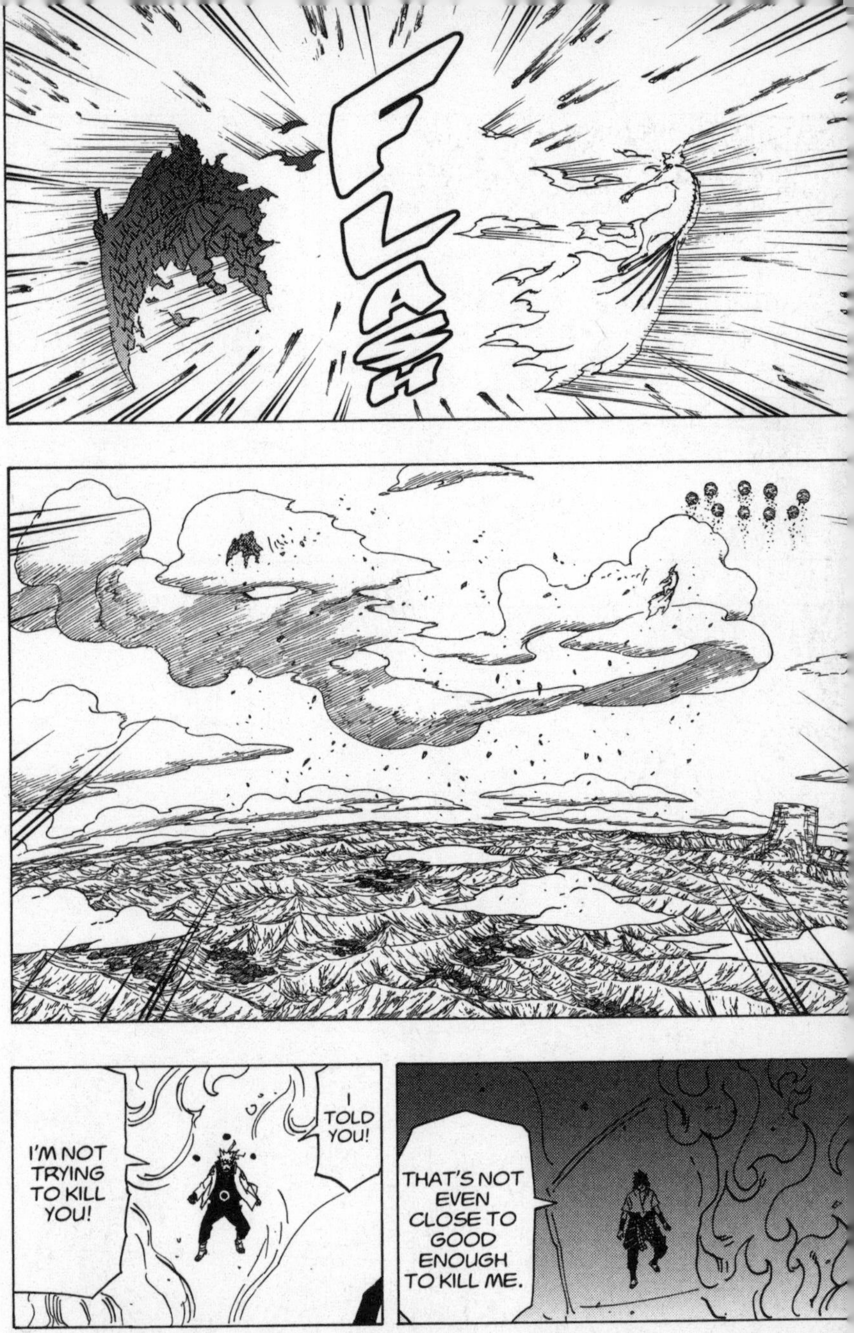
FLASH
THAT'S NOT EVEN CLOSE TO GOOD ENOUGH TO KILL ME.
I TOLD YOU!
I'M NOT TRYING TO KILL YOU!

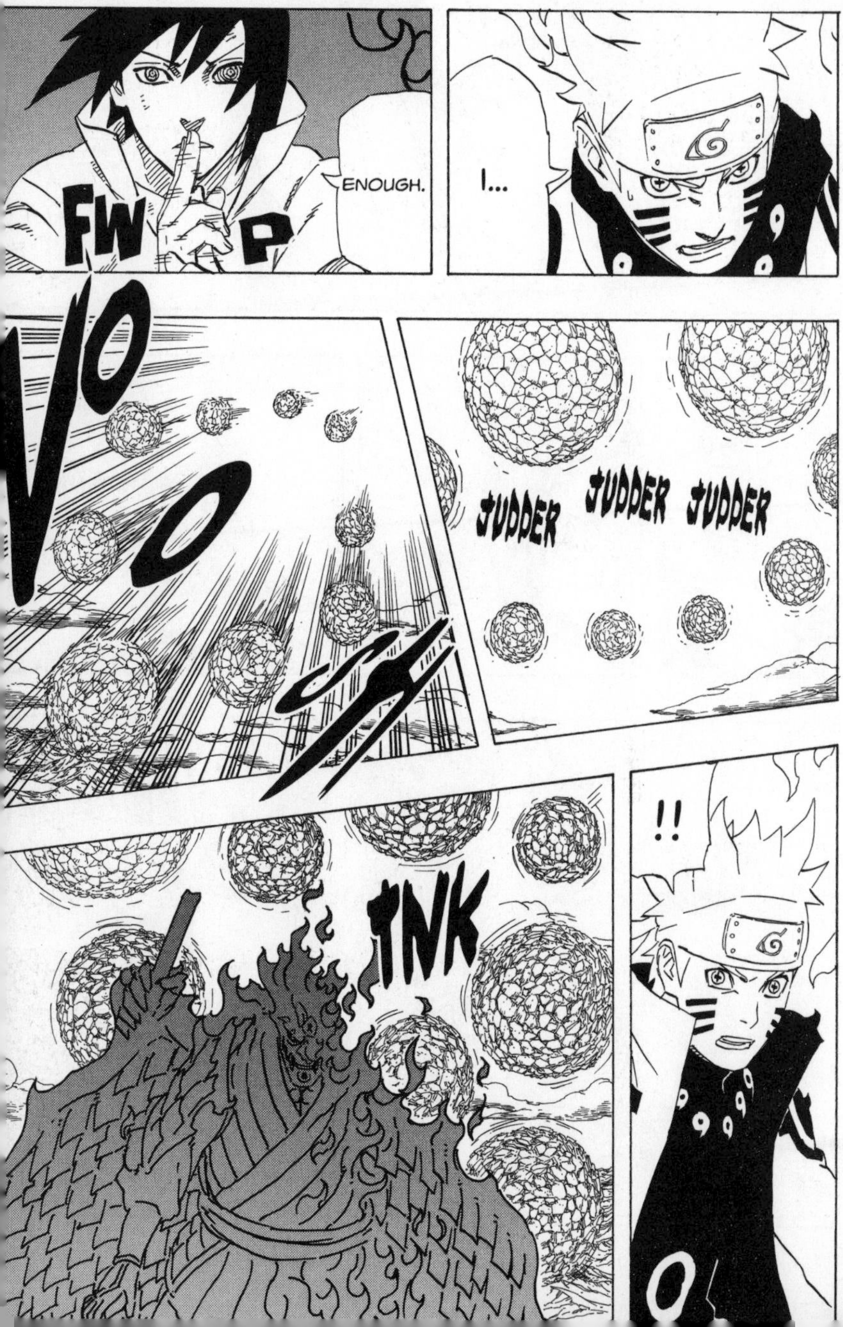
I...
ENOUGH.
FWP
JUDDER JUDDER JUDDER
VOOSH
!!
TNK

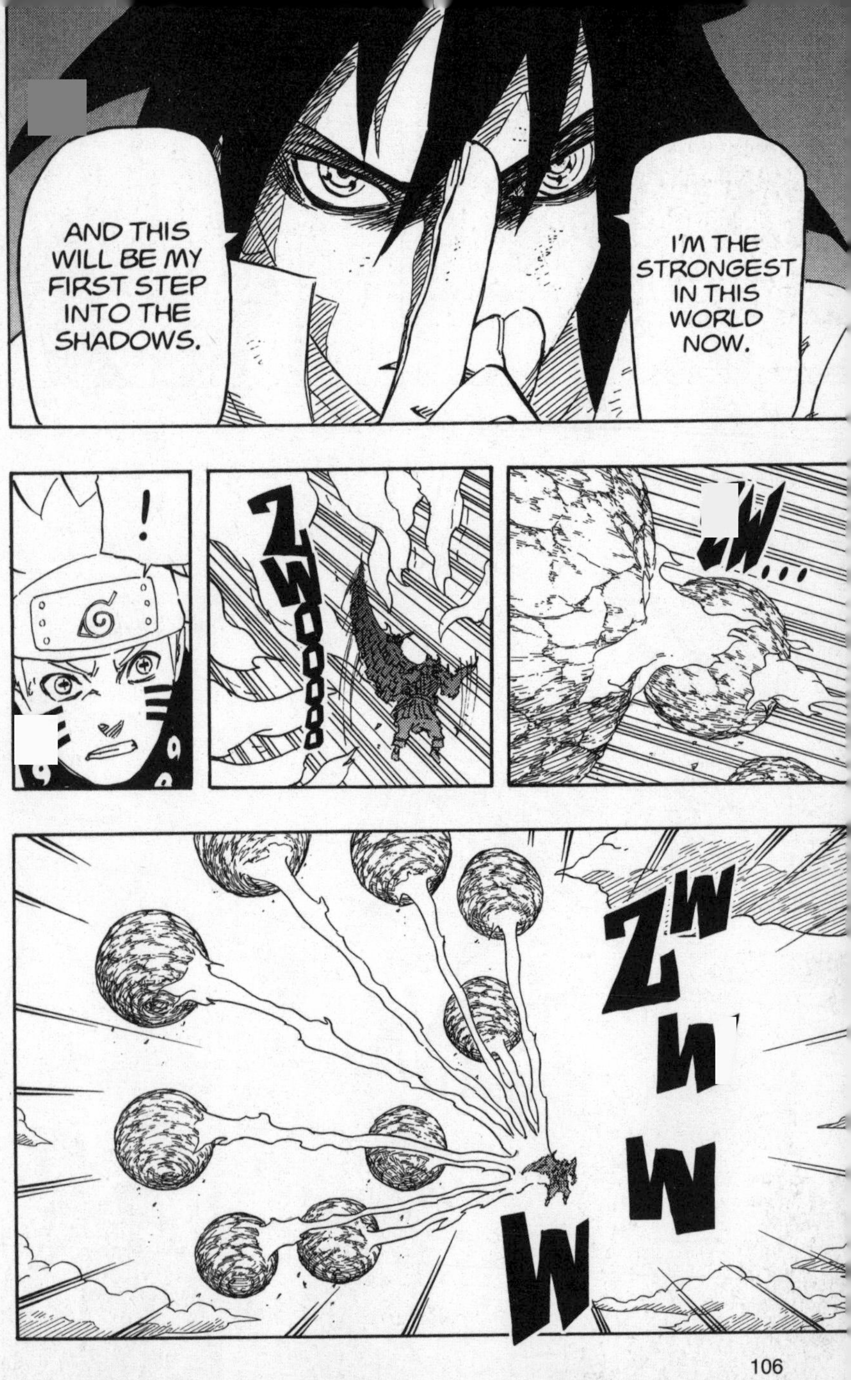

I'M THE STRONGEST IN THIS WORLD NOW.
AND THIS WILL BE MY FIRST STEP INTO THE SHADOWS.
W...
ZWOOOOOO
!
ZWWWW

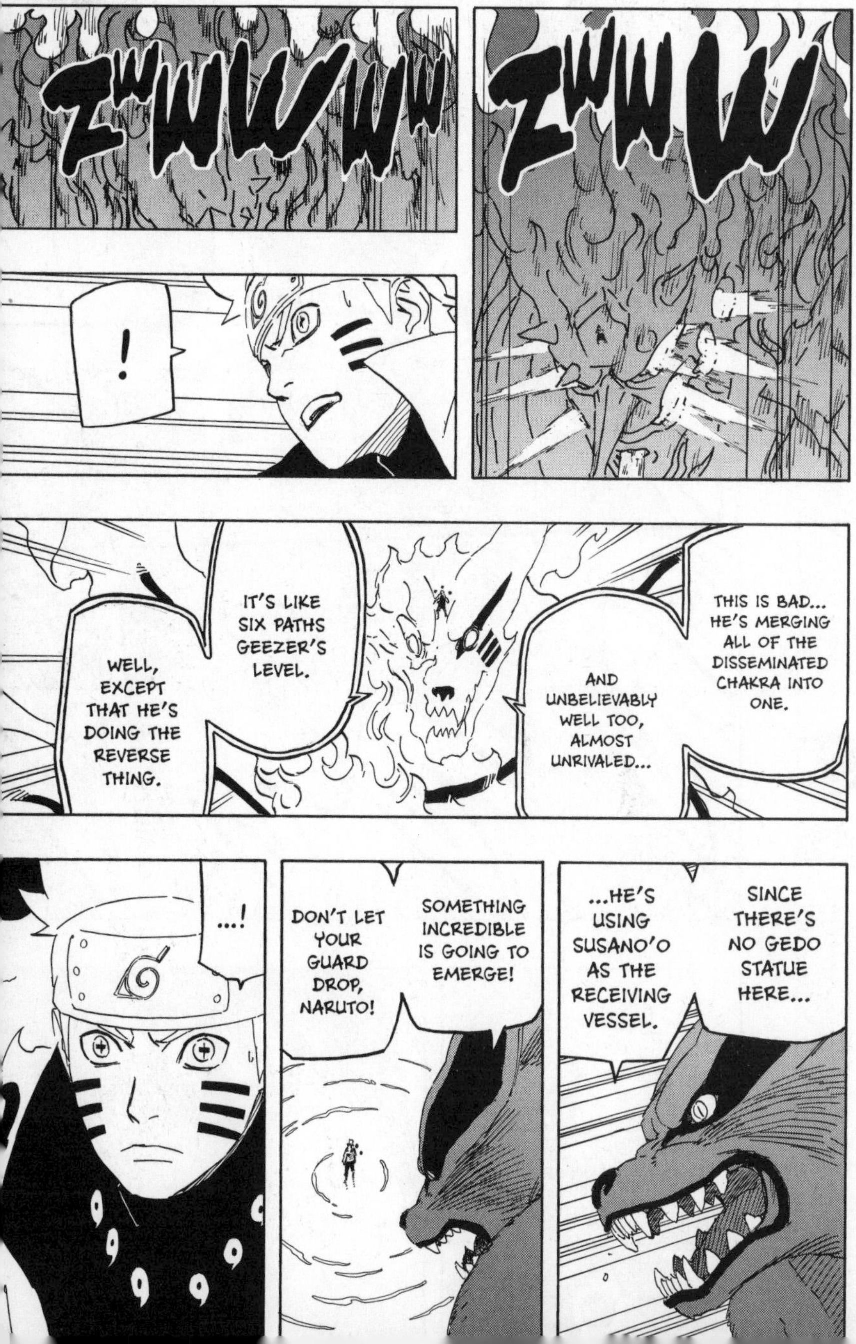
ZWWU
ZWWUWWW
!
THIS IS BAD... HE'S MERGING ALL OF THE DISSEMINATED CHAKRA INTO ONE.
AND UNBELIEVABLY WELL TOO, ALMOST UNRIVALED...
IT'S LIKE SIX PATHS GEEZER'S LEVEL.
WELL, EXCEPT THAT HE'S DOING THE REVERSE THING.
SINCE THERE'S NO GEDO STATUE HERE...
...HE'S USING SUSANO'O AS THE RECEIVING VESSEL.
SOMETHING INCREDIBLE IS GOING TO EMERGE!
DON'T LET YOUR GUARD DROP, NARUTO!
...!

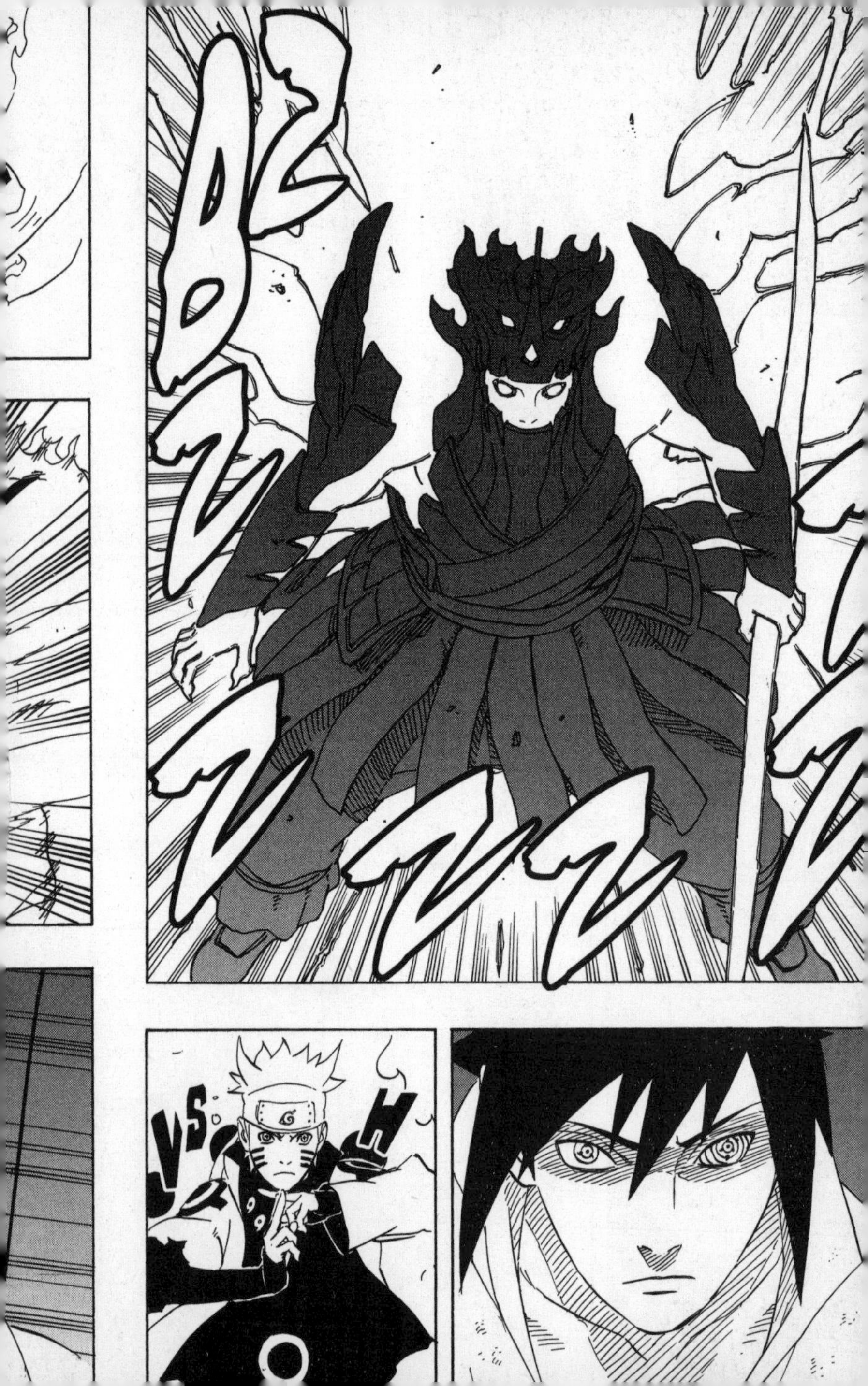

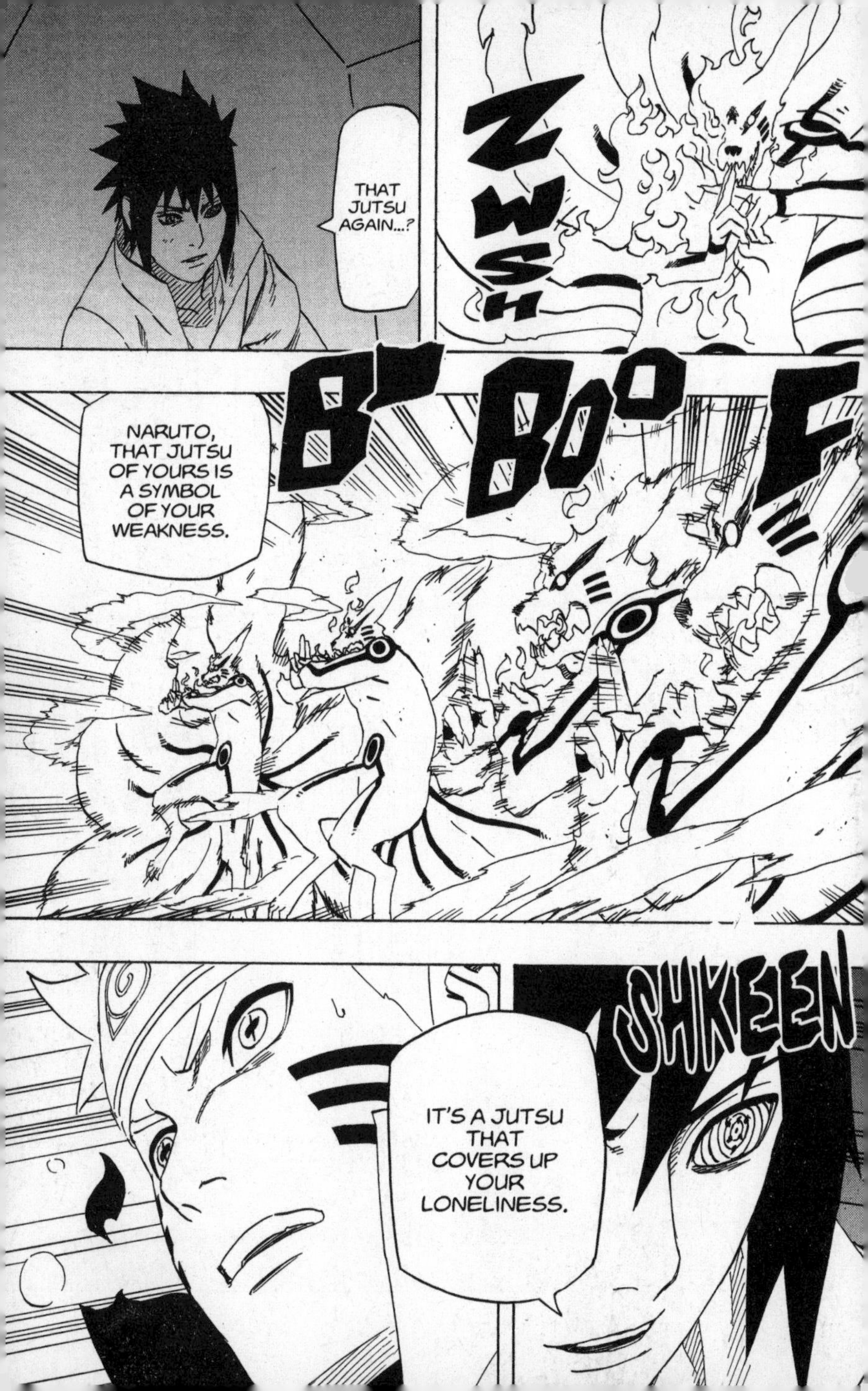
ZWSH
THAT JUTSU AGAIN...?
BBOOF
NARUTO, THAT JUTSU OF YOURS IS A SYMBOL OF YOUR WEAKNESS.
SHKEEN
IT'S A JUTSU THAT COVERS UP YOUR LONELINESS.

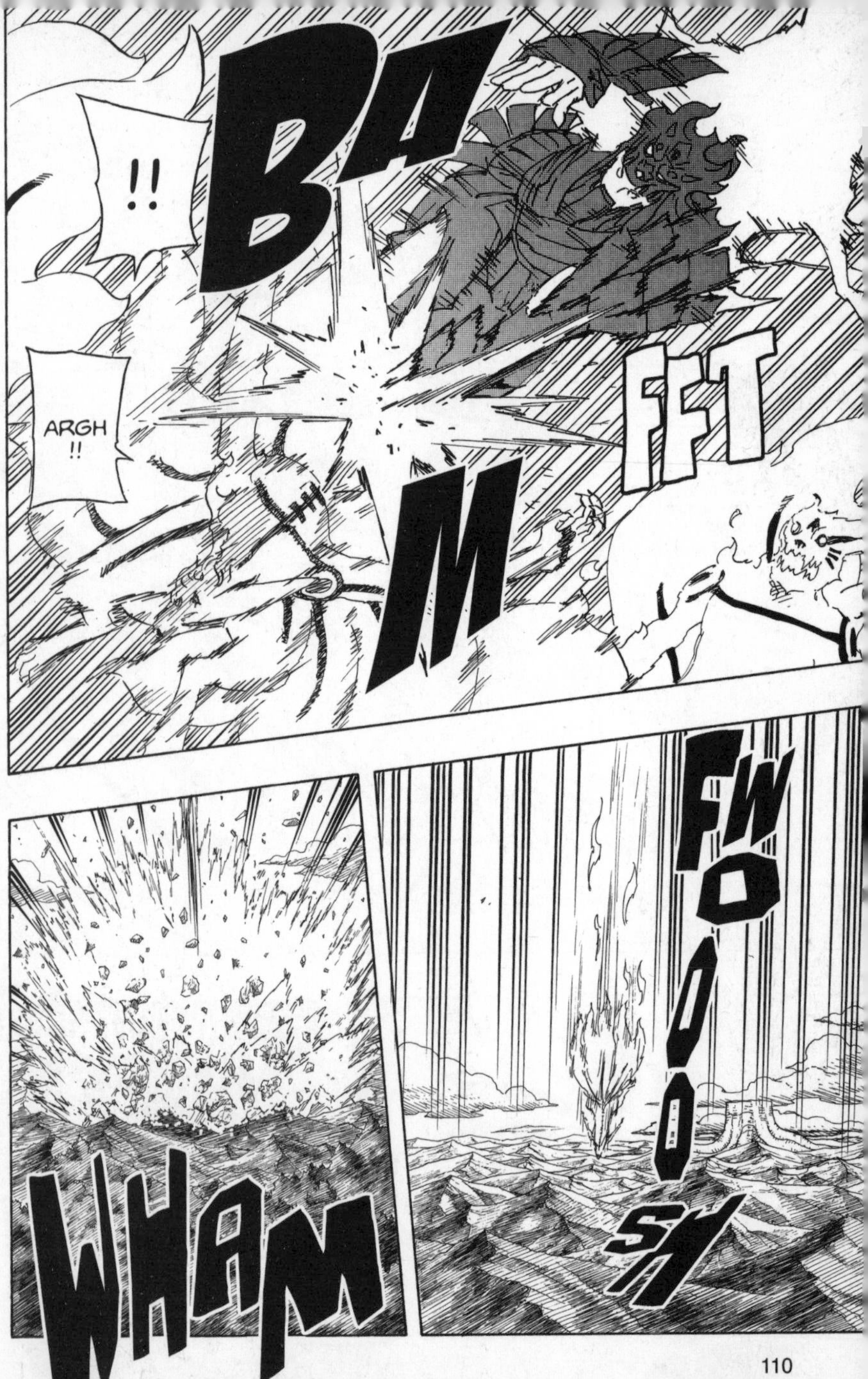
BAM
FFT
!!
ARGH !!
FWOOOSH
WHAM

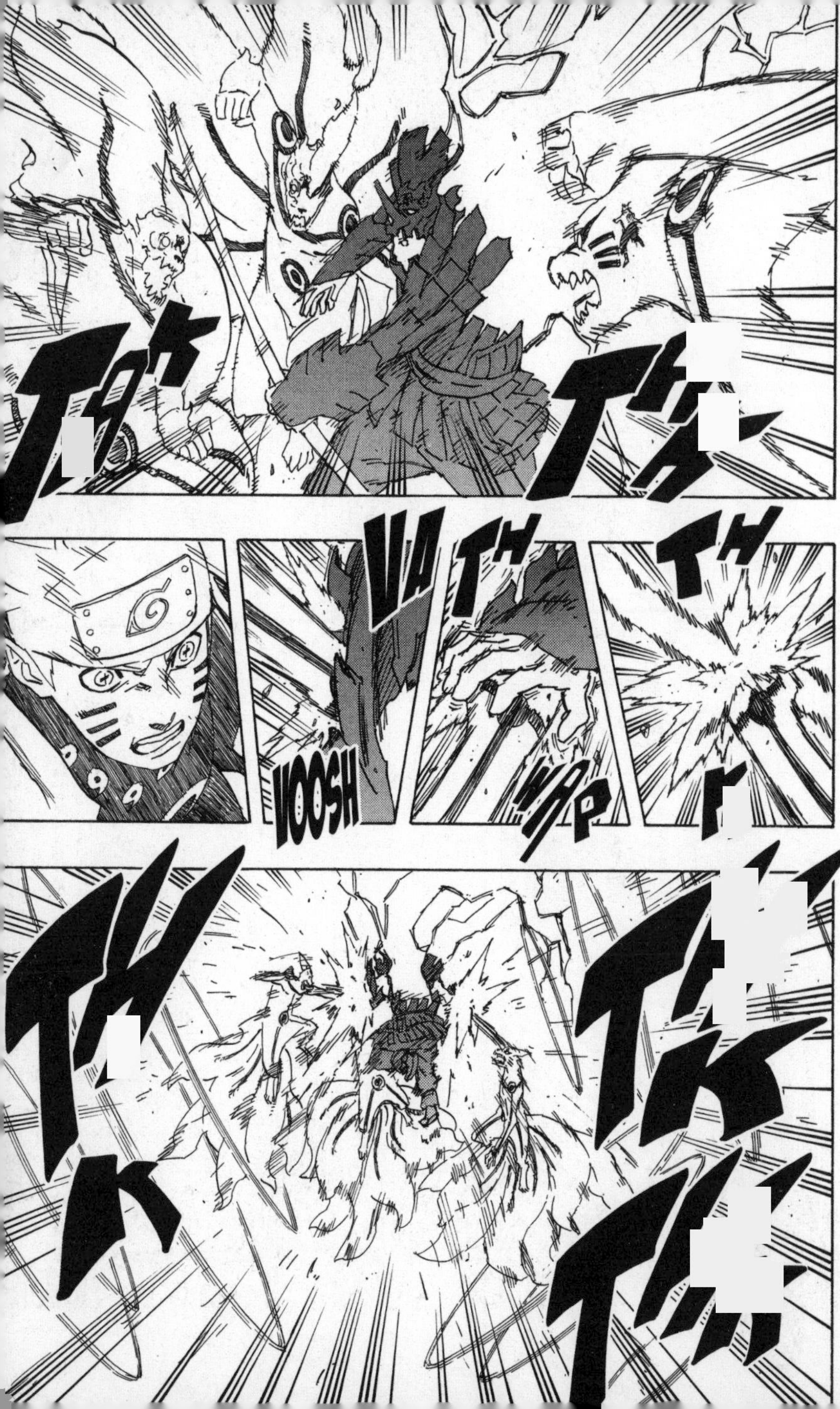
WAP
VOOSH

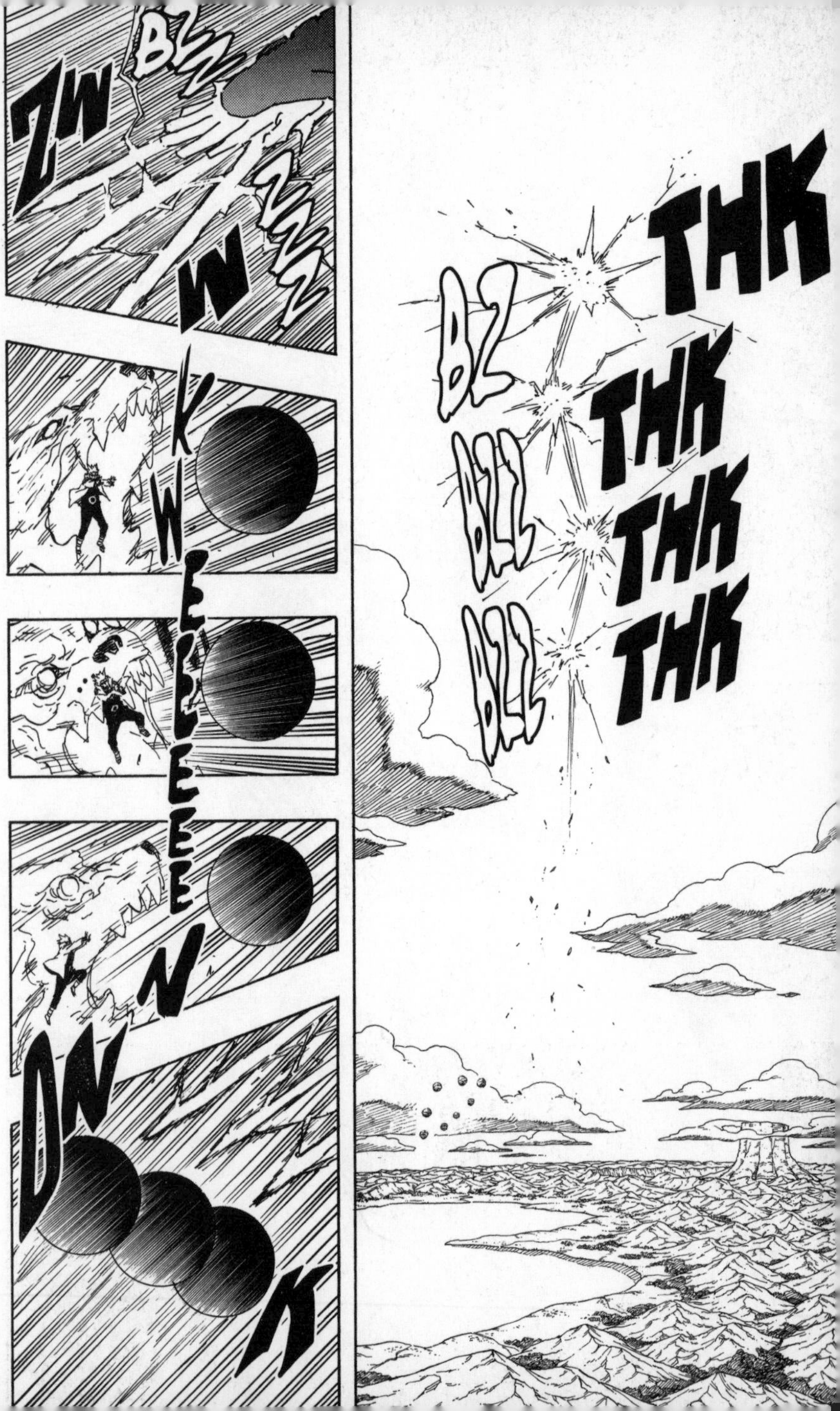
THK
THK
THK
THK
BZ
BZZ
BZZ
ZW
BZZZZZ
W
KWEEEEEEN
DN
K

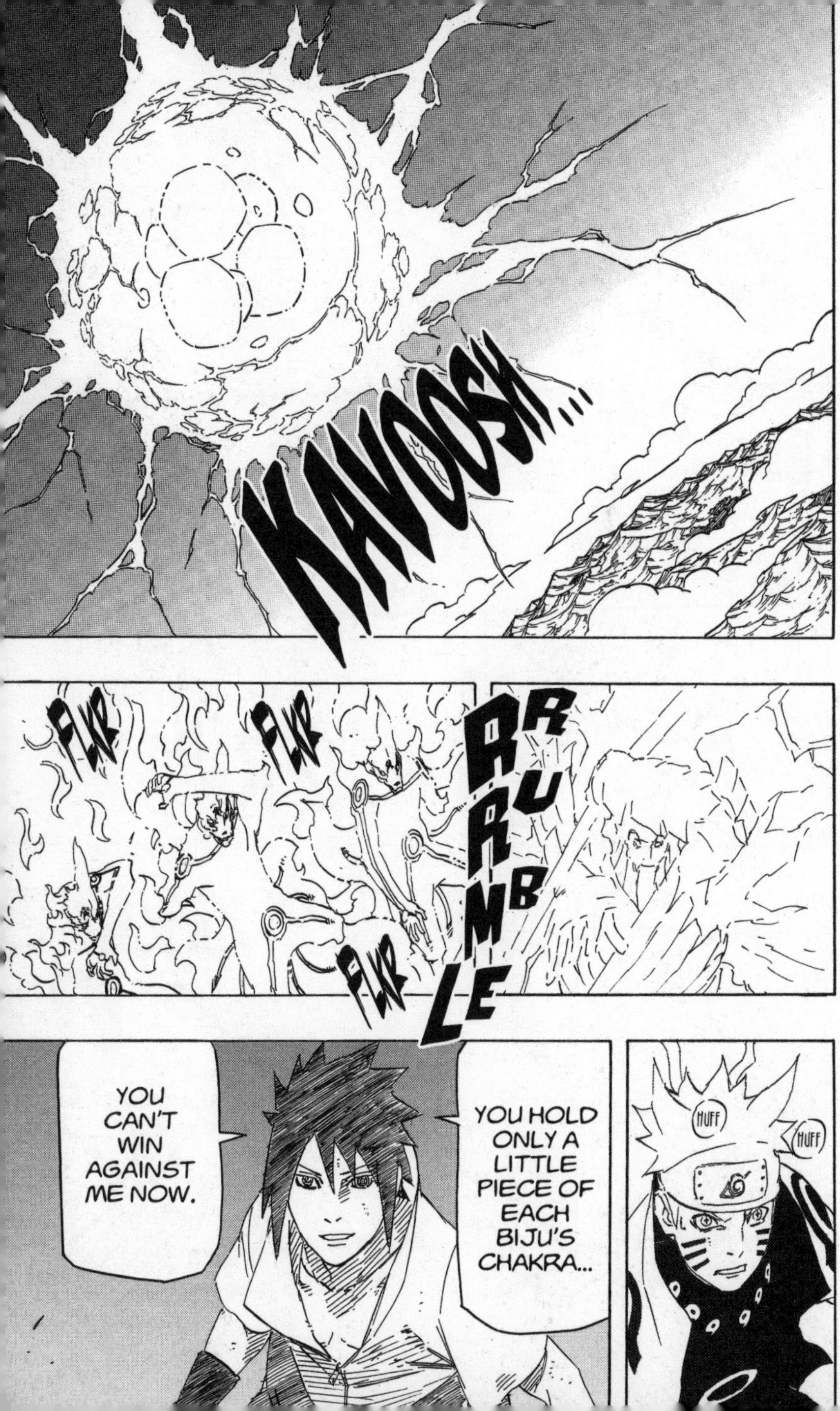
KAVOOSH...
RRUMBLE
FLKP
FLKP
FLKP
HUFF
HUFF
YOU HOLD ONLY A LITTLE PIECE OF EACH BIJU'S CHAKRA...
YOU CAN'T WIN AGAINST ME NOW.

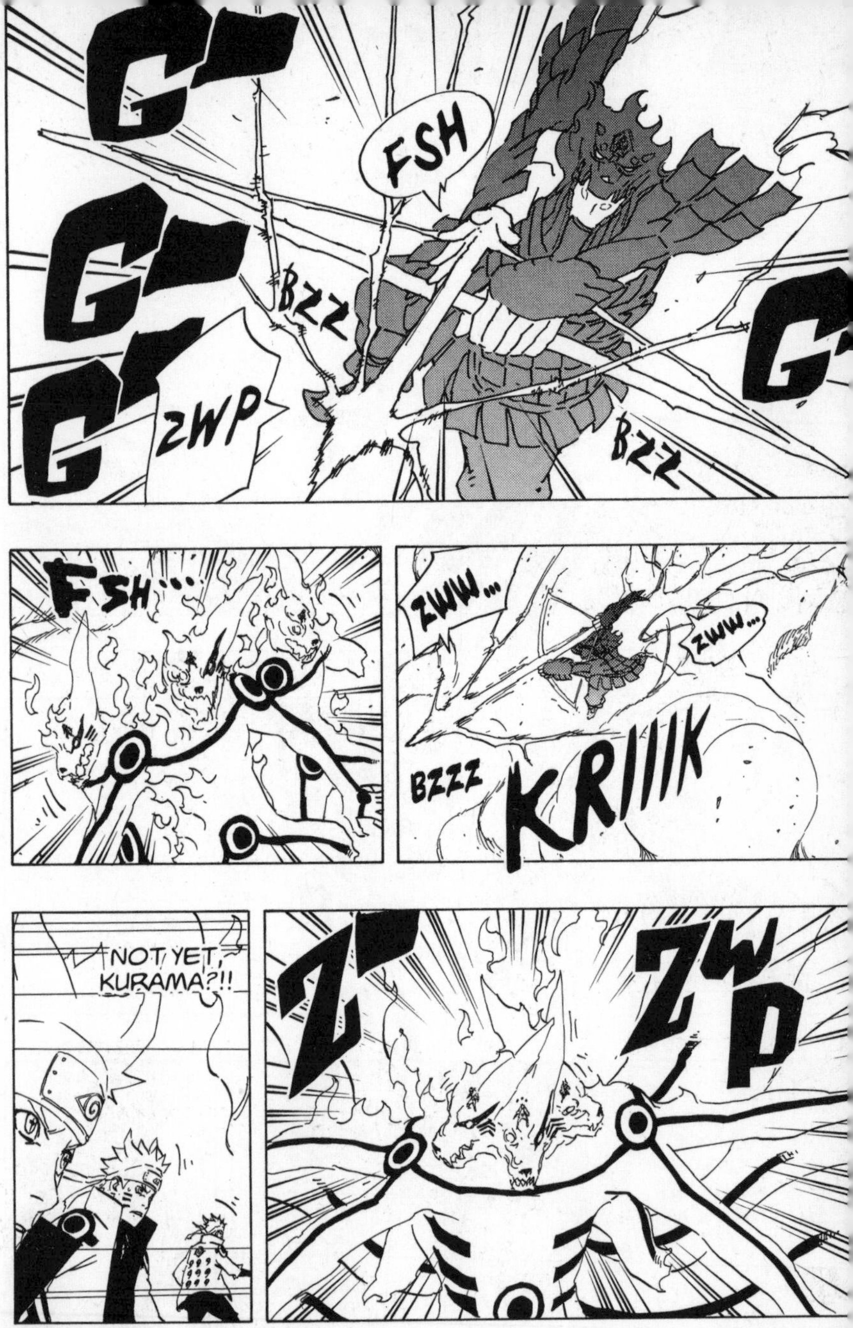
G
FSH
BZZ
G
G
G
ZWP
BZZ
ZWW...
ZWW...
KRIIIK
BZZZ
FSH...
ZWP
Z
NOT YET, KURAMA?!!

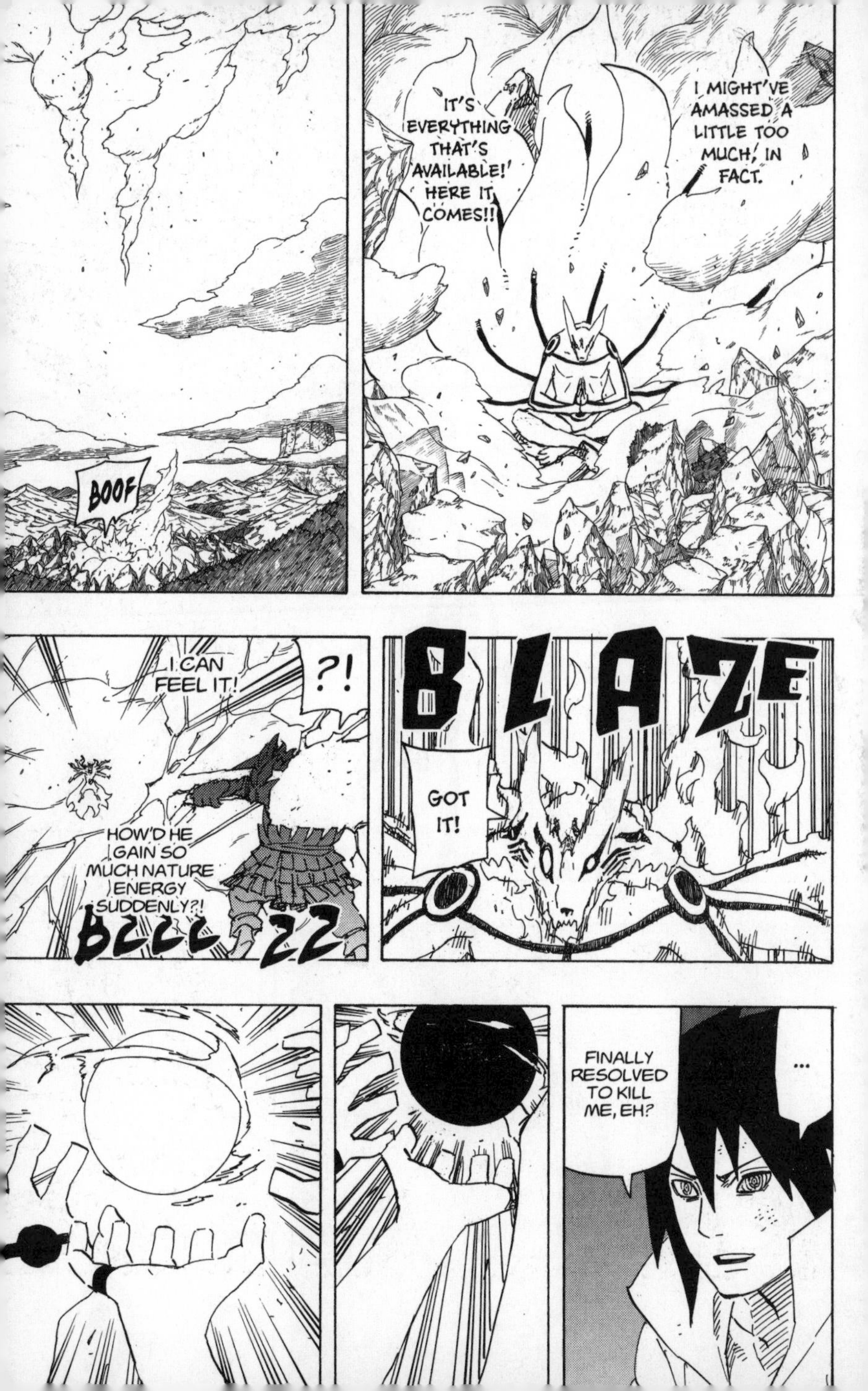
I MIGHT'VE AMASSED A LITTLE TOO MUCH, IN FACT.
IT'S EVERYTHING THAT'S AVAILABLE! HERE IT COMES!!
BOOF
BLAZE
GOT IT!
?!
I CAN FEEL IT!
HOW'D HE GAIN SO MUCH NATURE ENERGY SUDDENLY?!
BZZZZZ
...
FINALLY RESOLVED TO KILL ME, EH?

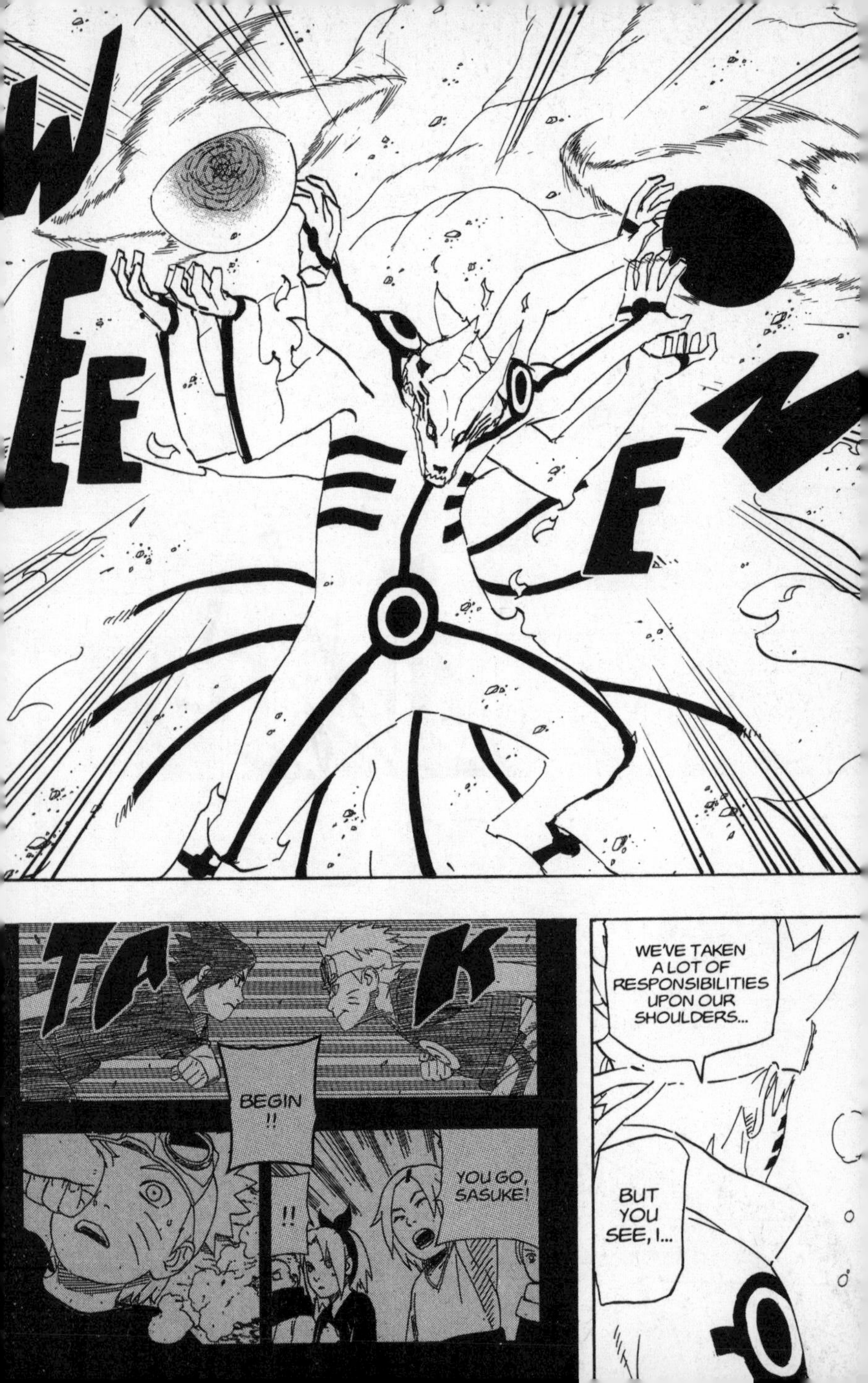
WEEEN
WE'VE TAKEN A LOT OF RESPONSIBILITIES UPON OUR SHOULDERS...
BUT YOU SEE, I...
TAK
BEGIN!!
YOU GO, SASUKE!
!!

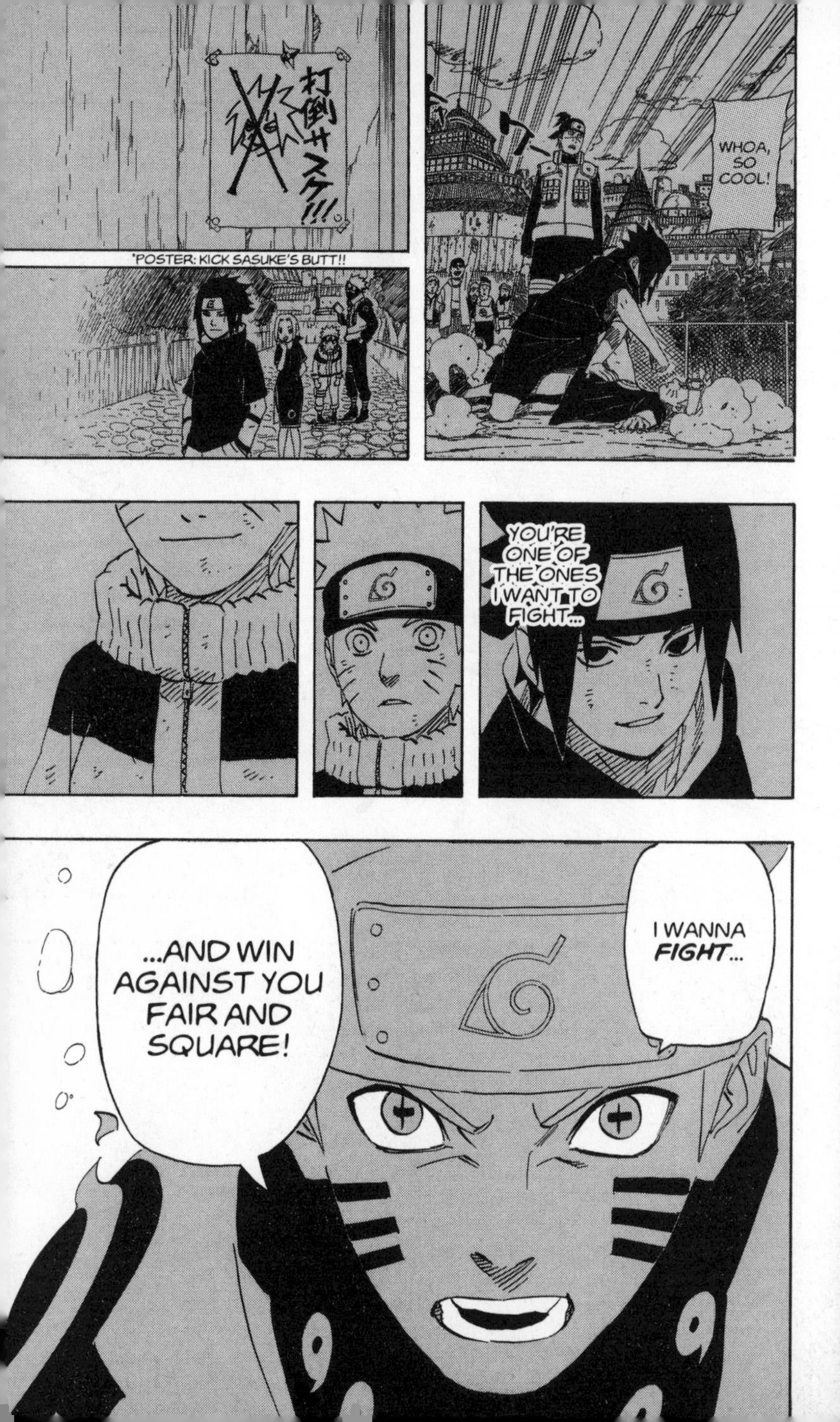
WHOA, SO COOL!
打倒サスケ!!!
*POSTER: KICK SASUKE'S BUTT!!
YOU'RE ONE OF THE ONES I WANT TO FIGHT...
I WANNA *FIGHT*...
...AND WIN AGAINST YOU FAIR AND SQUARE!

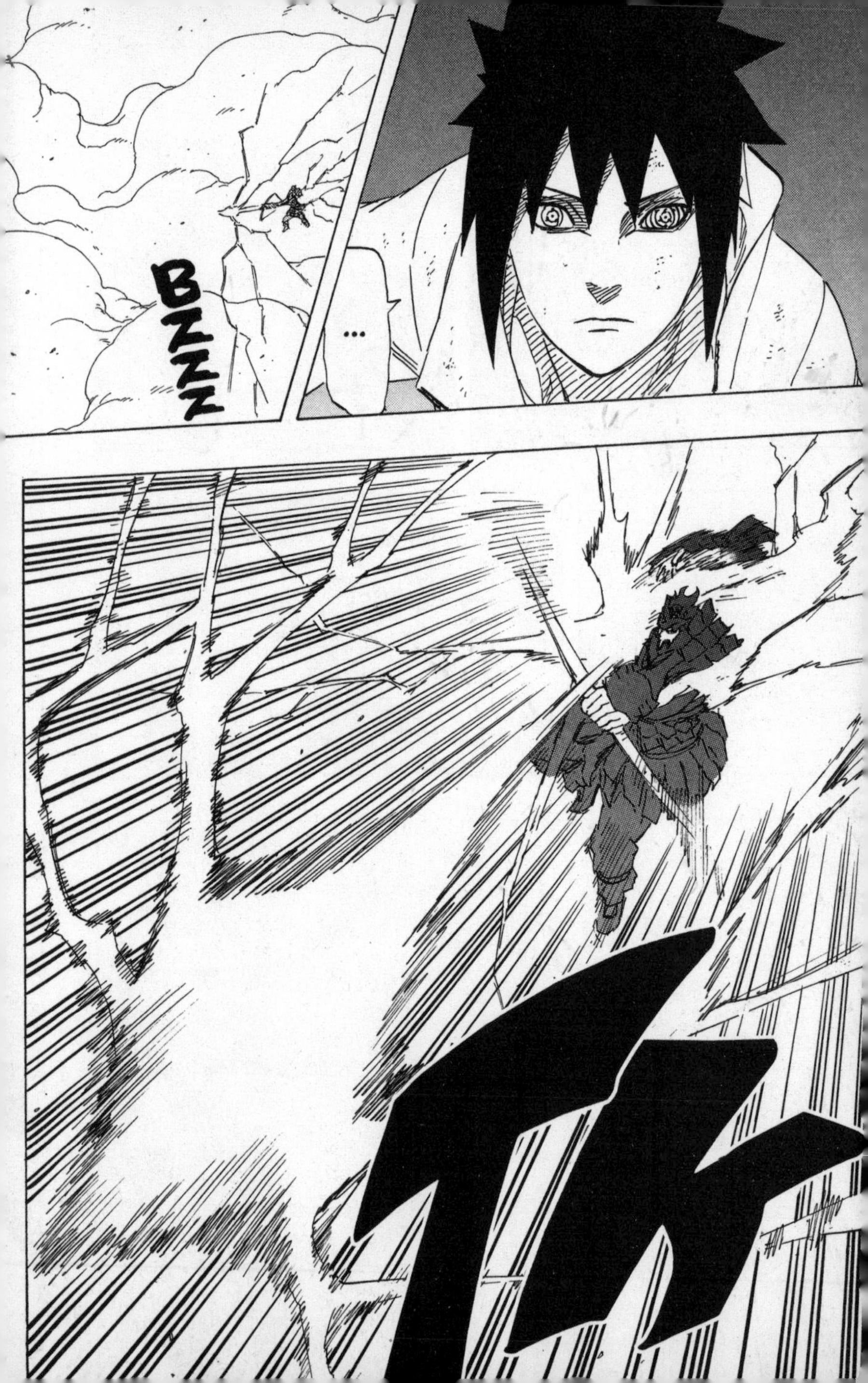
...
BZZZ

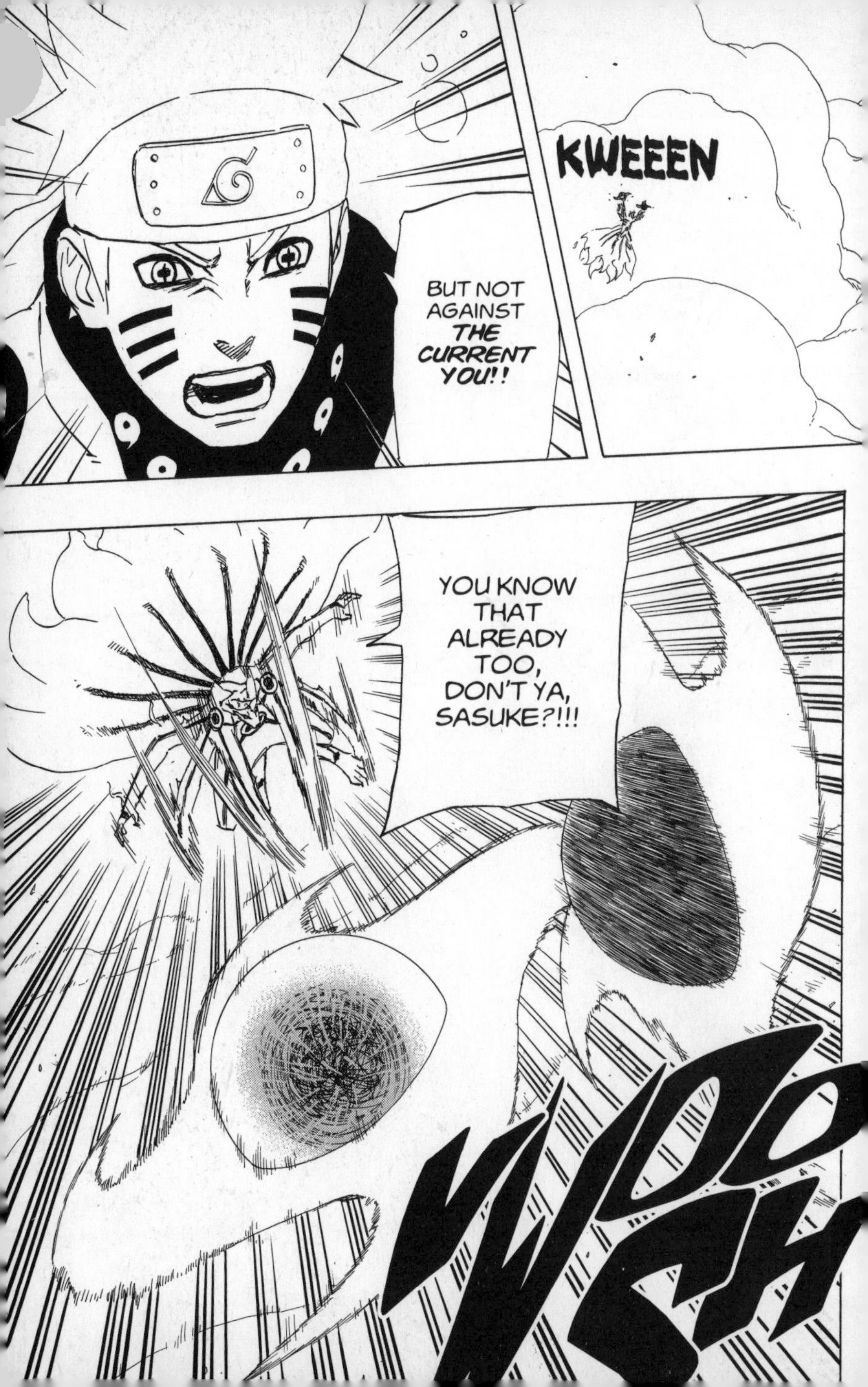
KWEEEN
BUT NOT AGAINST THE CURRENT YOU!!
YOU KNOW THAT ALREADY TOO, DON'T YA, SASUKE?!!!

END OF SERIES COMMEMORATION ILLUSTRATION (G) AKIRA OKUBO

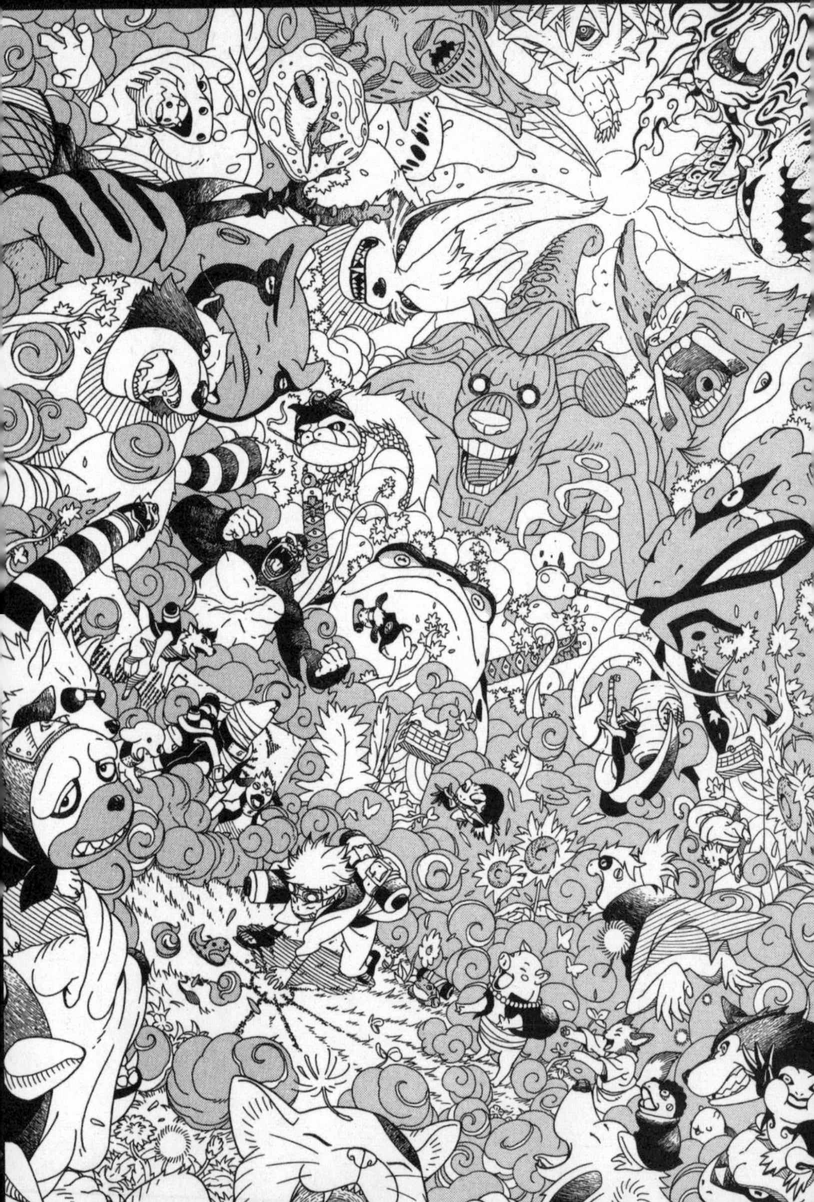

Number 697: Naruto and Sasuke, Part 4

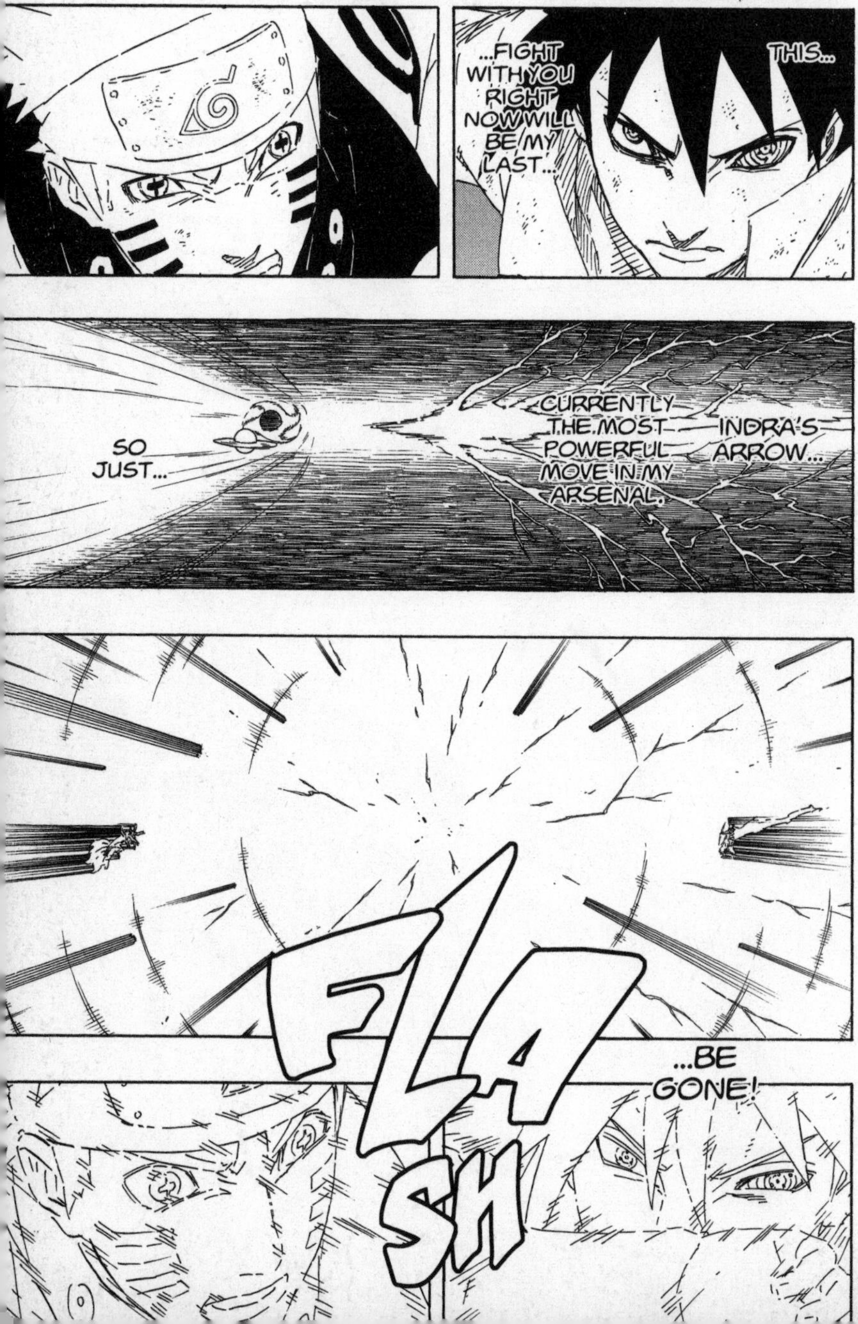
THIS...
...FIGHT WITH YOU RIGHT NOW WILL BE MY LAST...
INDRA'S ARROW...
CURRENTLY THE MOST POWERFUL MOVE IN MY ARSENAL.
SO JUST...
FLASH
...BE GONE!

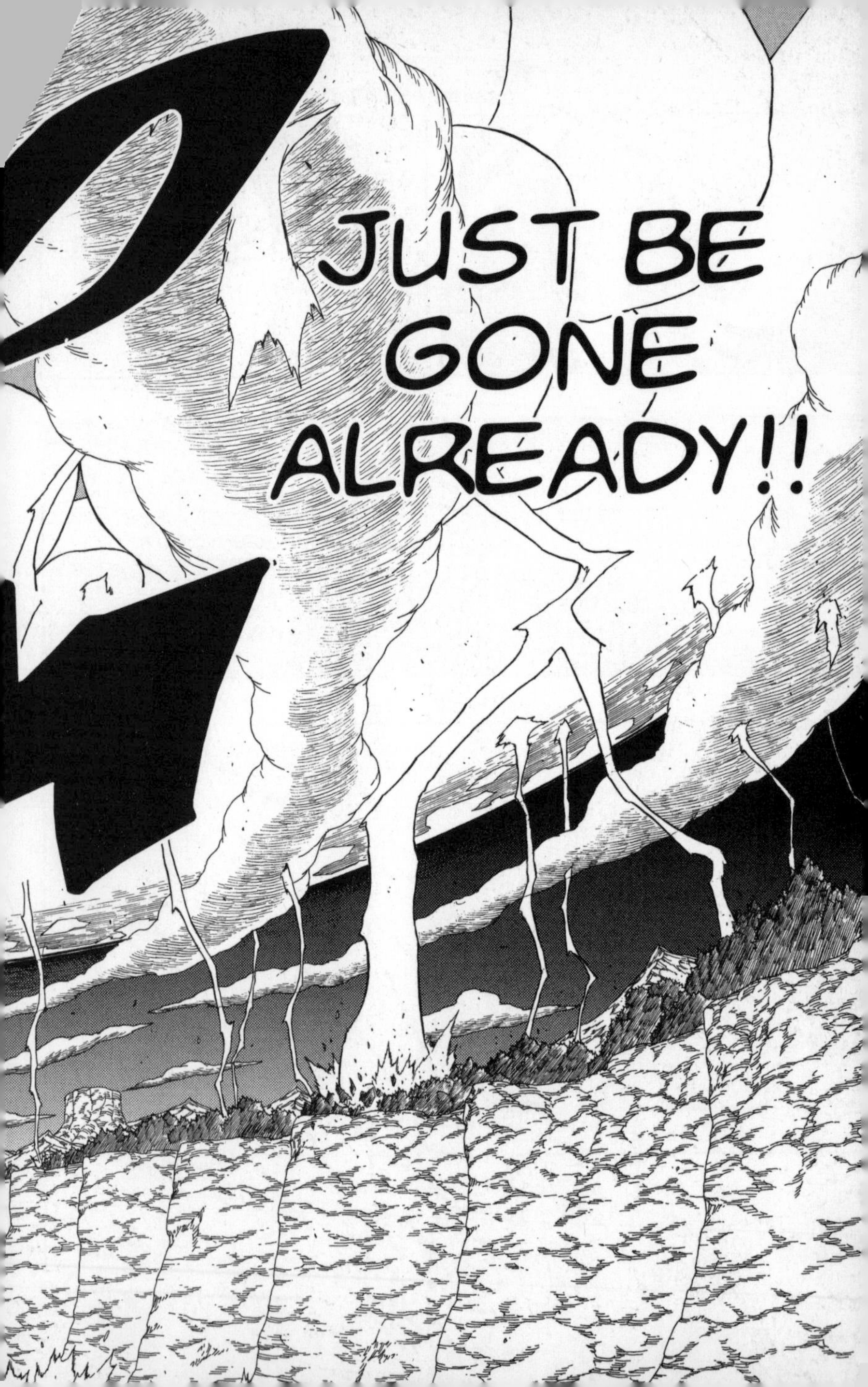
JUST BE GONE ALREADY!!

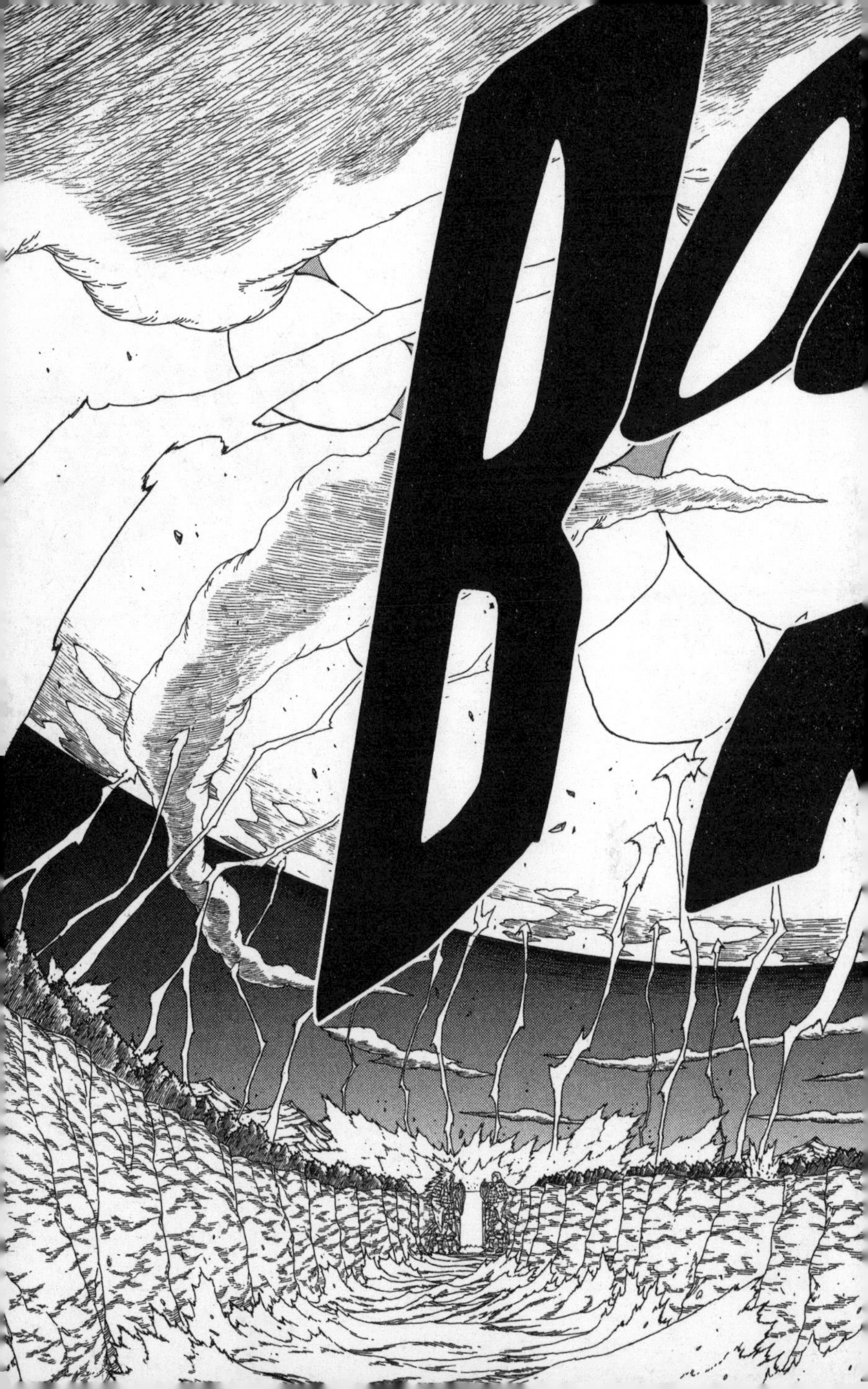

BOO

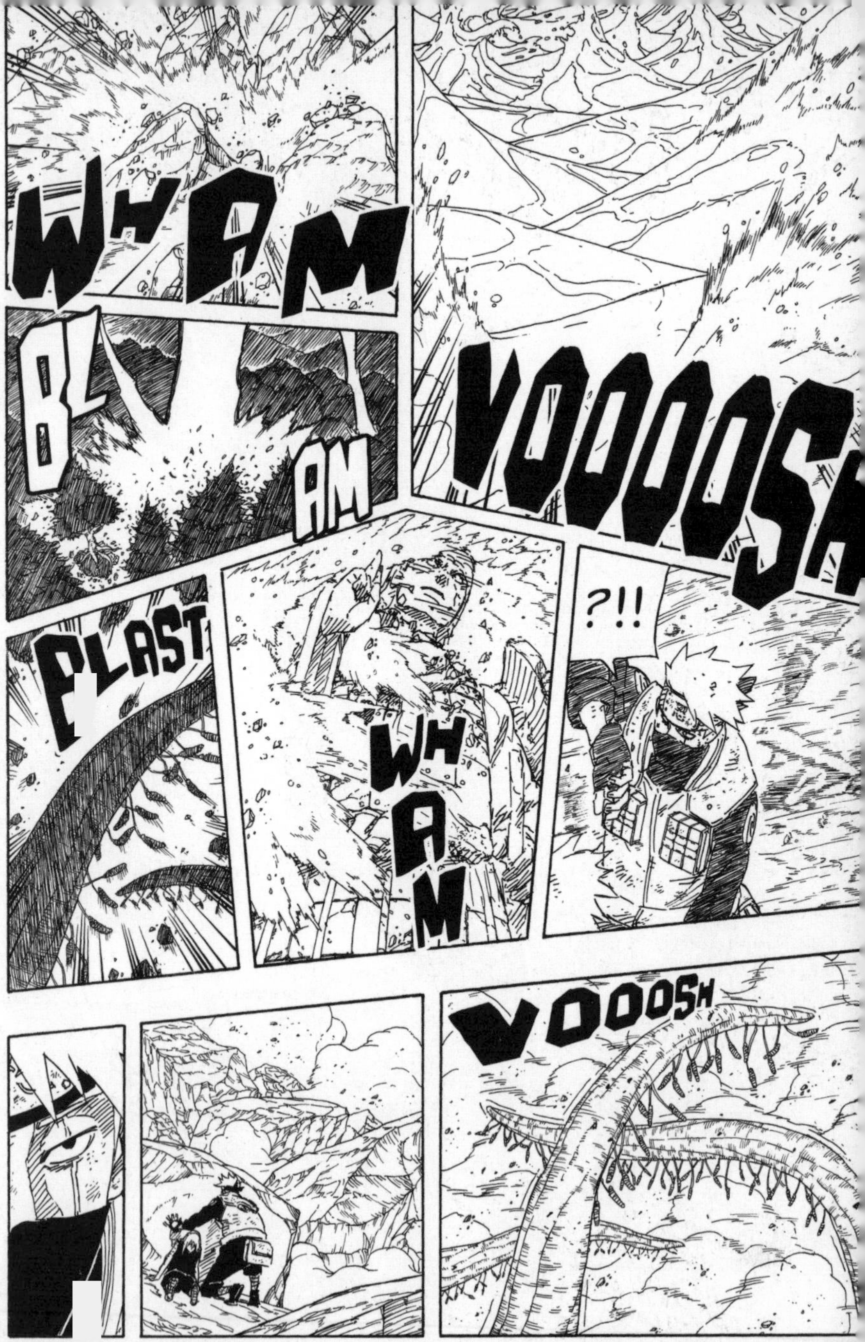
VOOOOSH
WHAM
BLAM
?!!
WHAM
BLAST
VOOOSH

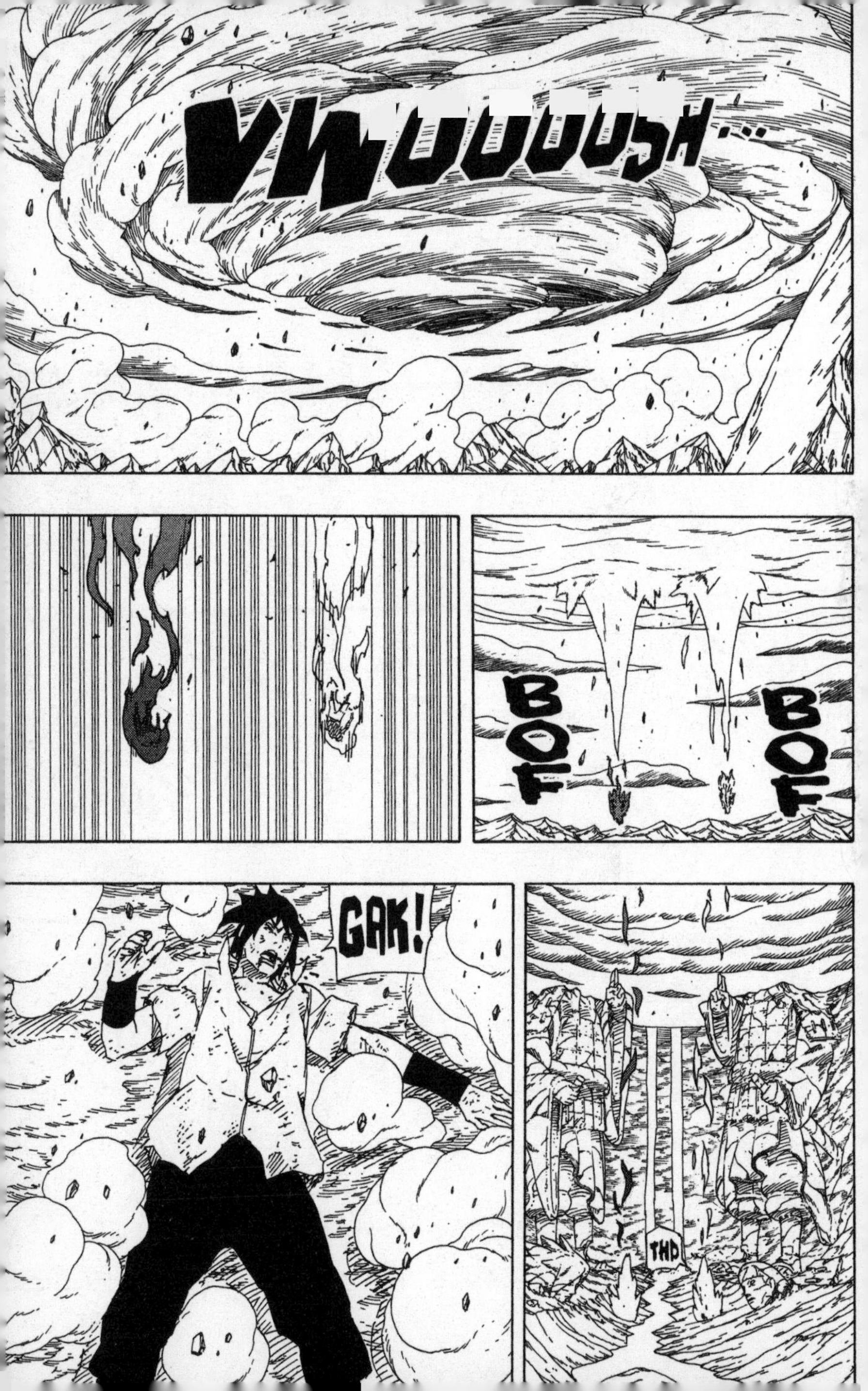
VWOOOOSH...
BOF
BOF
THD
GAK!

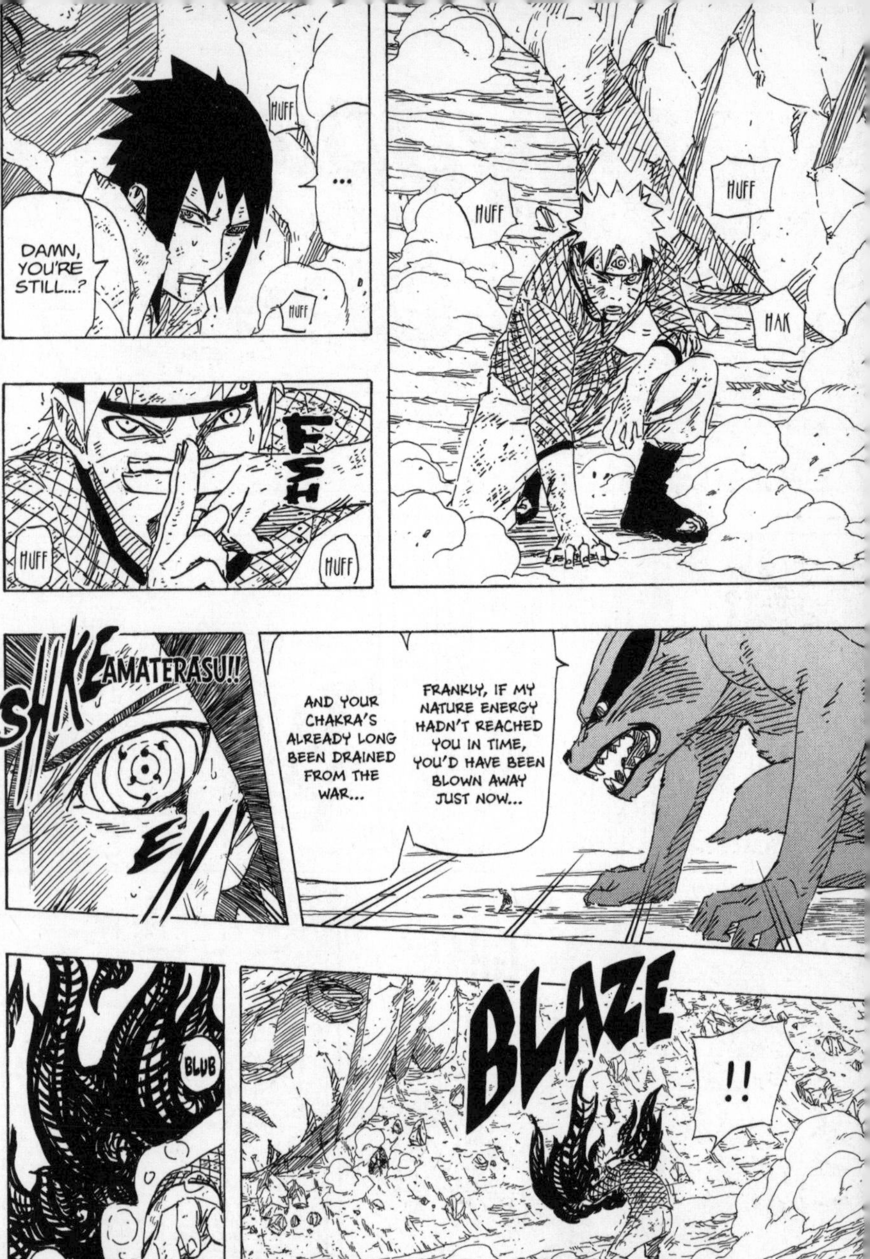
HUFF
HUFF
HAK
HUFF
...
DAMN, YOU'RE STILL...?
HUFF
FSH
HUFF
HUFF
FRANKLY, IF MY NATURE ENERGY HADN'T REACHED YOU IN TIME, YOU'D HAVE BEEN BLOWN AWAY JUST NOW...
AND YOUR CHAKRA'S ALREADY LONG BEEN DRAINED FROM THE WAR...
SHKE
AMATERASU!!
EN
BLAZE
!!
BLUB
BLUB

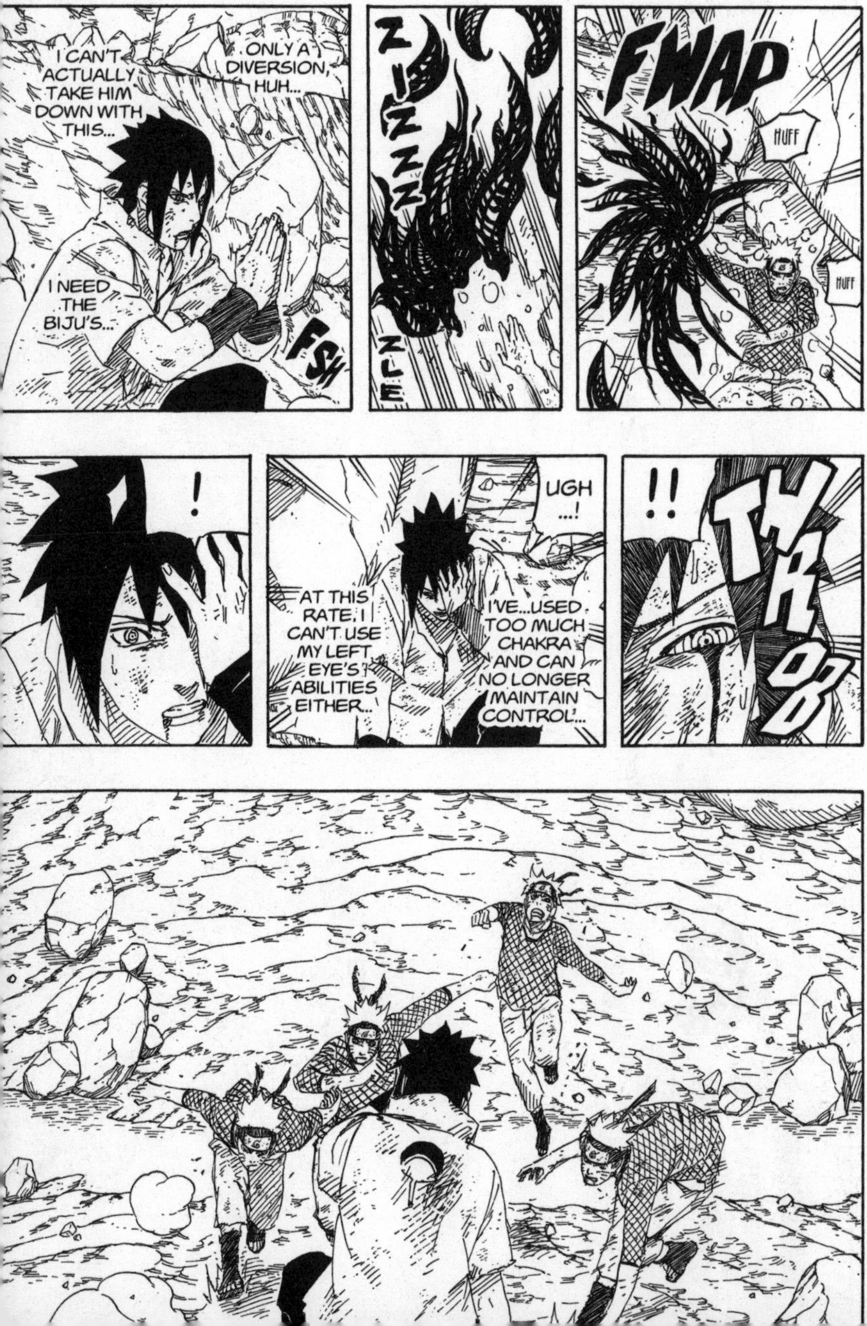
FWAP
HUFF
HUFF
ZIZZZ
ZLE
ONLY A DIVERSION, HUH...
I CAN'T ACTUALLY TAKE HIM DOWN WITH THIS...
I NEED THE BIJU'S...
FSH
!!
THROB
UGH ...!
I'VE...USED TOO MUCH CHAKRA AND CAN NO LONGER MAINTAIN CONTROL...
AT THIS RATE, I CAN'T USE MY LEFT EYE'S ABILITIES EITHER...
!

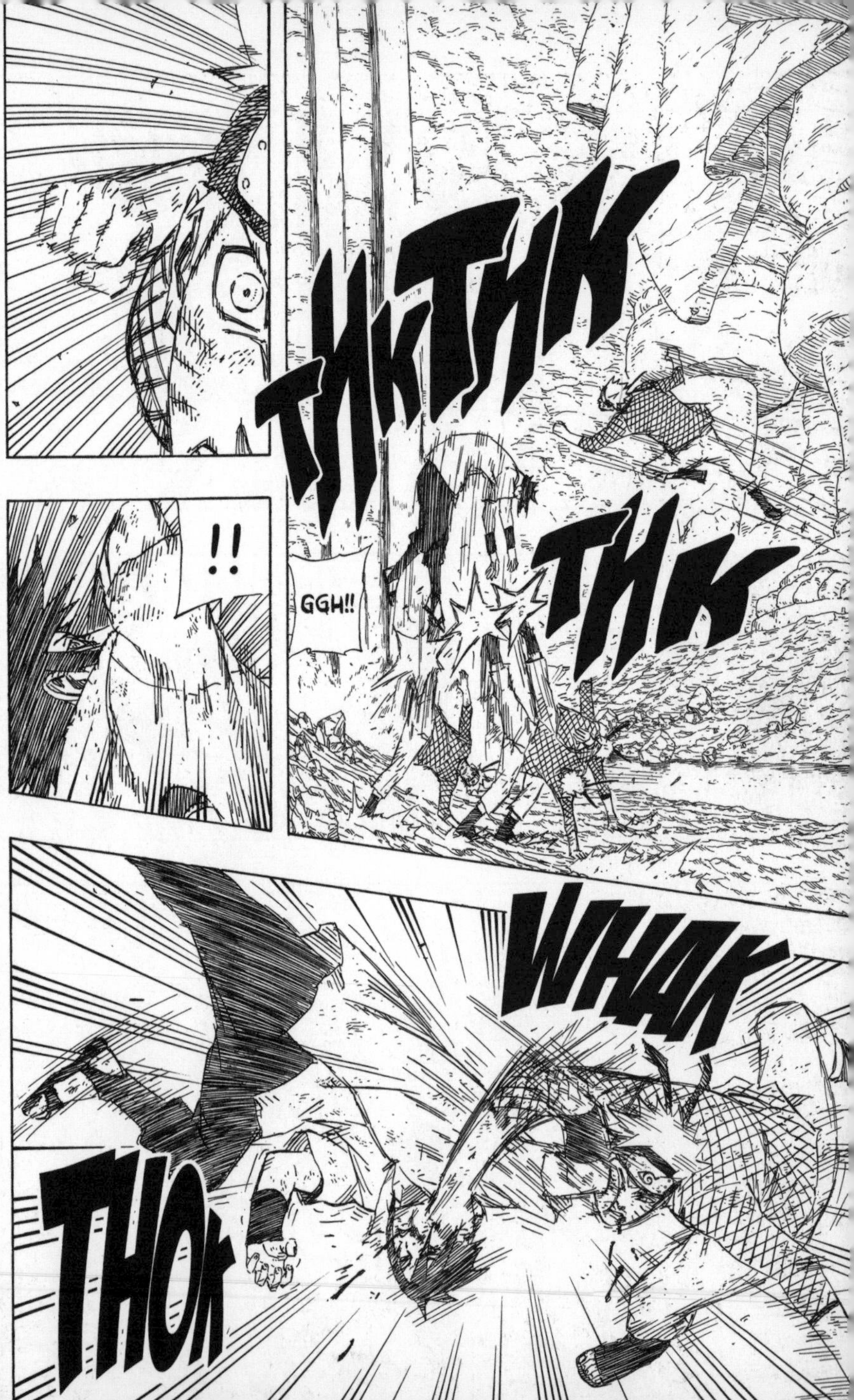
THKTHK
GGH!!
THK
!!
WHAK
THOK

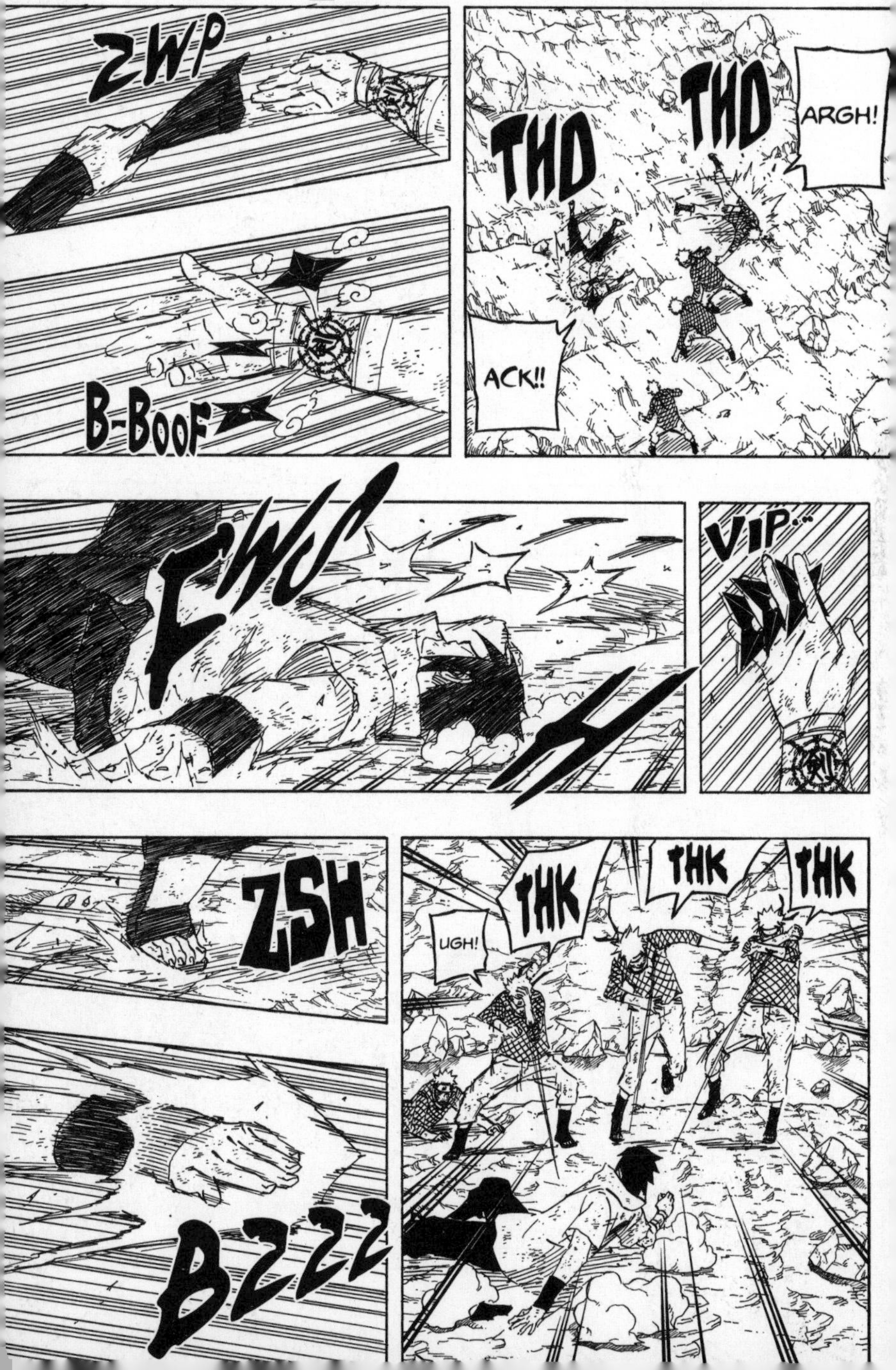
ARGH!
THD
THD
ACK!!
ZWP
B-BOOF
VIP...
FWUP
ZSH
THK
THK
THK
UGH!
BZZZ

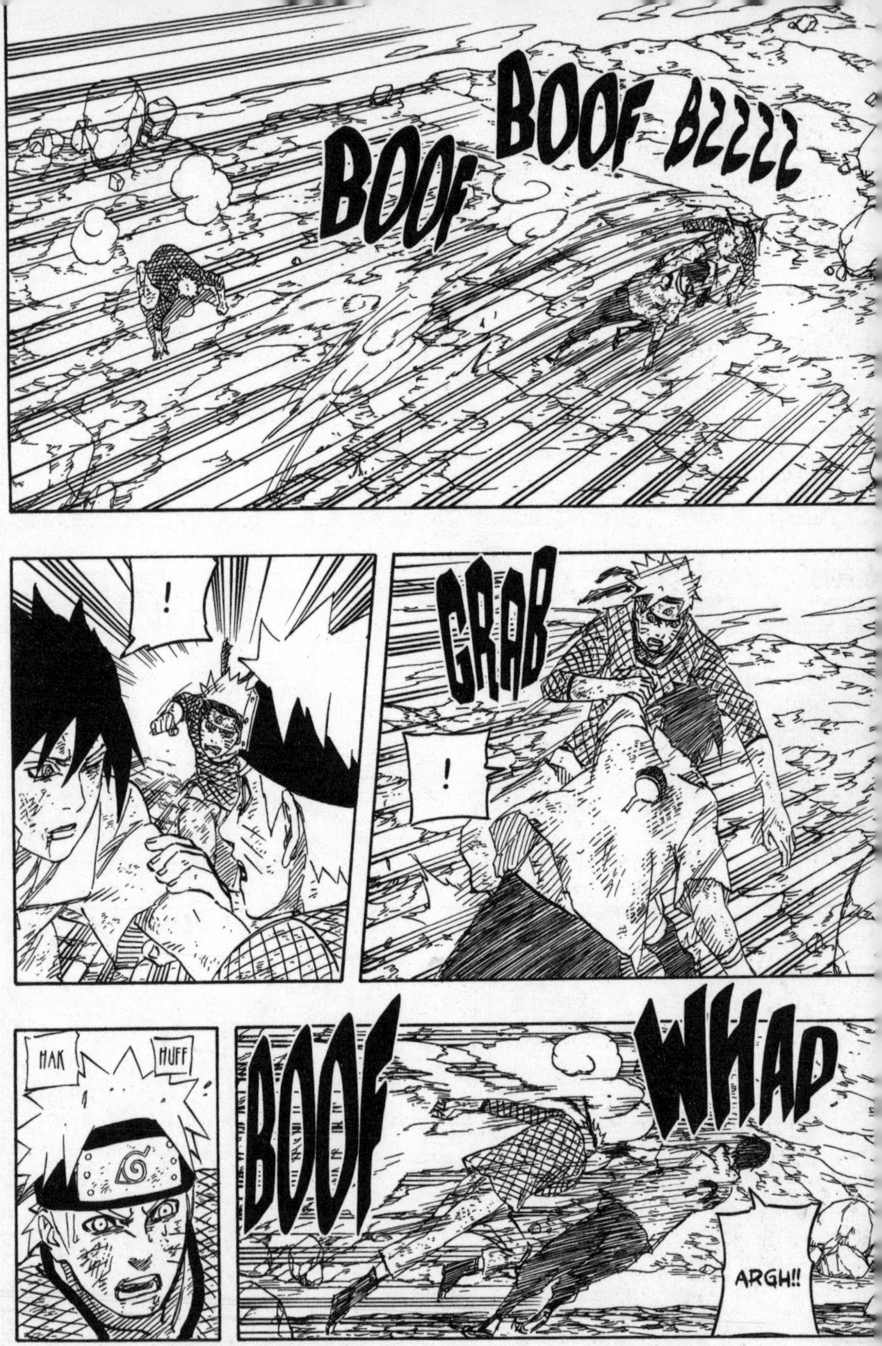
BOOF BOOF BZZZZ
BOOF
GRAB
!
!
WHAP
BOOF
ARGH!!
HUFF
HAK

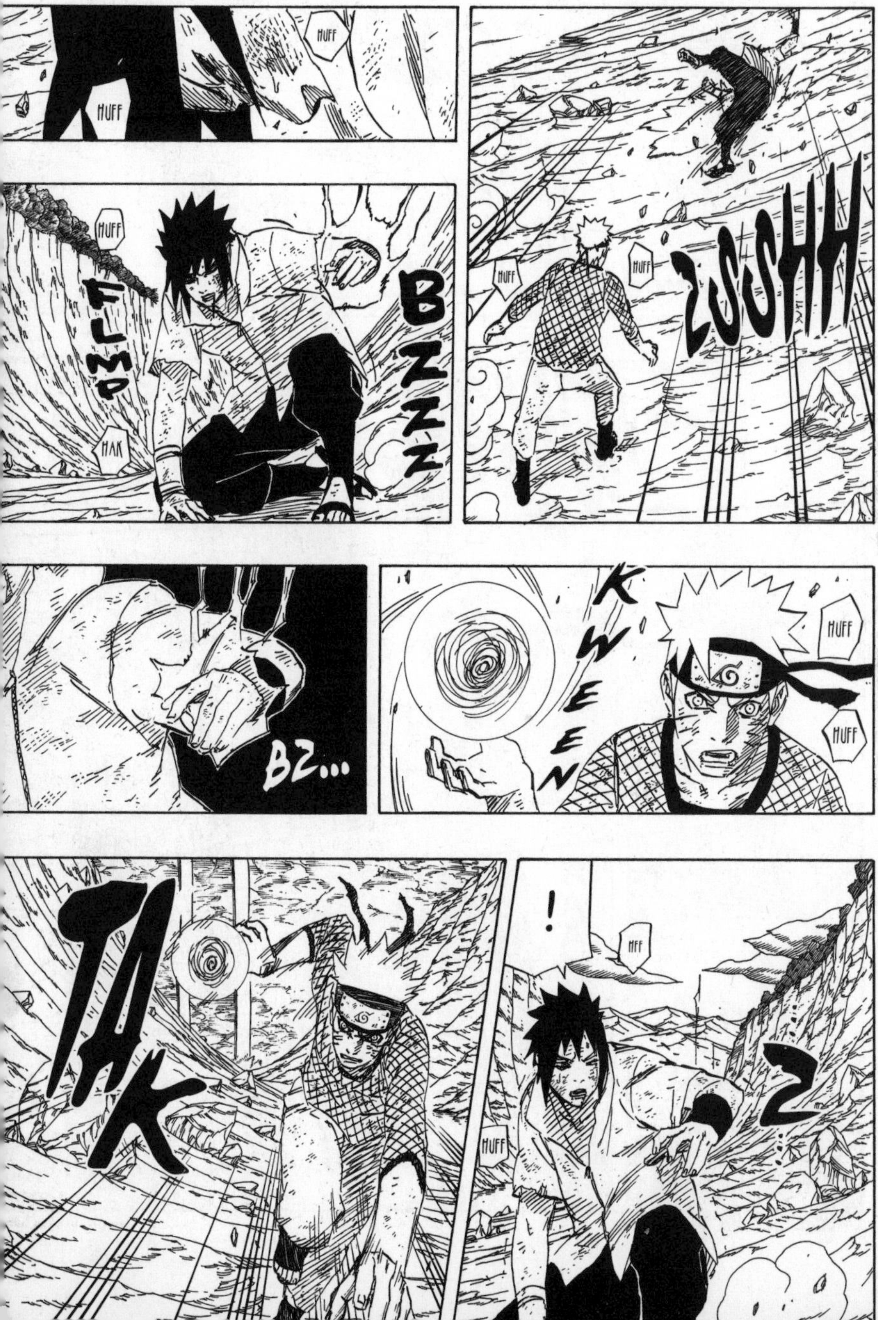
ZSSHH
HUFF
HUFF
HUFF
HUFF
HUFF
FLMP
HAK
BZZZ
HUFF
HUFF
KWEEEN
BZ...
!
HFF
Z
HUFF
TAK

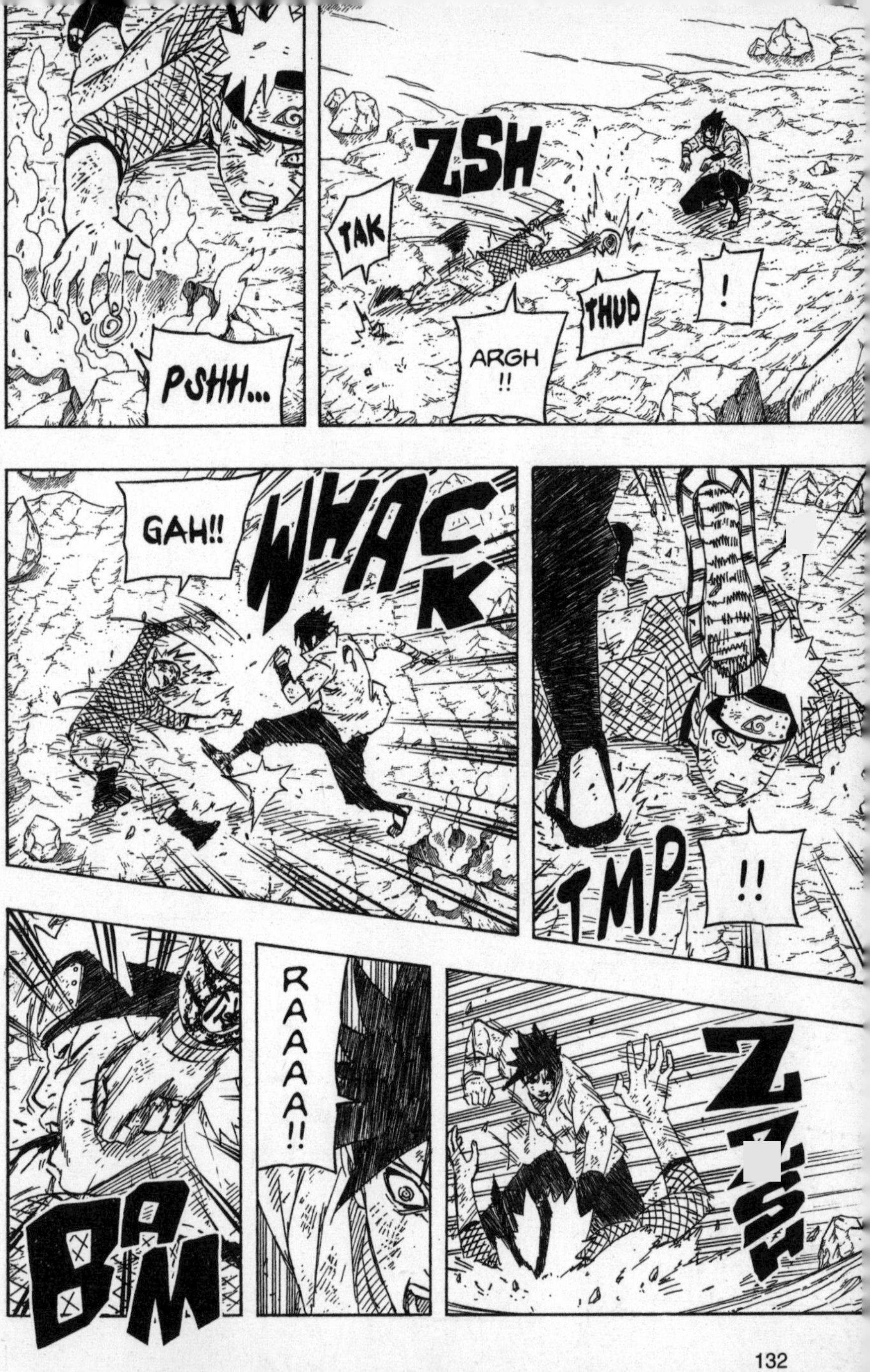
ZSH
!
THUD
TAK
ARGH!!
PSHHH...
TMP
!!
WHACK
GAH!!
ZZSH
RAAAAA!!
BAM

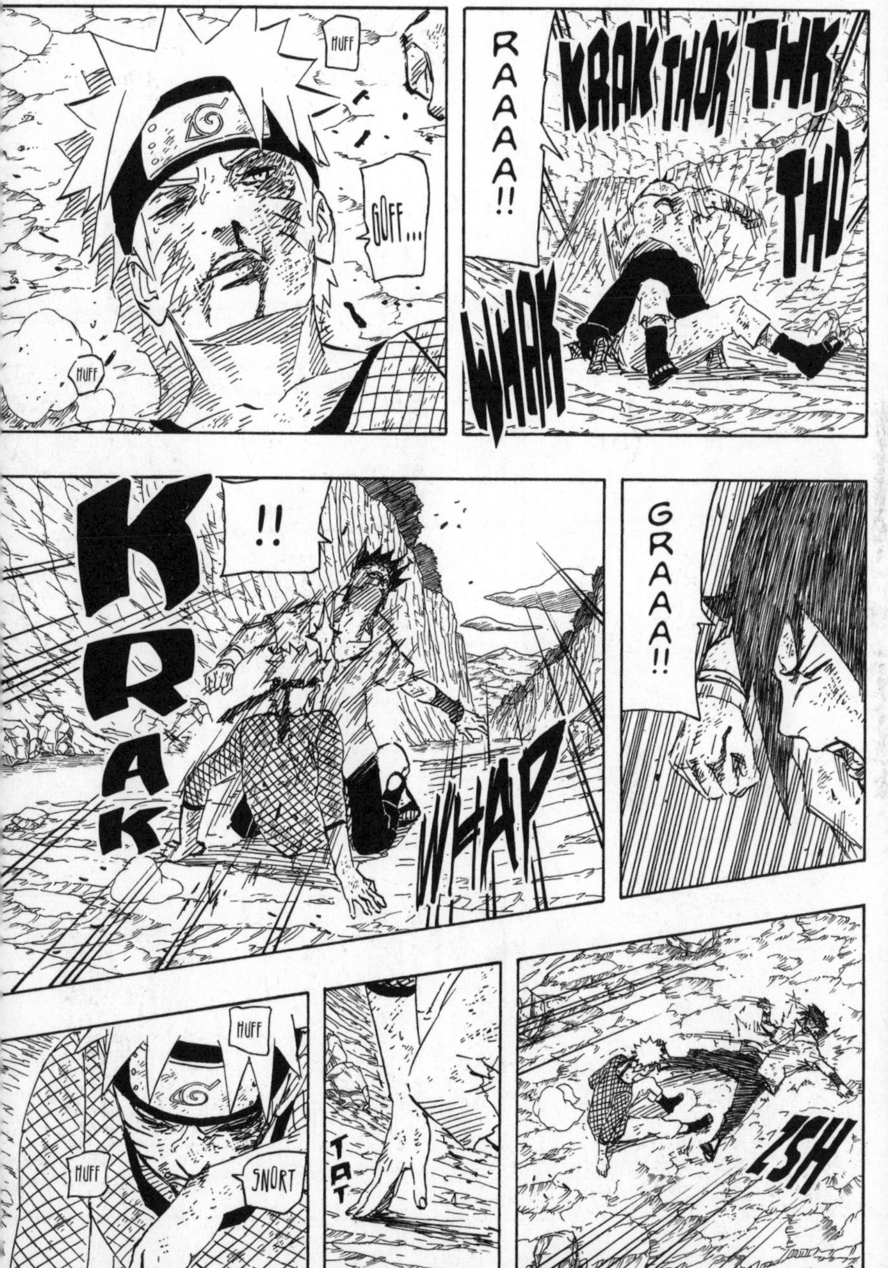
RAAAAA!!
KRAK THOK THK
THD
WHAK
HUFF
GOFF...
HUFF
GRAAAA!!
!!
KRAK
WHAP
TSH
TAT
HUFF
HUFF
SNORT

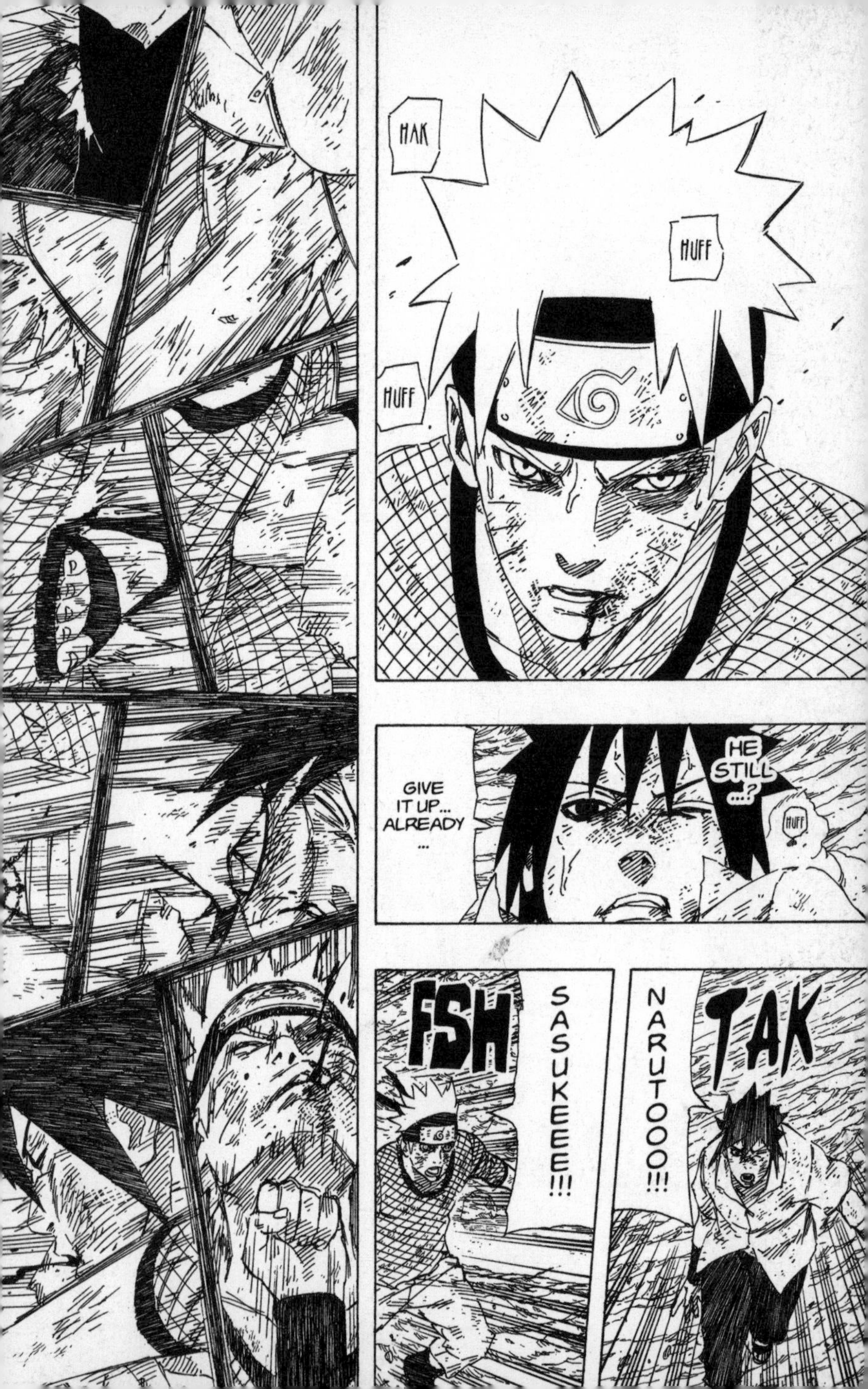
HAK
HUFF
HUFF
HE STILL ...?
HUFF
GIVE IT UP... ALREADY ...
TAK
NARUTOOO!!!
FSH
SASUKEEE!!!

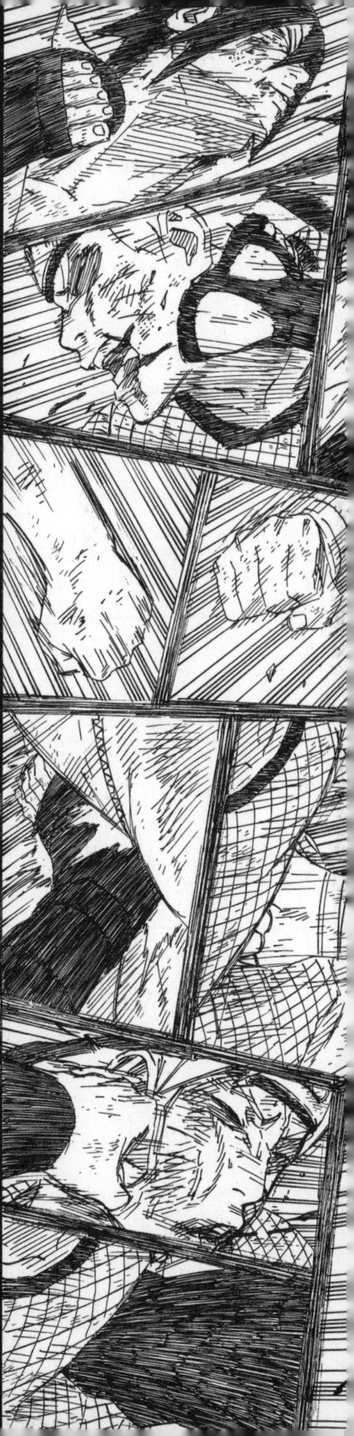

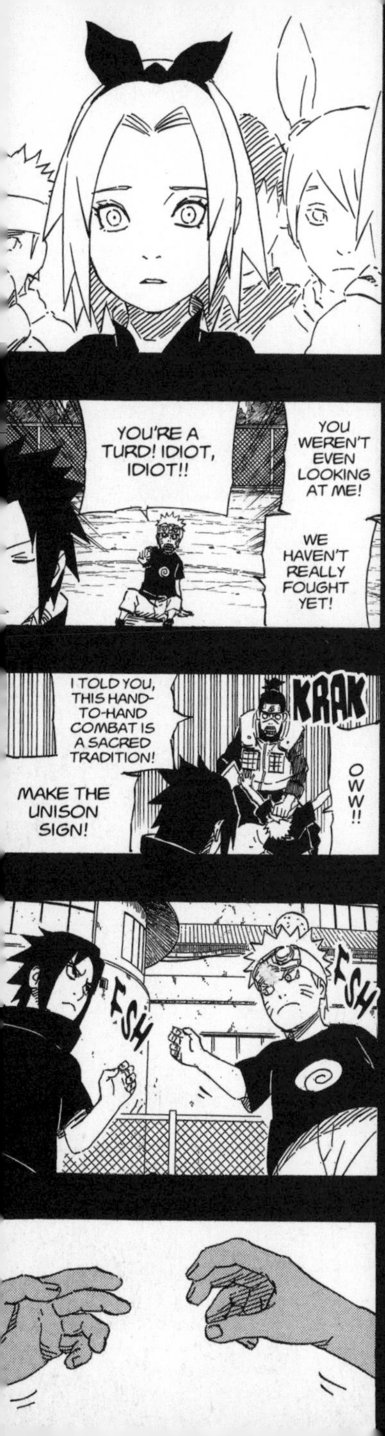
YOU WEREN'T EVEN LOOKING AT ME!
WE HAVEN'T REALLY FOUGHT YET!
YOU'RE A TURD! IDIOT, IDIOT!!
KRAK
OWW!!
I TOLD YOU, THIS HAND-TO-HAND COMBAT IS A SACRED TRADITION!
MAKE THE UNISON SIGN!
FSH
FSH

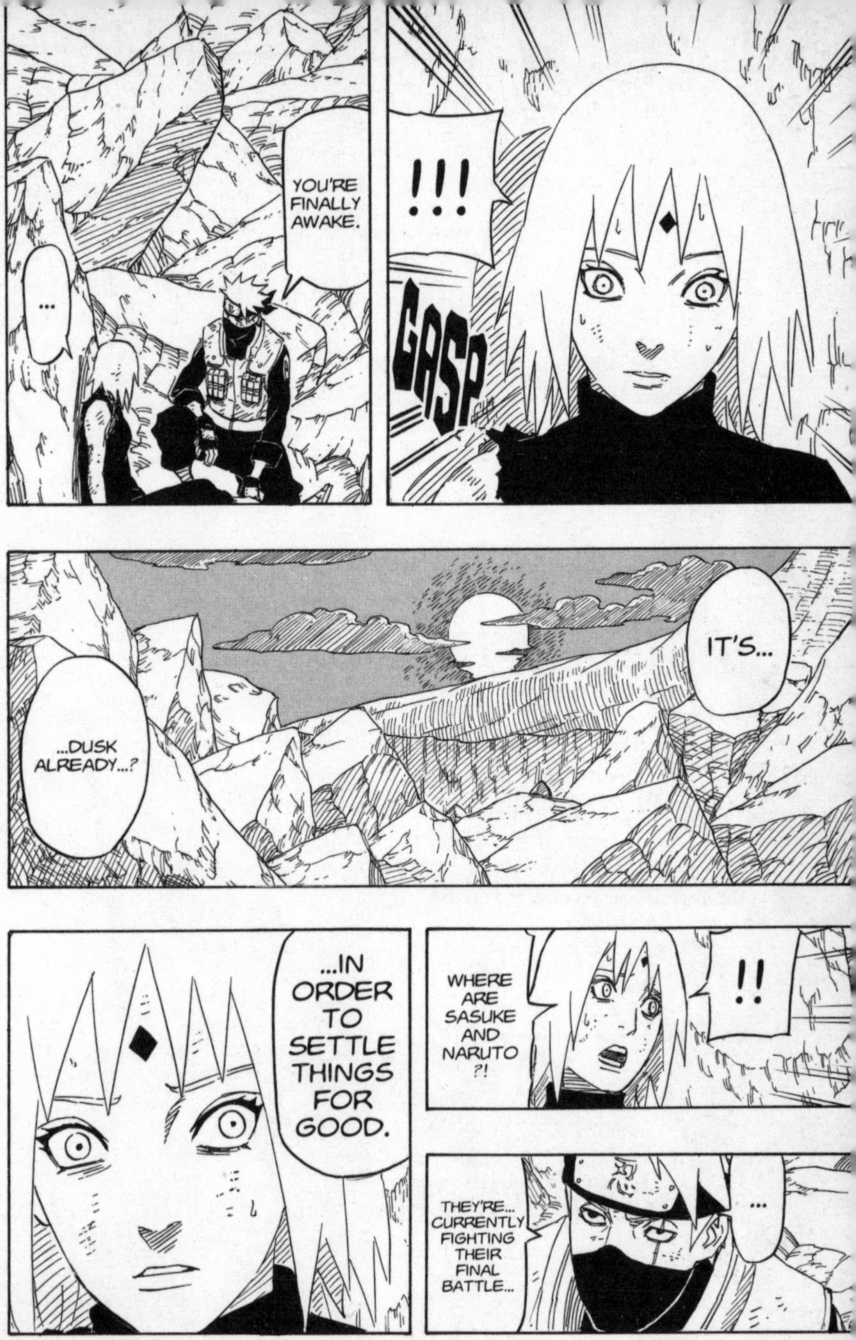
!!!
GASP
YOU'RE FINALLY AWAKE.
...
IT'S...
...DUSK ALREADY...?
!!
WHERE ARE SASUKE AND NARUTO?!
...
THEY'RE... CURRENTLY FIGHTING THEIR FINAL BATTLE...
...IN ORDER TO SETTLE THINGS FOR GOOD.

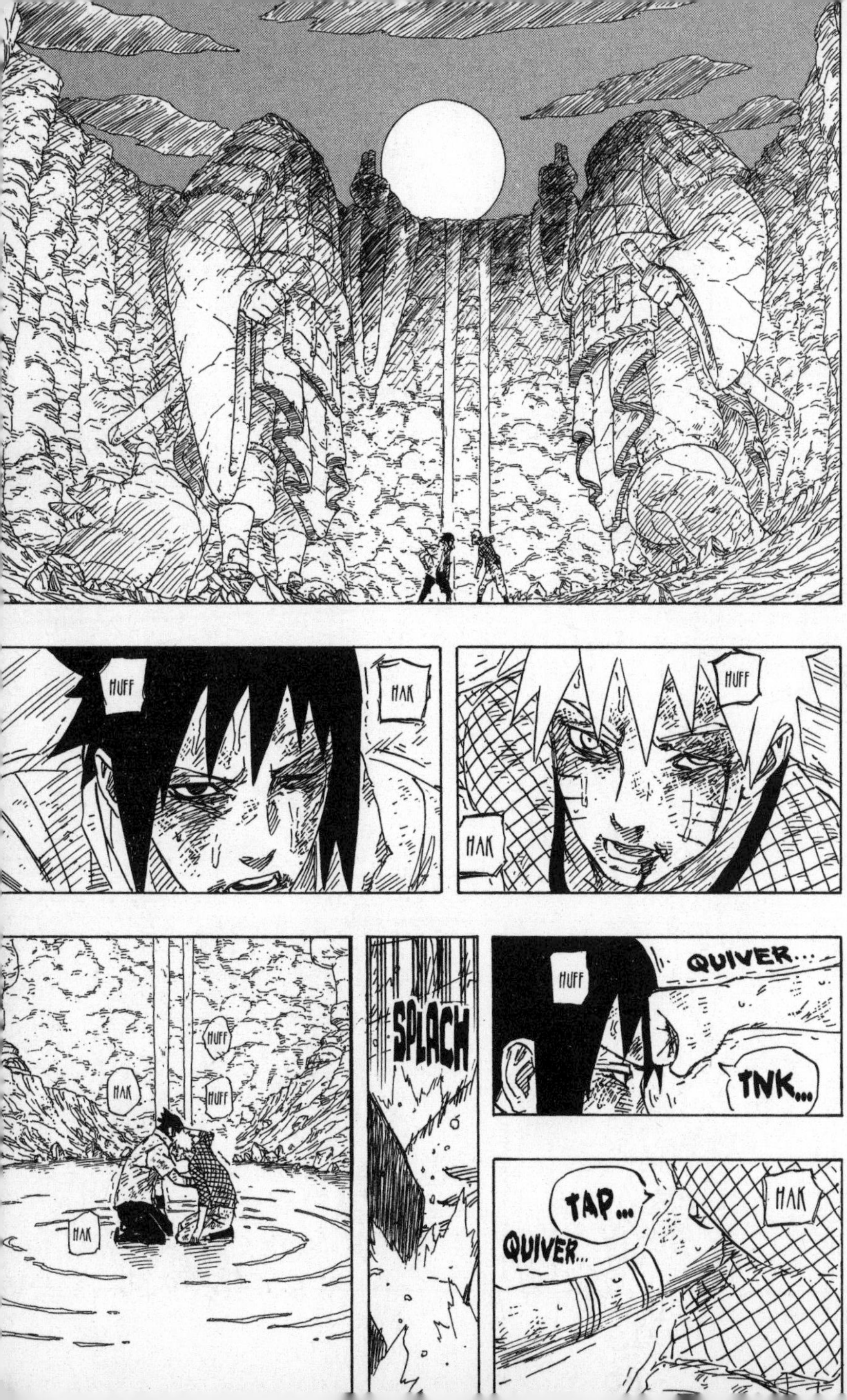
HUFF
HAK
HAK
HUFF
QUIVER...
HUFF
TNK...
HAK
TAP...
QUIVER...
SPLACH
HUFF
HUFF
HAK
HAK

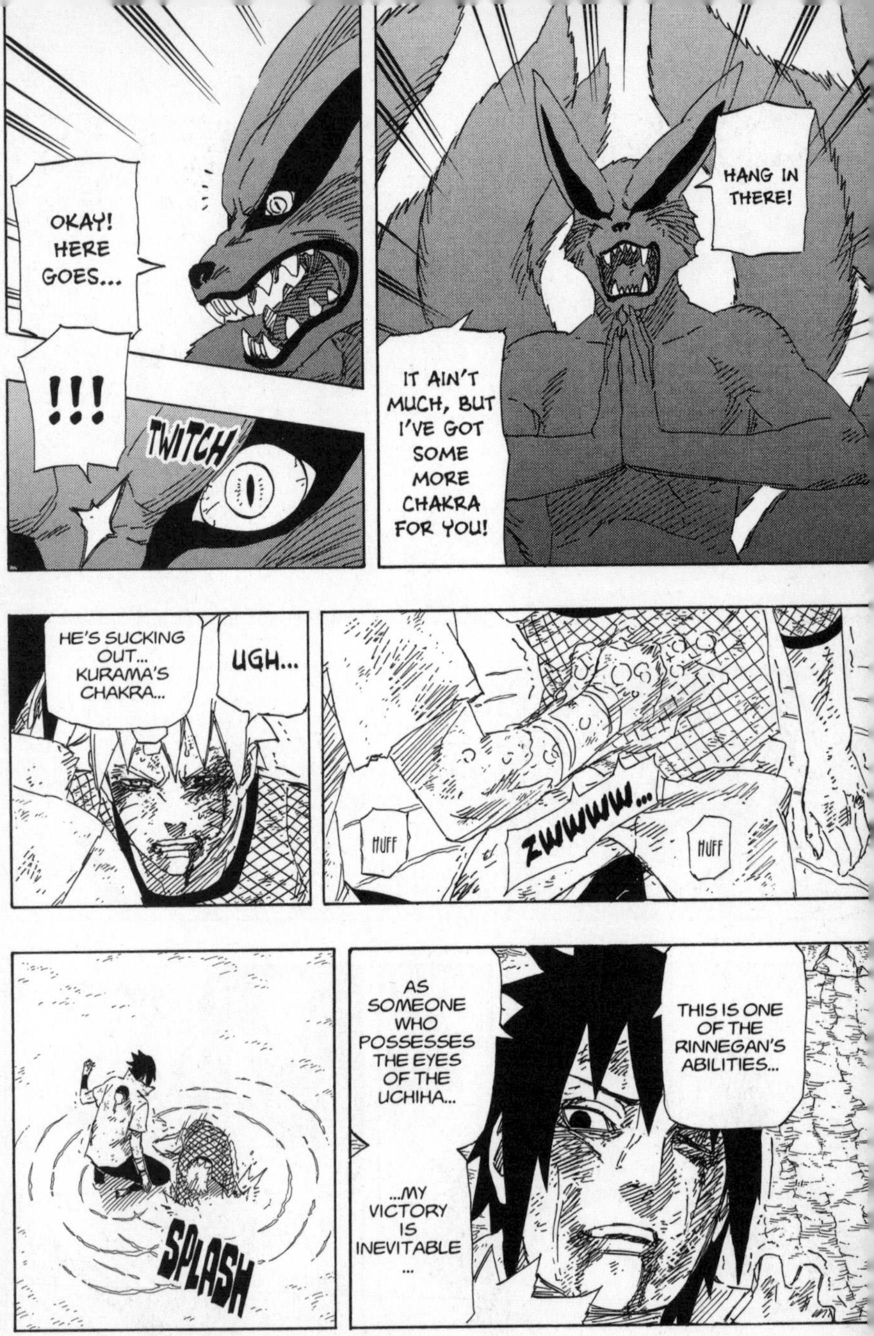

HANG IN THERE!
IT AIN'T MUCH, BUT I'VE GOT SOME MORE CHAKRA FOR YOU!
OKAY! HERE GOES...
!!!
TWITCH
HUFF
ZWWWW...
HUFF
UGH...
HE'S SUCKING OUT... KURAMA'S CHAKRA...
THIS IS ONE OF THE RINNEGAN'S ABILITIES...
AS SOMEONE WHO POSSESSES THE EYES OF THE UCHIHA...
...MY VICTORY IS INEVITABLE...
SPLASH

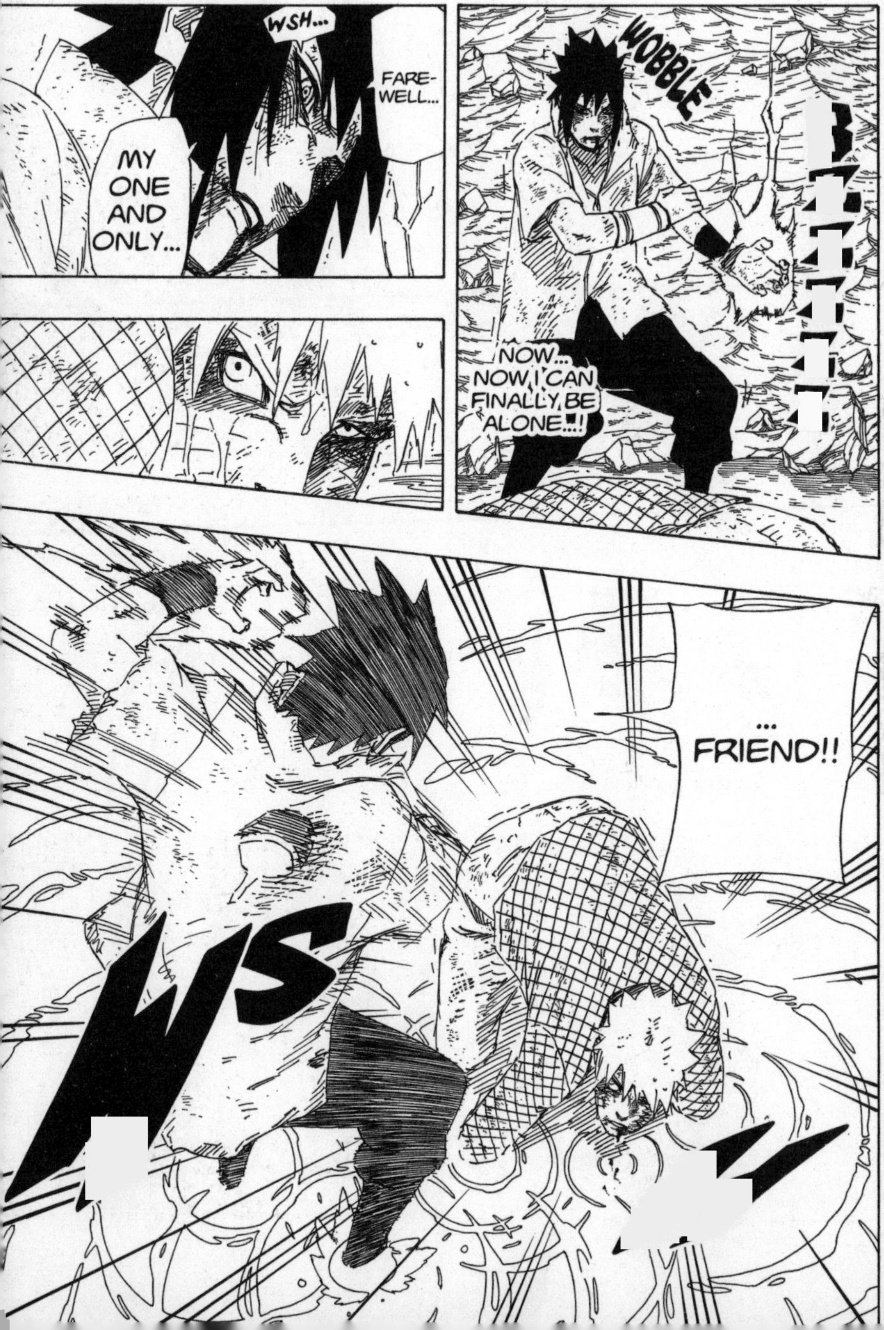
WOBBLE
NOW... NOW I CAN FINALLY BE ALONE...!!
WSH...
FARE-WELL...
MY ONE AND ONLY...
...FRIEND!!
WS

END OF SERIES COMMEMORATION ILLUSTRATION (7)

THANK YOU, THANK YOU, THANK YOU FOR ALL YOUR HARD WORK ON THE SERIES THESE PAST 15 YEARS! -MASAKI MURAKAMI

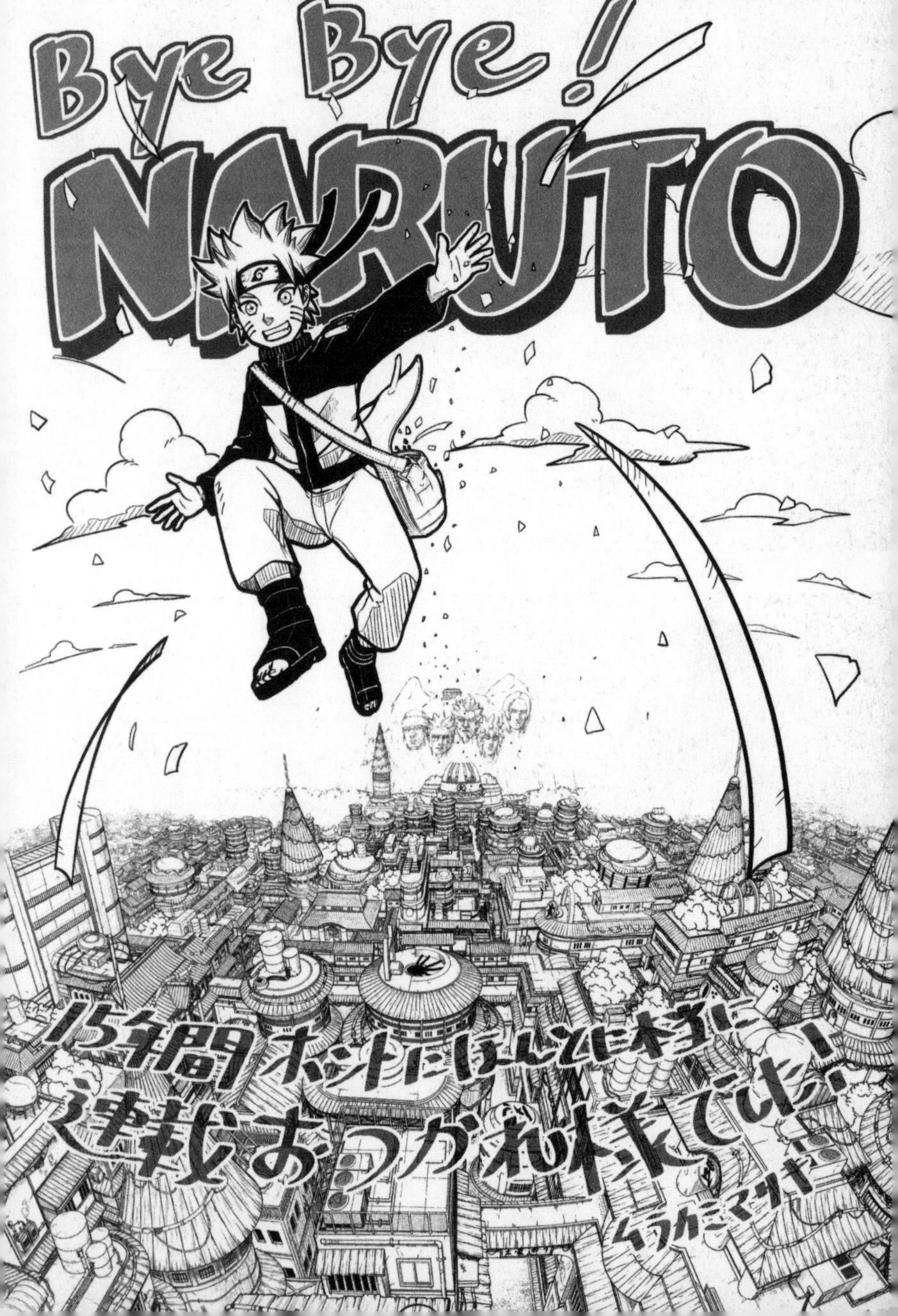
Bye Bye! NARUTO
15年間ホントにほんとに本当に！
連載おつかれ様でした！
ムラカミマサキ

Number 698: Naruto and Sasuke, Part 5

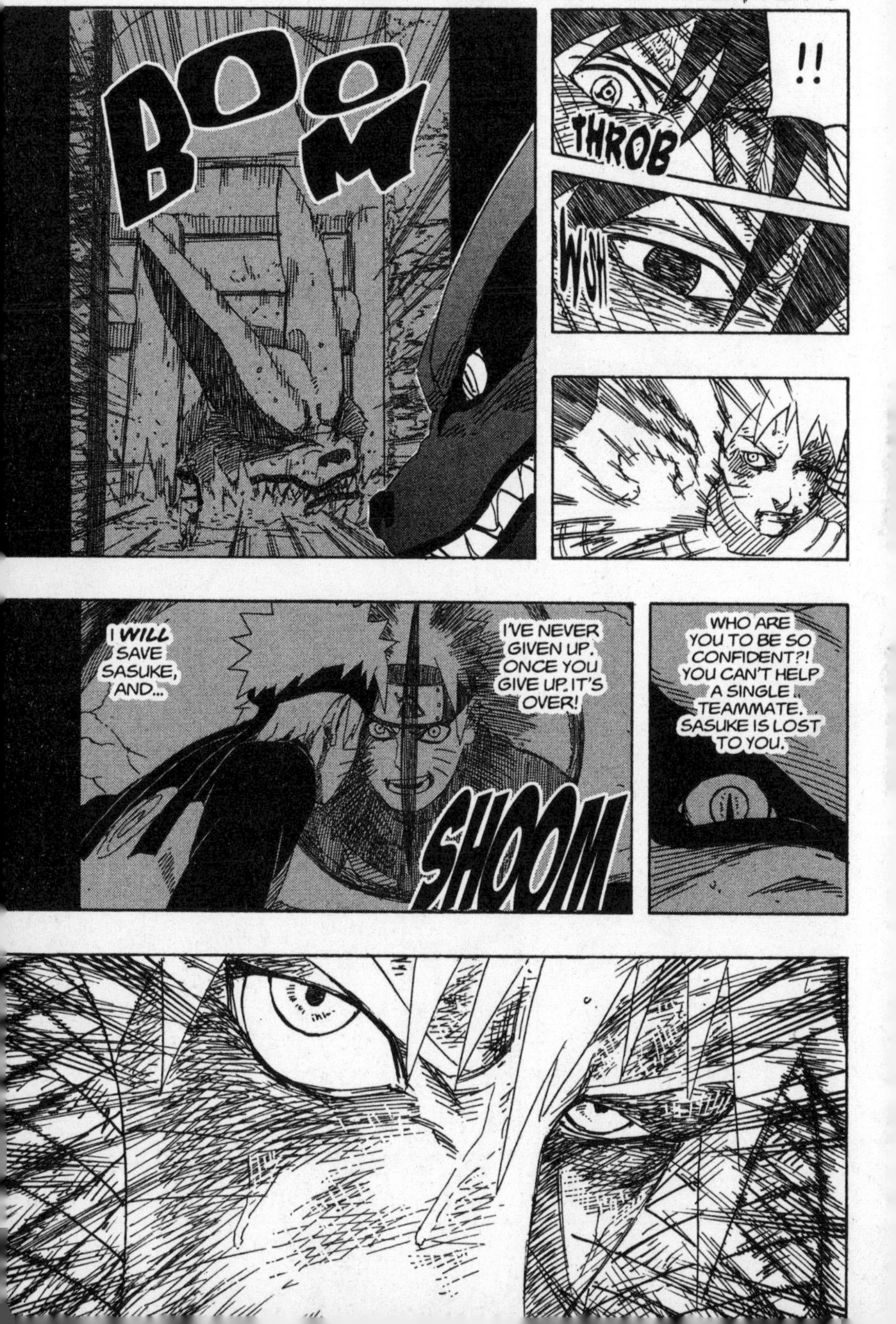
!!
THROB
WISH
BOOM
WHO ARE YOU TO BE SO CONFIDENT?! YOU CAN'T HELP A SINGLE TEAMMATE. SASUKE IS LOST TO YOU.
I'VE NEVER GIVEN UP. ONCE YOU GIVE UP, IT'S OVER!
I WILL SAVE SASUKE, AND...
SHOOM

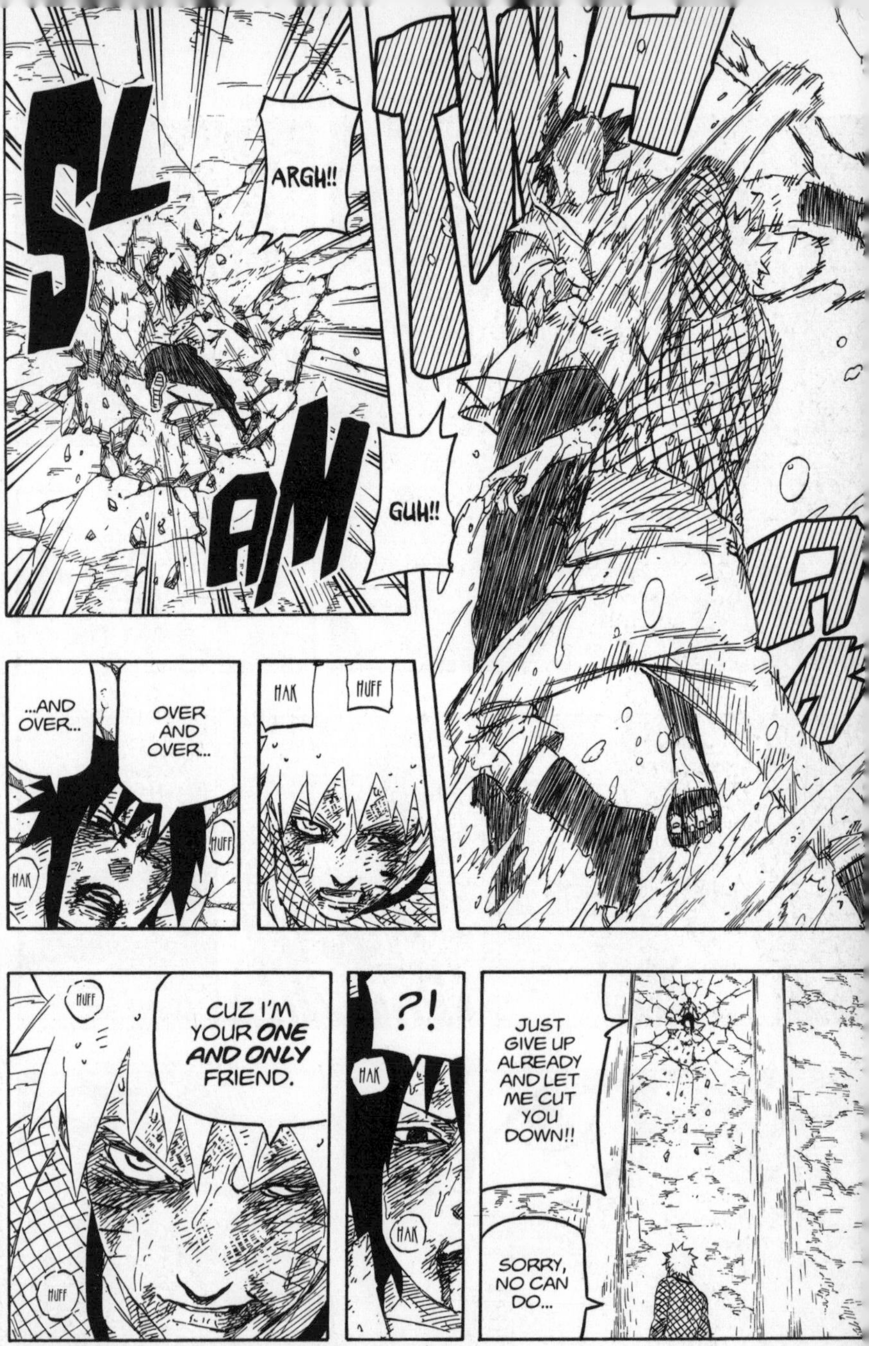
ARGH!!
GUH!!
SLAM
HAK
HUFF
OVER AND OVER...
...AND OVER...
HUFF
HAK
JUST GIVE UP ALREADY AND LET ME CUT YOU DOWN!!
SORRY, NO CAN DO...
?!
HAK
HAK
CUZ I'M YOUR ***ONE AND ONLY*** FRIEND.
HUFF
HUFF

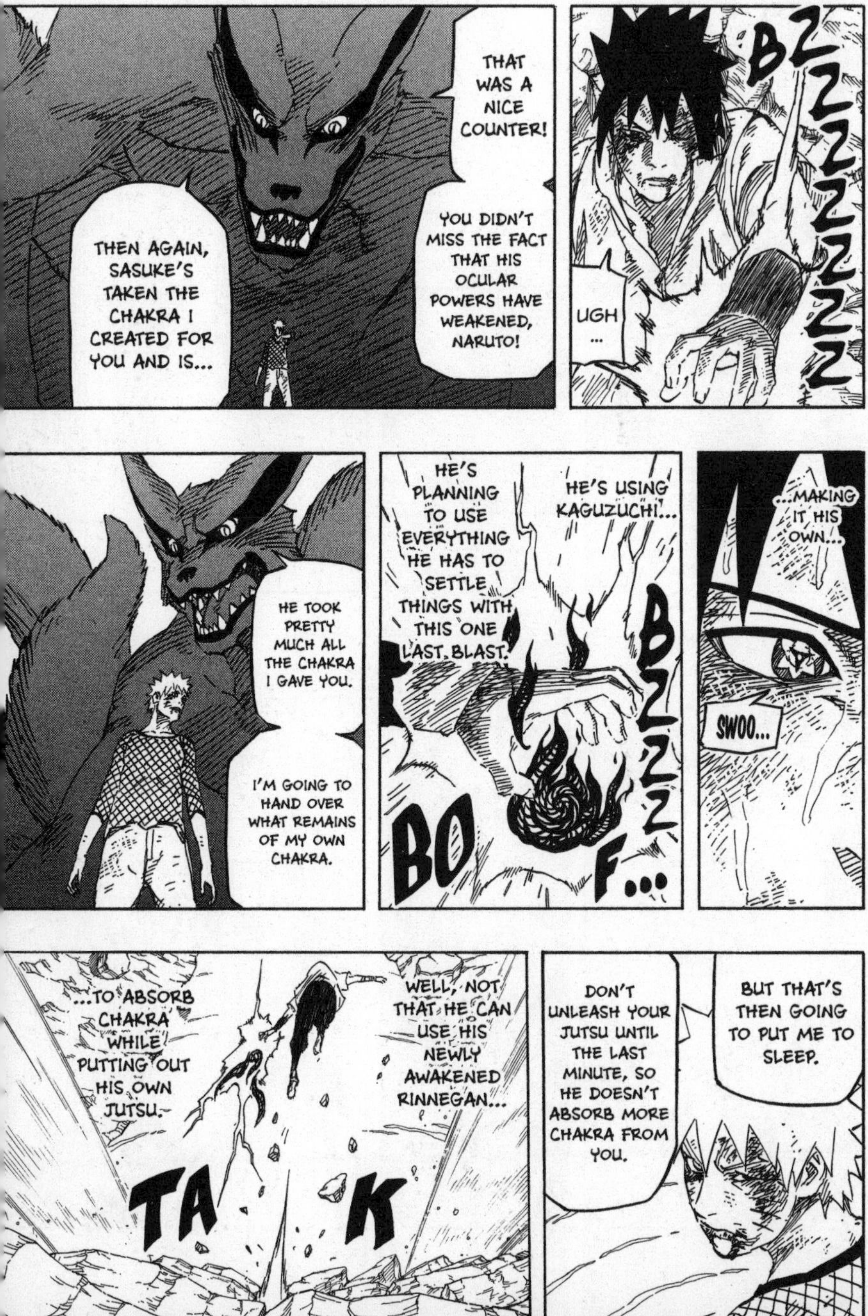
BZZZZZZZZ
UGH...
THAT WAS A NICE COUNTER!
YOU DIDN'T MISS THE FACT THAT HIS OCULAR POWERS HAVE WEAKENED, NARUTO!
THEN AGAIN, SASUKE'S TAKEN THE CHAKRA I CREATED FOR YOU AND IS...
...MAKING IT HIS OWN...
SWOO...
HE'S USING KAGUZUCHI...
HE'S PLANNING TO USE EVERYTHING HE HAS TO SETTLE THINGS WITH THIS ONE LAST BLAST.
BZZZ
BOF...
HE TOOK PRETTY MUCH ALL THE CHAKRA I GAVE YOU.
I'M GOING TO HAND OVER WHAT REMAINS OF MY OWN CHAKRA.
BUT THAT'S THEN GOING TO PUT ME TO SLEEP.
DON'T UNLEASH YOUR JUTSU UNTIL THE LAST MINUTE, SO HE DOESN'T ABSORB MORE CHAKRA FROM YOU.
WELL, NOT THAT HE CAN USE HIS NEWLY AWAKENED RINNEGAN...
...TO ABSORB CHAKRA WHILE PUTTING OUT HIS OWN JUTSU.
TAK

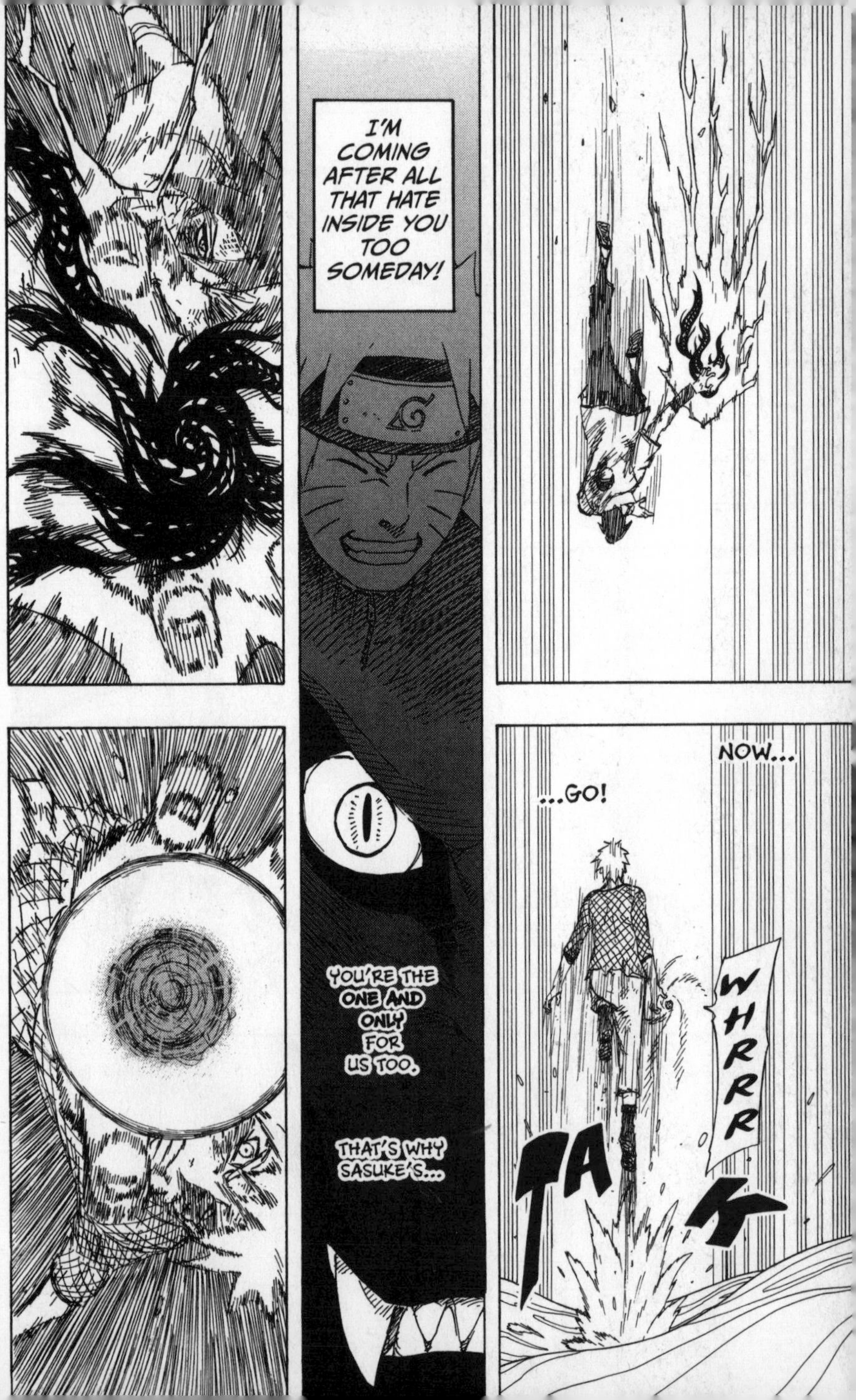
NOW...
...GO!
WHRRR
TAK
I'M COMING AFTER ALL THAT HATE INSIDE YOU TOO SOMEDAY!
YOU'RE THE ONE AND ONLY FOR US TOO.
THAT'S WHY SASUKE'S...

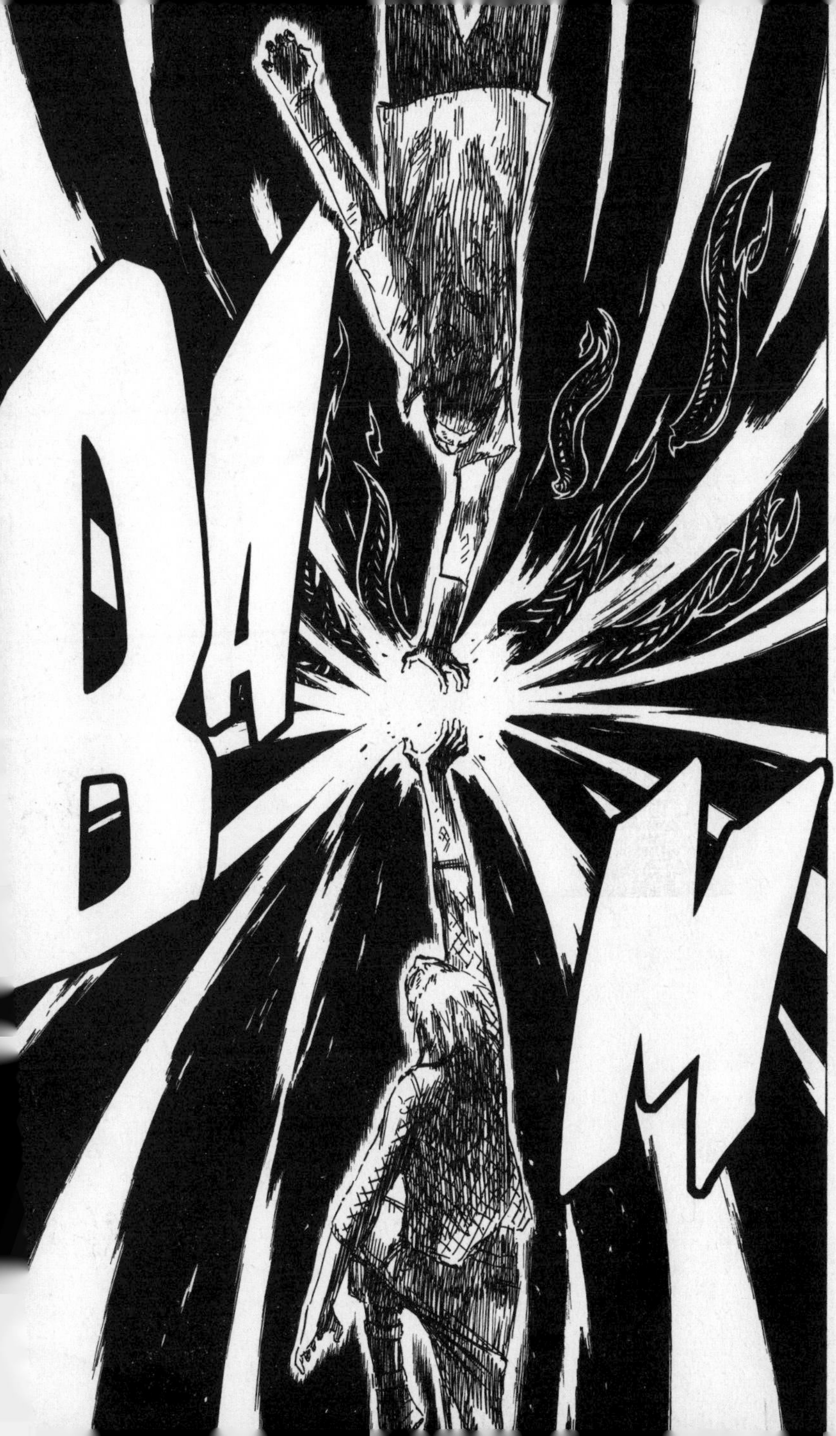
BAM

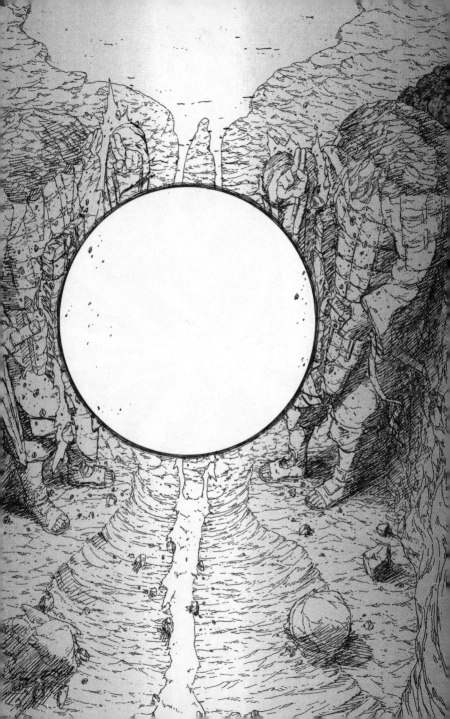

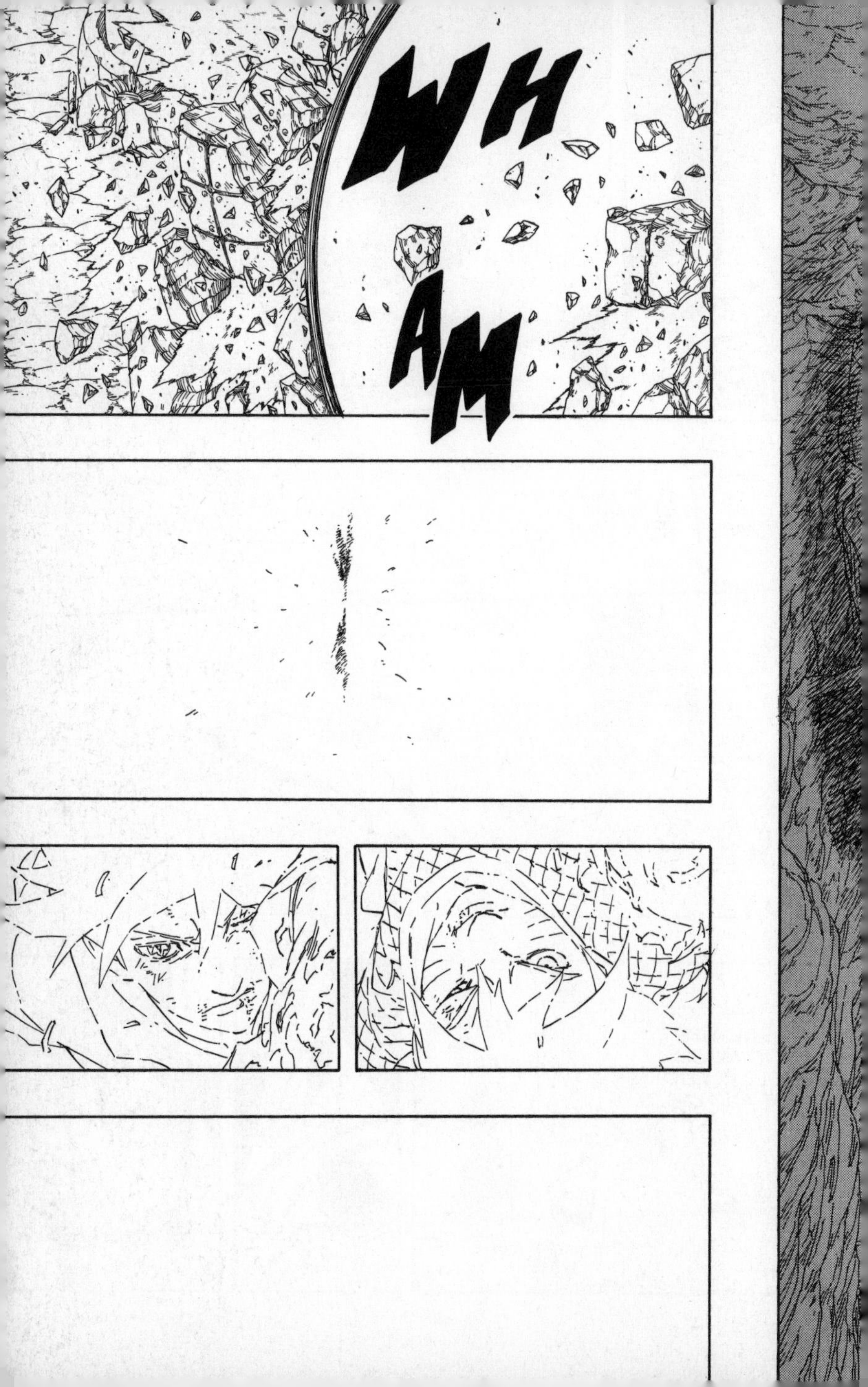
WHAM

UNH...

...

TWITCH

OW...

YOU'VE FINALLY COME TO, EH...

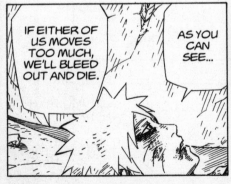

IF EITHER OF US MOVES TOO MUCH, WE'LL BLEED OUT AND DIE.

AS YOU CAN SEE...

!

...

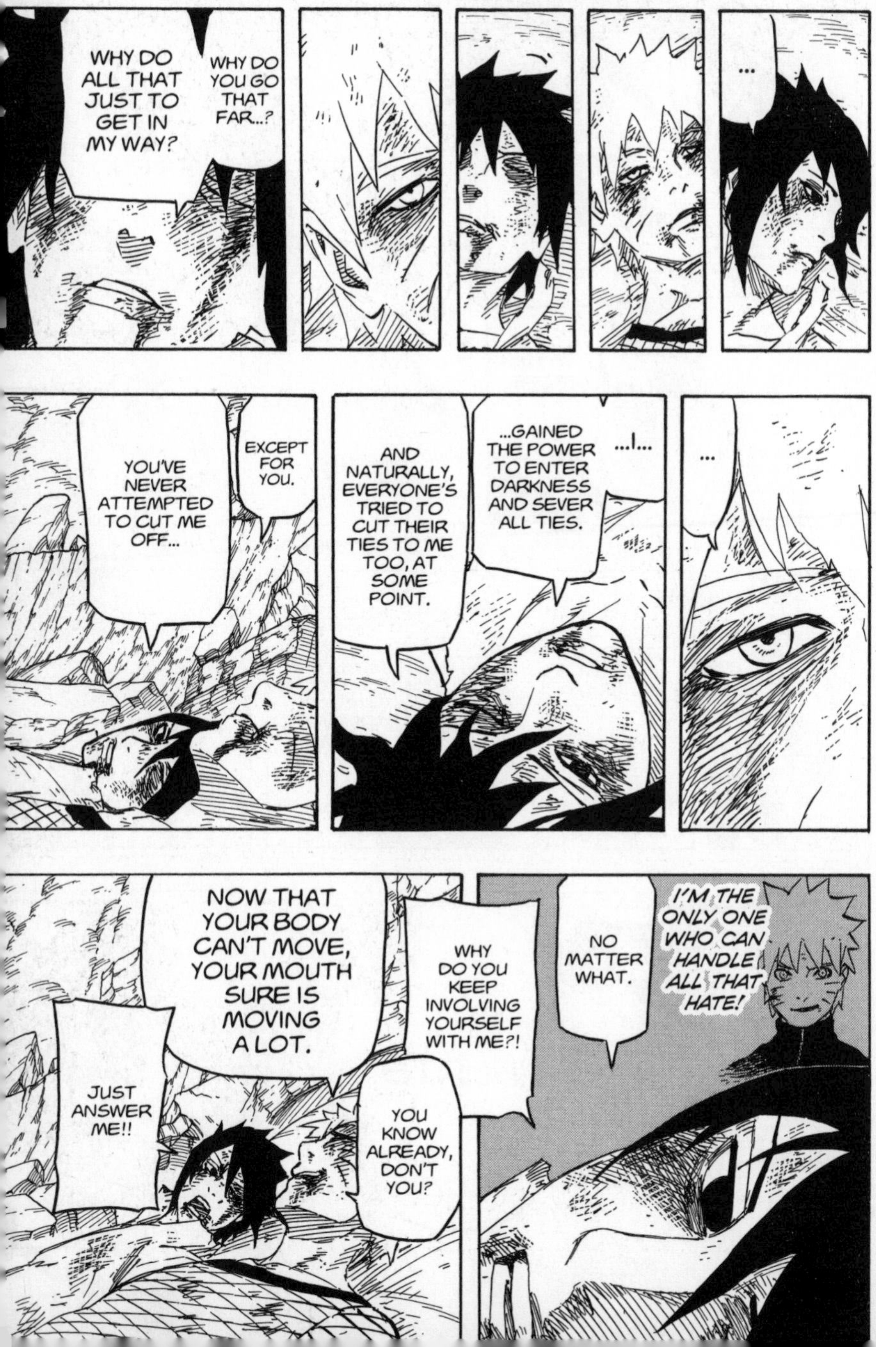
...
WHY DO YOU GO THAT FAR...?
WHY DO ALL THAT JUST TO GET IN MY WAY?
...
...I...
...GAINED THE POWER TO ENTER DARKNESS AND SEVER ALL TIES.
AND NATURALLY, EVERYONE'S TRIED TO CUT THEIR TIES TO ME TOO, AT SOME POINT.
EXCEPT FOR YOU.
YOU'VE NEVER ATTEMPTED TO CUT ME OFF...
I'M THE ONLY ONE WHO CAN HANDLE ALL THAT HATE!
NO MATTER WHAT.
WHY DO YOU KEEP INVOLVING YOURSELF WITH ME?!
NOW THAT YOUR BODY CAN'T MOVE, YOUR MOUTH SURE IS MOVING A LOT.
JUST ANSWER ME!!
YOU KNOW ALREADY, DON'T YOU?

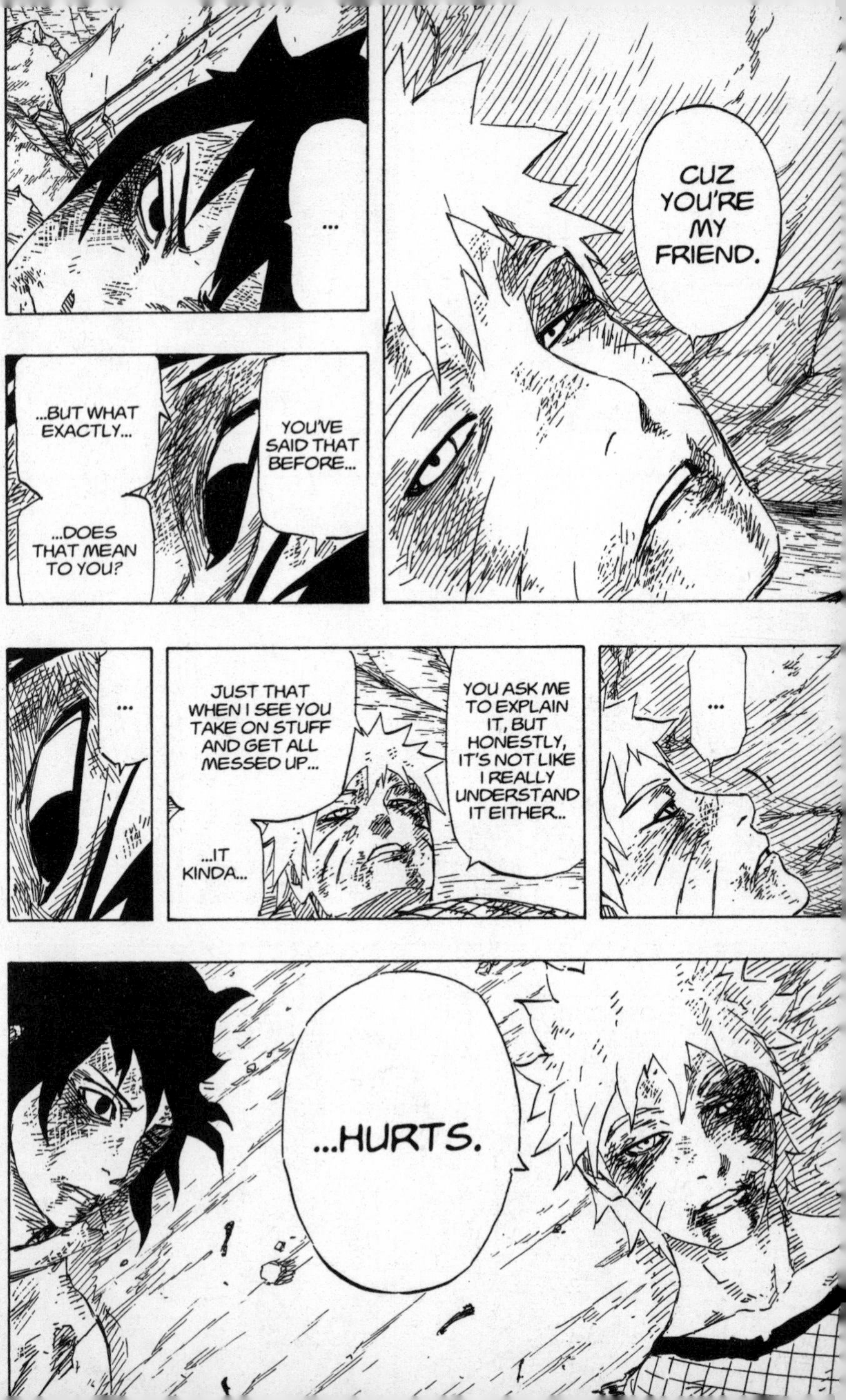
CUZ YOU'RE MY FRIEND.
...
YOU'VE SAID THAT BEFORE...
...BUT WHAT EXACTLY...
...DOES THAT MEAN TO YOU?
...
YOU ASK ME TO EXPLAIN IT, BUT HONESTLY, IT'S NOT LIKE I REALLY UNDERSTAND IT EITHER...
JUST THAT WHEN I SEE YOU TAKE ON STUFF AND GET ALL MESSED UP...
...IT KINDA...
...
...HURTS.

...INSIDE SO MUCH, I CAN'T JUST LEAVE IT ALONE!

IT HURTS...

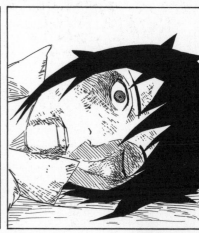

THOUGH TODAY I'M IN A TON OF PAIN EVERYWHERE.

...

OWW...

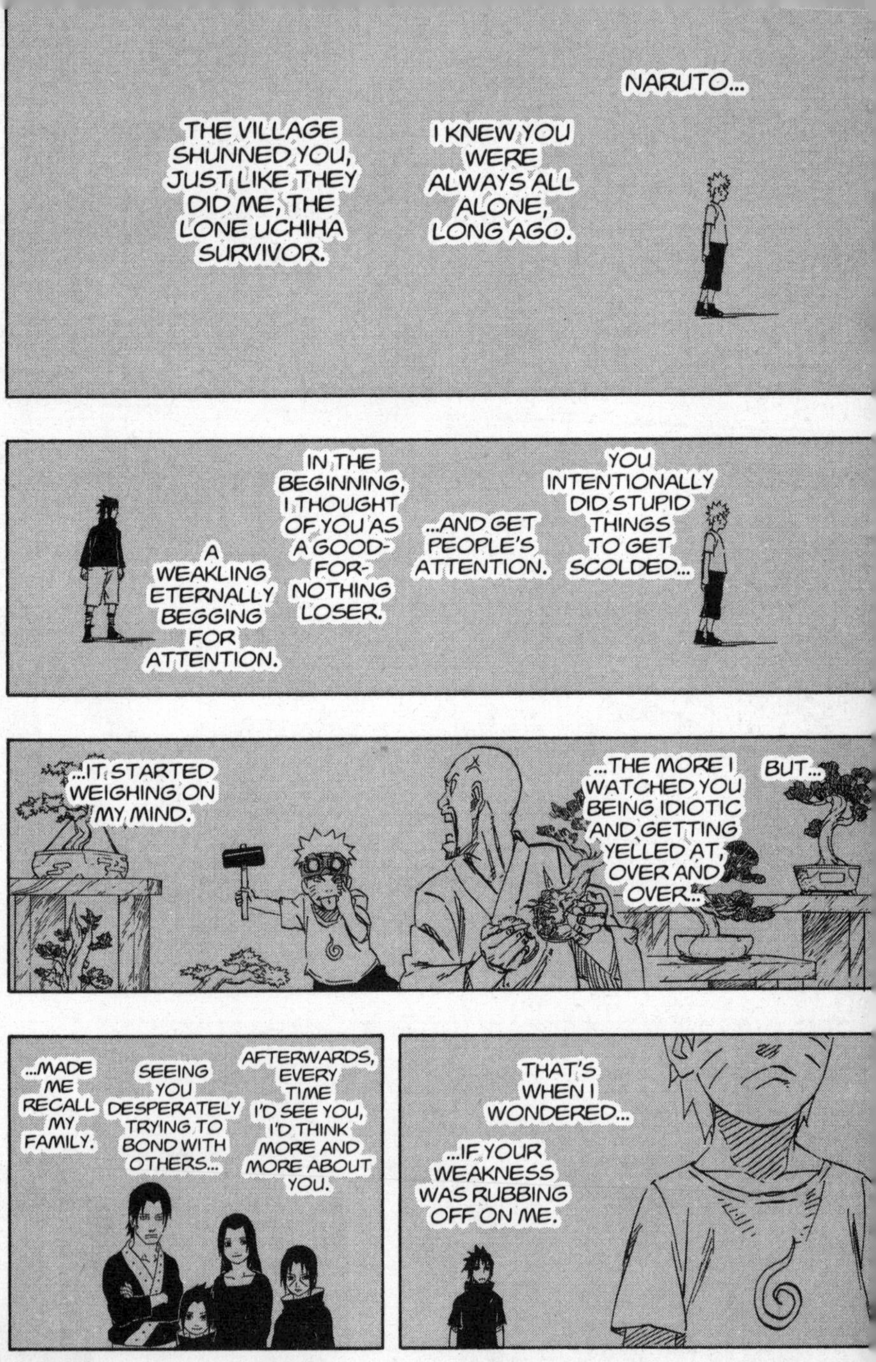
NARUTO...
I KNEW YOU WERE ALWAYS ALL ALONE, LONG AGO.
THE VILLAGE SHUNNED YOU, JUST LIKE THEY DID ME, THE LONE UCHIHA SURVIVOR.
YOU INTENTIONALLY DID STUPID THINGS TO GET SCOLDED...
...AND GET PEOPLE'S ATTENTION.
IN THE BEGINNING, I THOUGHT OF YOU AS A GOOD-FOR-NOTHING LOSER.
A WEAKLING ETERNALLY BEGGING FOR ATTENTION.
BUT...
...THE MORE I WATCHED YOU BEING IDIOTIC AND GETTING YELLED AT, OVER AND OVER...
...IT STARTED WEIGHING ON MY MIND.
THAT'S WHEN I WONDERED...
...IF YOUR WEAKNESS WAS RUBBING OFF ON ME.
AFTERWARDS, EVERY TIME I'D SEE YOU, I'D THINK MORE AND MORE ABOUT YOU.
SEEING YOU DESPERATELY TRYING TO BOND WITH OTHERS...
...MADE ME RECALL MY FAMILY.

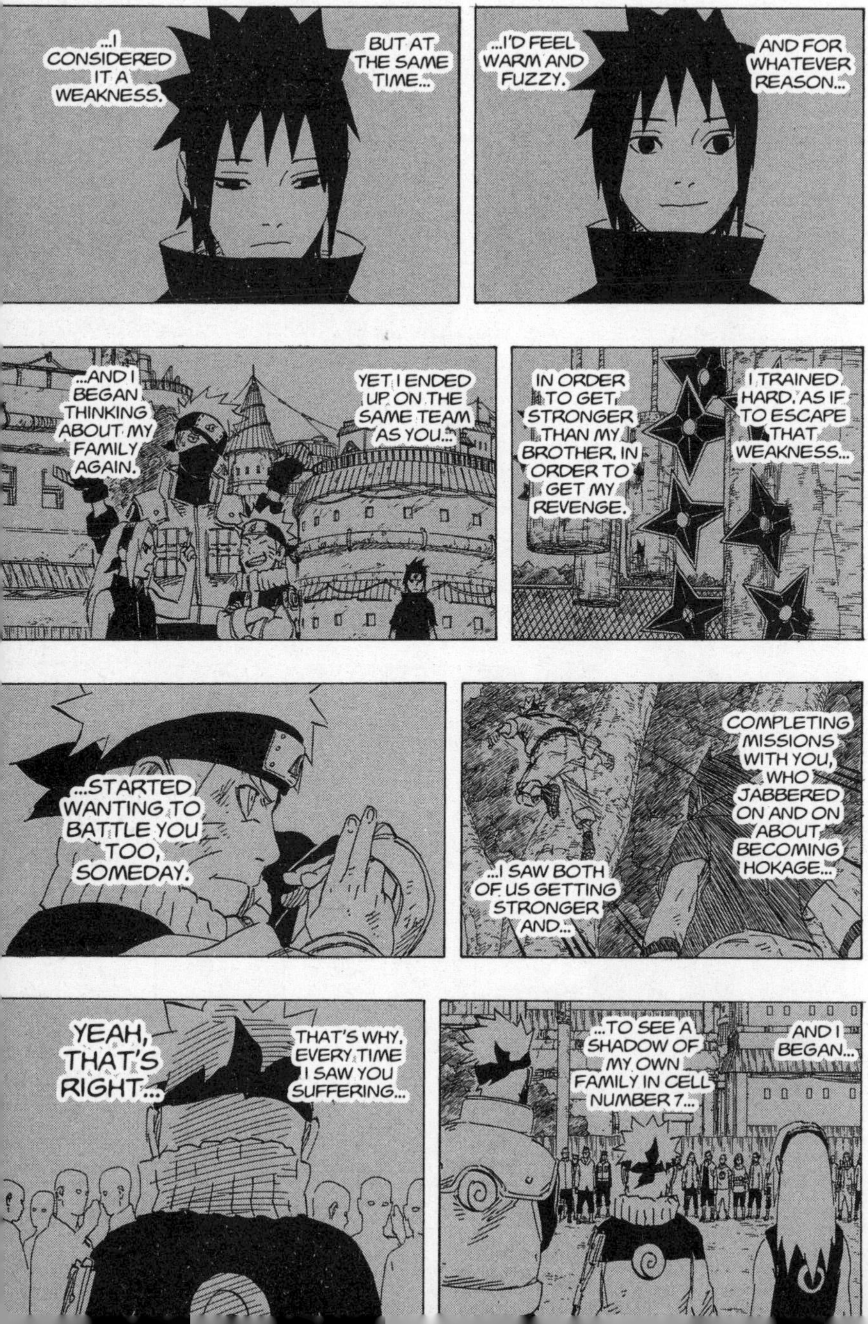
AND FOR WHATEVER REASON...
...I'D FEEL WARM AND FUZZY.
BUT AT THE SAME TIME...
...I CONSIDERED IT A WEAKNESS.
I TRAINED HARD, AS IF TO ESCAPE THAT WEAKNESS...
IN ORDER TO GET STRONGER THAN MY BROTHER, IN ORDER TO GET MY REVENGE.
YET I ENDED UP ON THE SAME TEAM AS YOU...
...AND I BEGAN THINKING ABOUT MY FAMILY AGAIN.
COMPLETING MISSIONS WITH YOU, WHO JABBERED ON AND ON ABOUT BECOMING HOKAGE...
...I SAW BOTH OF US GETTING STRONGER AND...
...STARTED WANTING TO BATTLE YOU TOO, SOMEDAY.
AND I BEGAN...
...TO SEE A SHADOW OF MY OWN FAMILY IN CELL NUMBER 7...
THAT'S WHY, EVERY TIME I SAW YOU SUFFERING...
YEAH, THAT'S RIGHT...

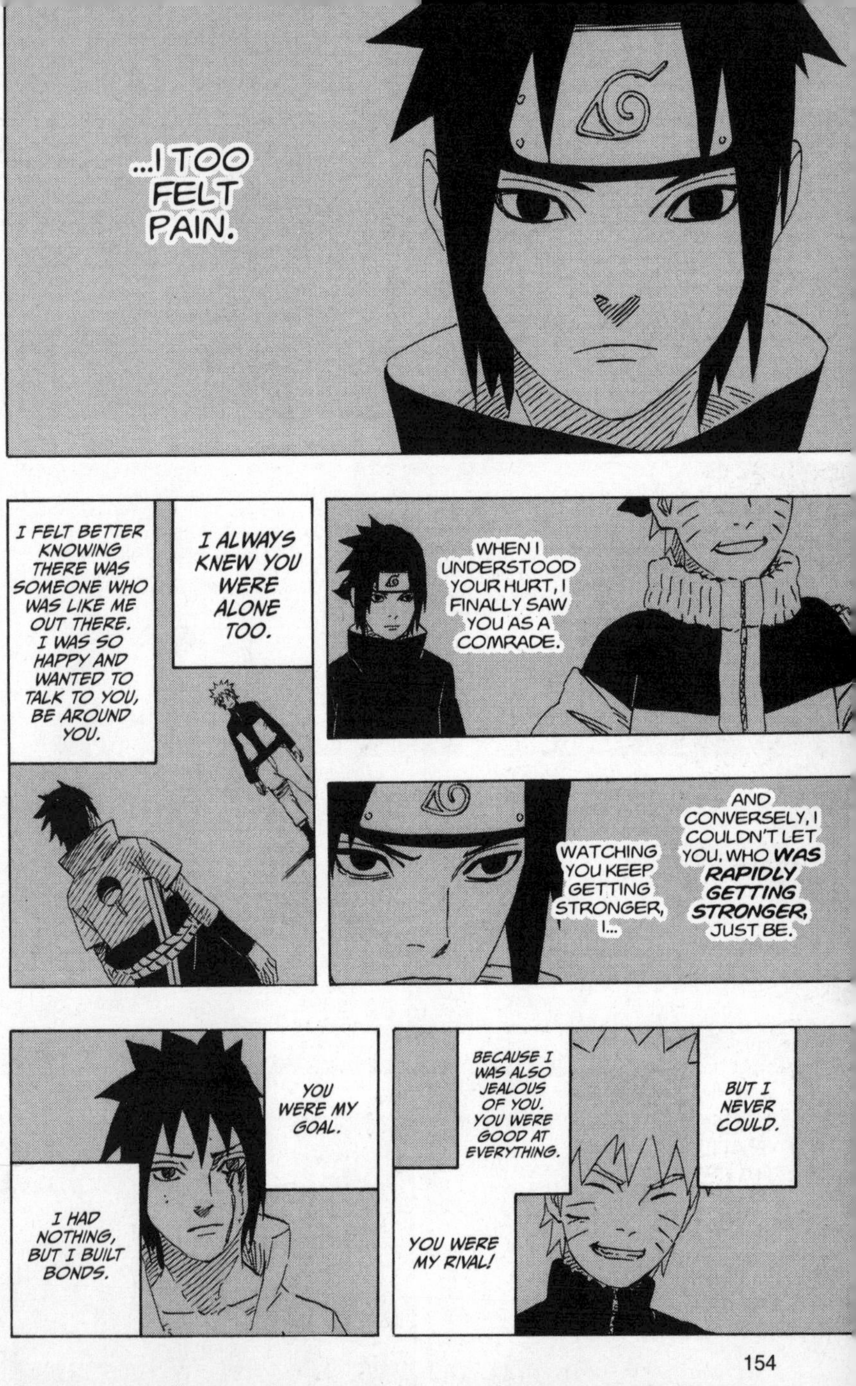

...I TOO FELT PAIN.
WHEN I UNDERSTOOD YOUR HURT, I FINALLY SAW YOU AS A COMRADE.
AND CONVERSELY, I COULDN'T LET YOU, WHO **WAS RAPIDLY GETTING STRONGER,** JUST BE.
WATCHING YOU KEEP GETTING STRONGER, I...
I ALWAYS KNEW YOU WERE ALONE TOO.
I FELT BETTER KNOWING THERE WAS SOMEONE WHO WAS LIKE ME OUT THERE. I WAS SO HAPPY AND WANTED TO TALK TO YOU, BE AROUND YOU.
BUT I NEVER COULD.
BECAUSE I WAS ALSO JEALOUS OF YOU. YOU WERE GOOD AT EVERYTHING.
YOU WERE MY RIVAL!
YOU WERE MY GOAL.
I HAD NOTHING, BUT I BUILT BONDS.

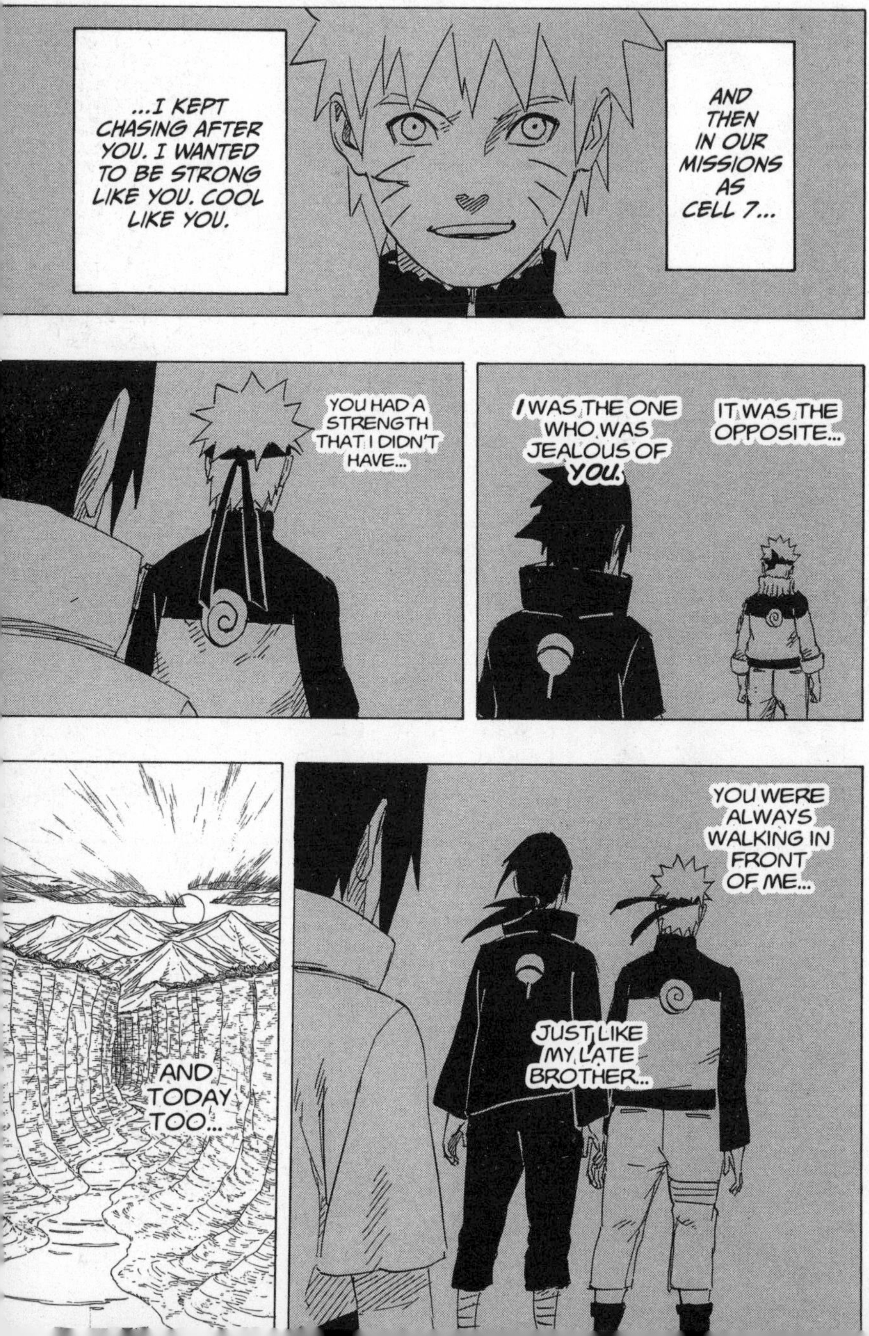
AND THEN IN OUR MISSIONS AS CELL 7...
...I KEPT CHASING AFTER YOU. I WANTED TO BE STRONG LIKE YOU. COOL LIKE YOU.
IT WAS THE OPPOSITE...
I WAS THE ONE WHO WAS JEALOUS OF YOU.
YOU HAD A STRENGTH THAT I DIDN'T HAVE...
YOU WERE ALWAYS WALKING IN FRONT OF ME...
JUST LIKE MY LATE BROTHER...
AND TODAY TOO...

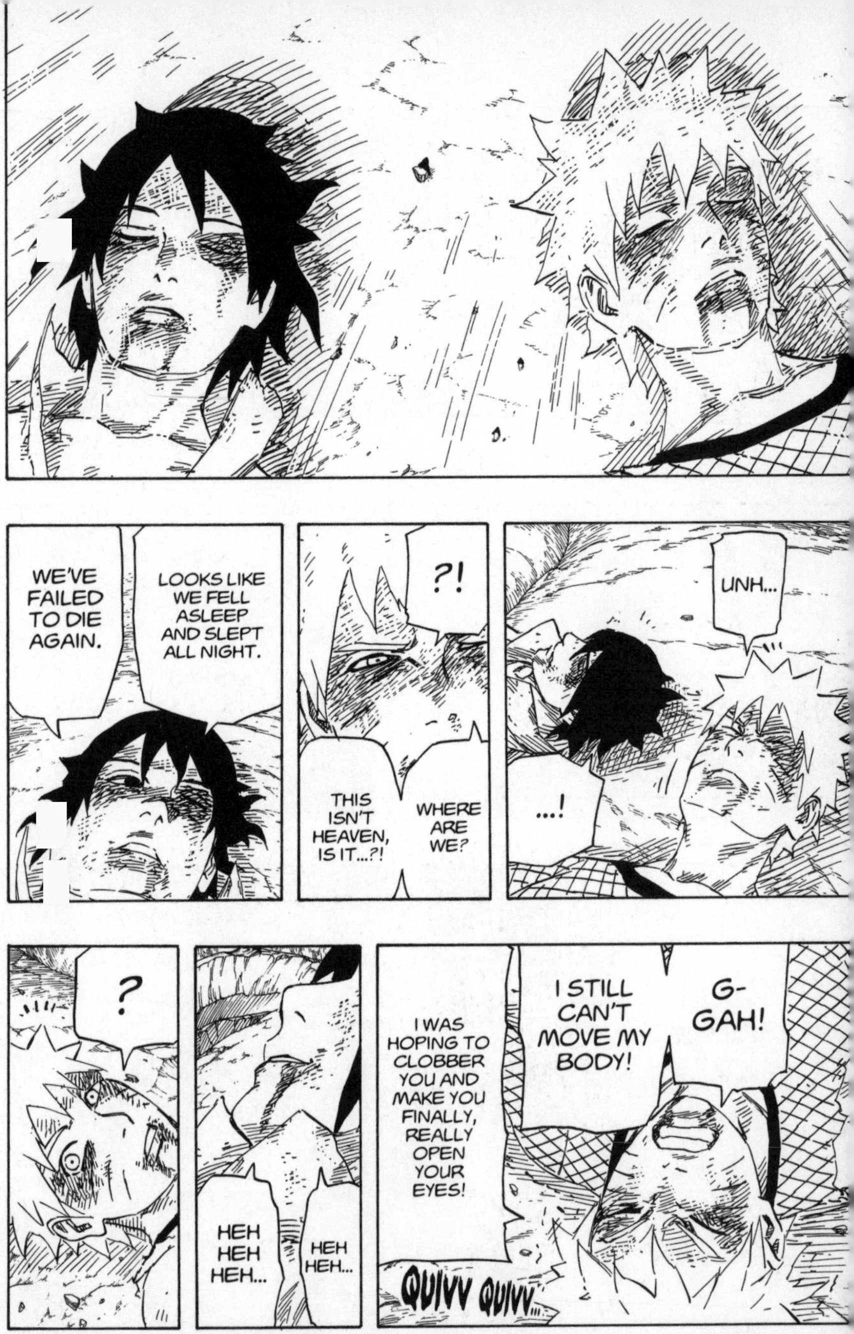
UNH...
...!
?!
WHERE ARE WE?
THIS ISN'T HEAVEN, IS IT...?!
LOOKS LIKE WE FELL ASLEEP AND SLEPT ALL NIGHT.
WE'VE FAILED TO DIE AGAIN.
G-GAH!
I STILL CAN'T MOVE MY BODY!
I WAS HOPING TO CLOBBER YOU AND MAKE YOU FINALLY, REALLY OPEN YOUR EYES!
QUIVV QUIVV...
HEH HEH...
HEH HEH HEH...
?

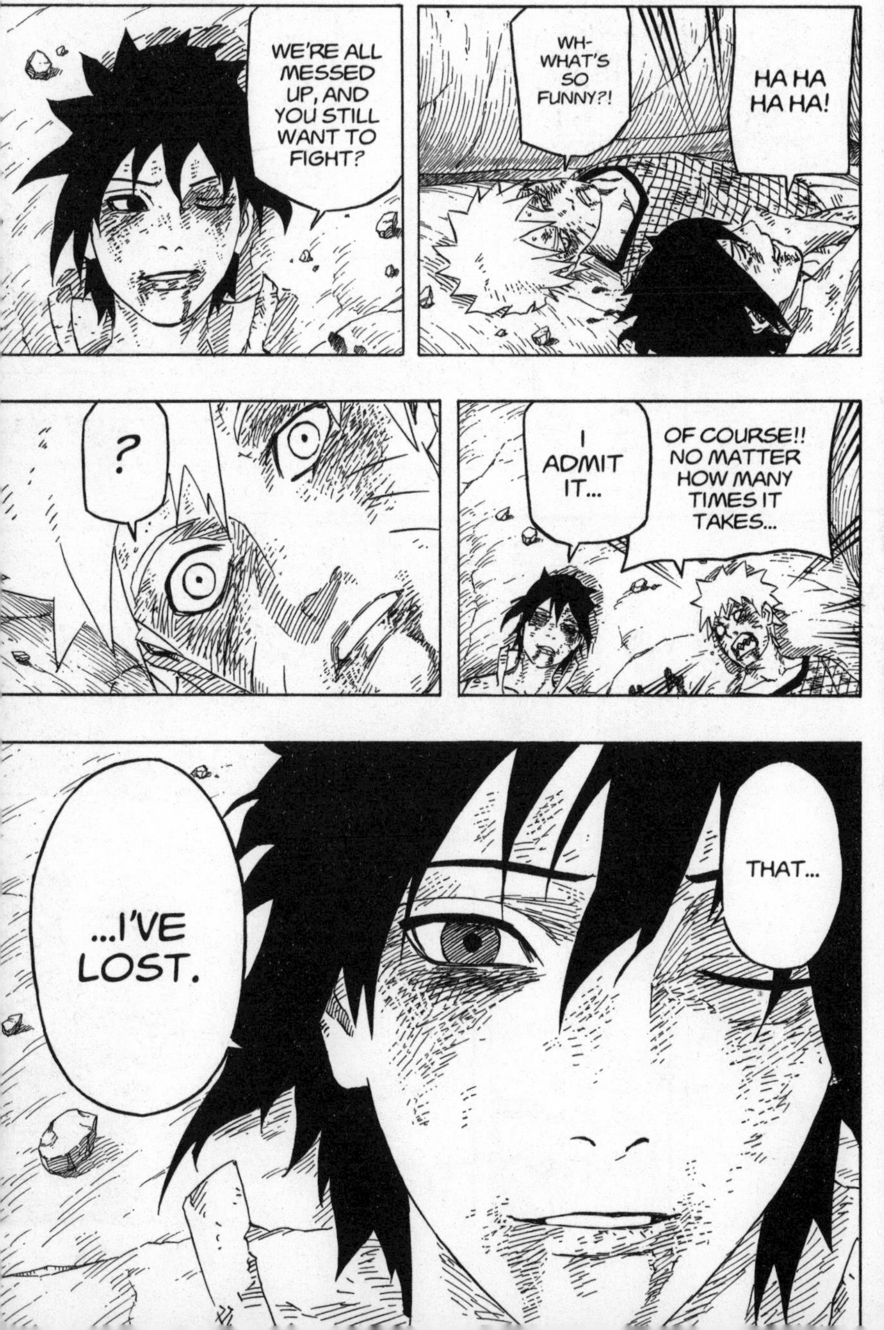
HA HA HA HA!
WH- WHAT'S SO FUNNY?!
WE'RE ALL MESSED UP, AND YOU STILL WANT TO FIGHT?
OF COURSE!! NO MATTER HOW MANY TIMES IT TAKES...
I ADMIT IT...
?
THAT...
...I'VE LOST.

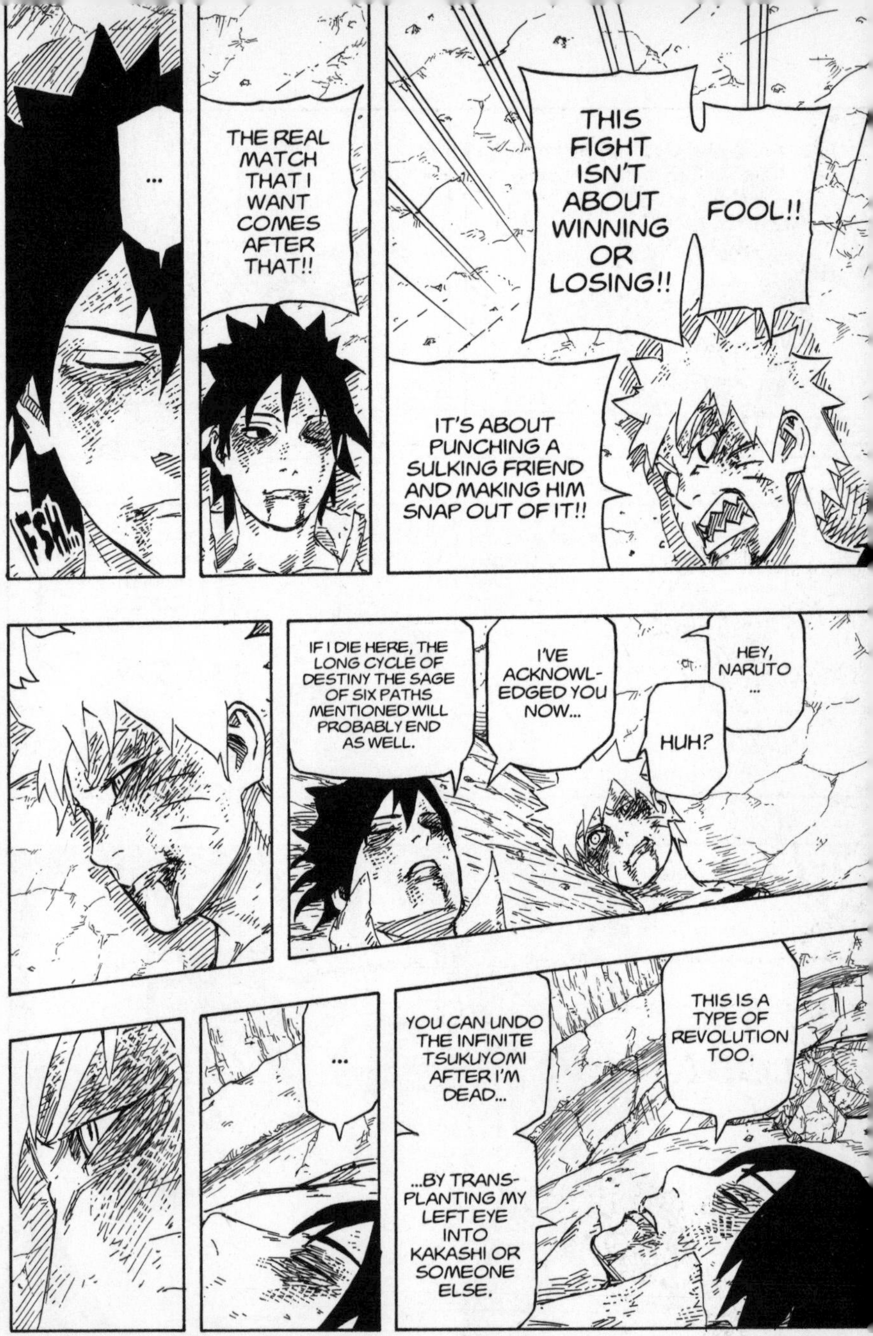
FOOL!!
THIS FIGHT ISN'T ABOUT WINNING OR LOSING!!
IT'S ABOUT PUNCHING A SULKING FRIEND AND MAKING HIM SNAP OUT OF IT!!
THE REAL MATCH THAT I WANT COMES AFTER THAT!!
...
FSH...
HEY, NARUTO ...
HUH?
I'VE ACKNOWL-EDGED YOU NOW...
IF I DIE HERE, THE LONG CYCLE OF DESTINY THE SAGE OF SIX PATHS MENTIONED WILL PROBABLY END AS WELL.
THIS IS A TYPE OF REVOLUTION TOO.
YOU CAN UNDO THE INFINITE TSUKUYOMI AFTER I'M DEAD...
...BY TRANS-PLANTING MY LEFT EYE INTO KAKASHI OR SOMEONE ELSE.
...

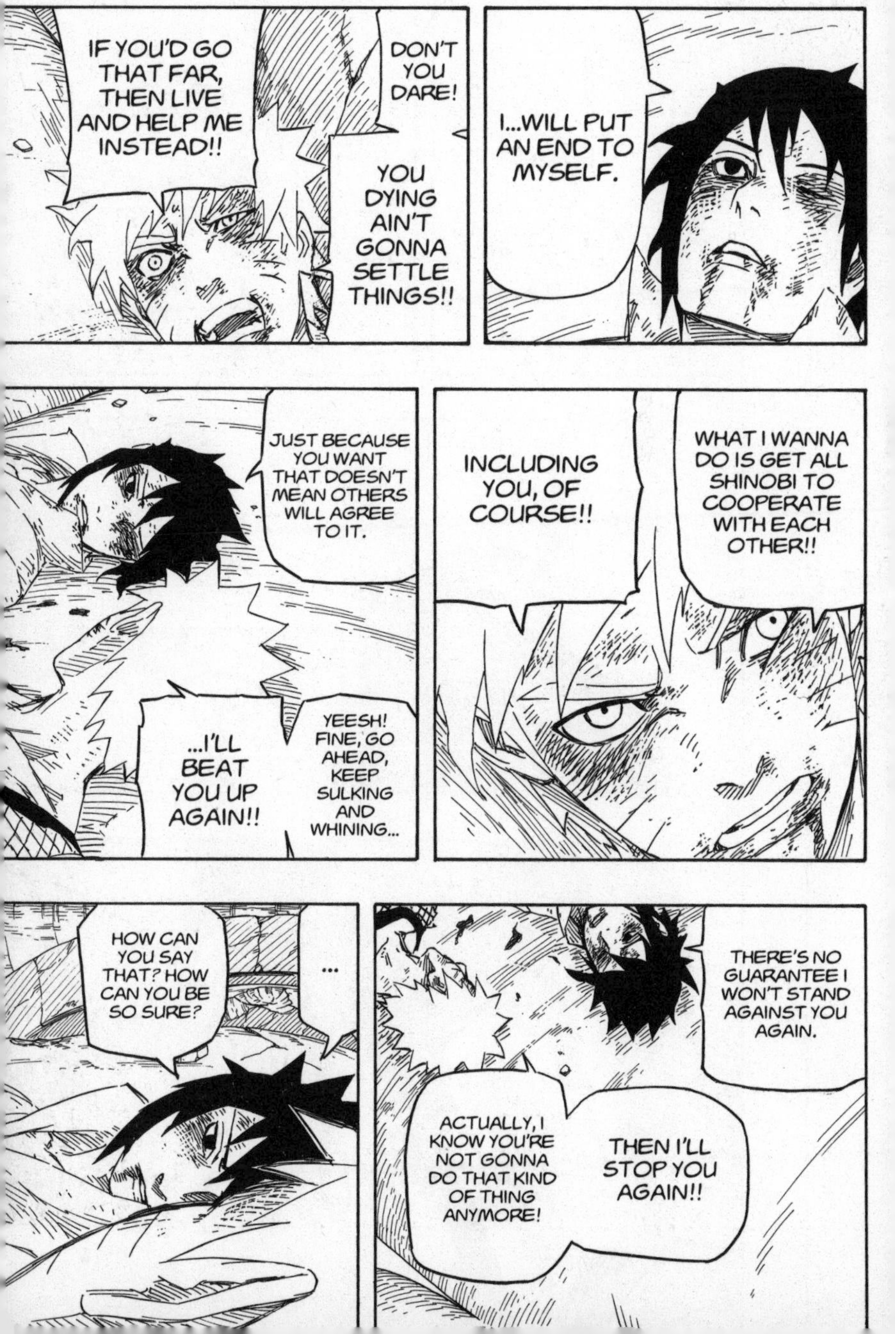
I...WILL PUT AN END TO MYSELF.
DON'T YOU DARE!
YOU DYING AIN'T GONNA SETTLE THINGS!!
IF YOU'D GO THAT FAR, THEN LIVE AND HELP ME INSTEAD!!
WHAT I WANNA DO IS GET ALL SHINOBI TO COOPERATE WITH EACH OTHER!!
INCLUDING YOU, OF COURSE!!
JUST BECAUSE YOU WANT THAT DOESN'T MEAN OTHERS WILL AGREE TO IT.
YEESH! FINE, GO AHEAD, KEEP SULKING AND WHINING...
...I'LL BEAT YOU UP AGAIN!!
THERE'S NO GUARANTEE I WON'T STAND AGAINST YOU AGAIN.
THEN I'LL STOP YOU AGAIN!!
ACTUALLY, I KNOW YOU'RE NOT GONNA DO THAT KIND OF THING ANYMORE!
...
HOW CAN YOU SAY THAT? HOW CAN YOU BE SO SURE?

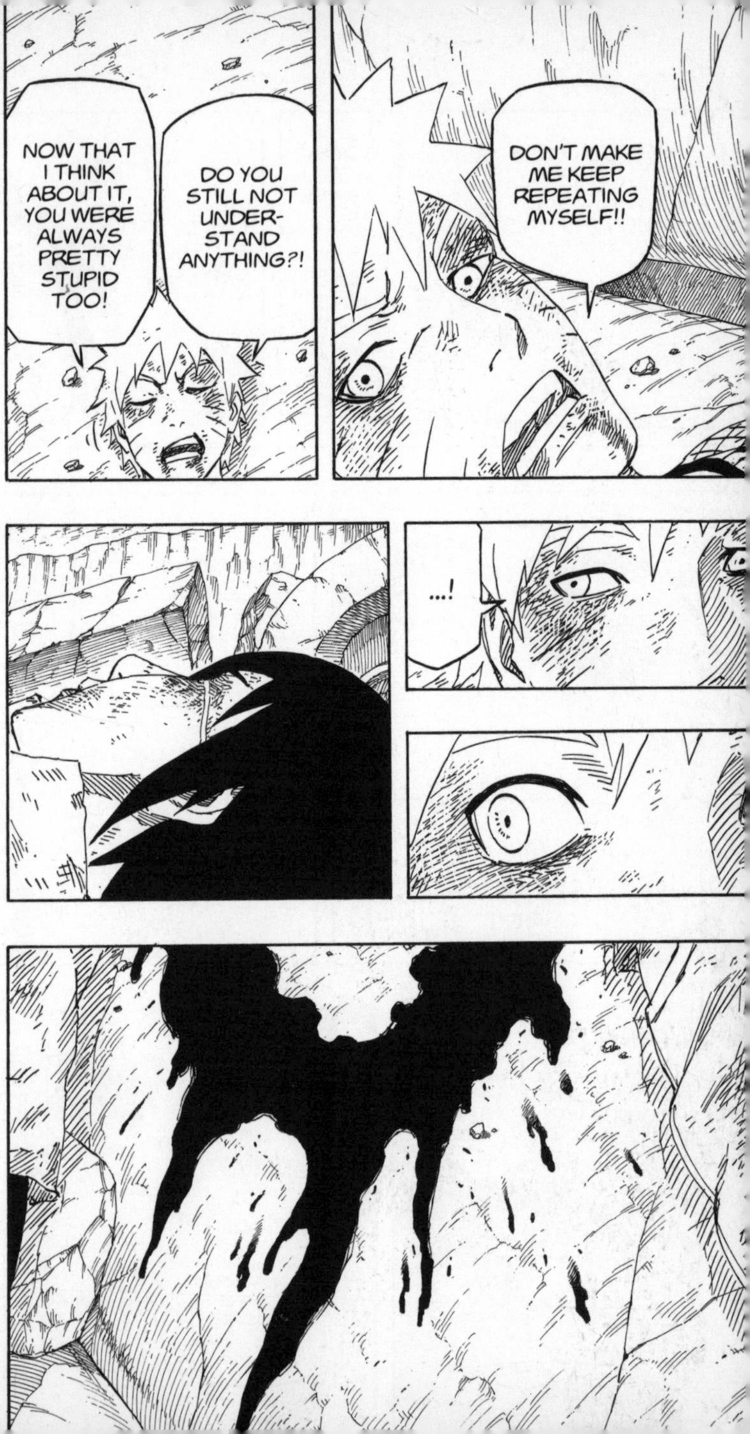
DON'T MAKE ME KEEP REPEATING MYSELF!!
DO YOU STILL NOT UNDER-STAND ANYTHING?!
NOW THAT I THINK ABOUT IT, YOU WERE ALWAYS PRETTY STUPID TOO!
...!

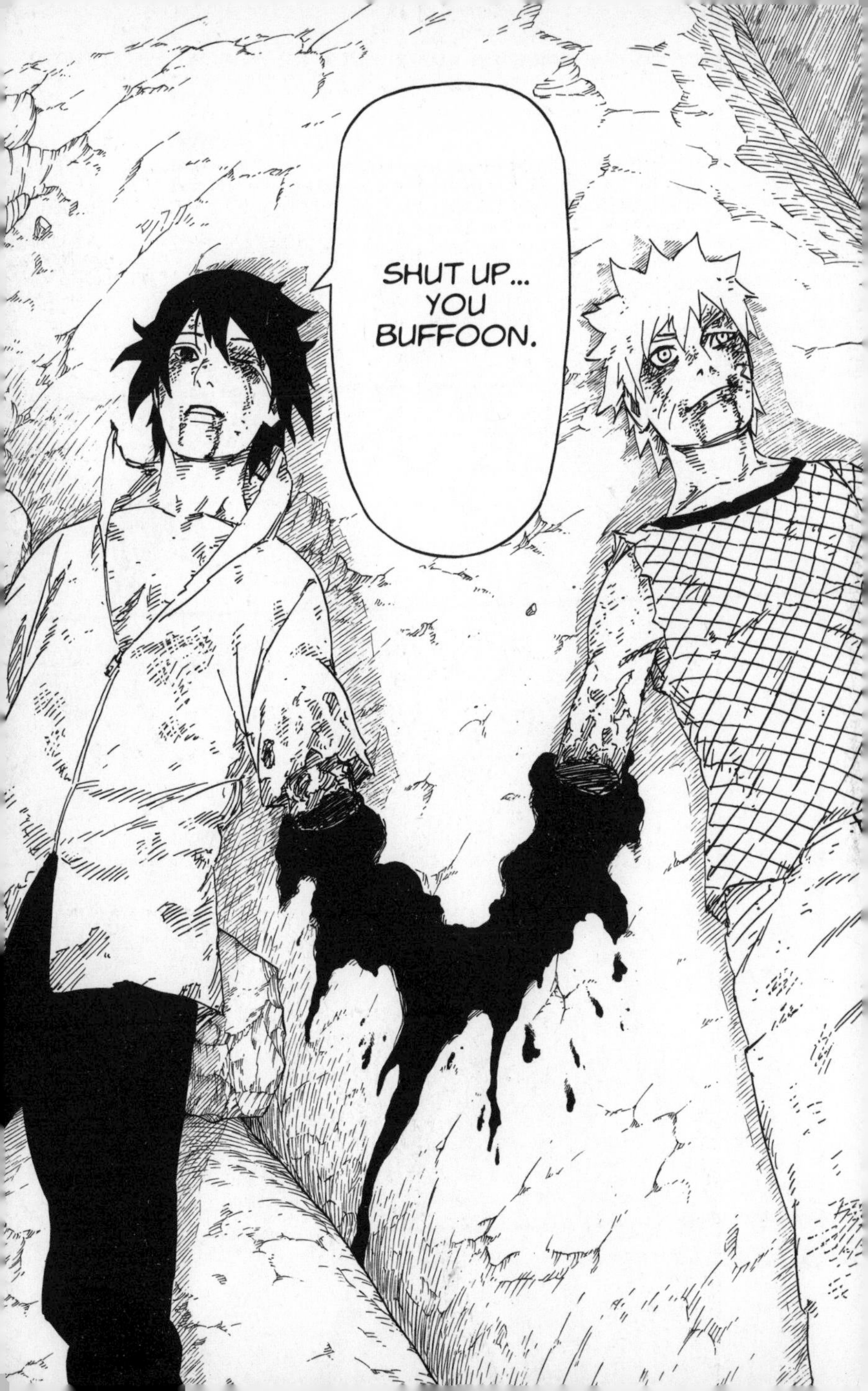
SHUT UP... YOU BUFFOON.

END OF SERIES COMMEMORATION ILLUSTRATION (8) MASARU MATSUBARA

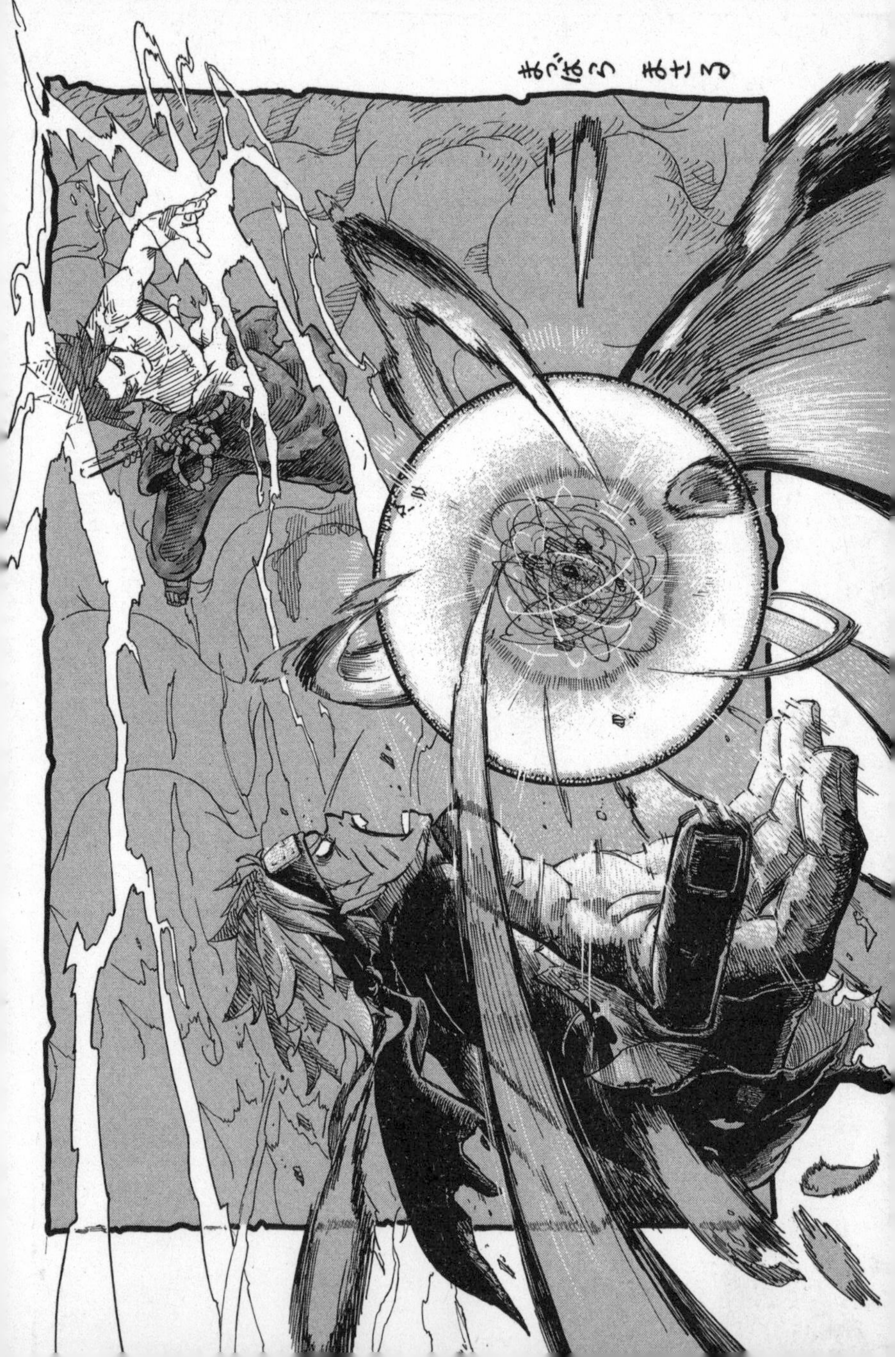

Number 699: Unison Sign

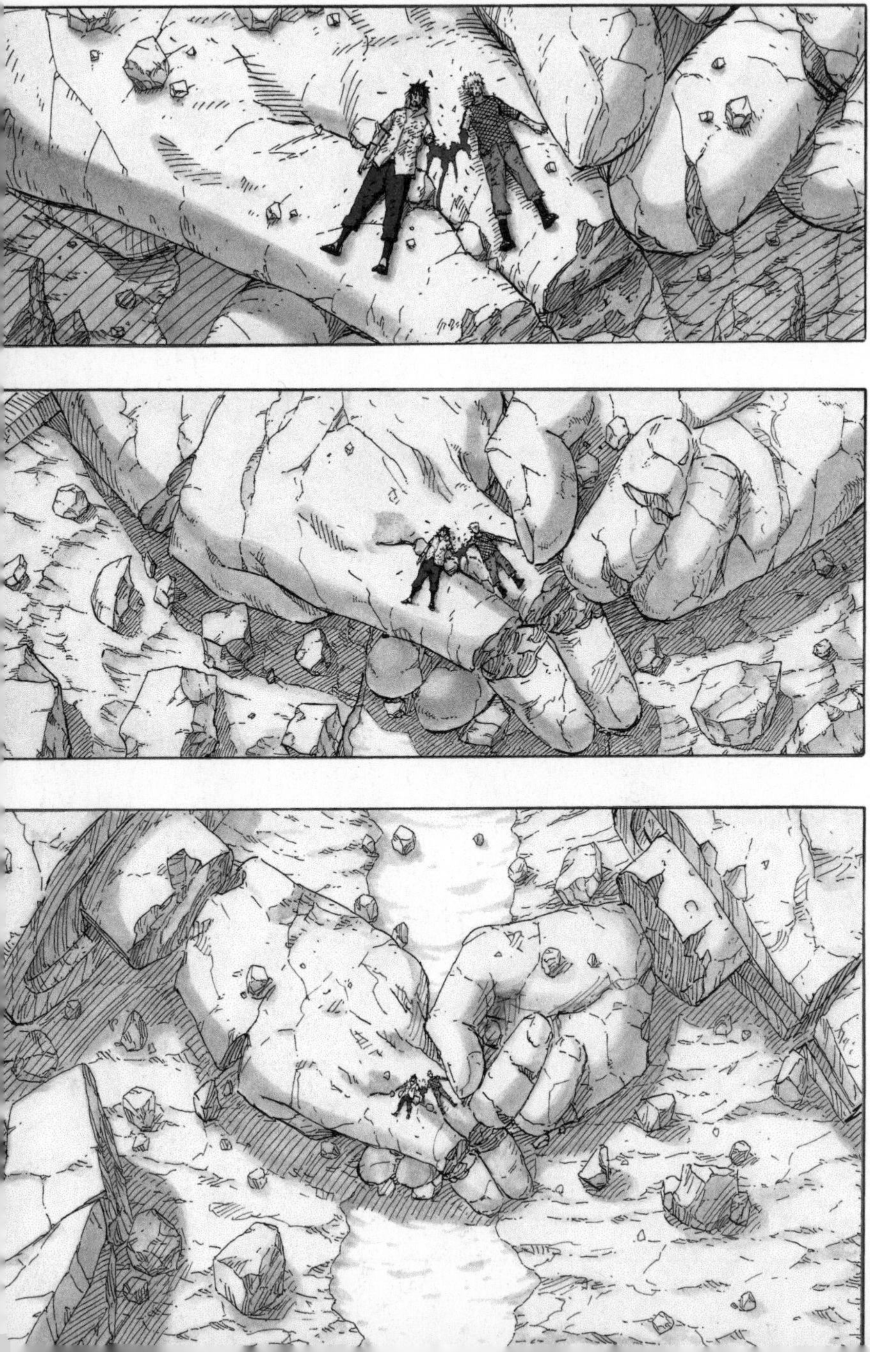

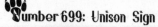

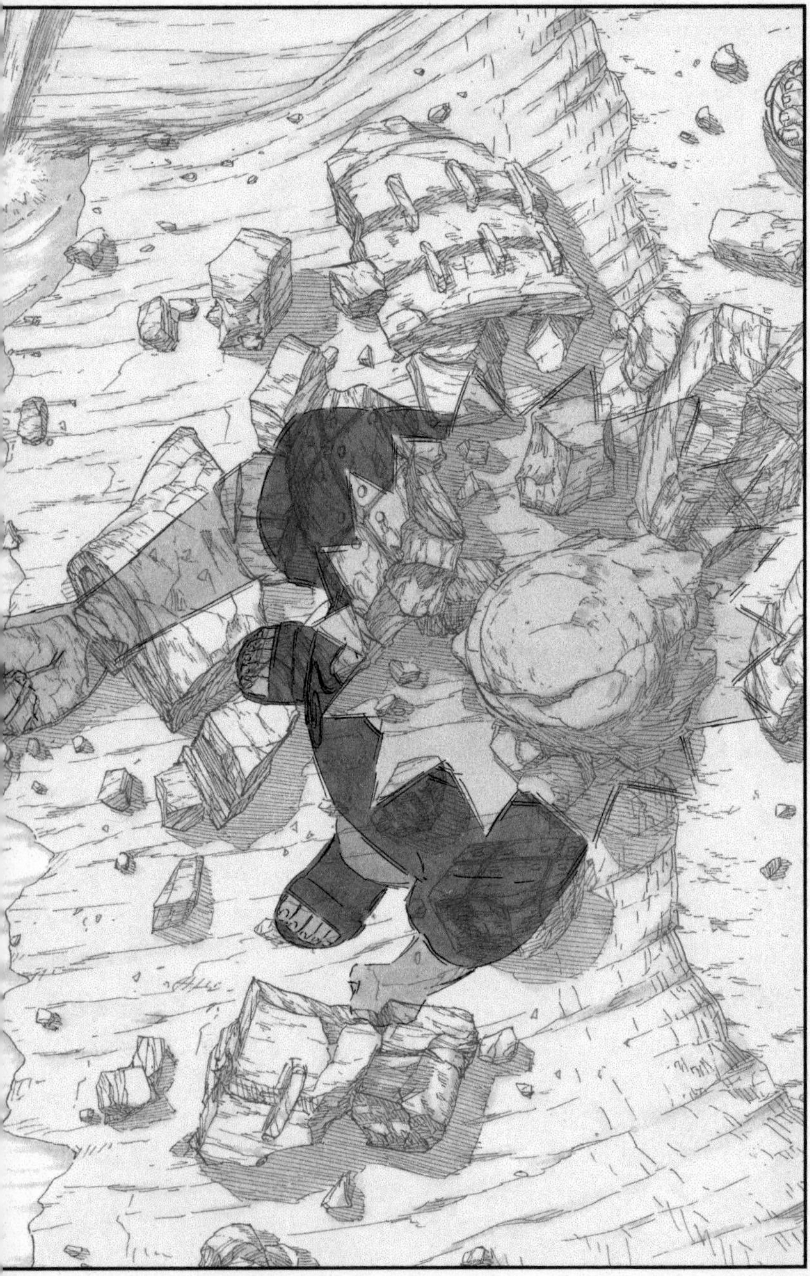

Number 699: Unison Sign

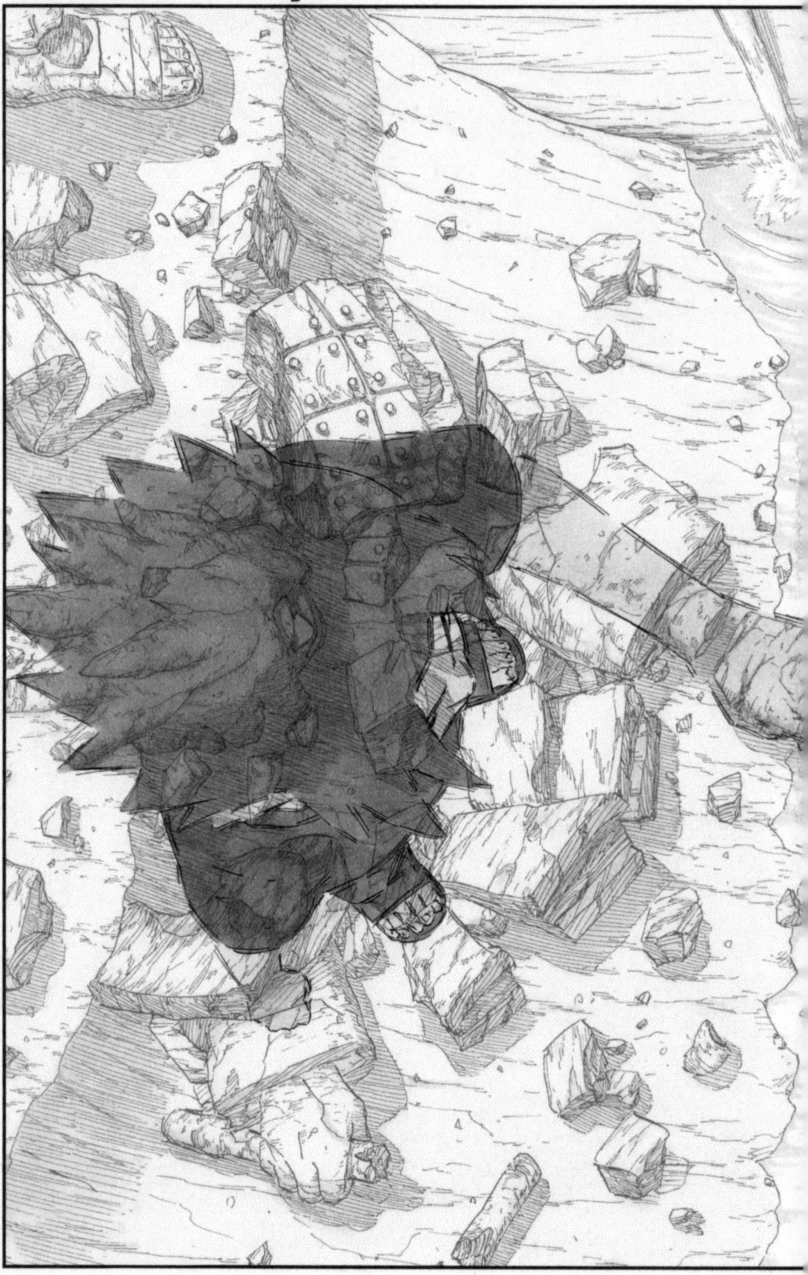

END OF SERIES COMMEMORATION ILLUSTRATION (9)

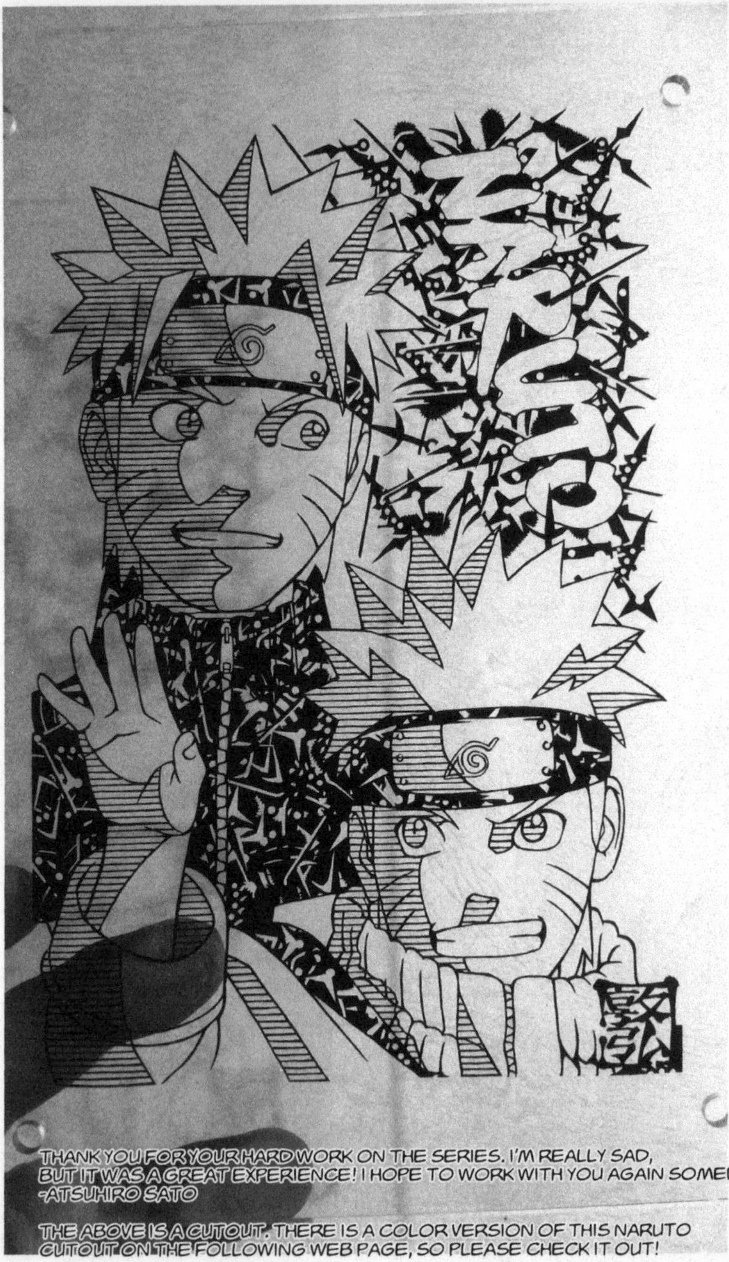

THANK YOU FOR YOUR HARD WORK ON THE SERIES. I'M REALLY SAD, BUT IT WAS A GREAT EXPERIENCE! I HOPE TO WORK WITH YOU AGAIN SOMEDAY.
-ATSUHIRO SATO

THE ABOVE IS A CUTOUT. THERE IS A COLOR VERSION OF THIS NARUTO CUTOUT ON THE FOLLOWING WEB PAGE, SO PLEASE CHECK IT OUT!

CUTOUT ARTIST ATSUHIRO   HTTP://KIRIEATSU.BLOG.FC2.COM/

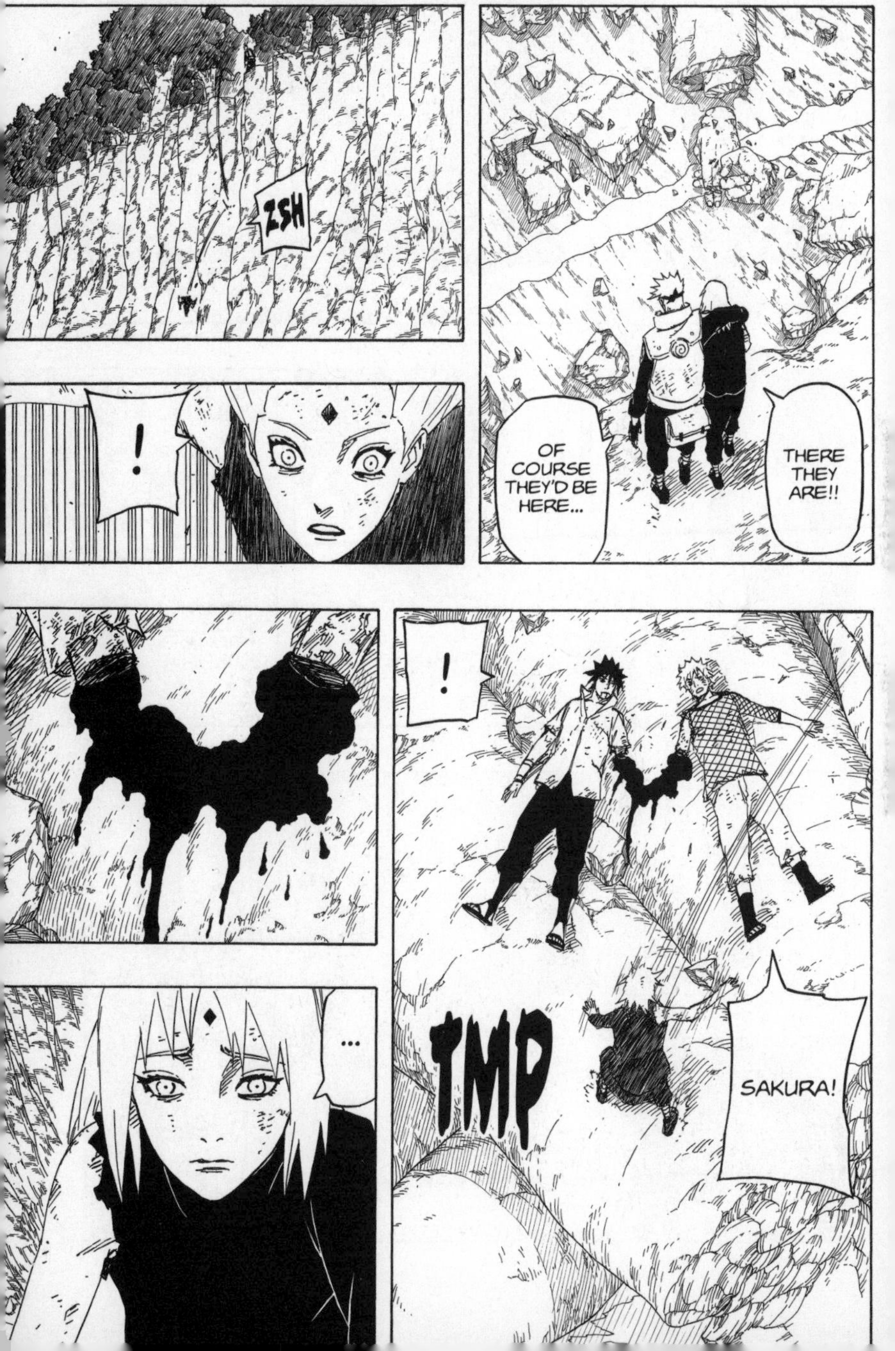
THERE THEY ARE!!
OF COURSE THEY'D BE HERE...
ZSH
!
!
SAKURA!
TMP
...

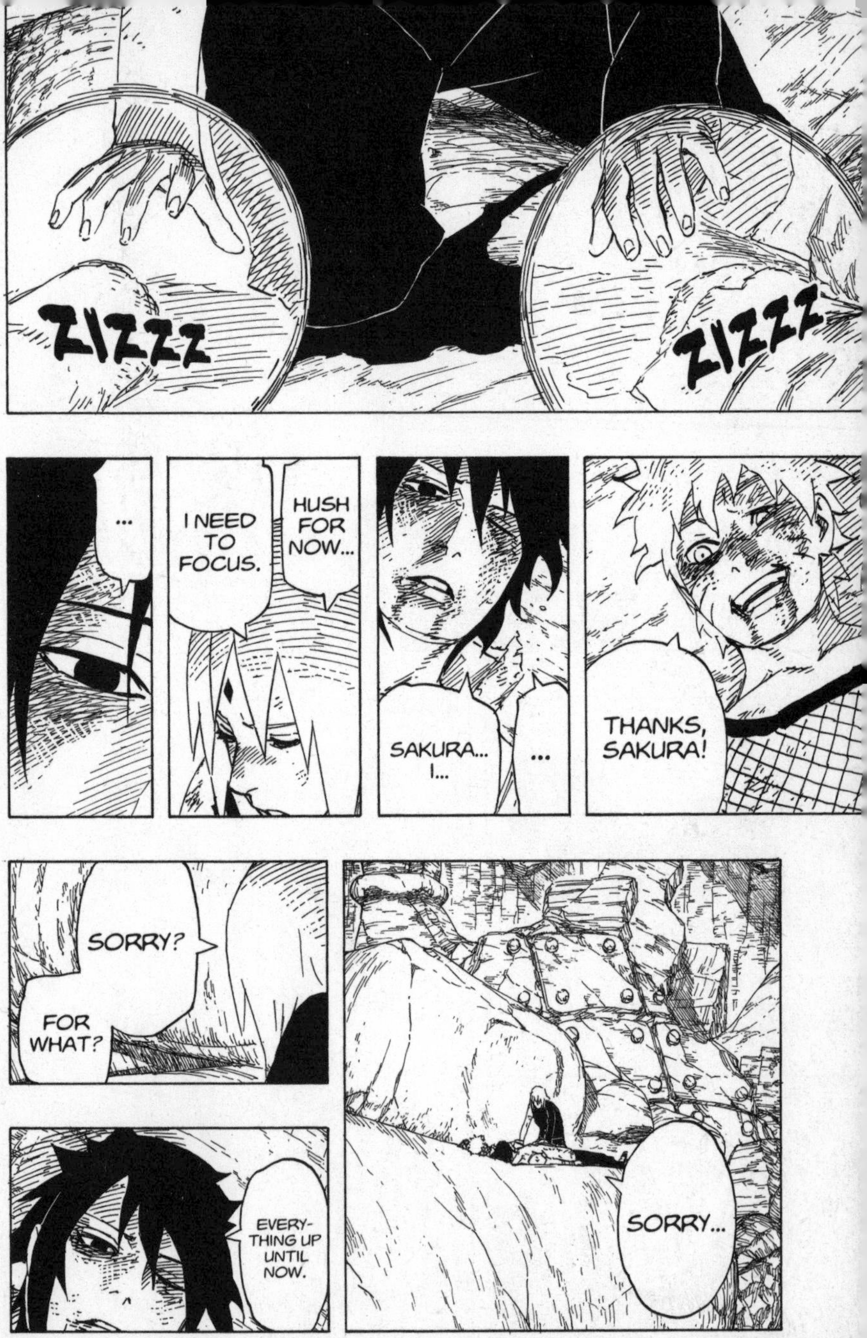
ZIZZZ
ZIZZZ
THANKS, SAKURA!
...
SAKURA... I...
HUSH FOR NOW...
I NEED TO FOCUS.
...
SORRY...
SORRY?
FOR WHAT?
EVERY-THING UP UNTIL NOW.

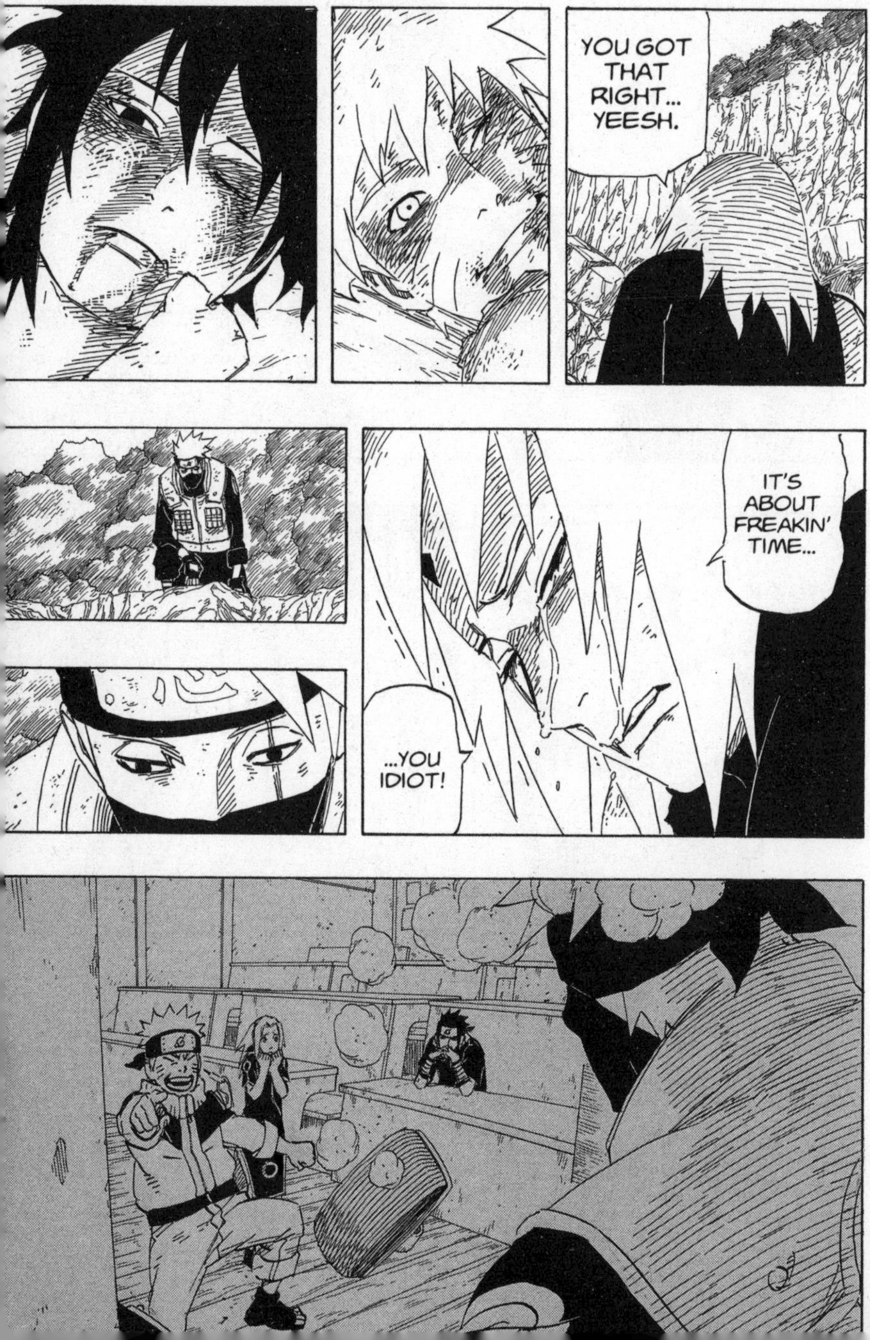
YOU GOT THAT RIGHT... YEESH.
IT'S ABOUT FREAKIN' TIME...
...YOU IDIOT!

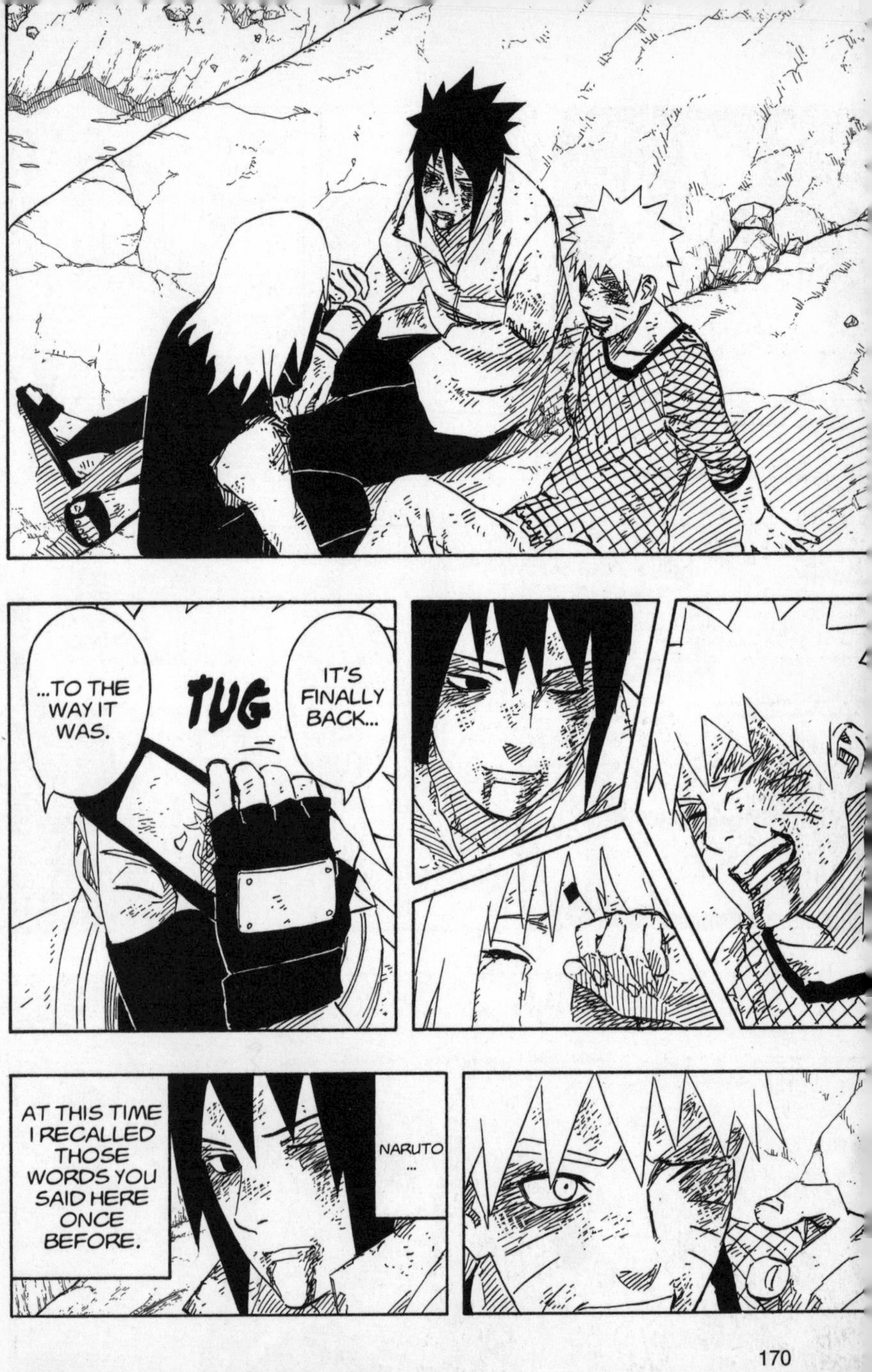
IT'S FINALLY BACK...
TUG
...TO THE WAY IT WAS.
NARUTO ...
AT THIS TIME I RECALLED THOSE WORDS YOU SAID HERE ONCE BEFORE.

HOW WHEN
YOU'RE WITH
ME YOU
WONDER IF
THIS IS WHAT
IT'S LIKE TO
HAVE A
BROTHER...

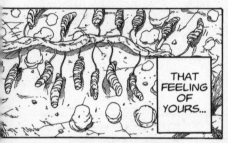

THAT
FEELING
OF
YOURS...

...I THINK I
FINALLY
GET WHAT
YOU
MEANT.

?!

UGH!

FWMP

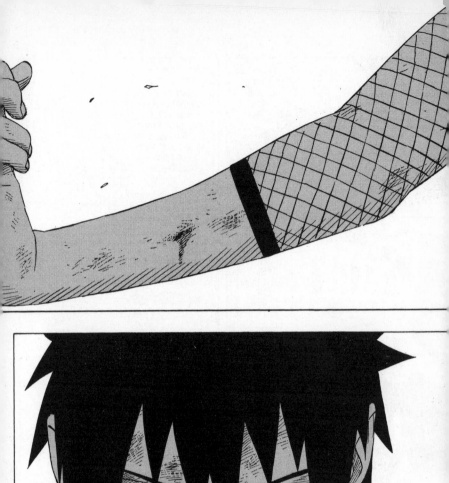

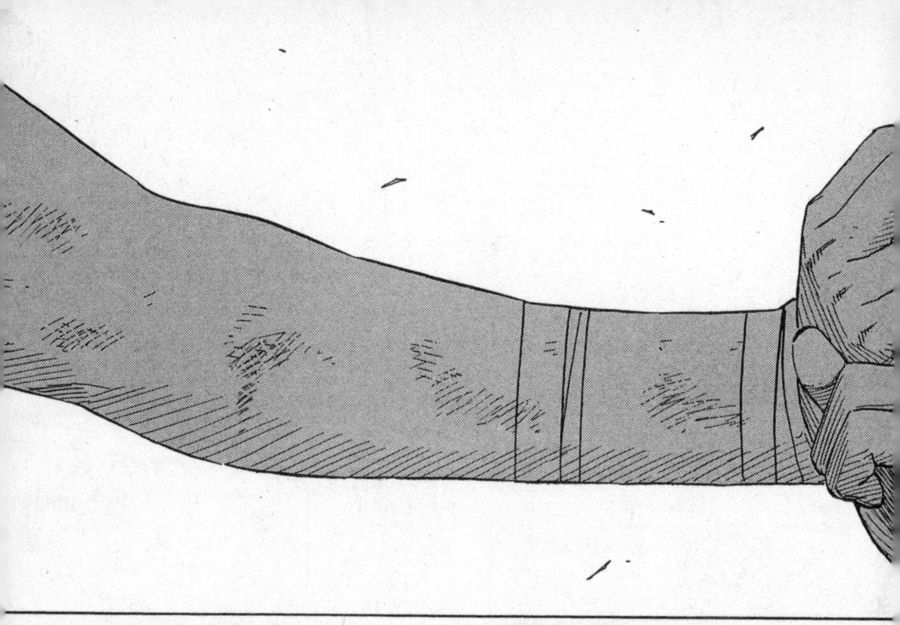

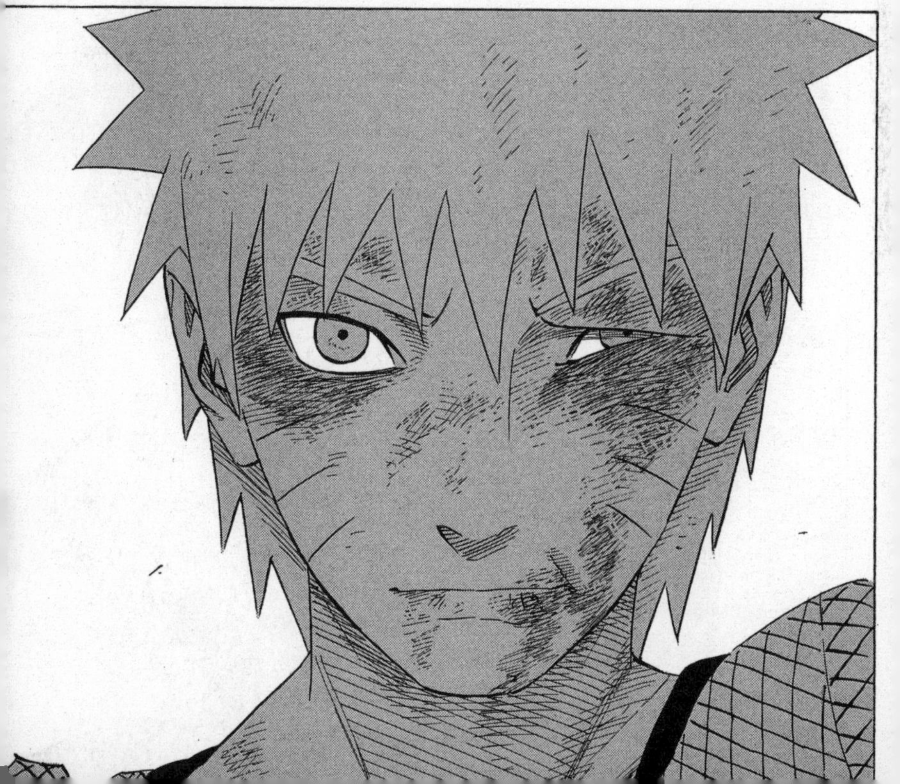

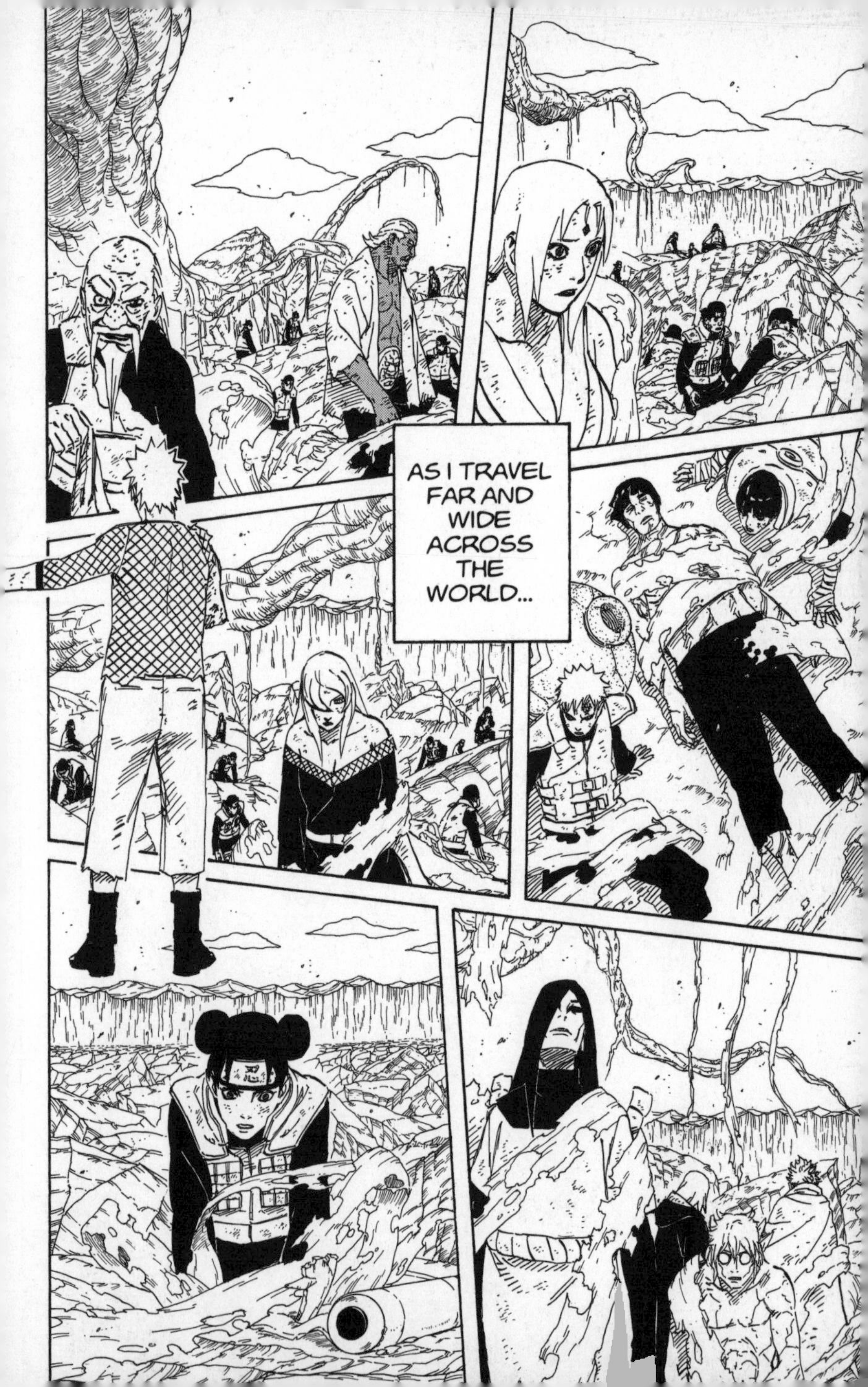
AS I TRAVEL FAR AND WIDE ACROSS THE WORLD...

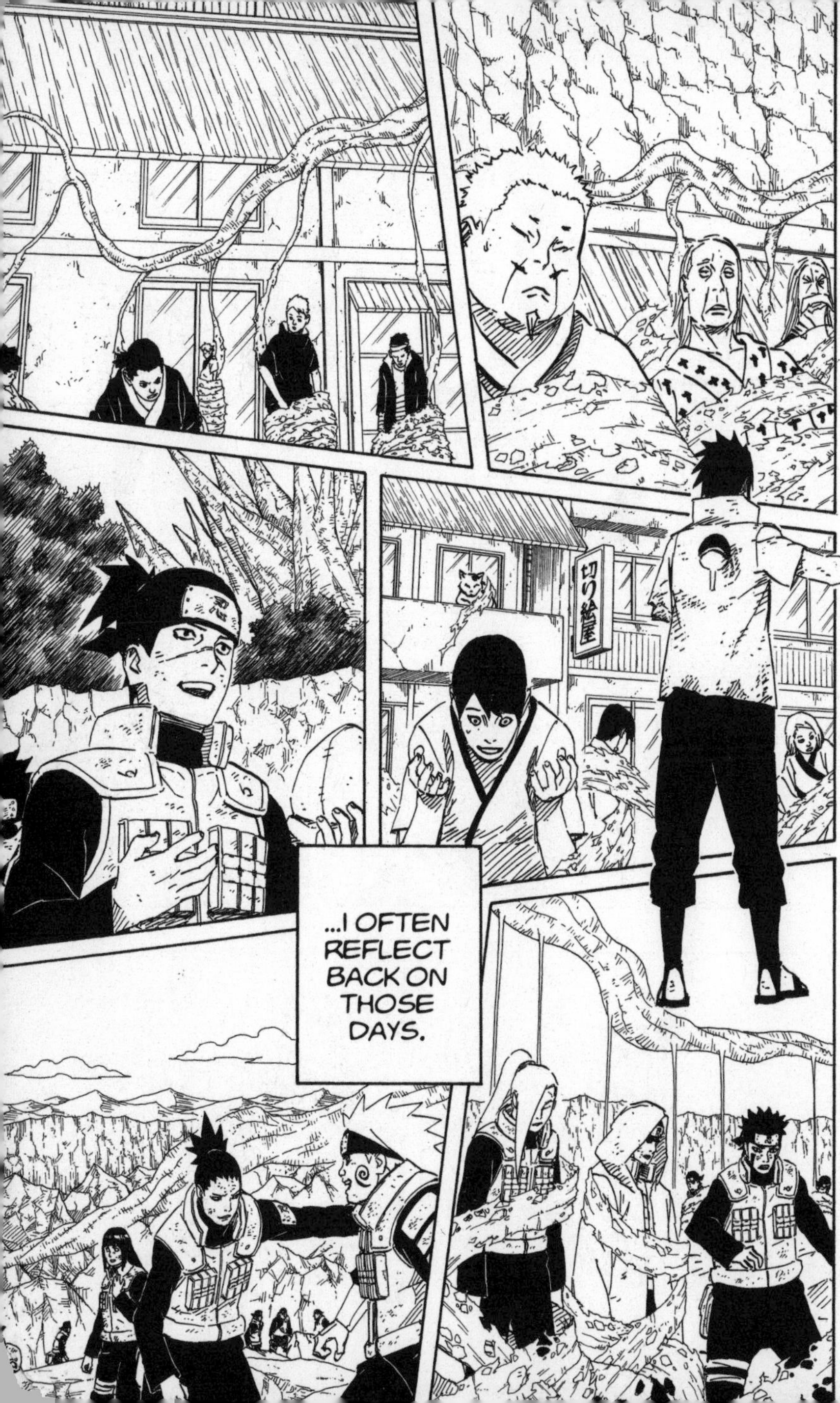
切り絵屋
...I OFTEN REFLECT BACK ON THOSE DAYS.

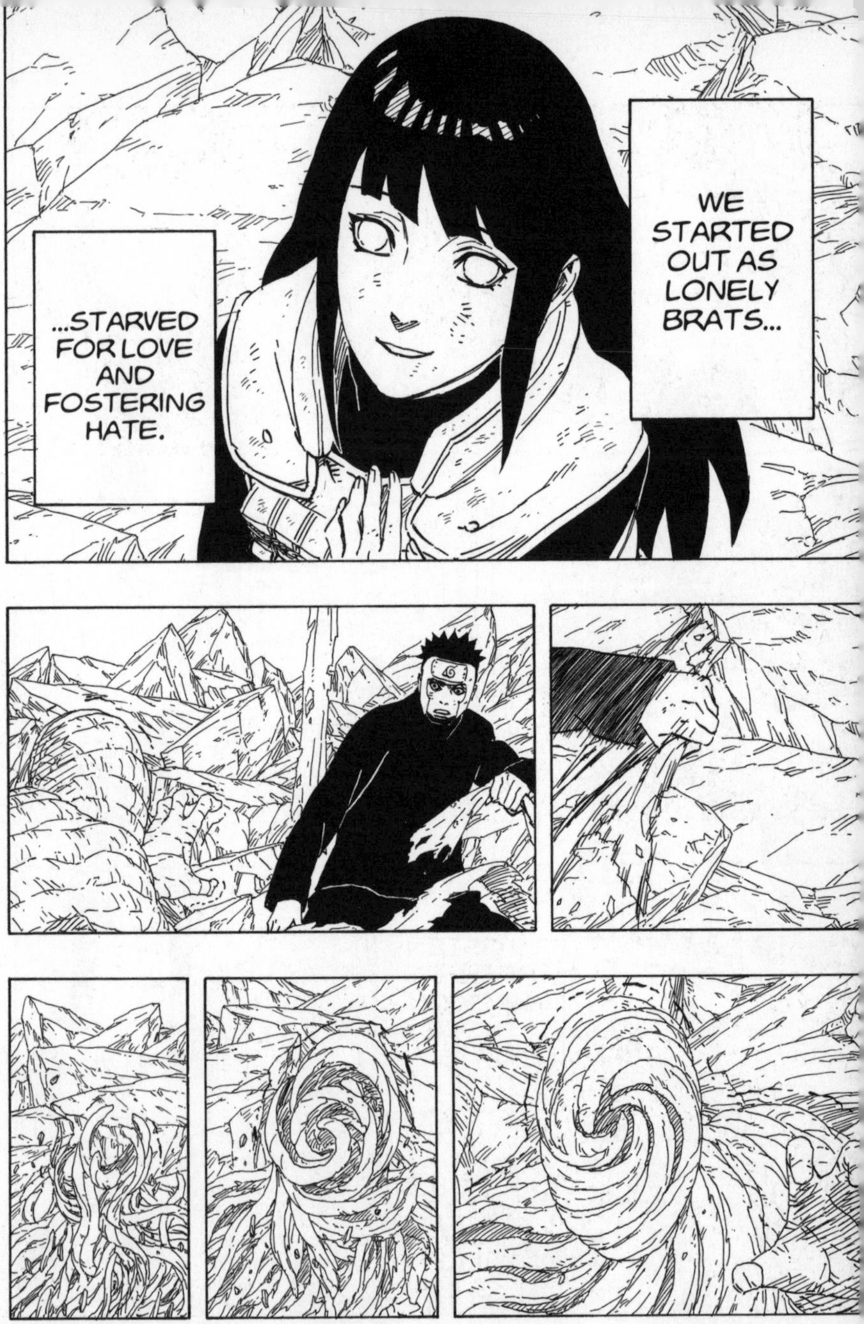
WE STARTED OUT AS LONELY BRATS...
...STARVED FOR LOVE AND FOSTERING HATE.

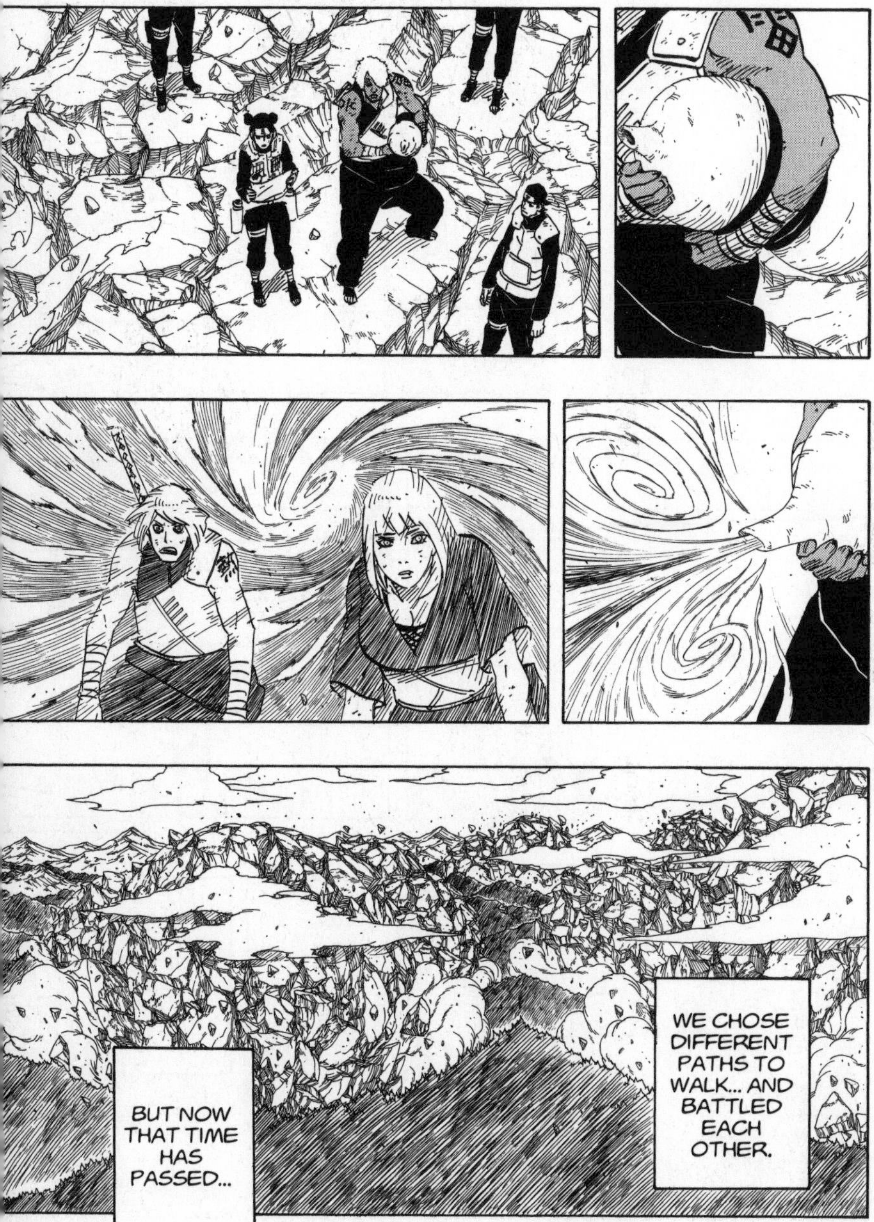
WE CHOSE DIFFERENT PATHS TO WALK... AND BATTLED EACH OTHER.
BUT NOW THAT TIME HAS PASSED...

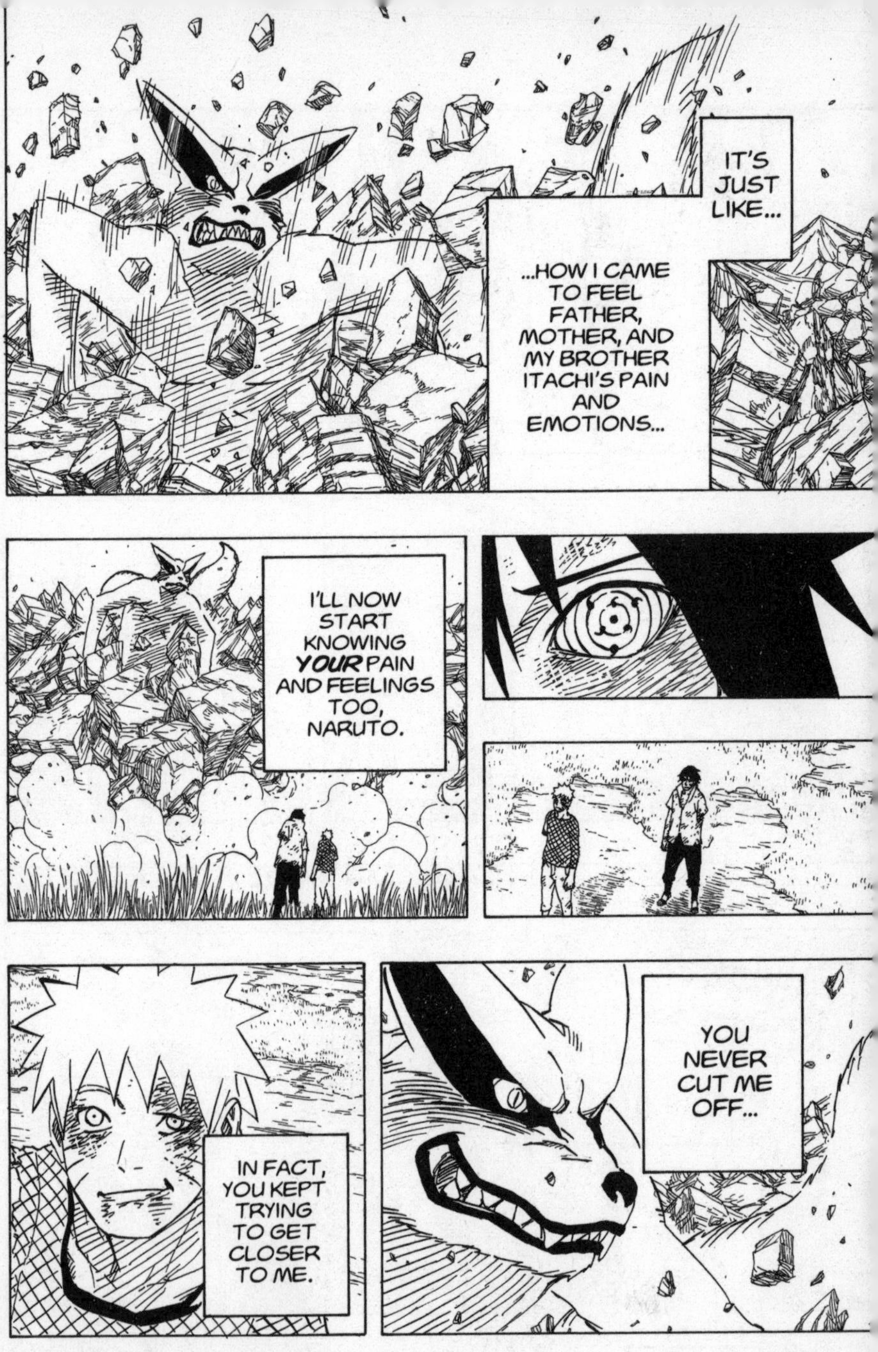
IT'S JUST LIKE...
...HOW I CAME TO FEEL FATHER, MOTHER, AND MY BROTHER ITACHI'S PAIN AND EMOTIONS...
I'LL NOW START KNOWING **YOUR** PAIN AND FEELINGS TOO, NARUTO.
YOU NEVER CUT ME OFF...
IN FACT, YOU KEPT TRYING TO GET CLOSER TO ME.

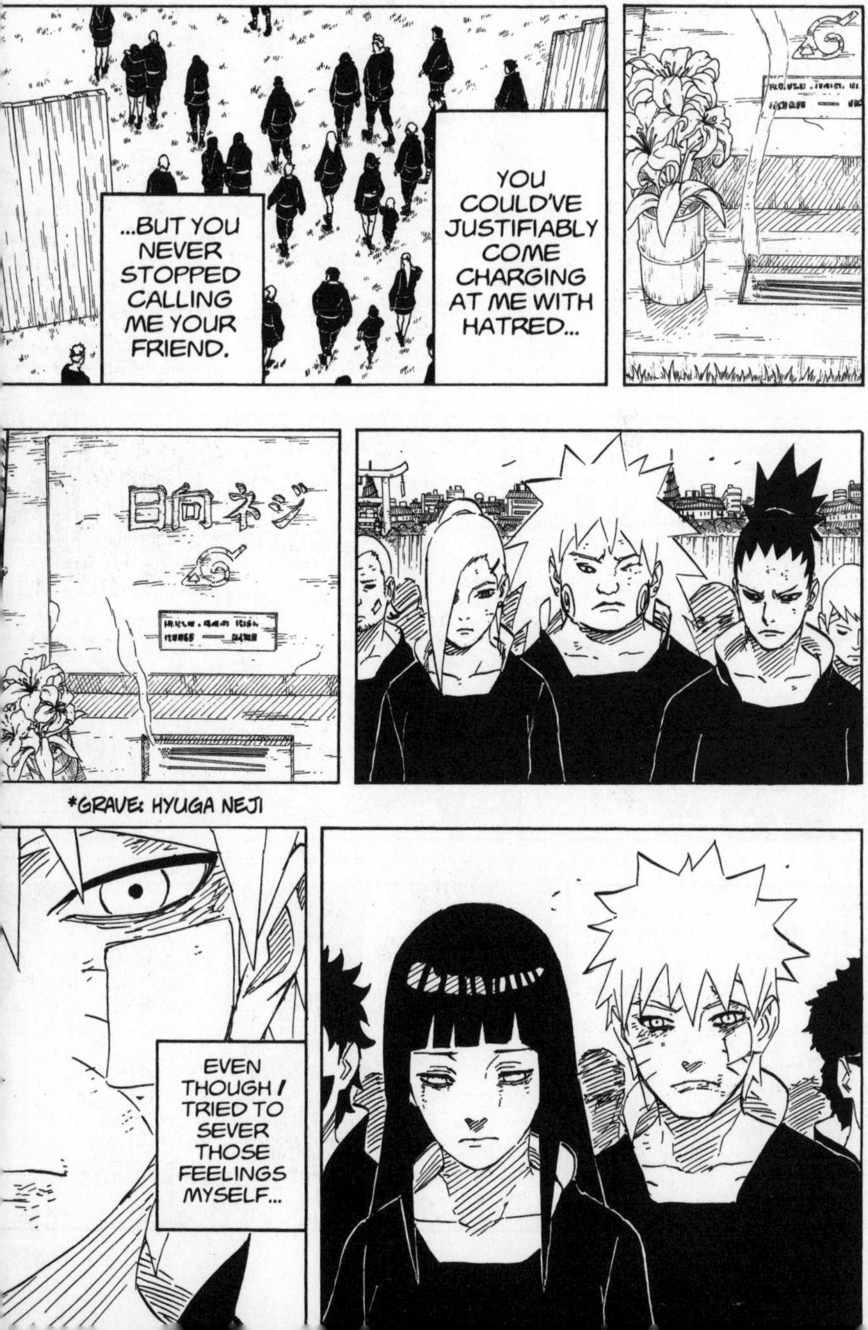
YOU COULD'VE JUSTIFIABLY COME CHARGING AT ME WITH HATRED...
...BUT YOU NEVER STOPPED CALLING ME YOUR FRIEND.
日向ネジ
*GRAVE: HYUGA NEJI
EVEN THOUGH I TRIED TO SEVER THOSE FEELINGS MYSELF...

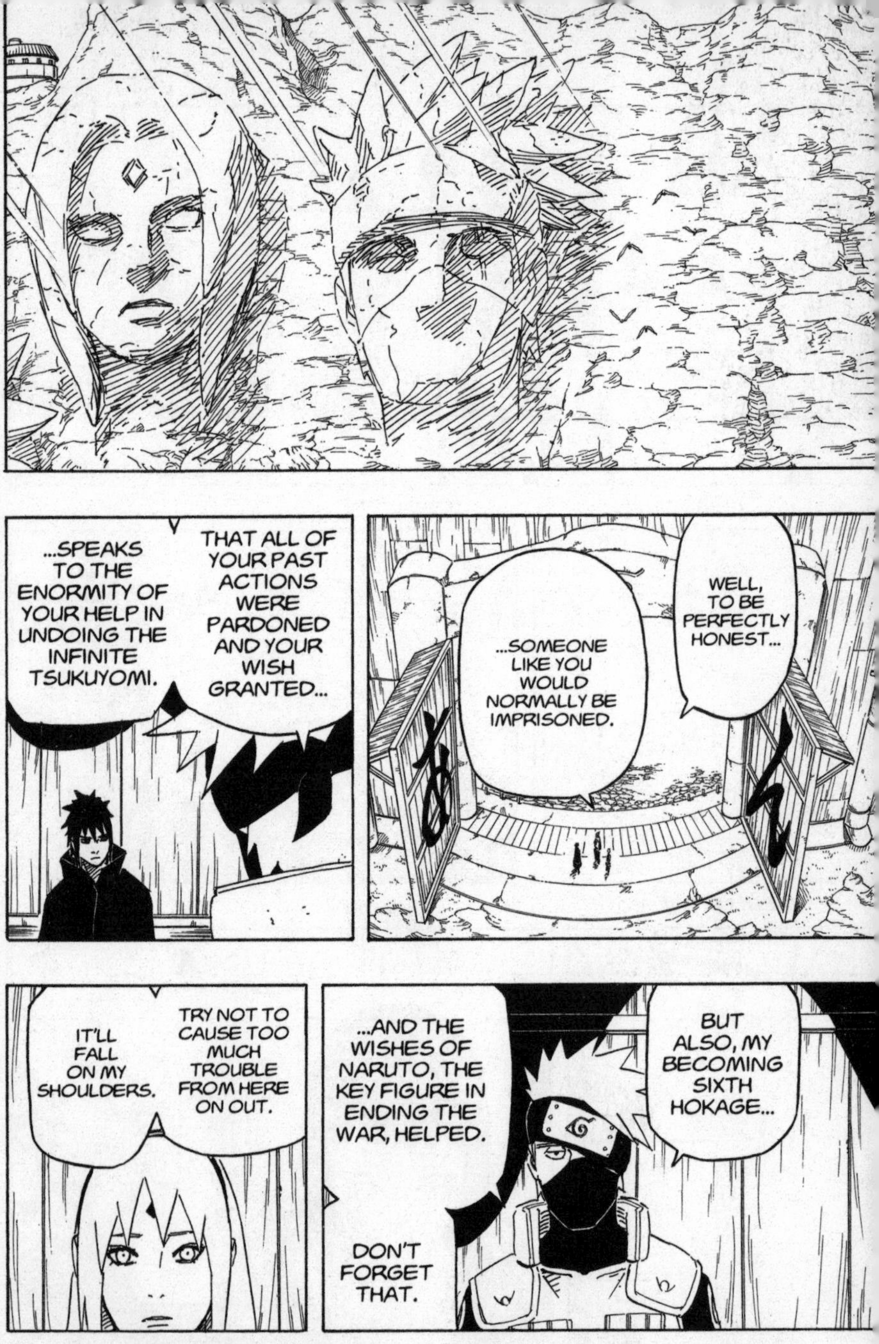
WELL, TO BE PERFECTLY HONEST...
...SOMEONE LIKE YOU WOULD NORMALLY BE IMPRISONED.
THAT ALL OF YOUR PAST ACTIONS WERE PARDONED AND YOUR WISH GRANTED...
...SPEAKS TO THE ENORMITY OF YOUR HELP IN UNDOING THE INFINITE TSUKUYOMI.
BUT ALSO, MY BECOMING SIXTH HOKAGE...
...AND THE WISHES OF NARUTO, THE KEY FIGURE IN ENDING THE WAR, HELPED.
DON'T FORGET THAT.
TRY NOT TO CAUSE TOO MUCH TROUBLE FROM HERE ON OUT.
IT'LL FALL ON MY SHOULDERS.

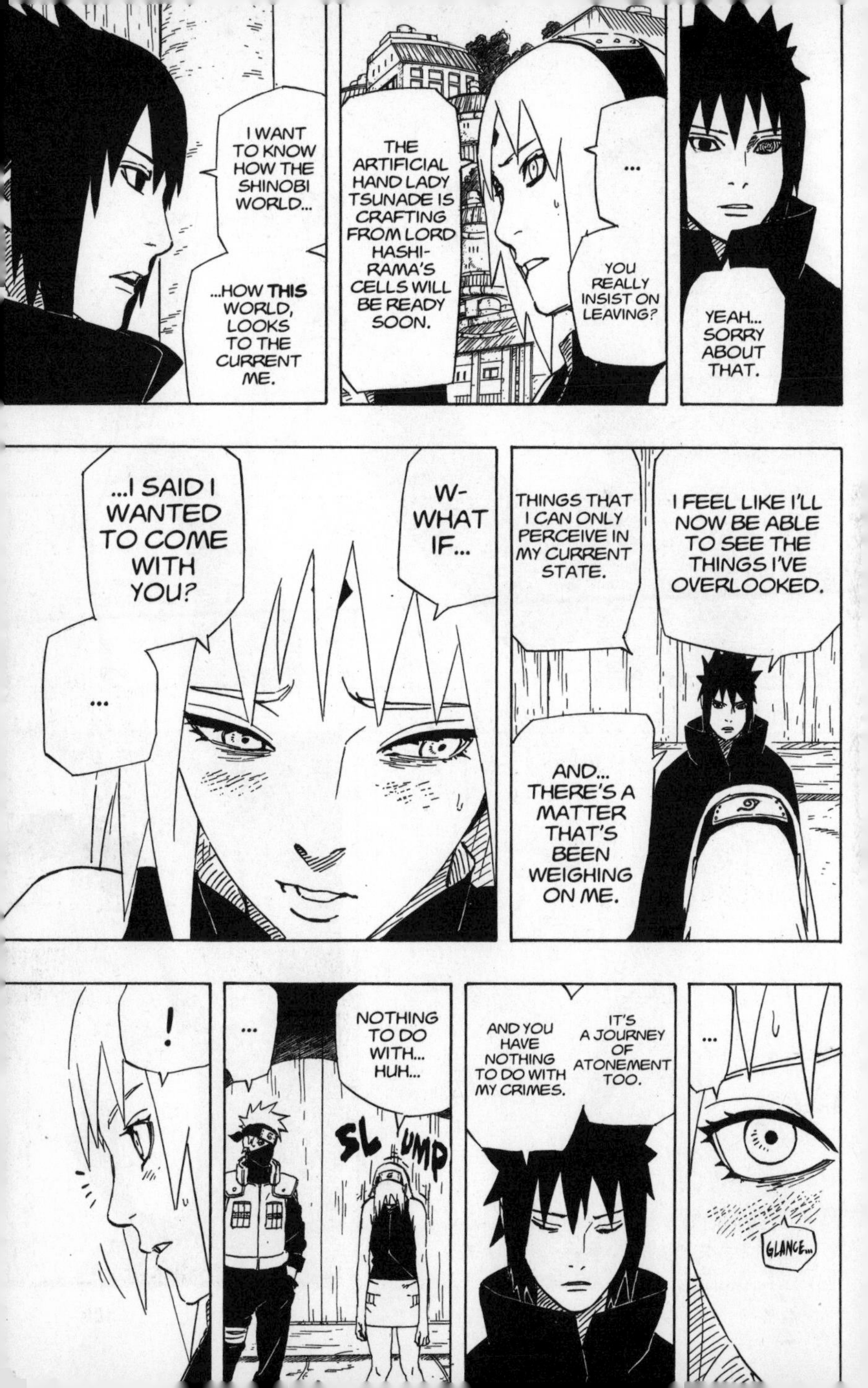
YEAH... SORRY ABOUT THAT.
...
YOU REALLY INSIST ON LEAVING?
THE ARTIFICIAL HAND LADY TSUNADE IS CRAFTING FROM LORD HASHI-RAMA'S CELLS WILL BE READY SOON.
I WANT TO KNOW HOW THE SHINOBI WORLD...
...HOW **THIS** WORLD, LOOKS TO THE CURRENT ME.
I FEEL LIKE I'LL NOW BE ABLE TO SEE THE THINGS I'VE OVERLOOKED.
THINGS THAT I CAN ONLY PERCEIVE IN MY CURRENT STATE.
AND... THERE'S A MATTER THAT'S BEEN WEIGHING ON ME.
W-WHAT IF...
...I SAID I WANTED TO COME WITH YOU?
...
...
GLANCE...
IT'S A JOURNEY OF ATONEMENT TOO.
AND YOU HAVE NOTHING TO DO WITH MY CRIMES.
NOTHING TO DO WITH... HUH...
SLUMP
...
!

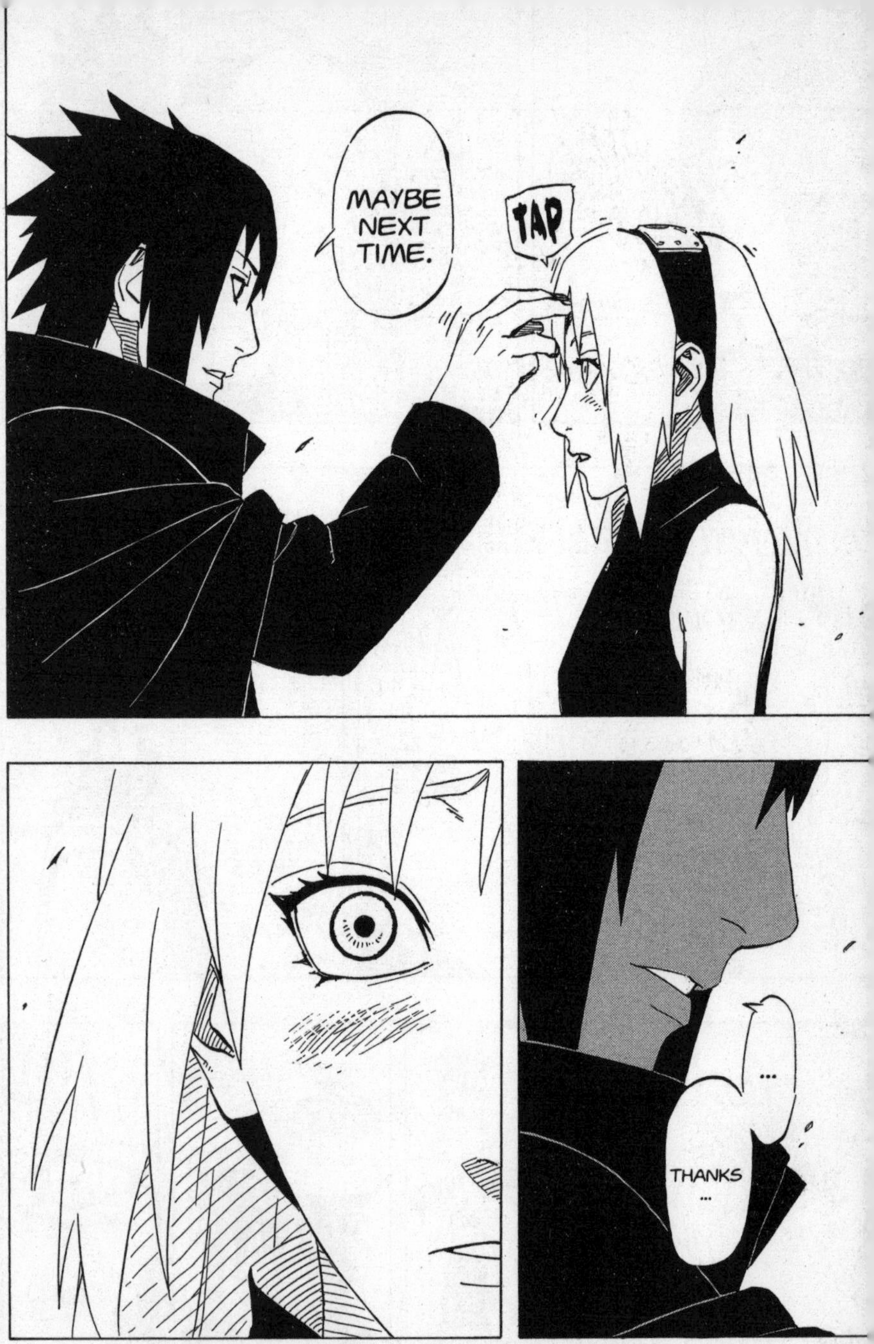
TAP
MAYBE NEXT TIME.
...
THANKS ...

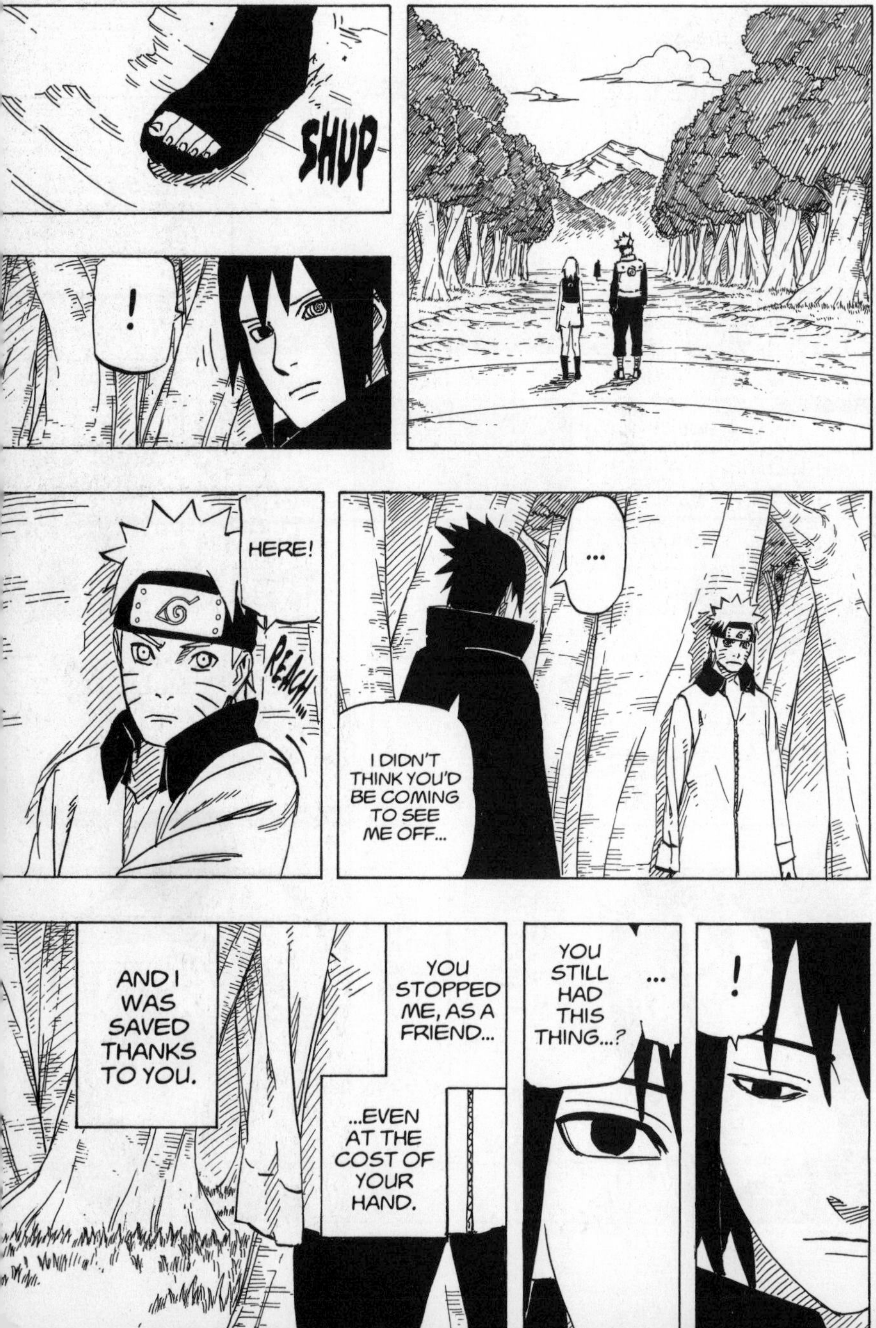
SHUP
!
...
I DIDN'T THINK YOU'D BE COMING TO SEE ME OFF...
HERE!
REACH
!
...
YOU STILL HAD THIS THING...?
YOU STOPPED ME, AS A FRIEND...
...EVEN AT THE COST OF YOUR HAND.
AND I WAS SAVED THANKS TO YOU.

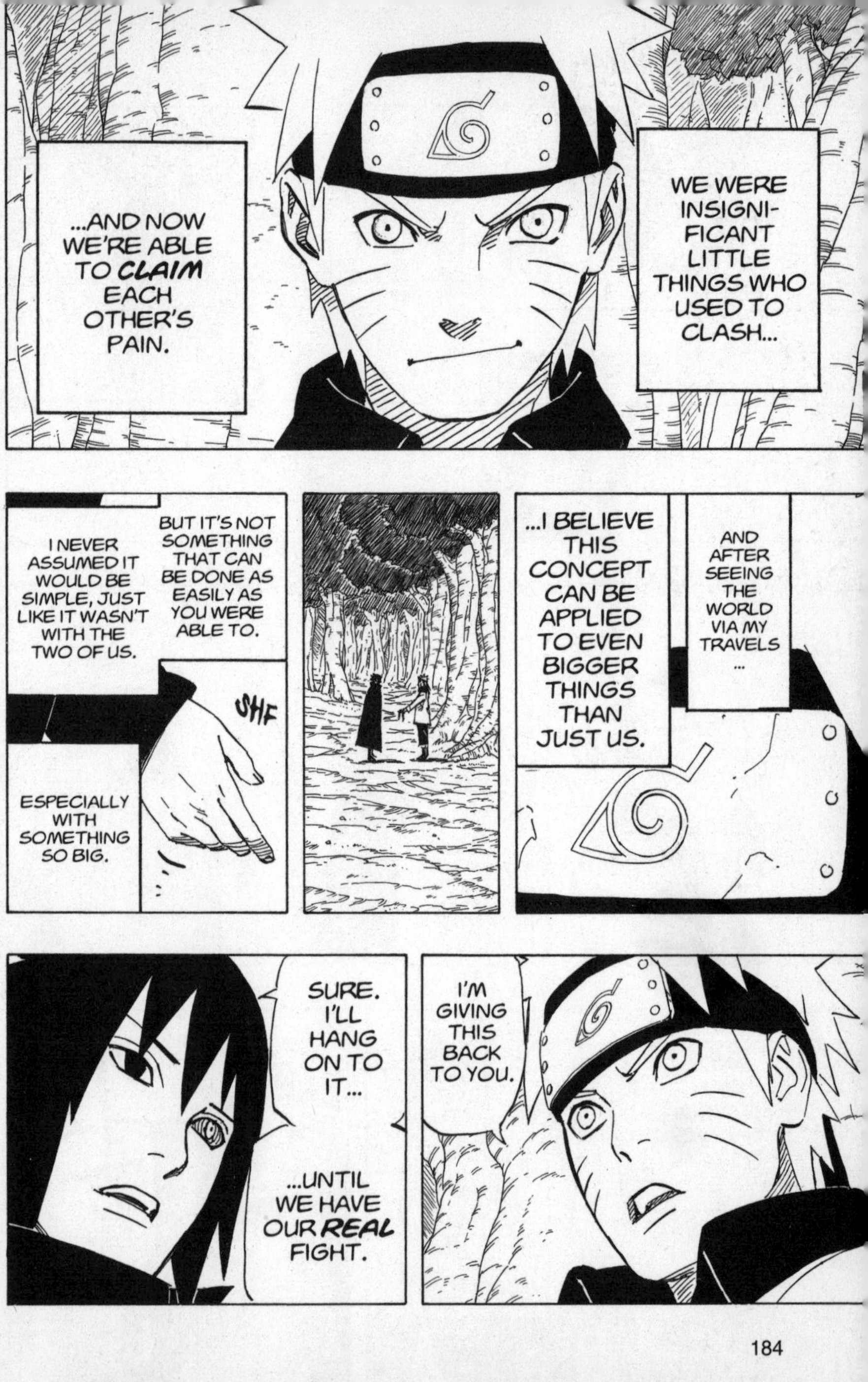

WE WERE INSIGNIFICANT LITTLE THINGS WHO USED TO CLASH...
...AND NOW WE'RE ABLE TO **CLAIM** EACH OTHER'S PAIN.
AND AFTER SEEING THE WORLD VIA MY TRAVELS ...
...I BELIEVE THIS CONCEPT CAN BE APPLIED TO EVEN BIGGER THINGS THAN JUST US.
BUT IT'S NOT SOMETHING THAT CAN BE DONE AS EASILY AS YOU WERE ABLE TO.
I NEVER ASSUMED IT WOULD BE SIMPLE, JUST LIKE IT WASN'T WITH THE TWO OF US.
SHF
ESPECIALLY WITH SOMETHING SO BIG.
I'M GIVING THIS BACK TO YOU.
SURE. I'LL HANG ON TO IT...
...UNTIL WE HAVE OUR **REAL** FIGHT.

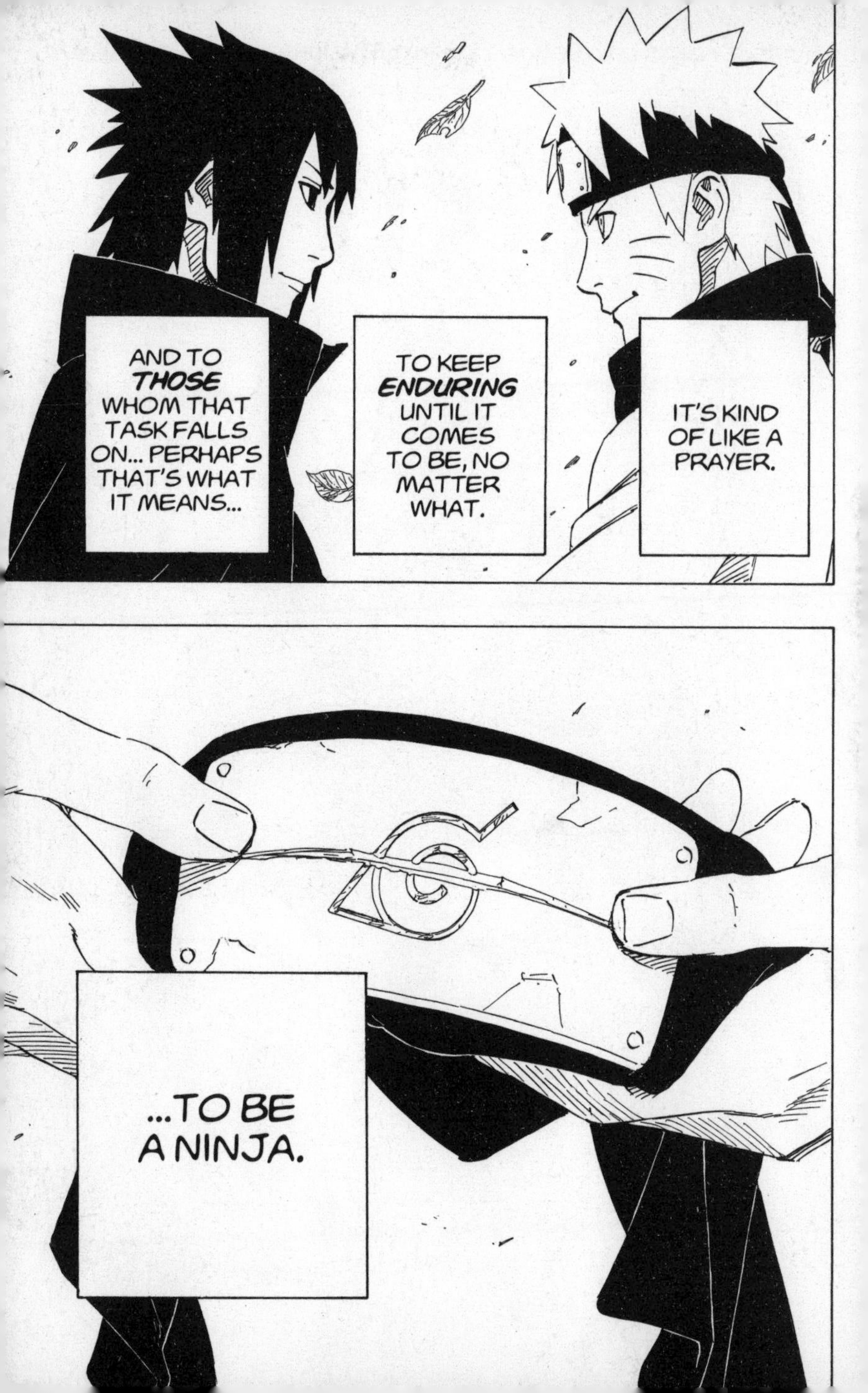
IT'S KIND OF LIKE A PRAYER.
TO KEEP **ENDURING** UNTIL IT COMES TO BE, NO MATTER WHAT.
AND TO **THOSE** WHOM THAT TASK FALLS ON... PERHAPS THAT'S WHAT IT MEANS...
...TO BE A NINJA.

END OF SERIES COMMEMORATION ILLUSTRATION (10) KANJI KAWAHARA

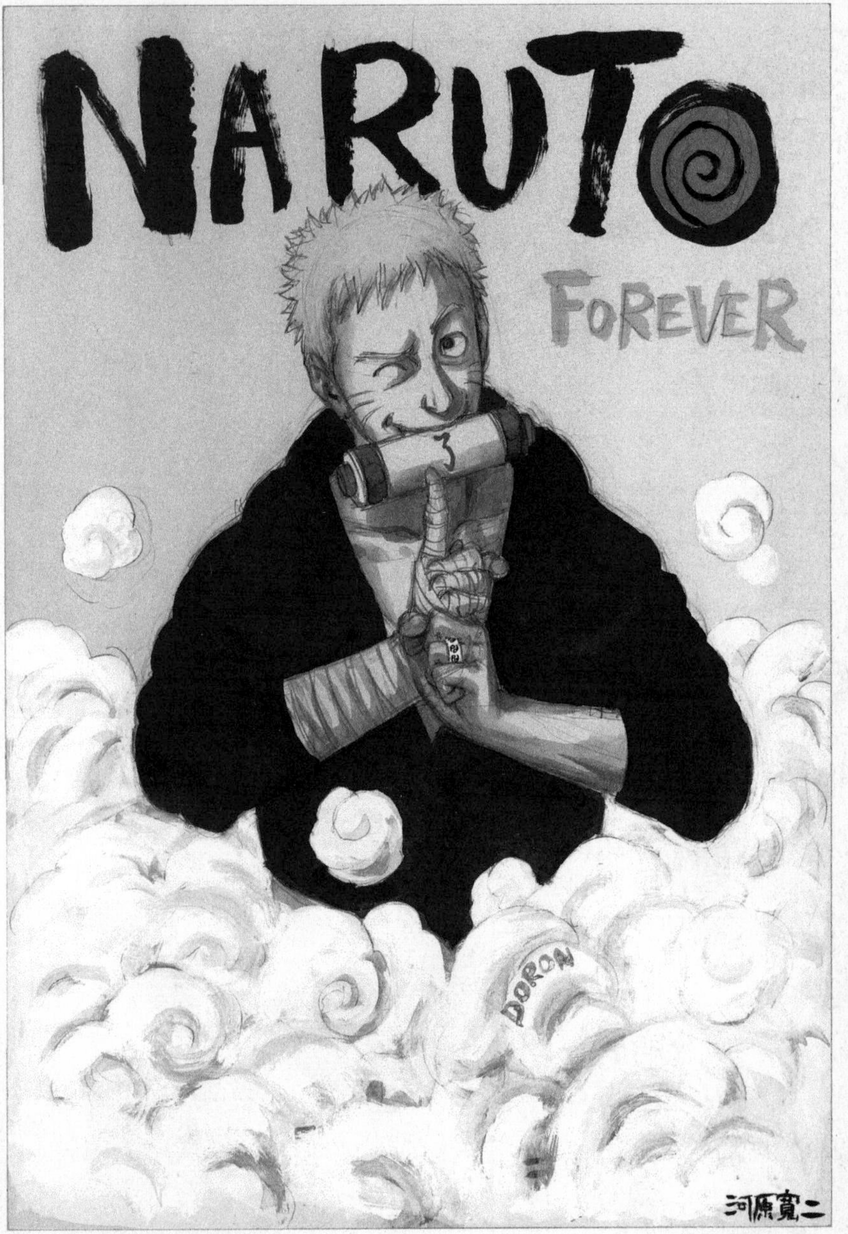
NARUTO
FOREVER
DORON
河原寛二

Number 700: Uzumaki Naruto!!

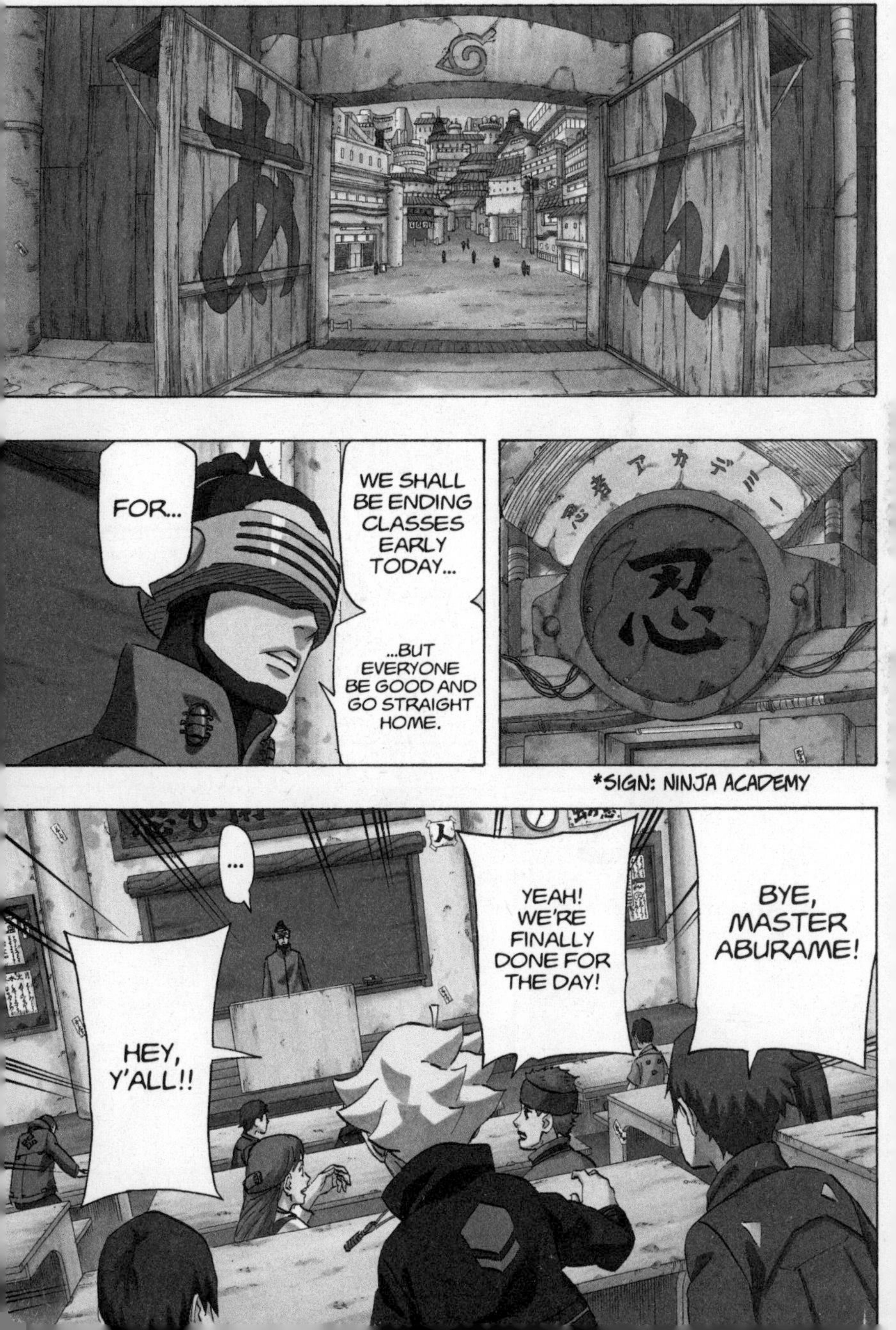
WE SHALL BE ENDING CLASSES EARLY TODAY...
FOR...
...BUT EVERYONE BE GOOD AND GO STRAIGHT HOME.
*SIGN: NINJA ACADEMY
BYE, MASTER ABURAME!
YEAH! WE'RE FINALLY DONE FOR THE DAY!
...
HEY, Y'ALL!!

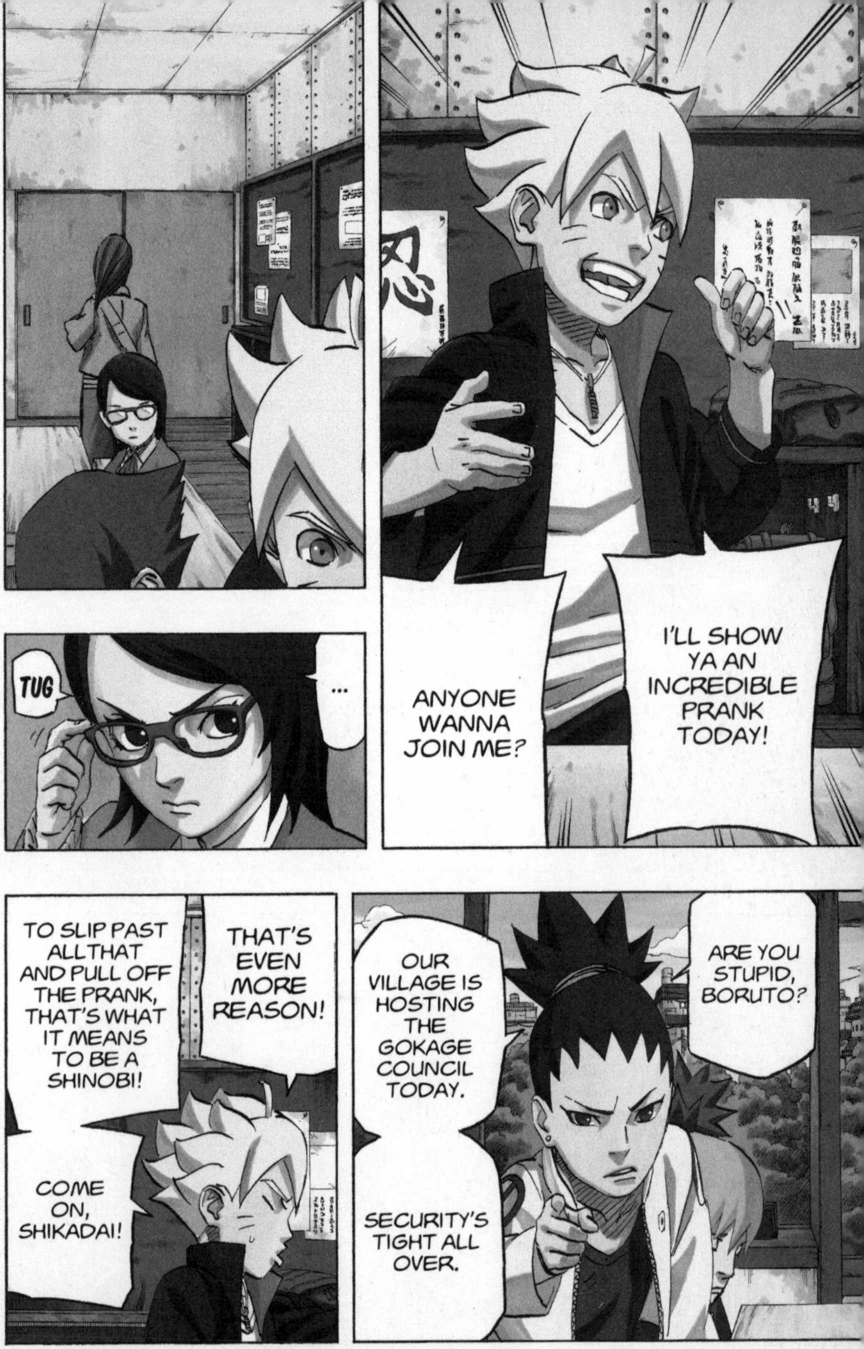
I'LL SHOW YA AN INCREDIBLE PRANK TODAY!
ANYONE WANNA JOIN ME?
TUG
...
ARE YOU STUPID, BORUTO?
OUR VILLAGE IS HOSTING THE GOKAGE COUNCIL TODAY.
SECURITY'S TIGHT ALL OVER.
THAT'S EVEN MORE REASON!
TO SLIP PAST ALL THAT AND PULL OFF THE PRANK, THAT'S WHAT IT MEANS TO BE A SHINOBI!
COME ON, SHIKADAI!

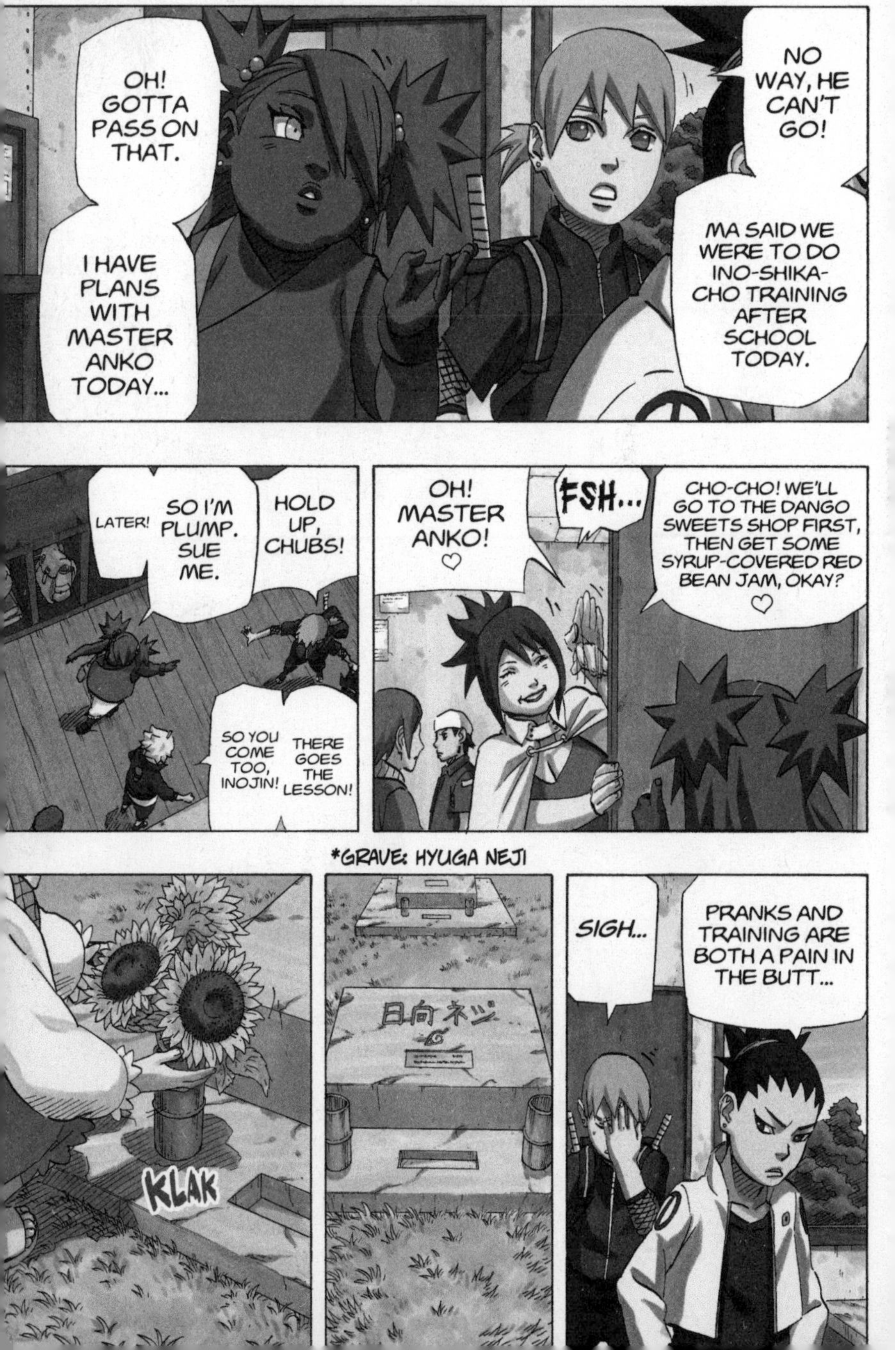
NO WAY, HE CAN'T GO!
MA SAID WE WERE TO DO INO-SHIKA-CHO TRAINING AFTER SCHOOL TODAY.
OH! GOTTA PASS ON THAT.
I HAVE PLANS WITH MASTER ANKO TODAY...
CHO-CHO! WE'LL GO TO THE DANGO SWEETS SHOP FIRST, THEN GET SOME SYRUP-COVERED RED BEAN JAM, OKAY? ♡
FSH...
OH! MASTER ANKO! ♡
HOLD UP, CHUBS!
SO I'M PLUMP. SUE ME.
LATER!
THERE GOES THE LESSON!
SO YOU COME TOO, INOJIN!
*GRAVE: HYUGA NEJI
PRANKS AND TRAINING ARE BOTH A PAIN IN THE BUTT...
SIGH...
日向ネジ
KLAK

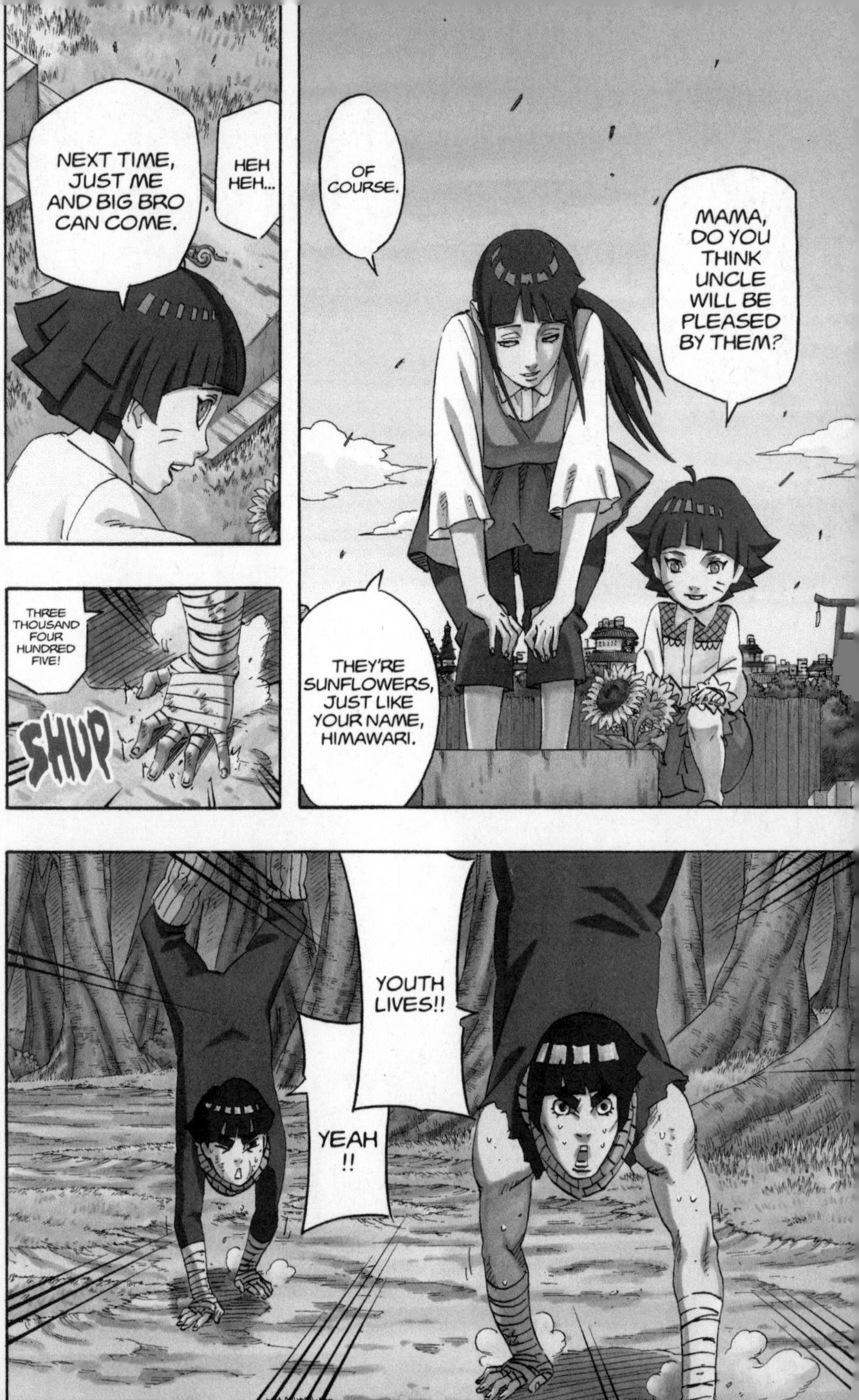
MAMA, DO YOU THINK UNCLE WILL BE PLEASED BY THEM?
OF COURSE.
THEY'RE SUNFLOWERS, JUST LIKE YOUR NAME, HIMAWARI.
HEH HEH...
NEXT TIME, JUST ME AND BIG BRO CAN COME.
THREE THOUSAND FOUR HUNDRED FIVE!
SHUP
YOUTH LIVES!!
YEAH !!

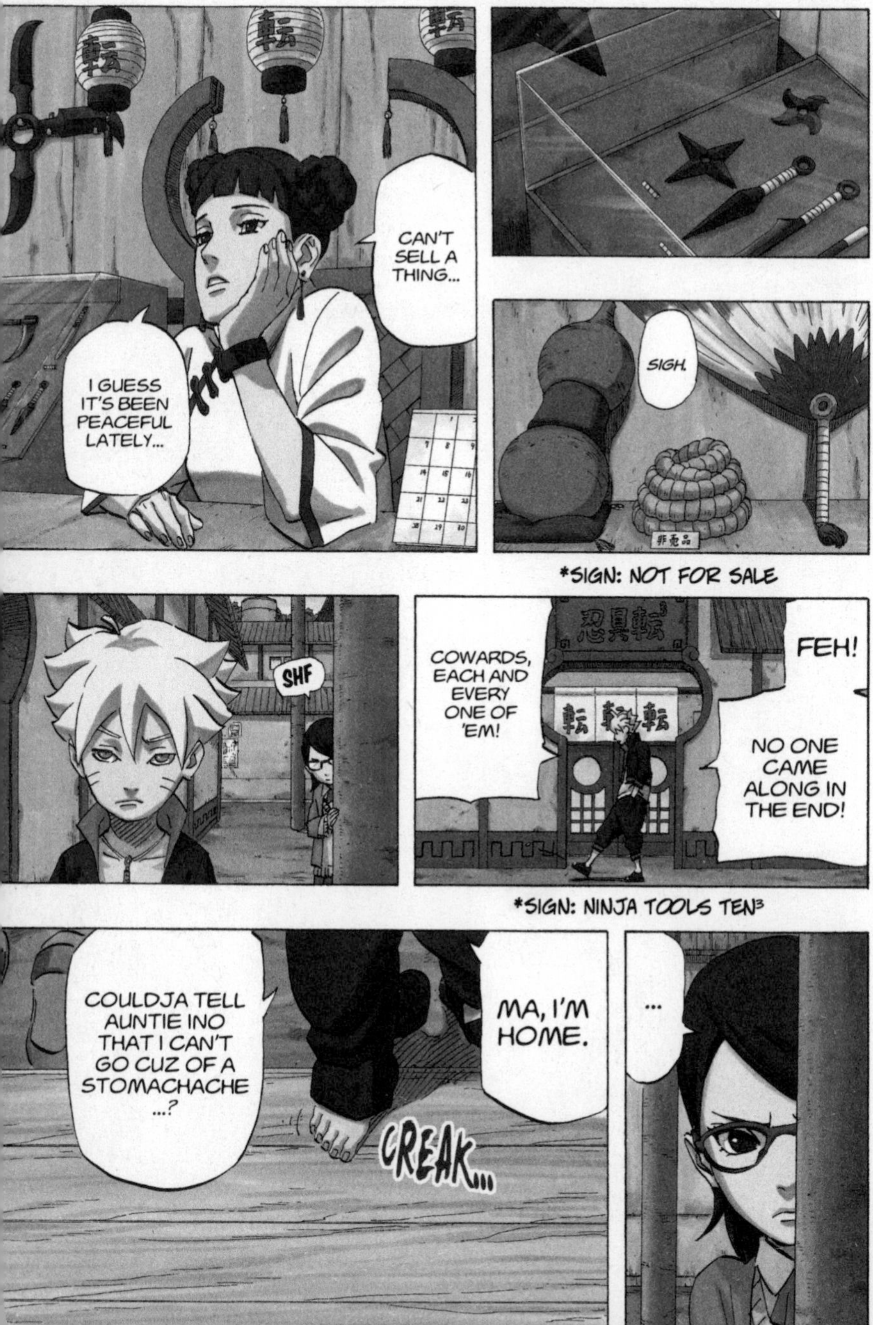
SIGH.
*SIGN: NOT FOR SALE
CAN'T SELL A THING...
I GUESS IT'S BEEN PEACEFUL LATELY...
FEH!
NO ONE CAME ALONG IN THE END!
COWARDS, EACH AND EVERY ONE OF 'EM!
*SIGN: NINJA TOOLS TEN³
SHF
...
MA, I'M HOME.
COULDJA TELL AUNTIE INO THAT I CAN'T GO CUZ OF A STOMACHACHE ...?
CREAK...

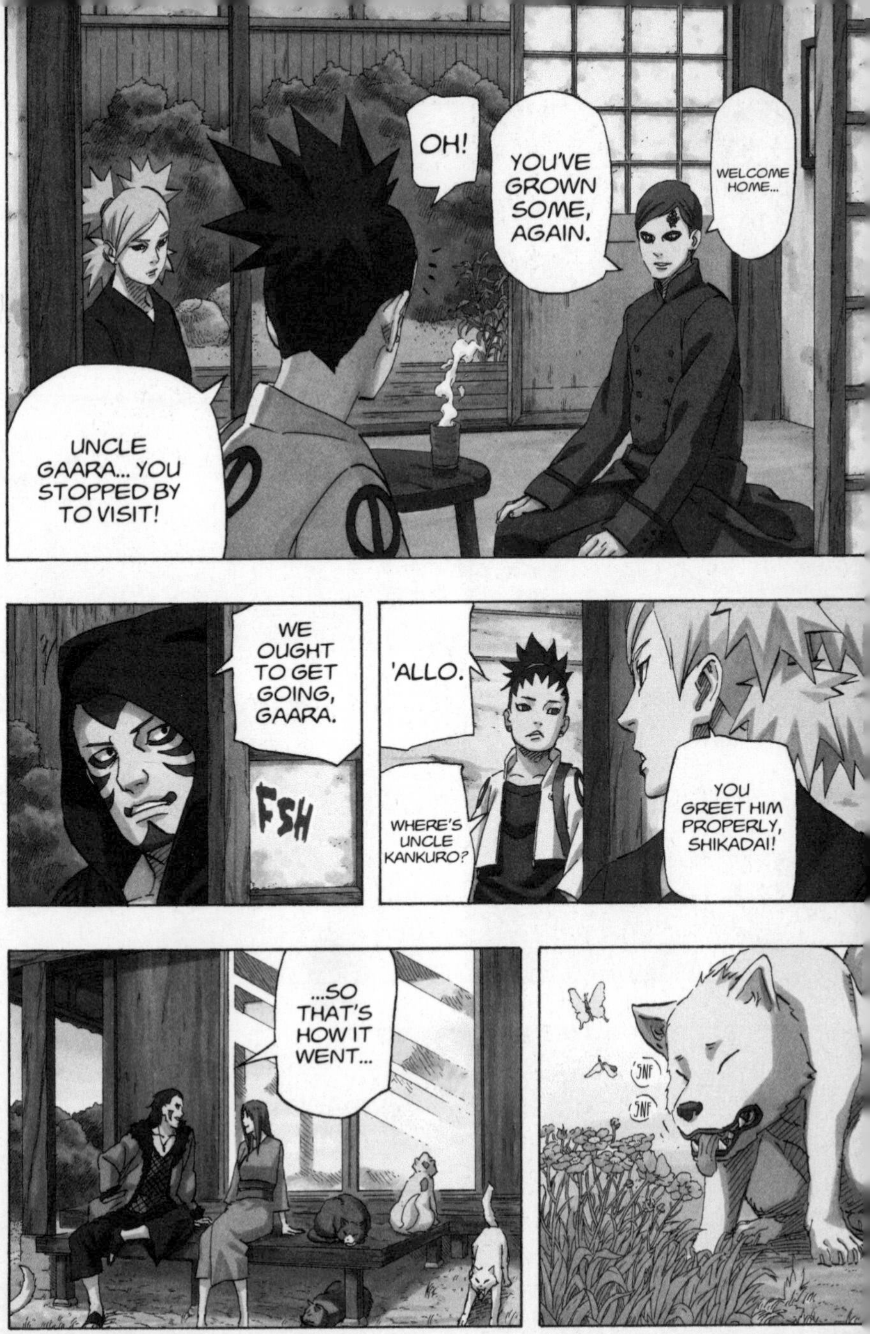
WELCOME HOME...
YOU'VE GROWN SOME, AGAIN.
OH!
UNCLE GAARA... YOU STOPPED BY TO VISIT!
'ALLO.
YOU GREET HIM PROPERLY, SHIKADAI!
WHERE'S UNCLE KANKURO?
WE OUGHT TO GET GOING, GAARA.
FSH
SNF
SNF
...SO THAT'S HOW IT WENT...

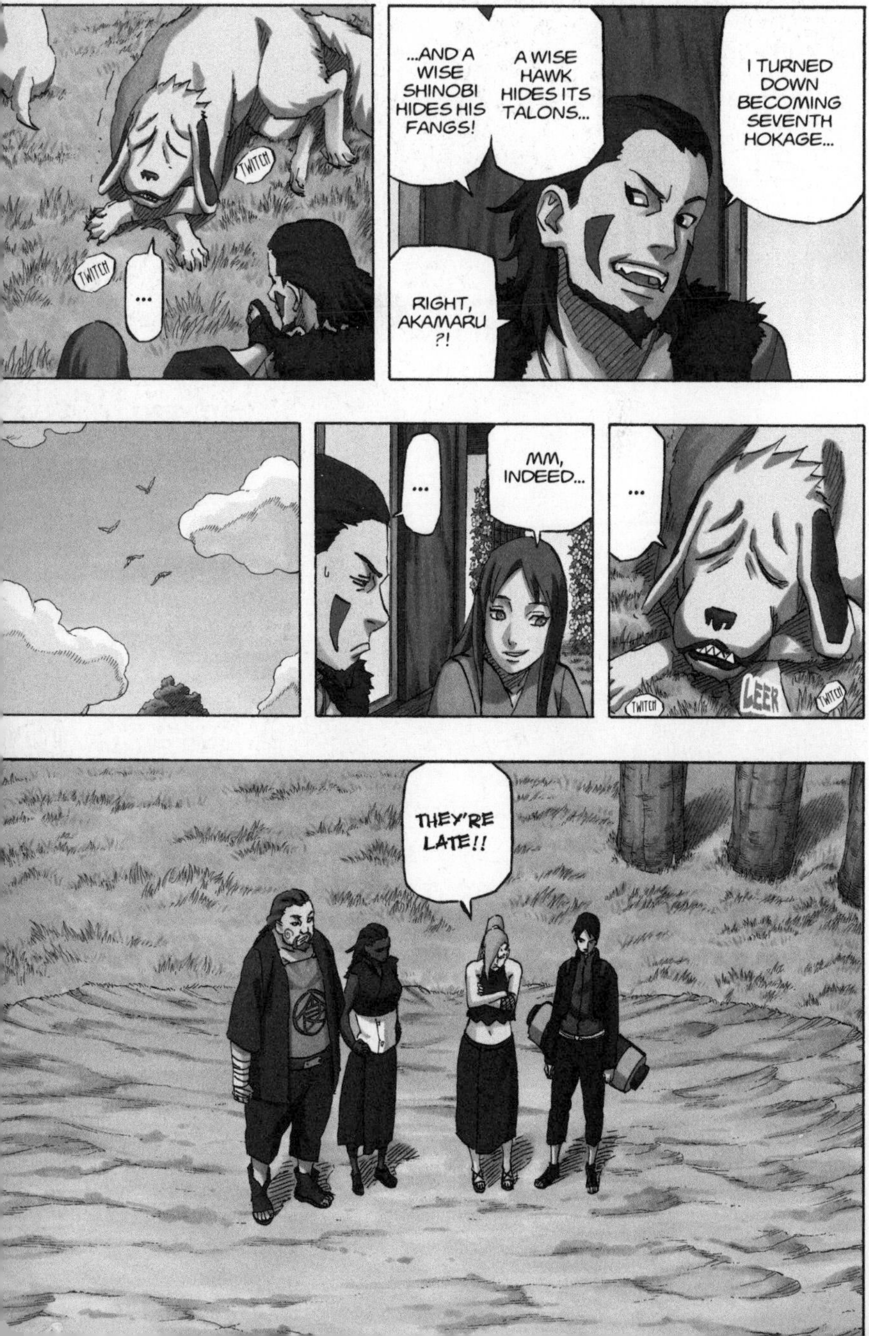
I TURNED DOWN BECOMING SEVENTH HOKAGE...
A WISE HAWK HIDES ITS TALONS...
...AND A WISE SHINOBI HIDES HIS FANGS!
RIGHT, AKAMARU ?!
TWITCH
...
TWITCH
...
LEER
TWITCH
TWITCH
MM, INDEED...
...
THEY'RE LATE!!

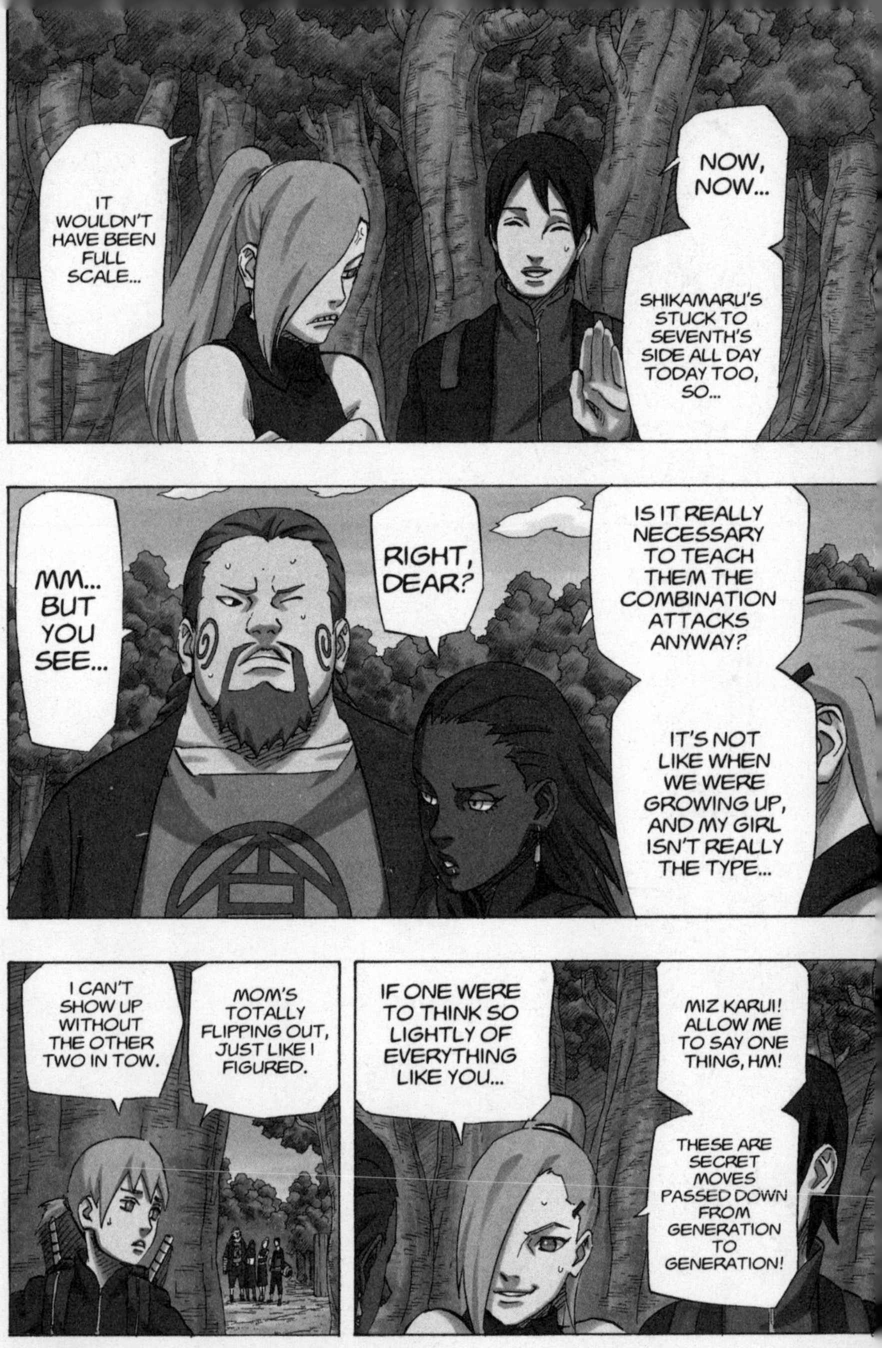
NOW, NOW...
SHIKAMARU'S STUCK TO SEVENTH'S SIDE ALL DAY TODAY TOO, SO...
IT WOULDN'T HAVE BEEN FULL SCALE...
IS IT REALLY NECESSARY TO TEACH THEM THE COMBINATION ATTACKS ANYWAY?
IT'S NOT LIKE WHEN WE WERE GROWING UP, AND MY GIRL ISN'T REALLY THE TYPE...
RIGHT, DEAR?
MM... BUT YOU SEE...
MIZ KARUI! ALLOW ME TO SAY ONE THING, HM!
THESE ARE SECRET MOVES PASSED DOWN FROM GENERATION TO GENERATION!
IF ONE WERE TO THINK SO LIGHTLY OF EVERYTHING LIKE YOU...
MOM'S TOTALLY FLIPPING OUT, JUST LIKE I FIGURED.
I CAN'T SHOW UP WITHOUT THE OTHER TWO IN TOW.

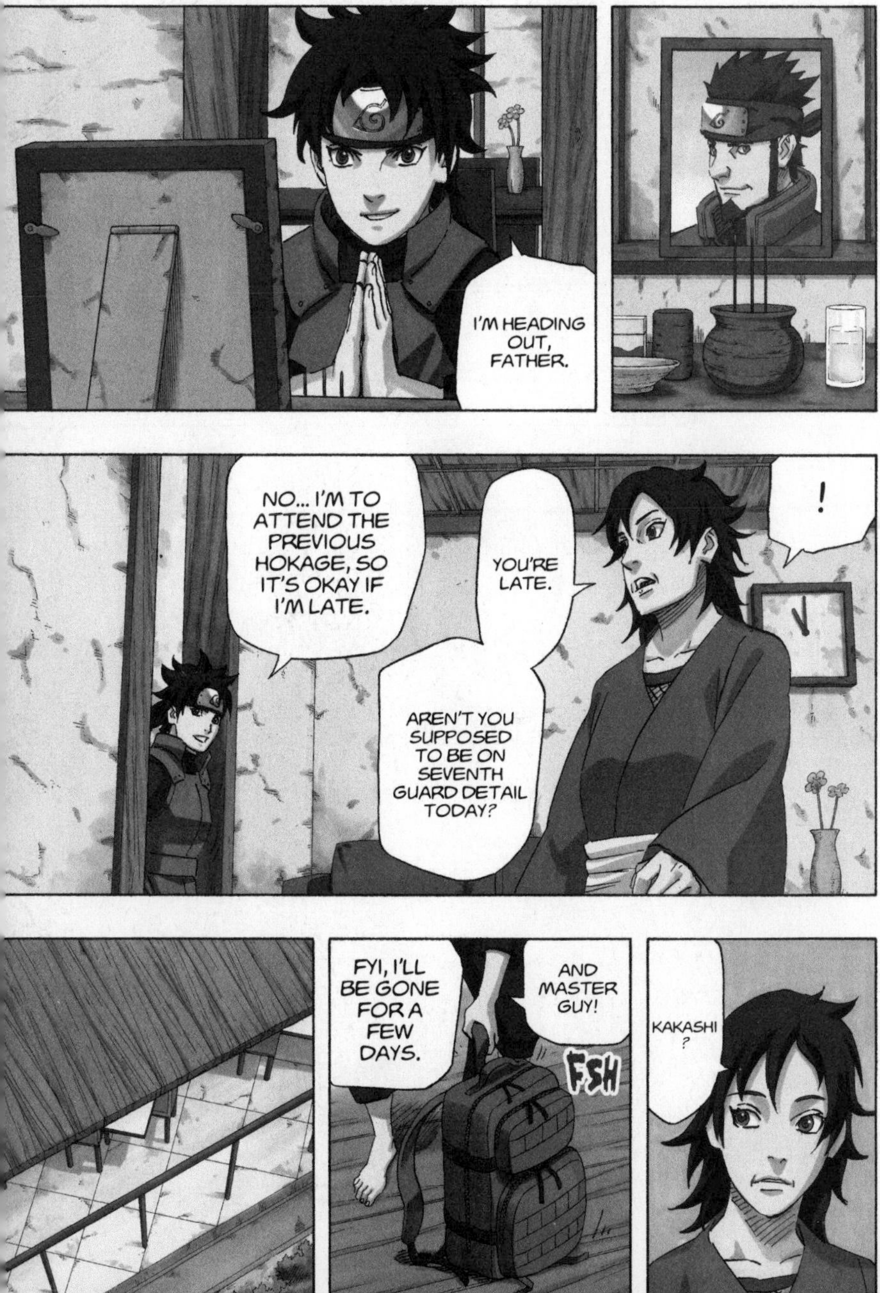
I'M HEADING OUT, FATHER.
!
YOU'RE LATE.
AREN'T YOU SUPPOSED TO BE ON SEVENTH GUARD DETAIL TODAY?
NO... I'M TO ATTEND THE PREVIOUS HOKAGE, SO IT'S OKAY IF I'M LATE.
KAKASHI?
AND MASTER GUY!
FSH
FYI, I'LL BE GONE FOR A FEW DAYS.

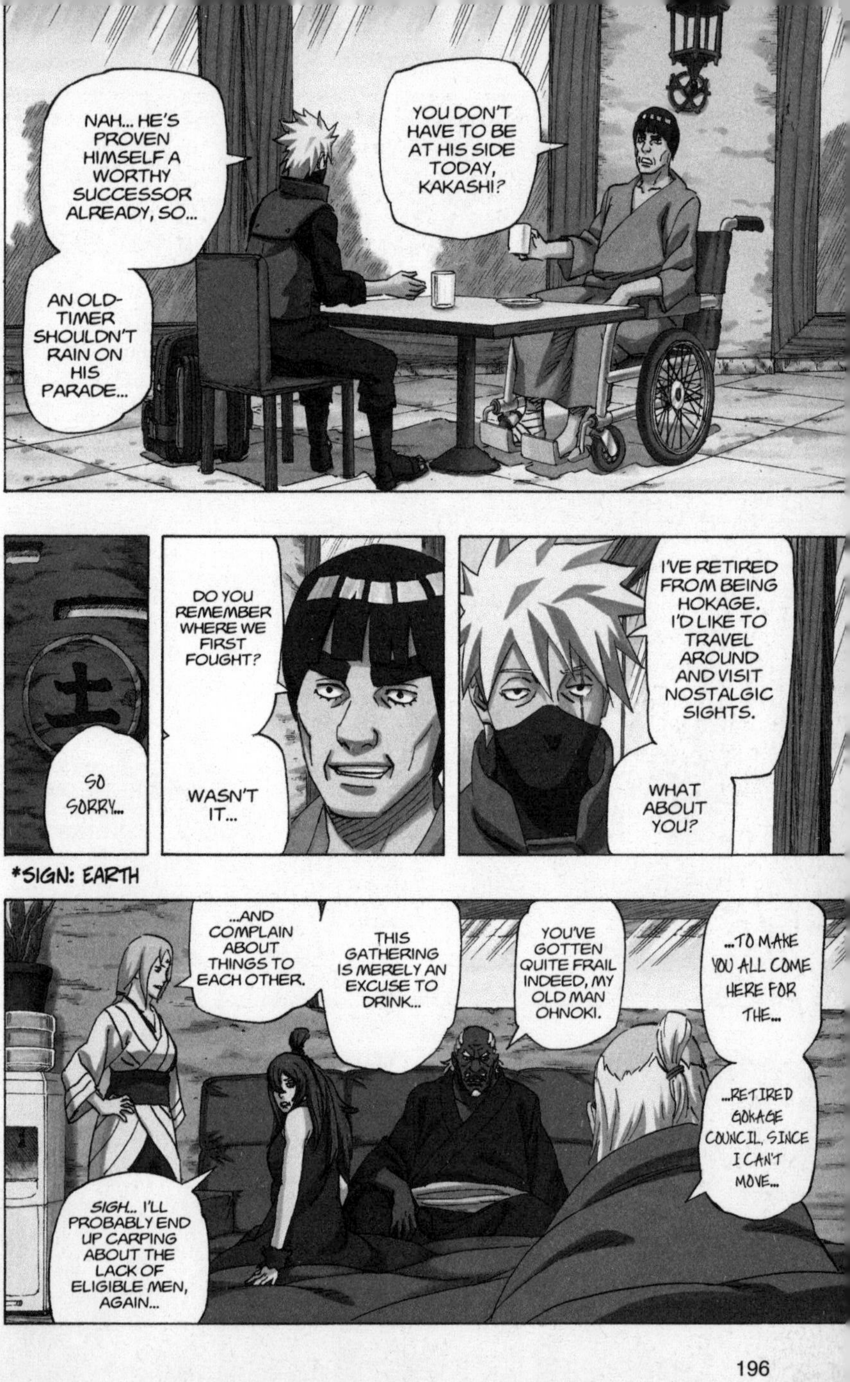
YOU DON'T HAVE TO BE AT HIS SIDE TODAY, KAKASHI?
NAH... HE'S PROVEN HIMSELF A WORTHY SUCCESSOR ALREADY, SO...
AN OLD-TIMER SHOULDN'T RAIN ON HIS PARADE...
I'VE RETIRED FROM BEING HOKAGE. I'D LIKE TO TRAVEL AROUND AND VISIT NOSTALGIC SIGHTS.
WHAT ABOUT YOU?
DO YOU REMEMBER WHERE WE FIRST FOUGHT?
WASN'T IT...
SO SORRY...
*SIGN: EARTH
...TO MAKE YOU ALL COME HERE FOR THE...
...RETIRED GOKAGE COUNCIL, SINCE I CAN'T MOVE...
YOU'VE GOTTEN QUITE FRAIL INDEED, MY OLD MAN OHNOKI.
THIS GATHERING IS MERELY AN EXCUSE TO DRINK...
...AND COMPLAIN ABOUT THINGS TO EACH OTHER.
SIGH... I'LL PROBABLY END UP CARPING ABOUT THE LACK OF ELIGIBLE MEN, AGAIN...

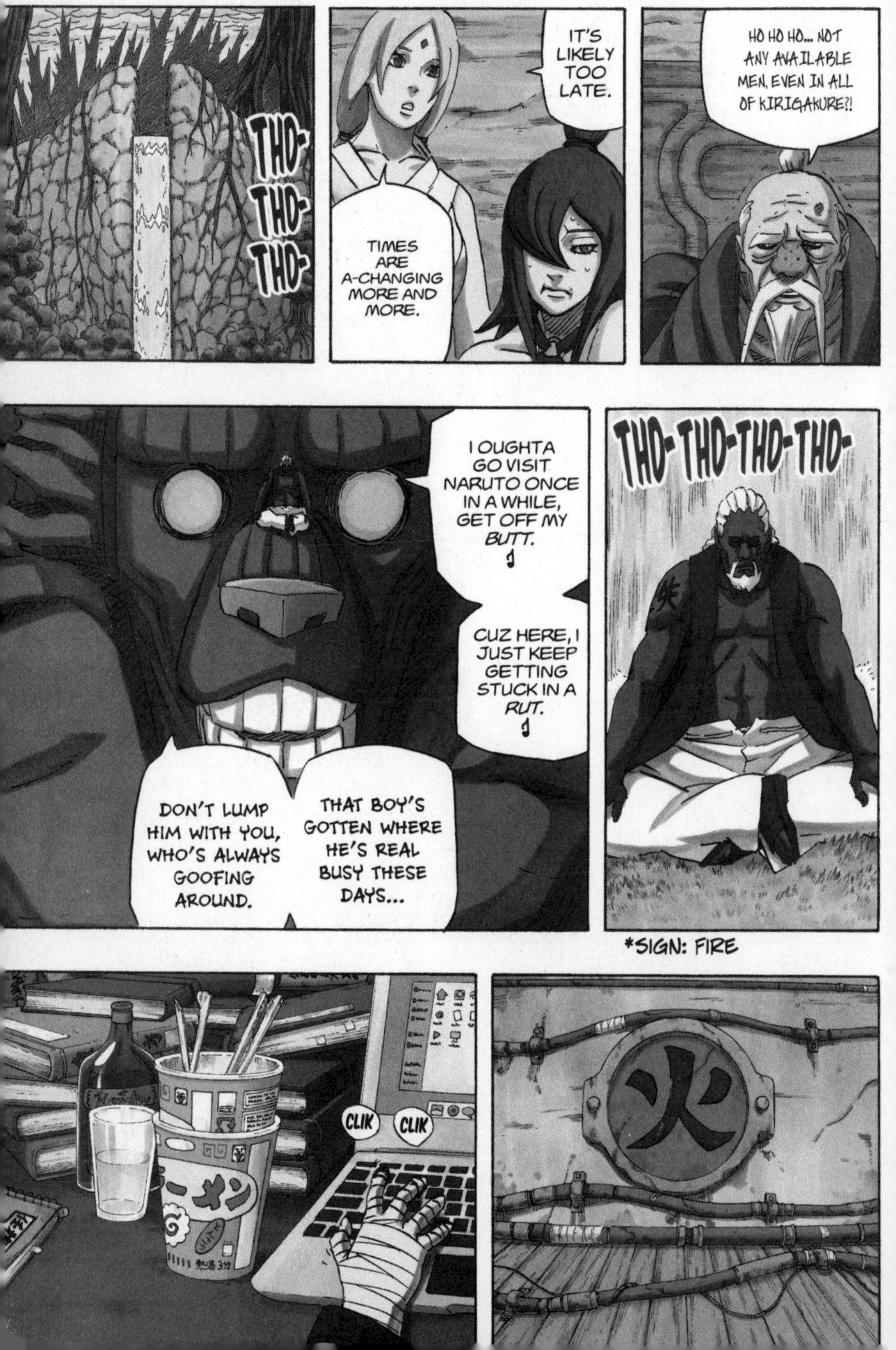
HO HO HO... NOT ANY AVAILABLE MEN, EVEN IN ALL OF KIRIGAKURE?!
IT'S LIKELY TOO LATE.
TIMES ARE A-CHANGING MORE AND MORE.
THO-THO-THO-
THO-THO-THO-THO-
I OUGHTA GO VISIT NARUTO ONCE IN A WHILE, GET OFF MY *BUTT.* ♪
CUZ HERE, I JUST KEEP GETTING STUCK IN A *RUT.* ♪
THAT BOY'S GOTTEN WHERE HE'S REAL BUSY THESE DAYS...
DON'T LUMP HIM WITH YOU, WHO'S ALWAYS GOOFING AROUND.
火
CLIK CLIK
*SIGN: FIRE

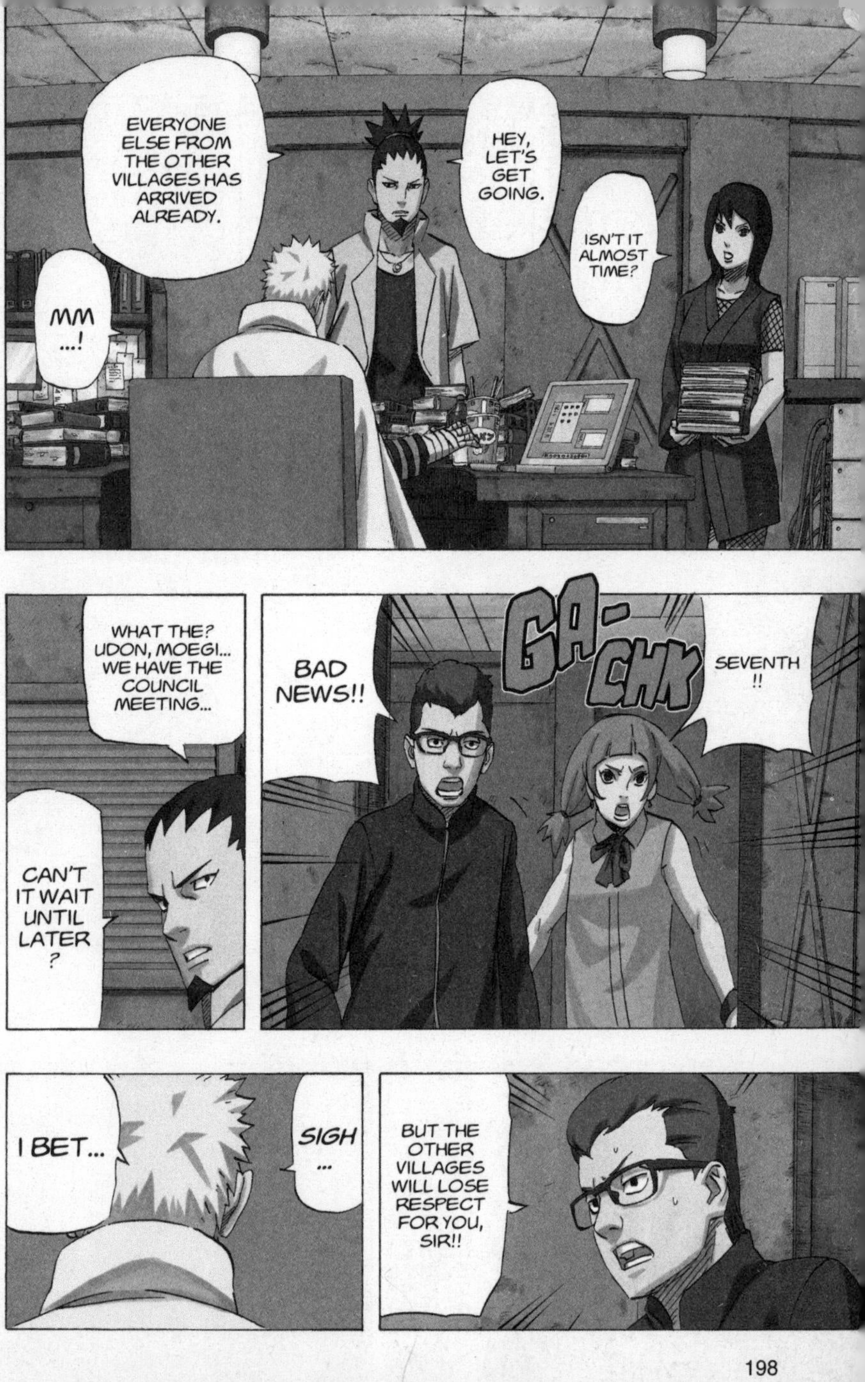
ISN'T IT ALMOST TIME?
HEY, LET'S GET GOING.
EVERYONE ELSE FROM THE OTHER VILLAGES HAS ARRIVED ALREADY.
MM ...!
SEVENTH!!
GA-CHK
BAD NEWS!!
WHAT THE? UDON, MOEGI... WE HAVE THE COUNCIL MEETING...
CAN'T IT WAIT UNTIL LATER?
BUT THE OTHER VILLAGES WILL LOSE RESPECT FOR YOU, SIR!!
SIGH ...
I BET...

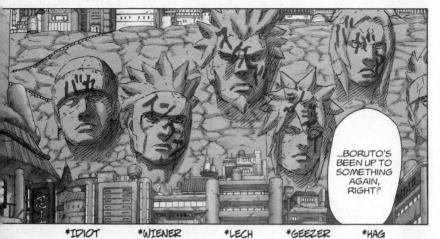

...BORUTO'S BEEN UP TO SOMETHING AGAIN, RIGHT?

*IDIOT   *WIENER   *LECH   *GEEZER   *HAG

PA SHOULD BE GETTING HERE ANY MINUTE!

HEH HEH!

TOSS

I HATE...

...THE HOKAGE!!!

FSH

GR

AB

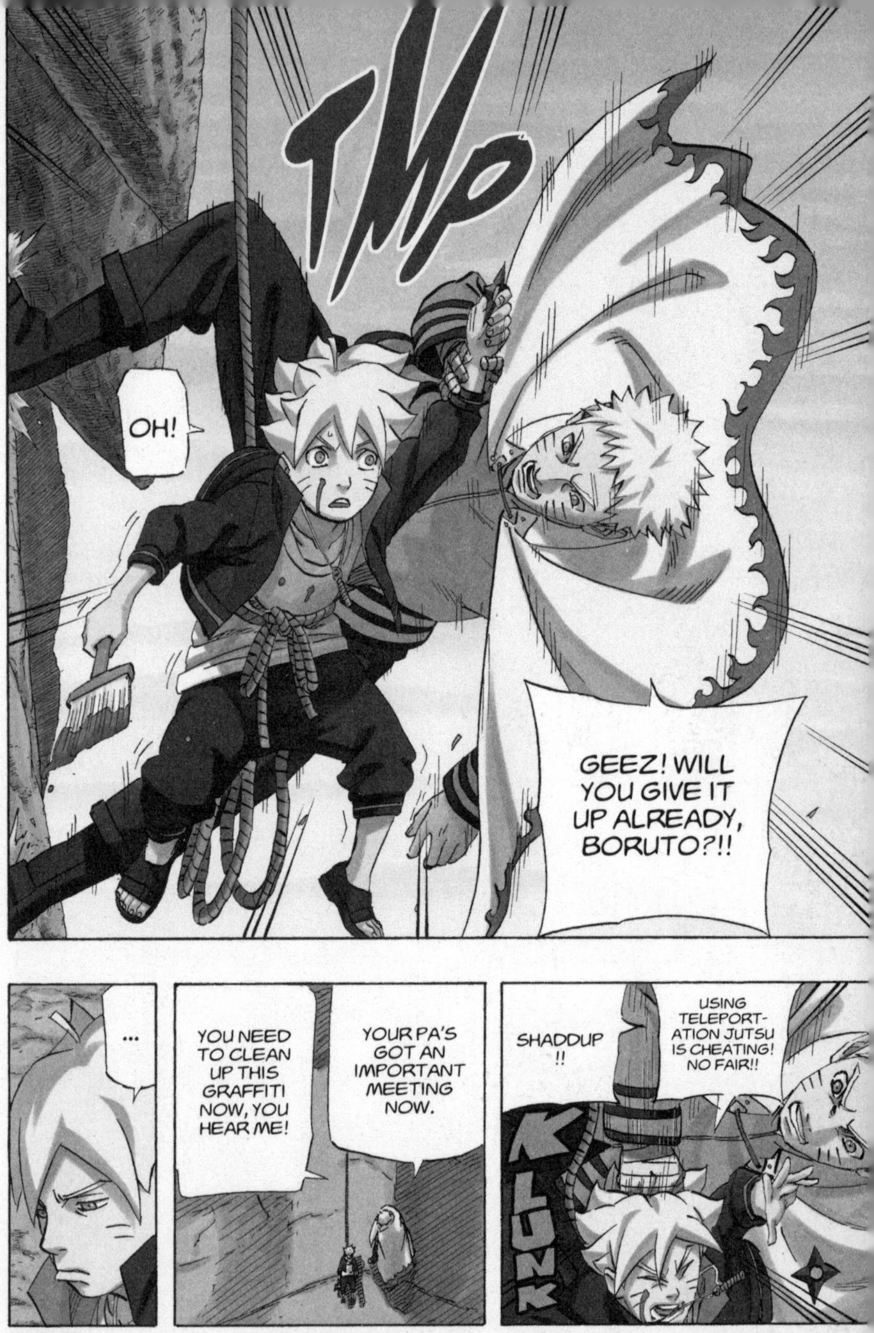
TMP
GEEZ! WILL YOU GIVE IT UP ALREADY, BORUTO?!!
OH!
USING TELEPORT-ATION JUTSU IS CHEATING! NO FAIR!!
SHADDUP!!
KLUNK
YOUR PA'S GOT AN IMPORTANT MEETING NOW.
YOU NEED TO CLEAN UP THIS GRAFFITI NOW, YOU HEAR ME!
...

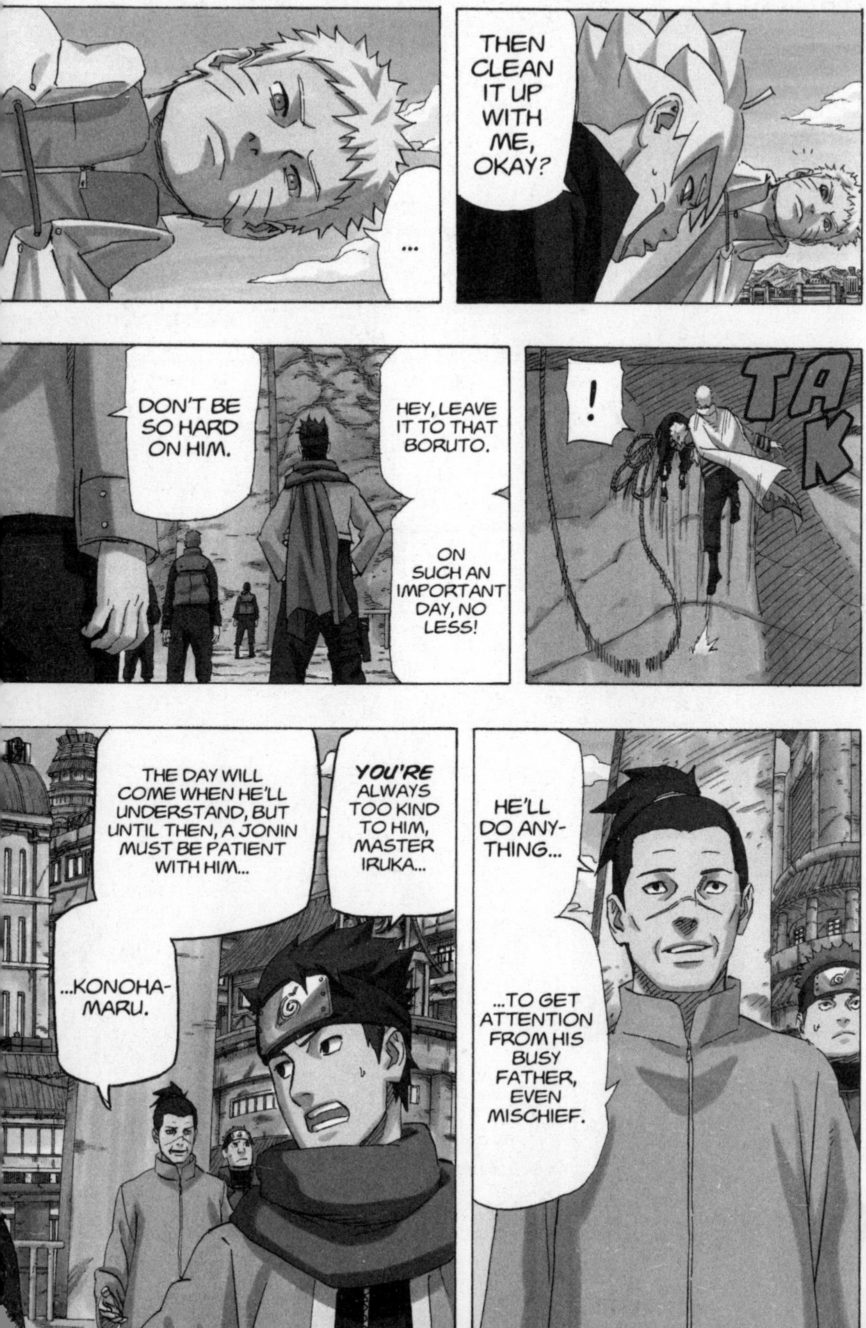

THEN CLEAN IT UP WITH ME, OKAY?
...
TAK
!
HEY, LEAVE IT TO THAT BORUTO.
ON SUCH AN IMPORTANT DAY, NO LESS!
DON'T BE SO HARD ON HIM.
HE'LL DO ANYTHING...
...TO GET ATTENTION FROM HIS BUSY FATHER, EVEN MISCHIEF.
YOU'RE ALWAYS TOO KIND TO HIM, MASTER IRUKA...
THE DAY WILL COME WHEN HE'LL UNDERSTAND, BUT UNTIL THEN, A JONIN MUST BE PATIENT WITH HIM...
...KONOHAMARU.

BORU-TO...

ALL OF THE PEOPLE IN THIS VILLAGE ARE LIKE FAMILY TO ME NOW.

THERE ARE TIMES WHEN I CAN'T BE PA JUST TO YOU.

I REALIZE IT MIGHT BE PAINFUL FOR YOU...

...BUT YOU GOTTA START LEARNING TO ENDURE...

PAT

...

...

...IF YOU'RE A NINJA TOO.

202

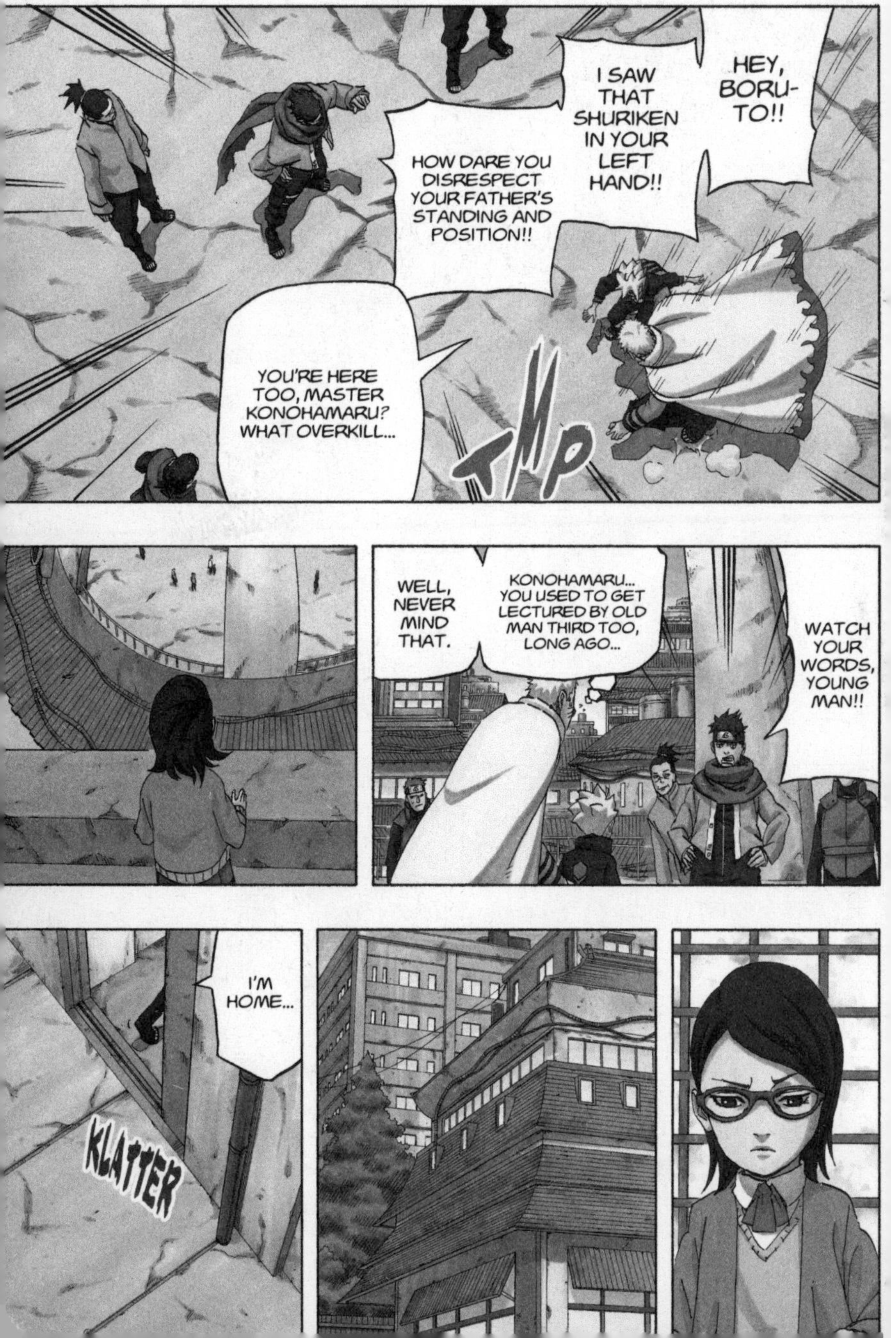
HEY, BORU-TO!!
I SAW THAT SHURIKEN IN YOUR LEFT HAND!!
HOW DARE YOU DISRESPECT YOUR FATHER'S STANDING AND POSITION!!
YOU'RE HERE TOO, MASTER KONOHAMARU? WHAT OVERKILL...
TMP
WATCH YOUR WORDS, YOUNG MAN!!
KONOHAMARU... YOU USED TO GET LECTURED BY OLD MAN THIRD TOO, LONG AGO...
WELL, NEVER MIND THAT.
I'M HOME...
KLATTER

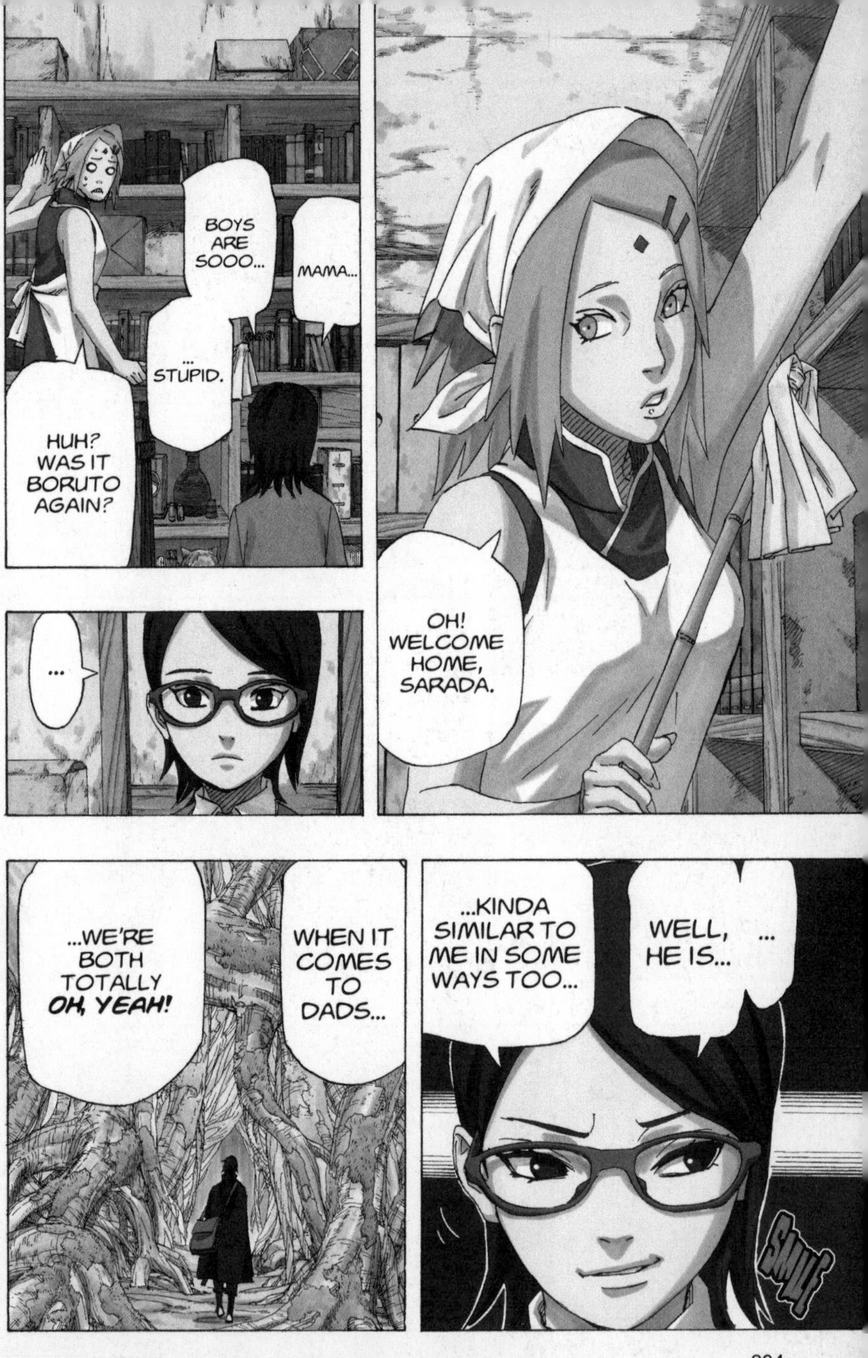
OH! WELCOME HOME, SARADA.
MAMA...
BOYS ARE SOOO...
... STUPID.
HUH? WAS IT BORUTO AGAIN?
...
...
WELL, HE IS...
...KINDA SIMILAR TO ME IN SOME WAYS TOO...
WHEN IT COMES TO DADS...
...WE'RE BOTH TOTALLY **OH, YEAH!**

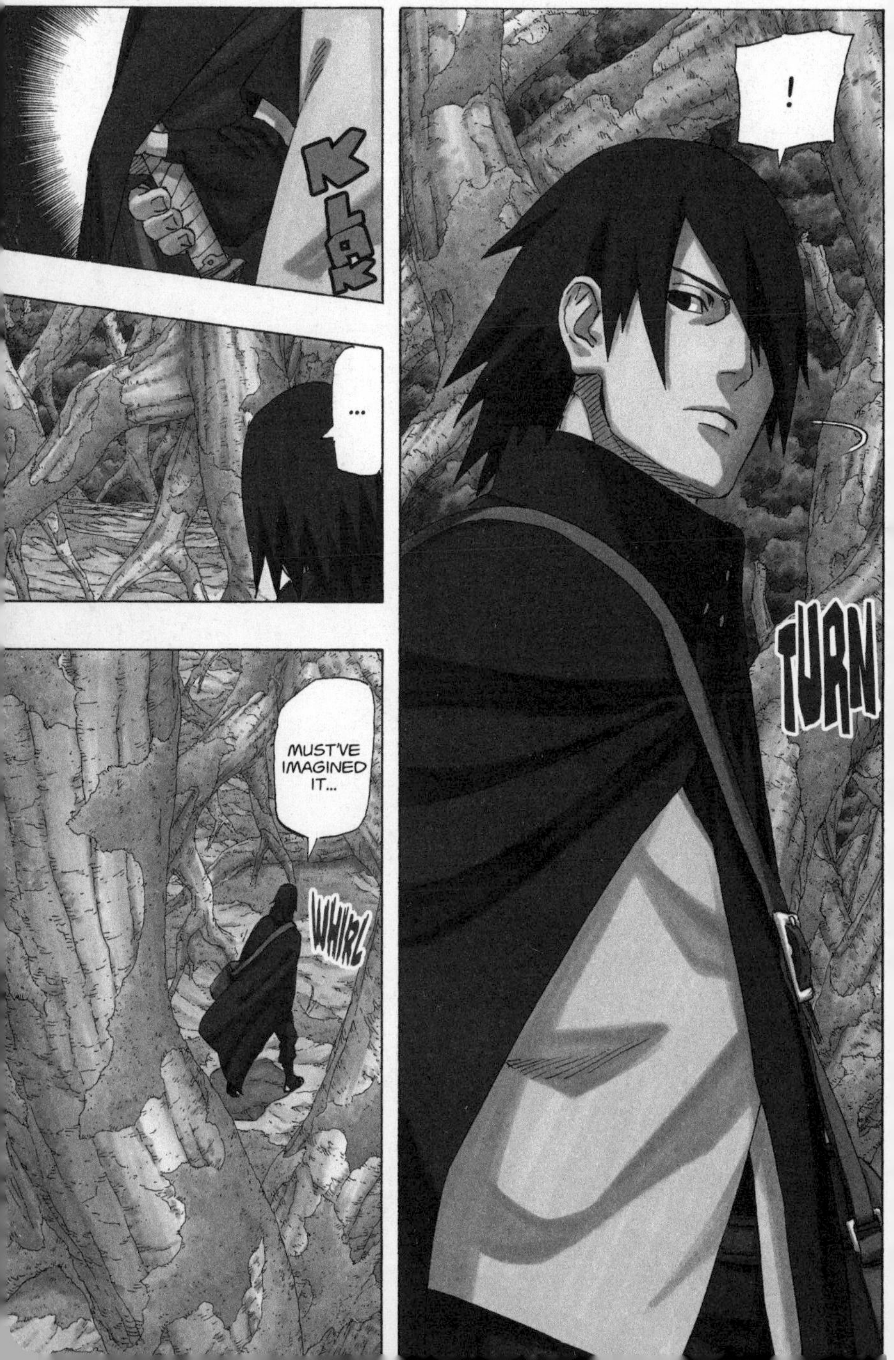
!
TURN
KLAK
...
MUST'VE IMAGINED IT...
WHIRL

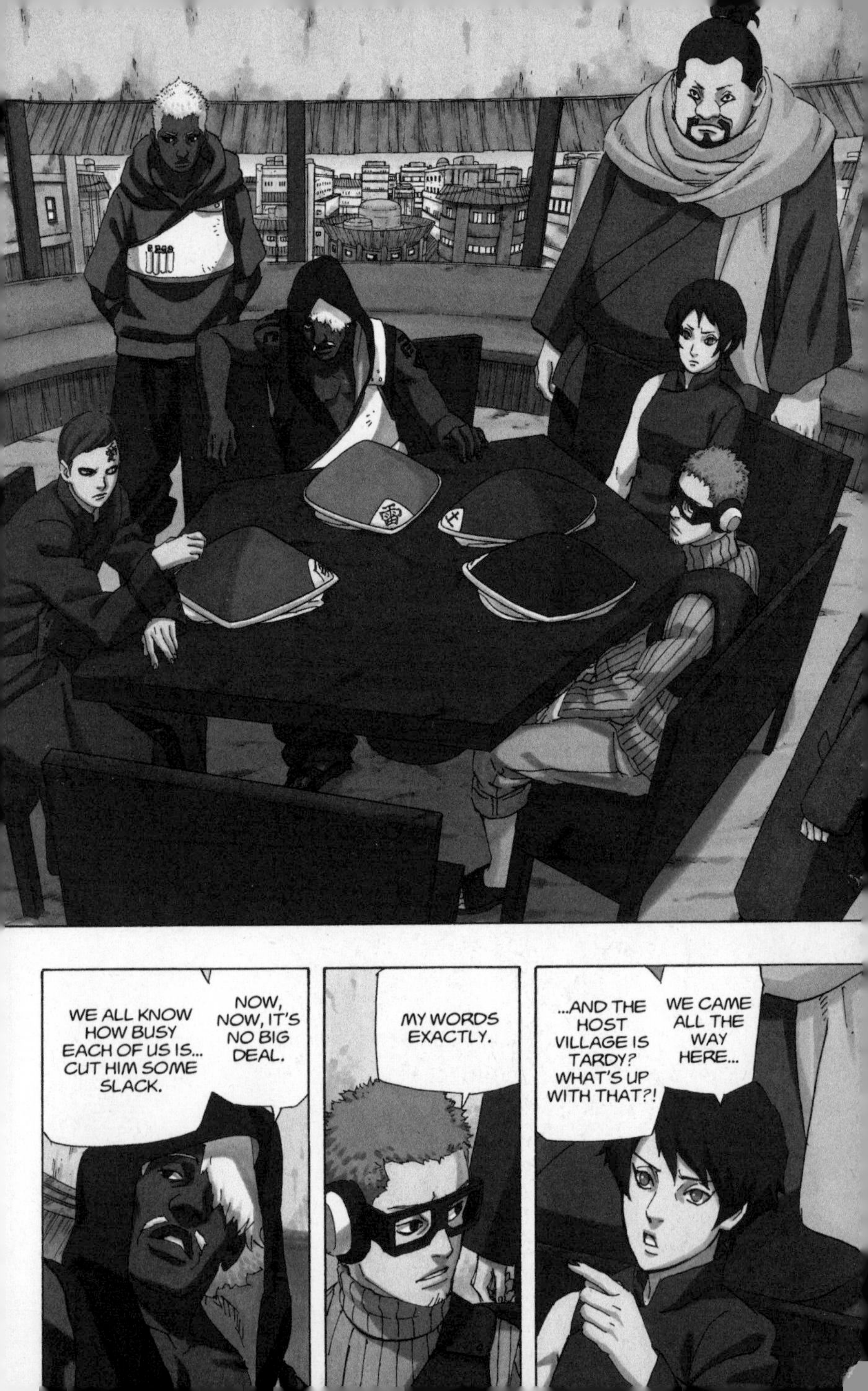
WE CAME ALL THE WAY HERE...
...AND THE HOST VILLAGE IS TARDY? WHAT'S UP WITH THAT?!
MY WORDS EXACTLY.
NOW, NOW, IT'S NO BIG DEAL.
WE ALL KNOW HOW BUSY EACH OF US IS... CUT HIM SOME SLACK.

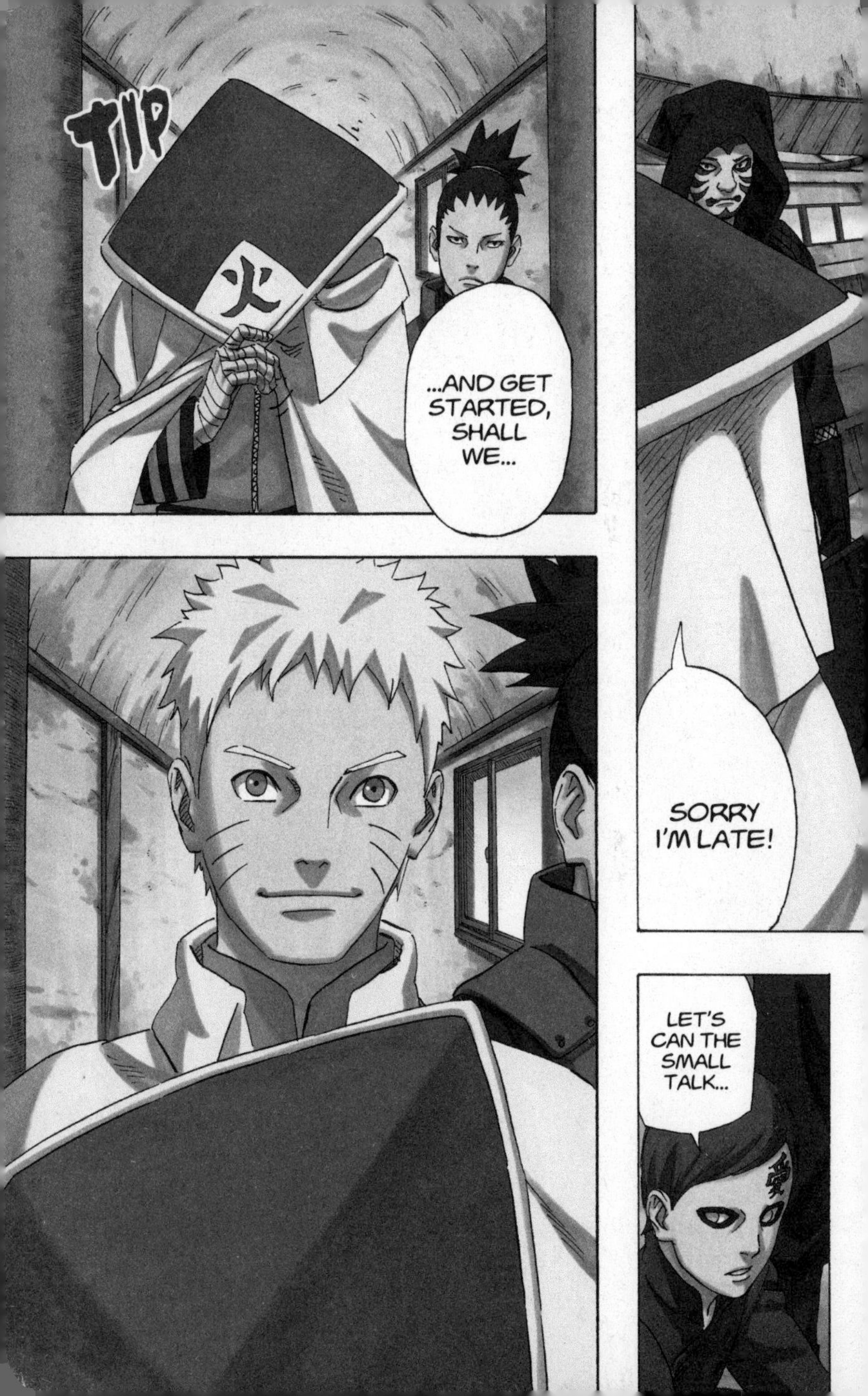
SORRY I'M LATE!
LET'S CAN THE SMALL TALK...
TIP
...AND GET STARTED, SHALL WE...

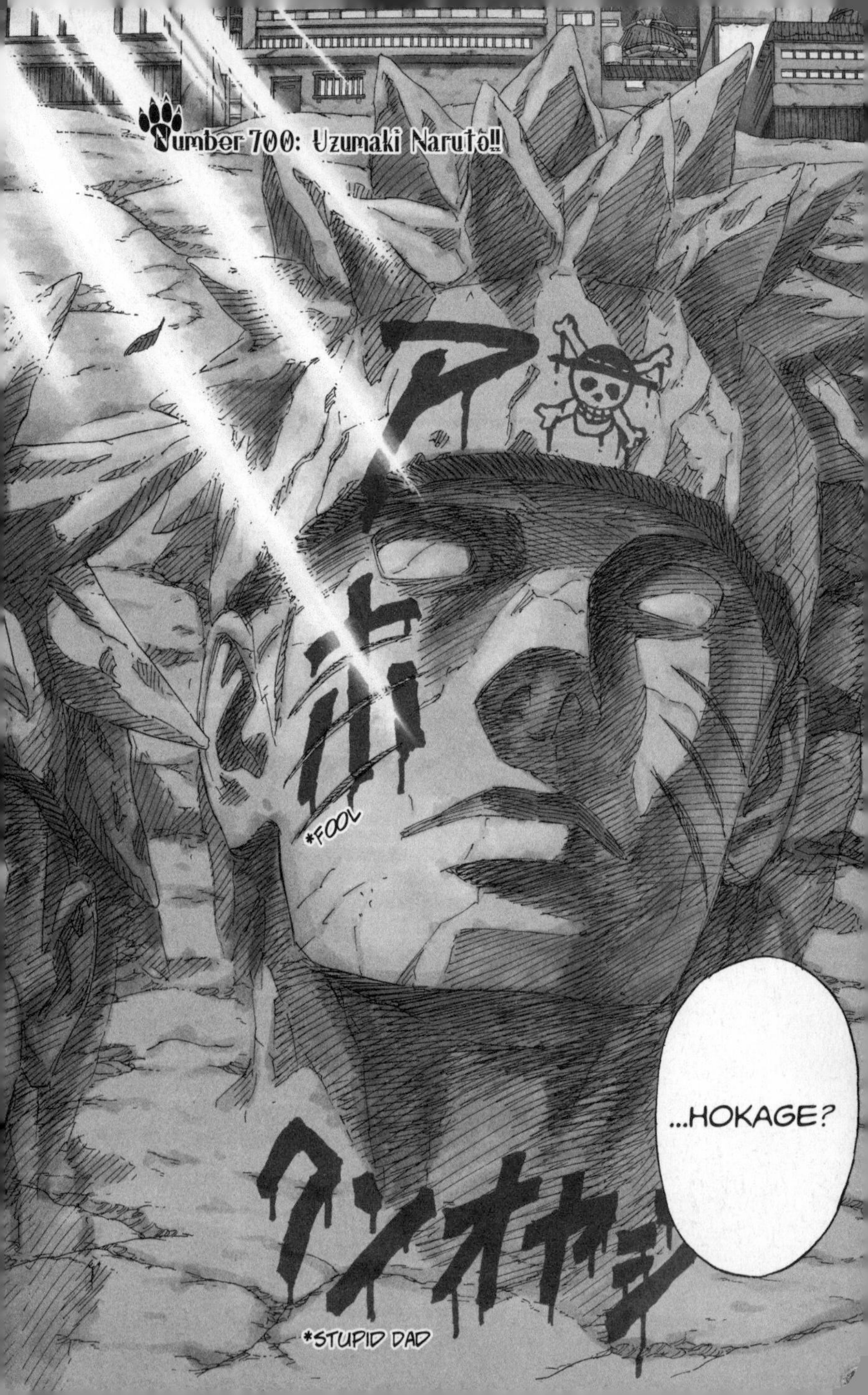
Number 700: Uzumaki Naruto!!
アホ
*FOOL
...HOKAGE?
クソオヤジ
*STUPID DAD

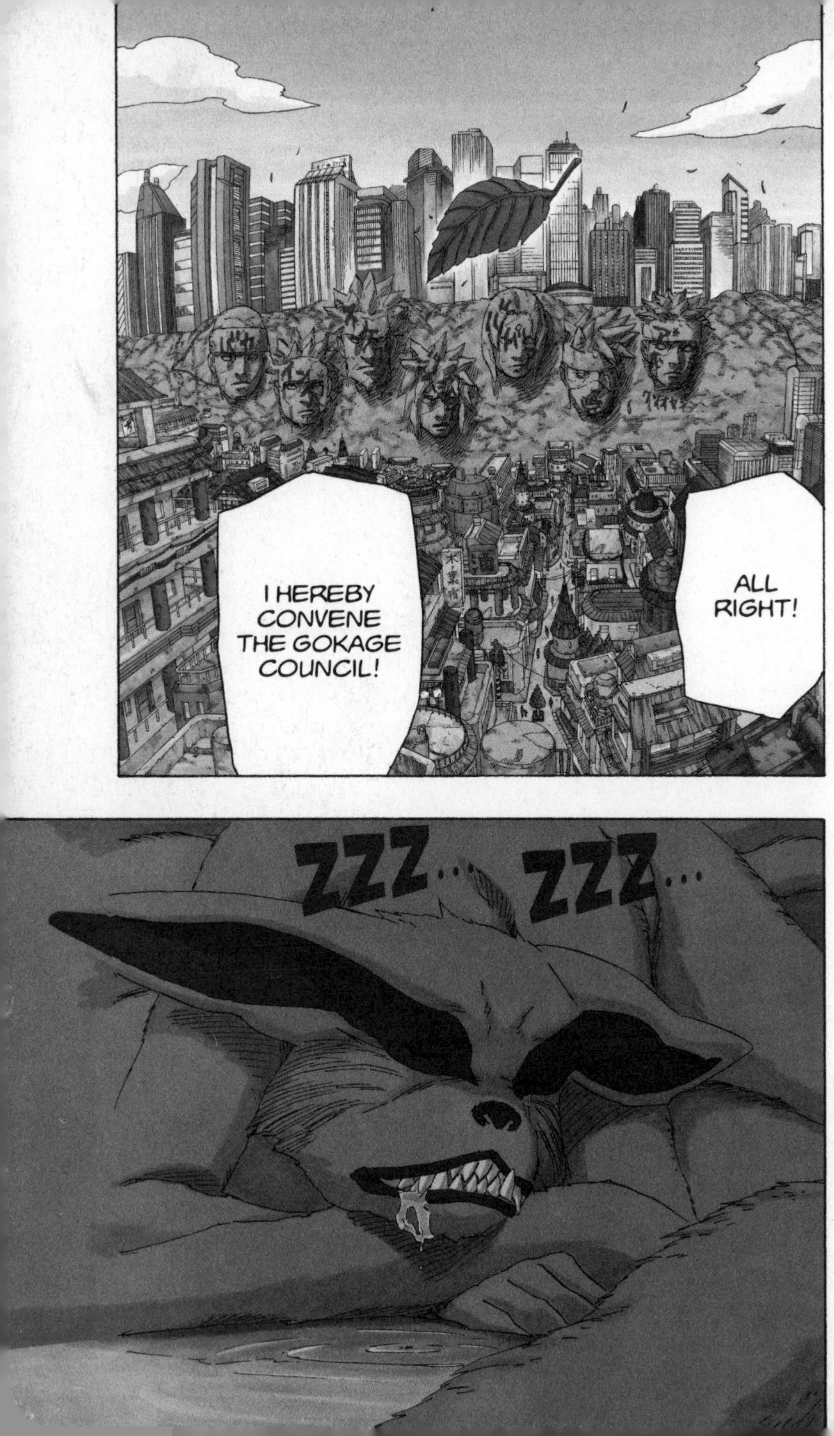
ALL RIGHT!
I HEREBY CONVENE THE GOKAGE COUNCIL!
ZZZ... ZZZ...

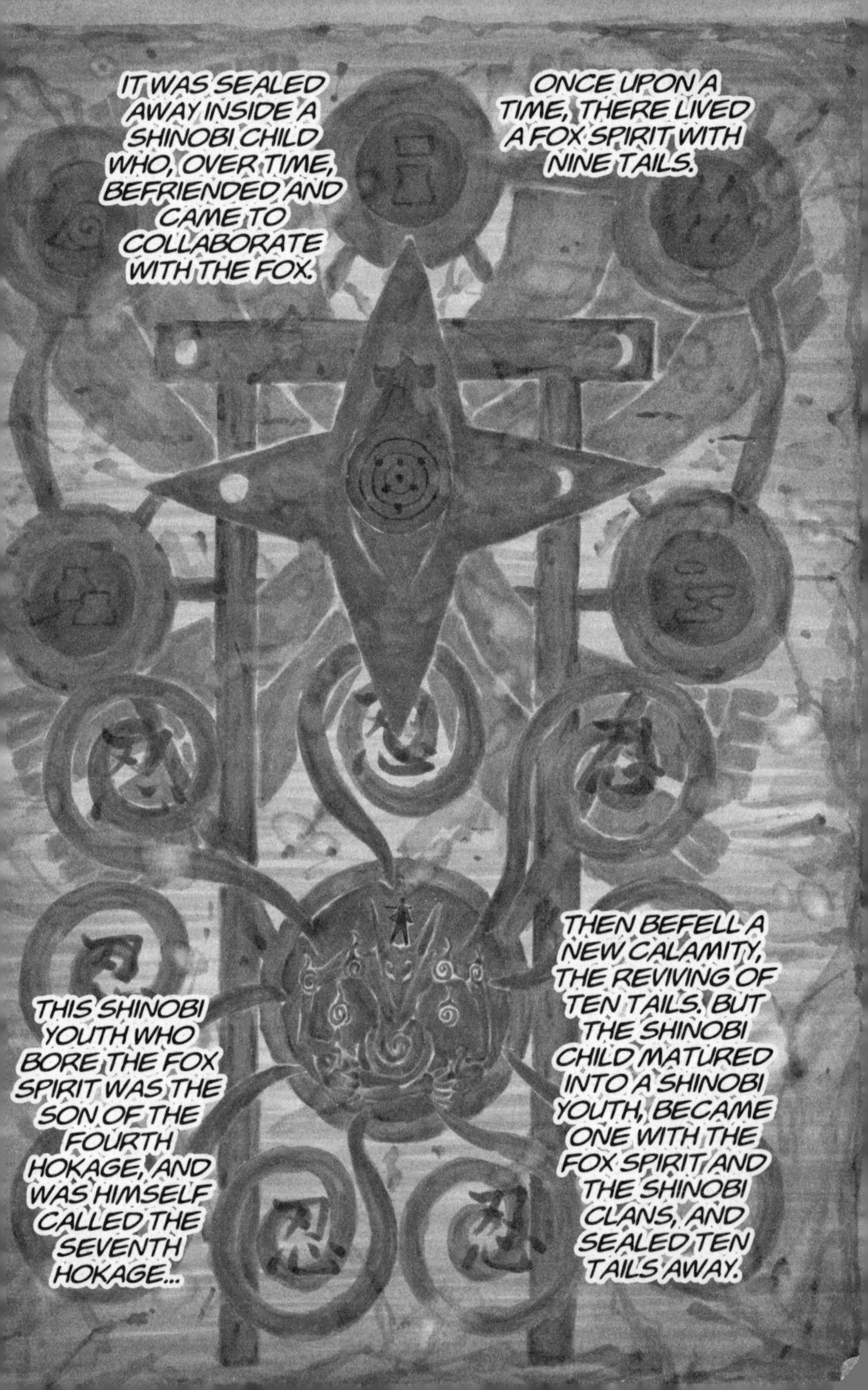
ONCE UPON A TIME, THERE LIVED A FOX SPIRIT WITH NINE TAILS.
IT WAS SEALED AWAY INSIDE A SHINOBI CHILD WHO, OVER TIME, BEFRIENDED AND CAME TO COLLABORATE WITH THE FOX.
THEN BEFELL A NEW CALAMITY, THE REVIVING OF TEN TAILS. BUT THE SHINOBI CHILD MATURED INTO A SHINOBI YOUTH, BECAME ONE WITH THE FOX SPIRIT AND THE SHINOBI CLANS, AND SEALED TEN TAILS AWAY.
THIS SHINOBI YOUTH WHO BORE THE FOX SPIRIT WAS THE SON OF THE FOURTH HOKAGE, AND WAS HIMSELF CALLED THE SEVENTH HOKAGE...

THE BEST SELLING MANGA SERIES IN THE WORLD!

ONE PIECE

Story & Art by EIICHIRO ODA

As a child, **Monkey D. Luffy** was inspired to become a pirate by listening to the tales of the buccaneer "Red-Haired" Shanks. But Luffy's life changed when he accidentally ate the Gum-Gum Devil Fruit and gained the power to stretch like rubber...at the cost of never being able to swim again! Years later, still vowing to become the king of the pirates, Luffy sets out on his adventure in search of the legendary "One Piece," said to be the greatest treasure in the world...

www.shonenjump.com   www.viz.com

A S S A S S I N A T I O N
CLASSROOM

STORY AND ART BY
YUSEI MATSUI

Ever caught yourself screaming, "I could just kill that teacher"?
What would it take to justify such antisocial behavior
and weeks of detention? Especially if he's the best
teacher you've ever had? Giving you an "F" on a quiz?
Mispronouncing your name during roll call...*again*? How about
blowing up the moon and threatening to do the same to
Mother Earth—unless you take him out first?! Plus a reward
of a cool 100 million from the Ministry of Defense!

Okay, now that you're committed... How are you going to
pull this off? What does your pathetic class of misfits have
in their arsenal to combat Teach's alien technology, bizarre
powers and...*tentacles*?!

ASSASSINATION
CLASSROOM

STORY AND ART BY
YUSEI MATSUI
1

SHONEN JUMP ADVANCED

You're Reading in the Wrong Direction!!

Whoops! Guess what? You're starting at the wrong end of the comic!

…It's true! In keeping with the original Japanese format, **Naruto** is meant to be read from right to left, starting in the upper-right corner.

Unlike English, which is read from left to right, Japanese is read from right to left, meaning that action, sound effects and word-balloon order are completely reversed… something which can make readers unfamiliar with Japanese feel pretty backwards themselves. For this reason, manga or Japanese comics published in the U.S. in English have sometimes been published "flopped"—that is, printed in exact reverse order, as though seen from the other side of a mirror.

By flopping pages, U.S. publishers can avoid confusing readers, but the compromise is not without its downside. For one thing, a character in a flopped manga series who once wore in the original Japanese version a T-shirt emblazoned with "M A Y" (as in "the merry month of") now wears one which reads "Y A M"! Additionally, many manga creators in Japan are themselves unhappy with the process, as some feel the mirror-imaging of their art alters their original intentions.

We are proud to bring you Masashi Kishimoto's **Naruto** in the original unflopped format. For now, though, turn to the other side of the book and let the ninjutsu begin…!

—Editor

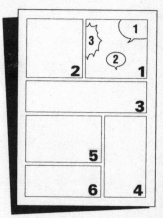